RHODE ISLAND
1790-1860

THE TRANSFORMATION

of

RHODE ISLAND

1790–1860

PETER J. COLEMAN

GREENWOOD PRESS, PUBLISHERS
WESTPORT, CONNECTICUT

Library of Congress Cataloging in Publication Data

Coleman, Peter J.
    The transformation of Rhode Island, 1790–1860.

    Reprint. Originally published: Providence, R.I. :
Brown University Press, 1963.
    1. Rhode Island--History--1775-1865. 2. Rhode
Island--Economic conditions. I. Title.
F83.C6 1985   974.5'03   84-27932
ISBN 0-313-24796-X (lib. bdg.)

Copyright © 1963 by Brown University

First printing 1963

Reprinted with the permission of the University Press of New England

Reprinted in 1985 by Greenwood Press
A division of Congressional Information Service, Inc.
88 Post Road West, Westport, Connecticut 06881

Printed in the United States of America

10 9 8 7 6 5 4 3 2 1

Preface

THE writing of Rhode Island history by professional historians, like their writing of national history, has been governed by a preconceived framework. Partly because they have been prone to accept political propaganda at face value and partly because they have been guilty of political partiality, they have produced polarized interpretations. Some aspects of the Rhode Island story, most notably the state's eighteenth century emissions of paper currency and its rôle in the ratification of the Constitution of the United States, have suffered especially badly at the hands of the professionals. The Hamiltonians turned the Rhode Islanders into scoundrels deliberately bent on inflating the currency in order to evade their lawful debts; the Jeffersonians made them the apostles of agrarian democracy manfully resisting the oppressive designs of the money changers. But as recent scholarly studies have shown, the paper money question was not the pervasive issue earlier students made it, and most modern historians concede at least the complexity of the constitutional question.

Rhode Island's history has also suffered from neglect. In their preoccupation with national issues and trends the trained scholars have left its study almost entirely to the non-professionals. Only four general histories have been published since 1900. Of these, the multi-volume works edited or written by Edward Field (1902), Thomas Williams Bicknell (1920), and Charles Carroll (1932) fall into the general class of amateur, antiquarian, or commercial publications characteristic of so much of the writing of local history in America. Accordingly, they embody some of the strengths and most of the weaknesses of their kind. They are strongest on information, especially the catalogues of raw data so appealing to

The Transformation of Rhode Island

antiquarians and genealogists, and weakest on organization and interpretation. Irving B. Richman's interpretative study of the separatist theme (1905) provides a welcome relief, but he focused primarily on the Colonial period and his treatment of the nineteenth century is impressionistic at best.

Monographic literature on ninteenth century Rhode Island hardly exists. Apart from Arthur M. Mowry's study of the Dorr War (1901), Joseph Brennan's dissertation on social conditions (1940), and a series of chronicles on the port of Bristol, the student must turn to larger histories, such as Arthur H. Cole's survey of the American woolen industry (1926), Caroline F. Ware's study of cotton manufacturing in New England (1931), or Chilton Williamson's analysis of the American suffrage (1960), for discussions of particular phases of Rhode Island history. There are no fulllength biographies of any important nineteenth century figures; there are no histories of commerce or industry, of individual mercantile houses or particular manufacturing enterprises; and there are no acceptable urban studies.

I have approached Rhode Island history with these weaknesses in mind. I was familiar at the outset with the common generalization that nineteenth century Rhode Island was the most densely inhabited state in the Union and that it also had the highest urban-rural ratio. However, a detailed demographic study of the seventy year period from 1790 to 1860 quickly revealed that these generalizations had relatively little meaning and even less utility. For example, in 1860 the density of population ranged from over 7,500 persons per square mile in Providence to a mere twenty-four persons per square mile in West Greenwich, a hill-country town only fifteen miles away. Moreover, though the proportion of urban Rhode Islanders rose from less than a fifth of the total in 1790 to nearly two-thirds in 1860, the Census Bureau's arbitrary system of classification concealed the true state of affairs. Most of Cumberland remained in farmland or in forest, yet, because a prescribed number of people lived in villages, it qualified as an urban area; and Bristol, though one of the most thickly settled towns in the state, did not receive an urban classification until 1850, when its population became large enough to meet the Bureau's definition.

Indeed, on the eve of the Civil War, when two out of three Rhode Islanders were classified as residents of urban centers, only nine of the state's thirty-two towns were so classified and they covered less than a quarter of the land area.

More important, the demographic analysis revealed a central factor in Rhode Island's history—the extraordinary disparity from one town to another. The state's limited area and tiny population notwithstanding, there were sharp local differences ranging from growth rates, density, and the degree of urbanization to ethnic composition, mobility, and the incidence of illiteracy. Clearly, though climate, topography, natural resources, and locale gave each community its unique and relatively stable physical characteristics, the rôle of each of these factors was continuously subject to the modifying influence of human activity. Far from being homogeneous, therefore, Rhode Island actually comprised a bundle of discrete entities, each of which responded distinctively to its opportunities.

Even though, for purposes of presentation, I have categorized the thirty-two Rhode Island towns as rapidly expanding, static, or declining communities, I have kept their individual differences in mind and have anchored my interpretation of Rhode Island's transformation from a maritime to an industrial society in the locally disparate response to changing conditions. This pluralistic orientation reflects a deliberate attempt to investigate themes imposed by the data and not by the historian and to approach American history from the local rather than from the national standpoint. This approach does not imply that each locality developed in a vacuum, receiving nothing from and contributing nothing to the outside world. It does imply dissatisfaction with the way some scholars have abdicated their professional responsibilities. By relegating the study of local history to the well-meaning antiquarians and aspiring amateurs, trained historians have assured the combination of a disembodied accumulation of data for its own sake and the study of locales as mere microcosms of national history that has characterized the products of local historians for more than half a century. Fortunately, the present generation is recognizing the significance of locality and diversity in America and one of the more heartening trends in recent historiography is the growing professionalization of scholarship in the field of local history. This study is in part a conscious effort to abet that trend.

Not that this study makes necessary radical alterations in the basic outlines of American history as it has been written. Given Rhode Island's size and its minor rôle in the affairs of the Union that would be expecting too much. Nevertheless, the findings derived from the pluralistic, non-deterministic approach are sufficiently encouraging to justify its application on a wider scale. In some particulars these findings confirm and in others they deny generally accepted interpretations; they point to some topics, both in Rhode Island and elsewhere, that require closer scrutiny; and, most of all, they suggest that comparable studies of other states, by heightening our understanding of the relationship of local to national history, might produce major changes in traditional views.

For example, entrepreneurship was the critical human factor in the transformation of Rhode Island. At each stage of economic change—in the rise and decline of oceanic enterprise, in the development of industrialization, in the emergence of Providence as a metropolitan center, and in the process of economic diversification —the entrepreneurial factor exerted a direct and vital influence on the location, timing, speed, and direction of economic change. In this respect the Providence entrepreneurs performed the parallel function assumed in Massachusetts by the Lawrences, Lowells, and Cabots. Perhaps the earlier decay of Connecticut's foreign trade and the Nutmeg State's slower rate of industrialization reflected a less vital entrepreneurial spirit.

These same Rhode Island entrepreneurs planned and executed a major transfer of risk capital from maritime to industrial uses at a time when they were conducting their mercantile operations on a larger and more profitable scale than ever before. Though the French Revolutionary and Napoleonic wars certainly made seafaring ventures increasingly hazardous, the most daring Rhode Islanders moved substantial resources into the even more speculative field of cotton manufacturing before maritime enterprise was seriously embattled either by the Anglo-French conflict or by the Jeffersonian embargo. Thus the Rhode Islanders, at least, did not conform to the widely accepted view that the cotton industry's period of accelerated growth occurred after Congressional restrictions and the War of 1812 had cut off the flow of imports.

The same Rhode Islanders who pioneered the cotton industry and who led the pack in shifting out of foreign trade and into manufacturing lagged a full generation behind other New Englanders in adopting the corporate form of business organization. Their conservatism in this matter, as in so many others, was pragmatic rather than philosophical and grew out of the mercantile tradition. Significantly, when the corporate innovators did emerge in Rhode Island they came from craft rather than commercial backgrounds. Even then, in sharp contrast to what has been assumed about the behavior of American businessmen, many Rhode Island industrialists refused to accept the corporate form of organization or the privilege of limited liability.

This otherwise-mindedness also manifested itself in Rhode Island's refusal to abolish imprisonment for debt and seemingly contradicted the traditional image of the Rhode Islanders as scoundrels, smugglers, cutthroats, and pirates. Yet just as they resisted limited liability out of sensitivity for their reputations as men of business integrity, so they acted in the mid-eighteenth century to develop what soon became a liberal bankruptcy procedure. They did not intend it to favor debtors. Rather, they developed this remedy for the benefit of creditors; they designed it to discourage debtors from absconding and to give creditors a greater possibility of realizing on their claims. Just as the emissions of paper money were designed to preserve credit, stimulate economic activity, and provide an acceptable medium for repaying debts, so the bankruptcy procedure was a method of preserving rather than impairing business integrity. If, as I believe, this is the correct view, then the Rhode Islanders have been harshly dealt with both by their contemporary critics and by some of their historians.

Finally, most students of industrialization in New England have slighted the rôle of steam power, particularly in the generation preceding the Civil War. The Rhode Islanders began substituting steam for water as the source of power as early as 1829. Within a decade the use of the steam engine was exerting a profound influence on both the rate of economic growth and on the locale of industrial activity. It even caused particular industries to migrate from one section of a town to another. By 1860 steam power had made Providence the leading manufacturing center in southern New England, and it had partially revived the economies of the depressed maritime centers.

In sum, then, if this study is a fair sample, the narrowly focused treatment of local history promises both to enrich and to modify prevailing interpretations at all levels of generalization, be it the locality itself, the region, the state, the section, or the nation. To be sure, it promises neither to shatter the accepted mold of American history nor to provide a short cut to meaningful analysis, but it does bring the historian closer to reality, to understanding, and, ultimately, to truth.

In addition to drawing on the general and monographic literature already noted, and the published city, state, and federal census data, I have also canvassed the articles, essays, sermons, collections of documents, directories, gazetteers, pamphlets, and town, county, and older state histories cited in the footnotes. Invaluable though these sources have been, the core of the study rests on five main categories of materials. I have made extensive use of newspapers for certain subjects, notably social and political affairs; of the manuscript census records for industrial activity in 1850 and 1860; of the Thomas Wilson Dorr Papers for the constitutional problem; of the published session laws for all manner of information; and, above all, of the state archival records, particularly the charters, petitions, journals, reports, and miscellaneous legislative papers, for data on virtually every facet of Rhode Island's transformation. Except for those collections cited in the footnotes, I have not consulted private papers. So far as I can judge from discussions with scholars who have, these materials would enrich but not fundamentally alter the interpretation advanced here. This study is not intended to be exhaustive. It merely attempts to provide a valid and meaningful framework for further investigation.

Throughout the research and writing I have incurred numerous obligations. I am indebted to the American History Research Cen-

ter, to the American Philosophical Society, and to the Graduate
School of Arts and Science and the Social Science Institute at
Washington University for grants-in-aid; to the Social Science
Research Council for the opportunity to broaden my understanding of the law and the legislative process; to the librarians at the
universities, historical societies, and other institutions where I have
gathered material for their kindnesses and courtesies, and particularly to Mr. Clifford P. Monahon and Mr. Clarkson A. Collins,
3rd, of the Rhode Island Historical Society for their generous
assistance, to Mr. Earl C. Borgeson and his staff at the Harvard
Law School Library, especially Miss Edith G. Henderson in the
Treasure Room, for helping me in countless ways, and to Miss
Mary T. Quinn for the privilege of working in a model state
archive. I am also under a heavy obligation to Professor Fulmer
Mood, formerly of the University of Texas, who first called my
attention to what he called "pluralistic localism"; to Professor
Charles Fairman and his colleagues in the Harvard Law School
for their wise counsel; to Professor Oscar Handlin, the director
of the Center for the Study of the History of Liberty in America,
for his encouragement, his criticism, and, perhaps most of all, for
his patience; to my wife, Evelyn Scherabon Coleman, for taking
time from her own philological studies to assist in the collection
of data; to Paul Hass, John Kush, and Arthur Moser, who drew
some of the maps; and to Professors Leslie E. Decker, Dietrich
Gerhard, Thomas P. Govan, Forrest McDonald, and Jules Zanger,
and to my colleague O. Lawrence Burnette, Jr., for giving me the
benefit of their knowledge, insights, wisdom, and editorial skills.
Forbearing throughout they have tempered my pen while sharpen-
ing my interpretation, and they have saved me from blunders too
numerous to count. This is not to imply that they are in any way
responsible for the errors and deficiencies that remain.

PETER J. COLEMAN

Madison, Wisconsin
November, 1962

Contents

	Preface	v
1.	Heritage	3
2.	The Maritime Economy	26
3.	Industrialization: The Era of Experimentation	71
4.	Industrialization: The Era of Expansion	108
5.	The Making of a Metropolis	161
6.	Society and Politics	218
7.	Legacy	295
	Index	303

Tables

1.	The Population of Rhode Island, 1708–1782	21
2.	Shipping Constructed at Rhode Island Ports, 1790–1859	35
3.	Whaling Activity of Rhode Island Ports, 1825–1859	64
4.	Shipping Registered, Enrolled, and Licensed at Rhode Island Customs Districts, 1790–1860	65
5.	The Rhode Island Cotton Industry, 1809–1812	86
6.	The Rhode Island Cotton Industry, November, 1815	87
7.	The Rhode Island Cotton Industry, 1832	93
8.	The Rhode Island Woolen Industry, 1832	98
9.	Cotton Manufacturing in the Blackstone and Branch Valleys, 1844	122
10.	The Rhode Island Cotton Industry, 1840	124
11.	The Rhode Island Cotton Industry, 1850	127
12.	The Rhode Island Cotton Industry, 1860	129

13. The Rhode Island Woolen Industry, 1836–1840   135
14. The Rhode Island Woolen Industry, 1850   137
15. The Rhode Island Woolen Industry, 1860   140
16. The Rhode Island Base Metal Industry in 1850 and 1860   149
17. The Rhode Island Precious Metal Industry in 1850 and
    1860   152
18. Rhode Island Industrial Capital, 1850   153
19. The Principal Occupations of Rhode Islanders, 1860   156
20. The Distribution of Banking Capital, 1800–1860   185
21. The Population of Rhode Island, 1790–1860   220
22. The Rate of Population Growth, 1790–1860   225
23. The Ratio of Representatives to Population, 1790–1840   256
24. Legislative Apportionment and Ratio of Seats to Population
    under the Charter, the People's, and the Freemen's Con-
    stitutions, 1841   280
25. Voting for the 1843 Constitution, with Legislative Appor-
    tionment in 1842, 1843, and 1851   286

Maps

 1. Physiographic Diagram   6
 2. Rhode Island Towns   12
 3. Population Growth, 1790–1860   72
 4. Cotton Spindles, 1832   94
 5. Woolen Capital, 1832   99
 6. Cotton Capital, 1850   126
 7. Woolen Capital, 1850   139
 8. Industrial Capital, 1850   155
 9. The Transportation System   170
10. Banking Capital, 1860   205
11. Population Density, 1790   222
12. Population Density, 1830   224
13. Population Density, 1860   226
14. Estimated Ratio of Freemen to Population   260
15. Constitutional Referendum, 1824   267
16. Referendum on the Freemen's Constitution, March, 1842   277

RHODE ISLAND

1790-1860

CHAPTER ONE

Heritage

THOUGH Colonial Rhode Island measured only forty-eight miles north to south and thirty-seven east to west, it was characterized by variety and contrast. An area of variegated topography —of islands, peninsulas, and inlets; of flat and fertile farmland in small quantity and of hilly and infertile land in large—the colony attracted an equally variegated population, in opinion if not in national origin. Most were English, but most were also religious nonconformists and political individualists whose settlements were often in political or religious turmoil and whose town-to-town relations were marked by almost constant bickering and by vigorous commercial rivalry. Yet, out of the complex political and geographic structure that was Rhode Island there developed a kind of unity, a unity that had, by the time of the Revolution, created a sort of model "Rhode Islander." Probably no actual resident fit the mold exactly, but most could occupy it with but slight discomfort.

Those Rhode Islanders who most closely resembled the model were those whose activities had created the stereotype, the Narragansett Bay merchant-adventurers. Separatist in religion and otherwise-minded in politics, these traders, naturally enough, pursued an individualistic and pragmatic course in business. A shrewd, hardheaded lot, they were forced by the tiny colony's deficiencies in natural resources and encouraged by its strategic location to make opportunities where none existed, to turn one difficulty after another to their advantage. In the process they learned to subordinate conscience to convenience. Thus, though the governor of New York, writing in 1699, could not distinguish many of Newport's privateering activities from piracy,[1] to Rhode Islanders such enterprises had

[1] John Russell Bartlett, ed., *Records of the Colony of Rhode Island, and Providence Plantations, in New England* (10 vols., Providence, 1856–1865), 3:387.

3

the supreme virtue of combining patriotism with profit. Not that love of King or country outweighed love of money. When merchant-shipowners lacked a plausible rationale for their acquisitiveness, they measured the possible profit against the probable risk and followed the dictates of the result. If this required trading with the enemy in wartime or fitting out clandestine Caribbean ventures, they wasted little time in conscience-wrestling.[2]

Other Rhode Islanders were equally pragmatic and almost equally on the lookout for the "main chance." The colony's liberal, humane, and "holier than thou" attitude notwithstanding, some settlers created a plantation system replete with enslaved Negroes and Indians; others pillaged the lands of Huguenot refugees; and still others juggled the laws to deceive the imperial authorities, or made a mockery of self-government by their chicanery. And plausible though the justifications were—the encouragement of trade, fisheries, and manufactures and the construction of piers and forts— the successive emissions of paper money added to the colony's notoriety. The ordinary colonists did not operate on the grand scale of the Newport merchant-grandees or their Providence rivals, but they grasped what opportunities came their way and struggled to make Nature's niggardly bounty support them as best they could. They turned the colonial wars to their advantage by forging swords and casting cannon; they exploited the streams and waterfalls for grist- and sawmills; and, in clearing their farms, they made and sought markets for ship timber, shingles, staves, and charcoal.

This "Rhode Islander," whether merchant-shipowner or farmer-artisan, was the product of his environment and origins, richly leavened by a shrewdness, adaptability, and perverseness that stemmed, in part, from the imaginative view he took of himself and of his world. The Narragansett Bay region had first been settled by refugees from Massachusetts. Though their opposition to the Bay Colony's Puritan theocracy gave them a common enemy, it did not induce them to make common cause. One wave of fugitives followed Roger Williams to Providence in 1636, but

[2] Carl Bridenbaugh, *Cities in Revolt: Urban Life in America, 1743–1776* (New York, 1955), 46–47, 65–67, 74–76.

the second wave chose to establish an independent colony at Portsmouth on the northern end of Aquidneck (Rhode) Island. Factionalism soon developed within the Portsmouth group, and in 1639 the dissidents emigrated to the southern tip of the island, where they founded Newport. This independent spirit attracted another quarrelsome individualist, Samuel Gorton, who, when he found neither Portsmouth nor Providence to this liking, took his sympathizers to what became Warwick on the western shore of Narragansett Bay. Despite the hostility of Massachusetts and the danger of Indian attack, these four original settlements valued their independence so highly that they refused to unite as a single colony until 1647. Even then, the towns soon quarrelled over various issues, separated, and remained apart until 1654.

Geography reinforced the separatist spirit. The distances between the two Aquidneck Island communities and those on the mainland were short, but a journey of only a few miles, especially in winter, was a hazardous undertaking. As late as 1672, when Roger Williams went from Providence to Newport to meet the English Quaker leader, George Fox, the aged founder had to paddle himself the length of the Bay by canoe. The trip took so long that Williams arrived after midnight to find that Fox had already left. But gradually, the spread of settlement reduced the dangers of overland travel, and the growth of shipping on Narragansett Bay slowly brought all coastal communities within access.

Geography also influenced the way the settlers supported themselves and it shaped the formation of new communities. Until the early eighteenth century, settlement was confined to the narrow strip of coastal lowlands extending along the shores of Block Island Sound and Narragansett Bay. The lowlands also included Conanicut, Prudence, and Aquidneck islands in the Bay, as well as Block Island out in the Atlantic. Though some of the land was either swampy or sandy, the coastal plains and gently rolling hills contained the colony's best farm land, including salt meadows for grazing and haying and light but fertile soils for raising grain and vegetable crops. Accessible both to supplies of seaweed and fish for fertilizer and to water transportation to carry produce to markets,

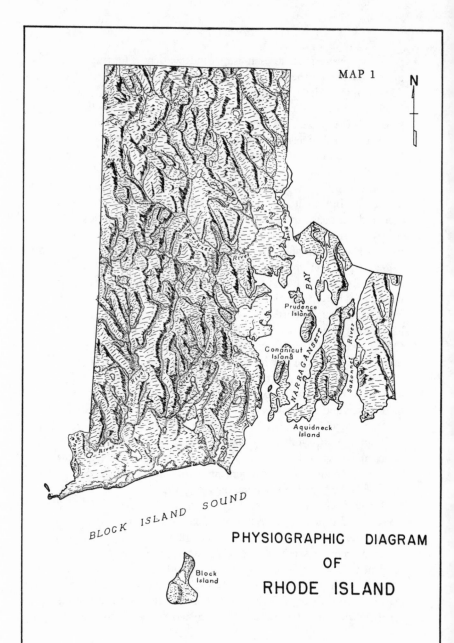

MAP 1

N

BLOCK ISLAND SOUND

PHYSIOGRAPHIC DIAGRAM
OF
RHODE ISLAND

these lands were also prized because the combination of a high water table and rich humus protected farmers in times of drought.

Only a small area in Rhode Island provided such attractive farming conditions. The relief map shows that the northwesterly two-thirds of the colony was upland. As the settlers pushed further inland, they found the hills becoming progressively higher until along the Connecticut border they reached a maximum altitude of 800 feet above sea level. Though the colonists discovered an occasional rich meadow in the Blackstone, Pawtuxet, and Pawcatuck valleys, usually they found rock-strewn, broken landscapes and thin, sterile soils. And, while the Atlantic Ocean and Narragansett Bay moderated climate throughout the colony, contrasts in temperature, rainfall, and the length of the growing season were sufficiently marked to penalize hill-country as compared to coastal farmers.

Despite these inhospitable conditions, the scarcity of coastal land eventually forced some families into the interior upland, where they eked out a precarious existence raising crops and livestock and paying for the few supplies they needed by selling farm produce and forest products. But most of the trees were so stunted that they had little commercial value and, when cleared, the land made poor farms. Some families supplemented their incomes by working scattered deposits of limestone, iron ore, and granite.

So it was that the forces of geography and economics which gave all northern colonies their maritime orientation were felt with particular strength along the shores of Narragansett Bay. Like other New England settlers, the Rhode Islanders had to import most of their manufactures and some of their food. The colony's extensive coastline, its abundance of excellent harbors, and, above all, its inability to support a large agricultural population, drew the colonists to mercantile rather than to agricultural pursuits. Rhode Island ports were favorably located for coastal trade, and, though not as conveniently situated as those of Massachusetts, they were also within reach of the major New England fishing grounds. Maritime affairs, then, gradually assumed the dominant position, and the fortunes of Rhode Islanders turned on their success as traders until long after the Revolution had run its course.

The seaward orientation developed slowly at first, but by the early years of the eighteenth century Rhode Island trading enterprises were growing rapidly and ranging far. Even as late as 1680, Governor Peleg Sanford could report that commerce and fishing languished for "the want of Merchants and Men of considerable Estate amongst us." Traders exchanged horses and provisions for Barbadoes goods, he wrote, but Rhode Island possessed only a few sloops, and "most of our Colloney live comfortably by improving the wilderness."[3] But conditions changed rapidly over the next half century. Newport established a customs house in 1681 and, with the outbreak of King William's War in 1689, began to reap large profits from privateering attacks on French and, later, Spanish shipping. Providence, too, built wharves and warehouses and developed a thriving commerce; and by 1698 Rhode Island's foreign trade had become sufficiently important for the legislature to regulate the export of provisions.

The colony's fleet increased from 29 vessels totaling probably less than 1,800 tons in 1708 to about 80 vessels totaling 5,000 tons in 1731, and the number of sailors employed rose from 140 to 400.[4] While a few of these craft were ships or brigs large enough to cross the Atlantic, most were small sloops specializing in the coastal trade. They picked up cargoes of English manufacturers, usually at Boston, for sale along the coast as far south as Philadelphia. Despite the small scale of these operations and despite Rhode Island's belated entry into commercial enterprises, merchant-shipowners prosecuted their business with such shrewd determination that they soon challenged Boston's long standing preëminence in northern intercolonial trade.

The perennial need for cargoes or cash to exchange for trading goods gradually forced Narragansett Bay merchants to extend their voyages into foreign waters. By 1740, the Rhode Island trading

[3] Samuel Greene Arnold, *History of Rhode Island, 1636–1790* (2 vols., New York, 1859–1860), 1:489–490.

[4] Bartlett, *Rhode Island Colonial Records*, 4:60; Arnold, *History of Rhode Island*, 2:106; Richard M. Bayles, ed., *History of Newport County* (New York, 1888), 530–531.

fleet numbered 120 vessels, many of which were engaged in African slaving operations or in West Indian commerce. The colony now imported most of its manufactures directly from England, and it had developed an extensive re-export business.[5] Following the abolition of the duty on slaves in 1732, Newport began a meteoric expansion which, by 1769, made it the principal northern slave mart and the most important commercial center in southern New England. Though the rate of growth had begun to decline after 1763, in its heyday Newport operated between five hundred and six hundred vessels, about a third of which (including fifty slavers) were employed in foreign commerce.[6]

Providence's maritime life, though slower to develop than Newport's, gradually gathered momentum. By the mid-eighteenth century, the town was growing prodigiously. A mercantile cabal, the match of any in New England in determination and singleness of purpose, gave direction to local affairs; a shipbuilding industry struggled to keep pace with the burgeoning demand for vessels; distillers and the packers of meat, fish, lime, and other provisions and commodities labored to keep the trading fleet supplied with cargoes; and captains soon became as familiar with foreign markets as they were with colonial ones. Providence merchants lost many vessels during the Anglo-French struggle for world supremacy—more than fifty craft during the Seven Year's War alone—but they recouped by privateering, which made "many rich and some poor," and by trading voyages, which, because of the shortage of goods and the disruption of commerce, often returned enormous profits.[7]

The drive to expand the trading area and the willingness to engage in high risk enterprises like privateering reflected the special problems faced by Rhode Island merchants. Though numerous and accessible, Narragansett Bay ports lacked the productive, thickly

[5] Arnold, *History of Rhode Island*, 2:130; Bridenbaugh, *Cities in Revolt*, 46–47, 53; Bayles, *Newport County*, 531.

[6] Edward Field, ed., *State of Rhode Island and Providence Plantations at the End of the Century: A History* (3 vols., Boston, 1902), 2:398; Bayles, *Newport County*, 532–533.

[7] Field, *Rhode Island*, 2:450. For additional data on privateering, see *ibid.*, 1:533–560, 567, 578–580, 582, 597–599; 2:405–423.

lish creditors. But the iron industry failed to meet expectations, and candle making, though it prospered throughout the third quarter of the eighteenth century, did not survive the Revolution.[10] Nevertheless, the export of these and other manufactured goods did help Rhode Island merchants overcome the unfavorable balance of trade and thus played an important rôle in the expansion of the mercantile economy.

The development of opportunism as a way of life was both reflected in and a reflection of the patterns of population growth and settlement. Scarcity of good farming land at first restricted growth. But this was only temporary, simply because the drive for trade mounted by the mercantile community created a demand for all manner of products incidental to land clearing and to expanding town economies. Burnt lime, charcoal, potash, tar, shingles, lumber, cider, and even perishable products—butter, cheese, and meat—entered the stream of commerce. To the farmer-artisan, producing partly for trade, was added the village-artisan, producing partly for the local and partly for the external market. Blacksmiths, tinners, cobblers, carpenters, and many others found homes in both country villages and seaport towns. And finally there were those who produced almost exclusively for the external market—the iron workers, the candlemakers, the rum distillers, the fishermen—or who serviced the growing merchant fleet—the cordwainers and sailmakers, the shipwrights and chandlers.

During the seventeenth century, before the trading orientation became pronounced, the colony grew relatively slowly.[11] On at least three occasions, the settlers encountered severe setbacks. In King Philip's War, which broke out in 1675, the Wampanoag and Narragansett Indians went on the rampage. They sacked and burned

[10] Hedges, *The Browns*, 86–122, 220–225, 309–311; Bayles, *Newport County*, 533.

[11] The analysis of population growth is based on Evarts B. Greene and Virginia D. Harrington, *American Population Before the Federal Census of 1790* (New York, 1932), 61–70; Edwin M. Snow, comp., *Report upon the Census of Rhode Island, 1865* (Providence, 1867), xxxii–xxxiii; Kurt B. Mayer, *Economic Development and Population Growth in Rhode Island* (Providence, 1953), 9–26. The data are summarized in Table 1 on p. 21.

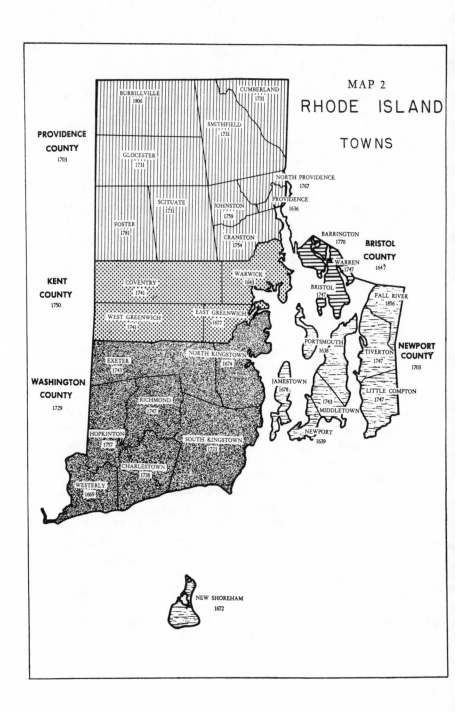

MAP 2

RHODE ISLAND

TOWNS

BURRILLVILLE
1806

CUMBERLAND
1731

SMITHFIELD
1731

PROVIDENCE
COUNTY
1703

GLOCESTER
1731

NORTH PROVIDENCE
1767

SCITUATE
1731

JOHNSTON
1759

PROVIDENCE
1636

FOSTER
1781

CRANSTON
1754

BARRINGTON
1770

BRISTOL
COUNTY
1647

WARREN
1747

KENT
COUNTY
1750

COVENTRY
1741

WARWICK
1643

BRISTOL
1747

FALL RIVER
1856

WEST GREENWICH
1741

EAST GREENWICH
1677

PORTSMOUTH
1638

NEWPORT
COUNTY
1703

TIVERTON
1747

WASHINGTON
COUNTY
1729

EXETER
1743

NORTH KINGSTOWN
1674

JAMESTOWN
1678

LITTLE COMPTON
1747

RICHMOND
1747

MIDDLETOWN
1743

HOPKINTON
1757

SOUTH KINGSTOWN
1723

NEWPORT
1639

CHARLESTOWN
1738

WESTERLY
1669

NEW SHOREHAM
1672

Providence, and drove the colonists from all the other mainland settlements. Aquidneck Island escaped the Indian torch, but a virulent pestilence swept Newport and Portsmouth in 1676, and in the winter of 1690–1691 the entire colony suffered from a deadly smallpox epidemic. Although Rhode Island gradually recovered from these disasters, the first census, taken in 1708, counted less than 7,200 people, at least three-quarters of whom sustained themselves by farming and fishing. Providence, which extended across the entire northern region and covered almost three hundred square miles of land, had only 1,450 residents. Most of them lived near the head of Narragansett Bay. Another 2,200 people resided in Newport, either in the commercial center itself or in the adjacent farming district to the northeast. Portsmouth, at the other end of Aquidneck Island, had barely 600 inhabitants. Jamestown on Conanicut Island to the west of Newport, and New Shoreham on Block Island to the south, each had a mere 200 people. Four towns, Warwick, Greenwich, Kingstown, and Westerly, occupied the mainland southwest of Providence. Together, they could count not quite 2,500 residents.

The rapid expansion of maritime trade, together with the extension of settlement into the more accessible interior regions, produced between 1708 and 1730 a quarter-century of extremely rapid growth. Providence, which emerged as the second-ranking commercial center, also benefited from the spread of farming into the more distant areas of the Blackstone, Woonasquatucket, and Pawtuxet valleys and grew from less than 1,450 residents to over 3,900. Newport, the chief beneficiary of the trade boom, more than doubled in size, reaching a population of 4,640. The three other towns in Newport County, Portsmouth, Jamestown, and New Shoreham, derived little benefit from the expansion of the maritime economy, and grew relatively slowly. Washington (or as it was known before the Revolution, King's) County occupied the southwestern mainland section of the colony and was the home of the Narragansett planters, a group of slave-owning families engaged in stock-raising on a comparatively large scale. Employing Negro and Indian slaves as well as indentured white servants, they produced wool, cheese, work animals, and the famous Narragansett pacers. One of these towns, Westerly, which lay along the Connecticut border, expanded particularly rapidly during the early eighteenth century. Its population rose from 570 in 1708 to over 1,900 in 1730, a threefold increase in less than a generation. Kingstown's plantation economy also developed significantly. The town was divided into two jurisdictions in 1723; by 1730 North and South Kingstown together contained over 3,600 people as compared to only 1,200 in 1708. South Kingstown had 965 whites, 333 Negroes, and 223 Indians.[12] The mainland farming towns to the north, Greenwich and Warwick, experienced a comparable upsurge in population, growing from 240 to 1,200 and from 480 to 1,800 inhabitants respectively. By 1730, then, Rhode Island's mixed agricultural, lumbering, manufacturing, fishing, and trading economy was supporting almost 18,000 people.

Because the colony was approaching the optimum population under prevailing economic conditions, the rate of growth slackened perceptibly over the ensuing quarter-century, from 1730 to 1755. By mid-century, Rhode Island numbered over 40,400 inhabitants, but many of them lived in towns newly acquired from Massachusetts, and in Newport, particularly, about a sixth of the residents (over 1,100 people) were Negroes. Thus the colony's actual rate of population growth had fallen from more than seven to not quite four per cent annually.

During this quarter-century population pressure on the intensively cultivated coastal lands forced many families either into the mercantile towns or into the interior hill country. The population of the area that had been Providence grew so rapidly—from barely 3,900 people to over 9,860—that Cranston, Smithfield, Glocester, and Scituate were carved out of it. These were quiet, rural jurisdictions with their inhabitants dispersed over a relatively wide area. Though Providence was reduced to about forty-six square miles, it still had some 3,160 residents, or only 750 less than in 1730.

[12] Edward Channing, "The Narragansett Planters: A Study of Causes," in *Johns Hopkins Studies in Historical and Political Science*, 4:109–127 (March, 1886).

The port itself was becoming a bustling trading center, but the outskirts were still in farmland. Newport was also divided. When the agricultural community of Middletown was set off in 1743, Newport was reduced to eight square miles. Some 6,750 inhabitants were crowded into this tiny area. The town was more dependent upon trade, especially slaving, than any other Rhode Island port, and, with the patronage of its cultivated merchant grandees, it had artistic, literary, and philosophic interests befitting its rank as a major commercial center. The agricultural and fishing towns in Newport County grew relatively slowly. The newly formed Middletown had only 780 people in 1755, and the older communities of Portsmouth, Jamestown, and New Shoreham grew from a total of 1,424 to 2,258, or at barely half the rate of the colony as a whole. Growth was much more rapid in Kent and Washington counties on the western shore of Narragansett Bay, where five new towns—Coventry, West Greenwich, Exeter, Richmond, and Charlestown—were formed. All except Charlestown were in the interior. Given over largely to farming, fishing, and the manufacture of forest products, these two counties grew from a total of less than 8,000 to almost 15,200 people.

The settlement of an old boundary dispute with Massachusetts in 1746 added three new areas, more than 120 square miles, and some 4,700 new residents to Rhode Island. Cumberland, an extensive tract of farming country lying to the east of the Blackstone River, added over 800 people to Providence County. Bristol and Warren, the second area, consisted of a series of promontories in Narragansett Bay southeast of Providence. They were accessible over land only by passing through Massachusetts. In these towns (which were organized as Bristol County) lived about 1,750 inhabitants; their principal pursuits were farming, fishing, and petty maritime ventures. The third area set off from Massachusetts comprised the eastern shore farming and fishing communities of Tiverton and Little Compton. They were joined to Newport County and added almost 2,200 people to its population.

By mid-century Rhode Island had entered a critical phase of development. The colony's agricultural settlement was reaching its natural limits; some mercantile towns, most notably Newport, were growing more slowly than previously; and Rhode Island's overall rate of population growth was declining to barely two and a half per cent annually.

Only two areas, Providence and the northern hill country, continued to grow rapidly. Providence again lost territory, being diminished (by the separation of Johnston in 1759 and North Providence in 1767) to a commercial and residential area covering only seven square miles. Even so, in 1774 the town had some 4,300 residents, a substantial increase over 1755. While this was still less than half the population of Newport, Providence, a relative pygmy, threatened to topple Newport's long-standing political and economic hegemony. Providence merchants were operating on such a substantial scale that each year saw the gap between the two ports growing steadily narrower. The concentration of settlement at the head of Narragansett Bay also strengthened Providence's position relative to Newport. Providence and its three surrounding towns of Cranston, Johnston, and North Providence had a total population of more than 8,000 people. Moreover, the hinterland area of Cumberland, Smithfield, Glocester, and Scituate was growing more rapidly than any other region in the colony. Between 1755 and 1774 these towns increased their population from 6,300 to almost 11,200. Altogether, Providence County contained over 19,000 people, or almost a third of the colony's population.

The older coastal towns, the eastern and southern commercial centers, and the western hill country all grew relatively slowly after 1755. Some towns grew hardly at all. The incorporation of Barrington in 1770 created a third town in Bristol County, but this merely set off a sparsely settled agricultural area from the port towns of Bristol and Warren, and the county's population totaled only 2,790 in 1774, an increase of barely 780 since 1755. Newport County grew even more slowly. No significant change occurred in Middletown, Portsmouth, Jamestown, Little Compton, and New Shoreham. The growth in Tiverton and Newport, though substantial, failed to keep pace with the colony's average. In Washington County, where the shortage of good land restricted the number of farming families that could be supported, most towns began to press the means of subsistence soon after the middle of the century. The county's total population increased from 9,675 in 1755 to 13,870 in 1774. North Kingstown and Exeter, the two most northerly towns in the county, all but stopped growing; in the southern part of the county settlement tended to move from the coastal towns of South Kingstown, Charlestown, and Westerly into the hill-country towns of Richmond and the newly formed Hopkinton. In Kent County, immediately to the north, the rate of population growth also declined. Warwick and East Greenwich on the coast grew from about 3,100 to about 4,100; Coventry and West Greenwich in the interior grew from about 2,440 to about 3,790.

By the eve of the Revolution, then, Rhode Island's population had ceased the rapid growth characteristic of the early years of the century. In fact, agricultural settlement had reached its natural limits almost twenty years before. Further growth, therefore, had become so dependent upon the ability of the commercial and manufacturing segments of the economy to absorb the population surplus, that any check to mercantile operations threatened Rhode Island's capacity to provide livelihoods for either the natural increase of population or additional immigrants.[13] Such a check had actually occurred as early as 1755, when a severe depression caused widespread distress in both the maritime and the agriculture communities. Intensified by the dislocation of normal trade during the war with France, the crisis sorely tested Rhode Island merchants. Most traders escaped permanent damage, but even those least injured emerged acutely aware of the colony's economic vulnerability. Having developed a delicately balanced economy based in Rhode Island rather than in England, and depending for its success on freedom to pursue profit wherever and whenever the opportunity appeared, the colony's merchants recognized that Britain's imperial wars and commercial regulations could cripple them. High

[13] For data on the shipbuilding, sailmaking, and ropemaking industries and for bounties to encourage flax and hemp production, see Field, *Rhode Island*, 1:168, 195; 2:399–400, 480–481; 3:327–329, 369, 579; Bartlett, *Rhode Island Colonial Records*, 4:399–400, 407–408, 512, 525–526.

wartime profits earned in legitimate trading voyages, privateering, smuggling, clandestine ventures, or in traffic with the French failed to dispel this concern.

So long as the imperial authorities enforced the Navigation system languidly, so long could traders pursue their self-interest; and only so long, too, could the colony sustain its growing population. Thus Britain's determination, after 1763, to strengthen its control of colonial affairs and especially its enforcement of the Acts of Trade, stung the colonists into bitter hostility. In particular, the Rhode Islanders regarded the enforcement of the Sugar Act of 1764 as an abomination. In their remonstrance against it they protested that it would destroy the molasses trade and thereby prevent their earning the exchange needed to sustain their other maritime operations.[14]

From the remonstrance against the Sugar Act in January, 1764, to the Rhode Island Declaration of Independence in May, 1776, the colony's merchants took whatever steps they judged best to defend their interests. Given the already firmly established tradition of pragmatic opportunism, they were American patriots when the occasion demanded, unpatriotic when there was profit in it. Thus, though both Providence and Newport adopted stringent sumptuary laws and nonimportation agreements in December, 1767, their effectiveness, especially in the case of Newport, was limited. As a result, Rhode Islanders acquired a reputation as exploiters of the patriotic self-sacrifice of others. Only in 1769, when pressure from Boston, New York, Philadelphia, and Charleston forced Newport to abandon the importation of enumerated British goods, did the Rhode Island position become unequivocal.[15]

When self-interest and devotion to the colonial cause were identical, Rhode Islanders proved themselves boldly patriotic. The interference of the revenue cutter *Gaspee* with the activities of Rhode Island vessels was a case in point. It gave John Brown, the most impetuous of the Providence merchant princes, the provocation he needed for organizing an expedition which, in June, 1772, de-

[14] Bartlett, *Rhode Island Colonial Records*, 4:378–383.
[15] Hedges, *The Browns*, 203–207.

stroyed the luckless craft as she lay stranded six miles down the bay from the family counting houses. In one stroke, Brown removed a major threat to commercial enterprise and identified the mercantile community with all determined opponents to British imperial policy.[16]

Since the importation of strategic materials vitally affected the success of American arms, the outbreak of hostilities in Massachusetts in April, 1775, gave many Rhode Islanders, especially Providence merchants and shipowners, an ideal opportunity to serve both the revolutionary cause and their own fortunes. Though they did contribute to independence, sometimes by taking risks exceeding the profits they earned, they kept a close watch for the main chance. Thus in November, 1775, John Brown coldly calculated the market for military supplies by the measure he understood best: acute shortage. Accordingly, when he furnished gunpowder to the Continental army encamped at Cambridge, he charged six shillings a pound, a price General Washington could only protest and pay.[17]

Such deals were typical of the shrewd ability of the Browns—and of families like them—to turn rapidly changing and often adverse conditions to their advantage. In the long run, the family fortune was not substantially affected one way or the other by the war. The Browns nevertheless escaped the disaster which engulfed many richer and more powerful American families, such as the Hancocks of Boston, and this by any standard was a notable achievement. Despite relatively little experience with continental merchants before 1775, the Browns speedily established relations with agents at Nantes, Gothenburg, and Amsterdam and, some costly mistakes notwithstanding, adjusted successfully to the new trading pattern. When the British seized control of Narragansett Bay, thereby rendering Providence useless as a trading port, the Browns stayed in business by fitting out their ships at Nantucket. The war crippled the candle industry, thereby depriving the Browns of a prime source of foreign remittance. But they took this disaster in their stride by concentrating their manufacturing effort

[16] *Ibid.*, 208–210.
[17] *Ibid.*, 219.

on casting cannon at their Hope Furnace and on the production of loaf sugar. Whether they were grappling with inflation, adjusting to the kaleidoscopic changes in Caribbean conditions, turning from trading to privateering ventures, or manipulating the value of public securities the Browns capitalized on each opportunity coming their way. In this fashion, the Browns in particular, and the Providence merchants in general, weathered the revolutionary crisis.[18]

In Newport, by contrast, the merchants were almost wiped out. During the three years the British occupied the town, this once proud commercial and cultural metropolis suffered more permanent damage than any other major center. Hundreds of buildings were destroyed, and the port's vitality was drained by the exodus of men, capital, and ships. Many prominent merchants, including the Portuguese Jewish community, fled when the British invaders arrived, and others, especially Loyalist sympathizers, abandoned the town when the British evacuated.[19]

Bristol also suffered considerable damage. The British bombarded the port to enforce their demand for supplies; they blockaded it with a frigate; and then, in May, 1778, they sent in troops to attack a battery commanding the channel between the town and Aquidneck Island and burned more than thirty homes. But while many sailors and vessels had to find employment away from the port, Bristol merchants retained their counting houses in the town, and when the war ended they resumed their maritime activities.[20]

During the war years Rhode Island's population fell from 59,700 to less than 52,000. Since almost half the loss was sustained by Newport alone, and since Providence lost only a negligible number of people, the net effect was to make the two ports more nearly equal in importance. Other commercial towns, especially Bristol, Warren, and Westerly, also gained relative to Newport, and Little Compton, Exeter, and Coventry actually attracted settlers, mainly

[18] *Ibid.*, 215–286 *passim.*
[19] Field, *Rhode Island*, 1:231–232, 234–236, 240–241, 244–246; Bridenbaugh, *Cities in Revolt*, 53, 264, 324, 378.
[20] George Howe, *Mount Hope: A New England Chronicle* (New York, 1959), 87–92.

refugees. All other towns declined substantially. But because they were agricultural rather than mercantile communities, their losses had little impact on the Narragansett Bay economy.

TABLE 1

THE POPULATION OF RHODE ISLAND, 1708–1782

Towns	Incorporated	1708	1730	1755	1774	1776	1782
Cranston	1754			1,460	1,834	1,701	1,589
Johnston	1759				1,031	1,022	996
Providence	1636	1,446	3,916	3,159	4,321	4,355	4,310
North Providence	1767				830	813	698
Cumberland	1747			1,083	1,756	1,686	1,548
Smithfield	1731			1,921	2,888	2,781	2,217
Glocester	1731			1,511	2,945	2,832	2,791
Foster	1781						1,763
Scituate	1731			1,813	3,601	3,289	1,628
Providence County	1703	1,446	3,916	10,947	19,206	18,479	17,540
Newport	1639	2,203	4,640	6,753	9,209	5,299	5,530
Middletown	1743			778	881	860	674
Portsmouth	1638	628	813	1,363	1,512	1,347	1,350
Jamestown	1678	206	321	517	563	322	345
Tiverton	1747			1,325	1,957	2,091	1,959
Little Compton	1747			1,170	1,232	1,302	1,341
New Shoreham	1672	208	290	378	575	478	
Newport County	1703	3,245	6,064	12,284	15,929	11,699	11,199
North Kingstown	1674	1,200	2,105	2,109	2,472	2,761	2,328
South Kingstown	1723		1,523	1,913	2,835	2,779	2,675
Exeter	1743			1,404	1,864	1,982	2,058
Richmond	1747			829	1,257	1,204	1,094
Charlestown	1738			1,130	1,821	1,835	1,523
Hopkinton	1757				1,805	1,845	1,735
Westerly	1669	570	1,926	2,291	1,812	1,824	1,720
Washington County	1729	1,770	5,554	9,676	13,866	14,230	13,133
Warwick	1643	480	1,178	1,911	2,438	2,376	2,112
Coventry	1741			1,178	2,023	2,300	2,107
East Greenwich	1677	240	1,223	1,167	1,663	1,664	1,609
West Greenwich	1741			1,246	1,764	1,653	1,698
Kent County	1750	720	2,401	5,502	7,888	7,993	7,526
Bristol	1747			1,080	1,209	1,067	1,032
Warren	1747			925	979	1,005	905
Barrington	1770				601	538	534
Bristol County	1747			2,005	2,789	2,610	2,471
Rhode Island		7,181	17,935	40,414	59,678	55,011	51,869

All Rhode Island, including Newport, seemed to recover rapidly from the Revolution. Freed from prewar British restrictions as well as from American wartime restraints, merchants quickly restored disrupted commercial ties and forged new and even more profitable ones. Though the postwar British duty on whale oil destroyed a formerly important method of remittance to English creditors and though the British Order in Council of July 2, 1783, closed West Indian ports to American shipping, thus depriving merchants of a valued market and source of raw materials, Rhode Island traders quickly found or created profitable substitutes. The European, African, Caribbean, and coastal trades quickly regained their former vigor, and in 1787 the Browns despatched the first Providence ship, the *George Washington*, to the East Indies. By 1790, Rhode Island had not only made up for the wartime exodus, but it had even expanded its population to almost 69,000, an increase of nearly 17,000 in less than a decade. Providence, in particular, had grown so rapidly that it threatened to replace Newport as the principal Rhode Island commercial center.

In one important respect appearances were deceptive. Rhode Island's population was only 9,000 more in 1790 than it had been in 1774. This represented a rate of growth over the sixteen year period of less than one per cent annually. Clearly, the Narragansett Bay economy had not outgrown its prewar weaknesses. The limits of agricultural expansion had been reached; the most accessible forest resources had been used up; and the Rhode Islanders were over-specialized. They were dangerously close to relying almost exclusively on maritime endeavor. To make matters worse, trading prospects were particularly uncertain at the beginning of 1790. For this state of affairs the mercantile community was largely responsible.

In the short span of nine years the merchants twice endangered their interests, first by helping to provoke the passage of state tariffs, then by almost failing to carry Rhode Island into the Union. To protect their re-export business, traders had marshalled opposition to the tariff recommended by the Confederation Congress in 1781, 1783, and 1786. Since the proposed impost did not grant a drawback on foreign goods shipped in interstate trade, a large proportion of Rhode Island's commerce would have been subject to an additional five per cent tax that merchants could not pass on to consumers. But, understandable though this opposition was, it indirectly jeopardized the Narragansett Bay economy by intensifying the pressures on state governments to take over the Revolutionary debt themselves and to service it through tariffs of their own. Thus Rhode Island merchants helped bring about the very burdens on interstate trade that they had been so anxious to prevent.[21]

The reorganization of the national government seemed to promise a satisfactory solution to this problem.[22] After delaying action long enough to satisfy themselves that they were serving their best interests, traders swung their support to ratification of the constitution drafted at Philadelphia in 1787. Though perhaps at first tempted to remain out of the Union in order to reap the immense profits from smuggling that such a situation would have made possible, in the end the merchants were swayed by two other considerations. First, both the Constitution and Hamilton's fiscal policies favored commercial interests. The states could not regulate interstate trade, and consumers, not merchants, paid duties on foreign goods imposed in the tariff of 1789. Moreover, the prospects for a drawback on goods re-exported in international trade seemed favorable. Second, Hamilton's proposal to fund the war debts promised substantial profits to holders of public securities, prominent among whom were Providence and Newport merchants. Ever mindful of the need for

[21] Hedges, *The Browns*, 323–325.

[22] Compare *ibid.*, 314–323, 326–328; Forrest McDonald, *We The People: The Economic Origins of the Constitution* (Chicago, 1958), 321–346; Hillman Metcalf Bishop, "Why Rhode Island Opposed the Federal Constitution: The Continental Impost; The Paper Money Era; Paper Money and the Constitution; Political Reasons," in *Rhode Island History*, 8:1–10, 33–44, 85–95, 115–126 (January to October, 1949); and Mack Thompson, *Moses Brown: Reluctant Reformer* (Chapel Hill, 1962), 239–243. For the vote to ratify, see *Providence Gazette*, June 5, 1790. Delegates from Newport and Bristol counties almost unanimously favored ratification. Elsewhere, sentiment against the Constitution ran high and only four other towns—Providence, Cumberland, Hopkinton, and Westerly—voted to ratify. Warwick divided on the issue. Thus, a coalition of the southeastern towns and the seaports carried Rhode Island into the Union by the narrow margin of thirty-four votes to thirty-two.

additional risk capital with which to finance their operations, Rhode Island traders would have been turning their backs on a successful history of opportunism had they failed to capitalize on the advantages the Constitution and the Hamiltonian program offered them.

But the earlier campaign against the tariff, directed of necessity at the threat of increased congressional power, had been so effective that a majority of Rhode Island voters were convinced that the proposed Constitution threatened liberty and democracy. Now the merchants had to reverse their position and preach centralization. They almost failed. For more than two years, from February, 1788, to May, 1790, the question hung in the balance. A convention finally ratified by a narrow majority, but only after Providence had seceded from Rhode Island and threatened to remain separate until the delegates voted to join the Union.

Looking back over the preceding century and a half, Rhode Islanders could pride themselves that they and their forebears had triumphed over adversity. From the moment of the colony's inception the settlers had faced an unfriendly, demanding world. They had preserved their political and religious independence despite pressure from a suspicious and overbearing Massachusetts; they had also resisted Connecticut's territorial demands. Little could be done to enrich the colony's natural resources, but, by shrewdly trading whatever surplus farm and forest products they could scrape together, they had parlayed Nature's parsimonious endowment into a sufficiency. In time, these maritime ventures had brought prosperity to many colonists and great wealth to a few.

Substantial though these achievements were, many Rhode Islanders had, along the way, won a reputation as pirates, smugglers, and cutthroats, or as shrewd, hard dealing, acquisitive mercenaries. And perhaps they did care more for Mammon than for God; certainly they had difficulty in shaking off the faint but unmistakable whiff of brimstone clinging to many of their exploits.[23] They were even uncertain where the truth lay themselves. For there was an element of self-delusion in the caricature of the "Rhode Islander."

[23] Bridenbaugh, *Cities in Revolt*, 140, 259, 266.

Part of his success lay in his belief that he could outsmart other traders; that he could succeed where others had failed; that he, better than others, could create and exploit opportunities; and that he could prosper even in adversity. And if, as he was wont to do, he grumbled about losses and poor business conditions, it was merely his way of discouraging others from crowding the field. In short, the Rhode Islander inherited from the Colonial and Revolutionary experiences an image of himself, the past, and why he had succeeded. Whether this amalgam of reality and fantasy would be an asset or a liability remained to be seen.

CHAPTER TWO

The Maritime Economy

WHEN Rhode Island entered the Union in 1790, the principal employment for risk capital was still in maritime activity, especially in international trade. As in colonial times, seafaring dominated economic life. Even in the most remote hamlets of the western hill country, the affairs of farmers, mechanics, craftsmen, and storekeepers were touched by the ocean. The far-ranging ventures of the Narragansett Bay traders drew down to the ports the surplus produce of every adjacent locality. And across the sea came the wares of a thousand markets. The economic difficulties of what has come to be called the "Critical Period" were already history, high hopes were entertained for the success of the newly opened East Indies trade, the Hamiltonian program was expected to dispel political and commercial uncertainties, and only confirmed pessimists saw reason to worry over the "sivel war in France."[1] The future was promising, and Rhode Island merchants had the organization and the experience, the capital and the ships to turn the promise into profits.

Most traders conducted their affairs according to a pattern that had become fairly standardized.[2] The common form of commercial

[1] Mark Anthony DeWolf to John DeWolf, quoted in Howe, *Mount Hope*, 100.
[2] The discussion of commercial practices is based on Vincent P. Carosso and Lawrence H. Leder, eds., "The Samuel Snow–Sullivan Dorr Correspondence," in *Rhode Island History*, 15:65–88 (July, 1956); *Clarke's Executors vs. Van Riemsdyk*, 9 *Cranch* 153 (1815); "Commerce of Rhode Island, 1775–1800," in *Massachusetts Historical Society Publications*, 7th series, vol. 10 (Boston, 1915), especially pp. 406–478; Howard Corning, ed., "Letters of Sullivan Dorr," in *Proceedings of the Massachusetts Historical Society*, 67:178–364 (Boston, 1941–1944); Corning, "Sullivan Dorr, An Early China Merchant," in *Essex Institute Historical Collections*, 78:158–175 (April, 1942); Corning, "Sullivan Dorr, China Trader," in *Rhode Island History*, 3:75–90 (July, 1944); Elizabeth

organization was the partnership. With its subordinate supercargoes, captains, agents, factors, and correspondents linking Rhode
Island counting houses with world markets, it constituted a flexible,
efficient, and effective method of organizing maritime affairs. Although a few merchants did operate alone, most firms consisted of
two members, and three or more partners were not unknown. Sometimes a partnership was an association of equals and involved a
pooling of resources. Other firms brought men of widely dissimilar
backgrounds and accomplishments together. Established merchants with diverse business interests frequently took promising
younger men into partnership. The senior member contributed
capital, experience, and commercial connections, and sometimes he
merely exercised general supervision. He left routine management
to the junior partner, who, in effect, contributed work rather than
capital. Depending upon the particular articles of agreement and
the status of individual members, partners were usually free to devote some of their energies to other ventures.

Since credit was the stuff of which commercial success was made,
partners were often selected with an eye to the effect an association would have upon the firm's standing in the market place.
From the inception of maritime trade Narragansett Bay merchants

Donnan, ed., *Documents Illustrative of the History of the Slave Trade to America*
(4 vols., Washington, D.C., 1930–1935), 3:346–404; Welcome Arnold Greene,
et al., *The Providence Plantations for Two Hundred and Fifty Years* (Providence, 1886), 247; Howard Greene and Alice E. Smith, eds., *The Journals of
Welcome Arnold Greene: The Voyages of the Brigantine Perseverence, 1817–
1820* (Madison, 1956), especially pp. 10–11, 30–35, 47–57, 64, 74–80, 85–86,
101, 111–124, 139–143, 147, 171–174, 182–184, 194–211; Hedges, *The
Browns*, especially pp. 289–291, 307, 309; Robert W. Kenny, "The Maiden
Voyage of *Ann and Hope* of Providence to Botany Bay and Canton, 1798–1799,"
in *The American Neptune*, 18:105–136 (April, 1958); Gertrude Selwyn Kimball, *The East-India Trade of Providence from 1787 to 1807* (Providence,
1896), 3–34; George Champlin Mason, *Reminiscences of Newport* (Newport,
1884), 371, 386; *Mathewson vs. Clarke*, 6 Howard 122 (1848); Earl C.
Tanner, "The Latin–American Trade of E. Carrington & Co., 1822," in *Rhode
Island History*, 13:33–44, 78–85 (April and July, 1954); Tanner, "The Voyage
of the *Mercury*," in *Rhode Island History*, 10:33–44, 65–79 (April and July,
1951); William B. Weeden, "Early Oriental Commerce in Providence," in
Proceedings of the Massachusetts Historical Society, 41:236–278 (December,
1907).

had been unusually dependent upon each other and upon their correspondents throughout the world for supplies of liquid capital. Concern for the ability to finance a new venture, to preserve the safety of one already underway, or to stave off a sudden crisis had gradually become part of the Rhode Island frame of mind and dominated mercantile thinking until well into the nineteenth century. According to the merchant's ethical code, the cardinal sin lay not in slaving, or smuggling, or privateering, or even in piracy and murder, nor did it lie in the dishonest dodges devised to cloak such practices. Rather, it lay in the inability to deliver on promises. The merchant's word was and had to be his bond. Whether this meant repaying a debt when it fell due, supplying goods of the promised quality at the time and place agreed upon, or honoring a note endorsed on behalf of a fellow merchant, the trader knew that such obligations had to be met promptly and fully. The man careless enough to endanger his credit was as foolhardy as the captain who deliberately sailed into a hurricane—and the results were usually just as disastrous.

Because a partnership normally expired with the death of any of its members, merchants generally tried to hedge against possible damage. Some merchants arranged to continue an association until all voyages were completed. Others trained their male heirs to succeed them, and still others, lacking qualified sons, selected promising youths who might eventually be taken into partnership. These arrangements were sometimes cemented by marriage and reflected dynastic ambitions, but most merchants prevented family loyalties from becoming excessively powerful. They selected partners and employees for ability, not kinship, and generally they refused to train their sons for responsibilities they would be unwilling or unable to assume.

The day-to-day operations of a large mercantile house, as well as the achievement of long range goals, required infinite care and constant attention. At home, merchants had to supervise clerks, draymen, truckers, coopers, warehousemen, shipwrights, sailmakers, watchmen, and a host of other workers; abroad, all was in the hands of supercargoes, captains, agents, factors, and correspondents.

A merchant's success depended largely on the skill and reliability of these men.

Supercargoes, usually young men starting a mercantile career, were commonly employed on all but the smallest vessels and were responsible for every aspect of a venture except navigation. Sometimes under specific instructions and sometimes not, they bought and sold cargoes on their own authority, and were constantly on watch to protect or promote their employers' interests. The wide discretion supercargoes traditionally enjoyed was particularly necessary from 1792 to 1815, when the Anglo-French and related conflicts made international commerce unusually hazardous. But even in peacetime, most voyages were complex; they rarely conformed to a routine pattern; and, not uncommonly, they lasted several years. On a typical voyage, a vessel might sail from Providence to Charleston, exchange its mixed cargo for products that could be sold for specie in the Mediterranean, freight another cargo to Canton, apply the specie and freight money to the purchase of Oriental goods, then return to Narragansett Bay via Amsterdam with a cargo of European manufactures. On such a venture, the supercargo carried general instructions about the route to be followed, the kinds of goods to be traded, and the prices to be paid. From time to time, commercial intelligence acquired in the course of business was despatched home and new counting-house directives were issued. Because many thousands of dollars were risked in a single venture, defective instructions from the entrepreneur or weak judgment by the supercargo could turn profits to losses and, as sometimes happened, send a partnership to the wall.

In effect, the supercargo system offered potential merchants an apprenticeship. They acquired firsthand understanding of the complex operations involved in international and domestic trade, a capacity for decision making, and qualities of leadership. They also learned to strike profitable bargains, often in foreign currencies of fluctuating values, acquired a smattering of other languages, and established valuable contacts with commission houses in ports scattered around the world. Supercargoes were compensated either by commission, generally two per cent on all transactions, or by salary.

In addition, they normally enjoyed cargo privileges—the right to ship a few tons of trading goods free of charge. An able super-cargo could reasonably expect to save enough from a few successful ventures to go into business for himself, or, if he were lucky, to be taken into partnership by an established firm.

The captain's function varied from venture to venture. He was always responsible for the navigation and safety of the ship, but if a supercargo was aboard, employers expected the captain "to con-form to his wishes and to consider him in our stead."[3] In such in-stances the captain received only general directions and did not even have supervision of the stowage of cargo. Captains received a monthly salary and cargo privileges and sometimes earned bonuses for particularly fast or successful voyages. If goods were carried on consignment, the captain assumed those responsibilities normally assigned to the supercargo, whose services were dispensed with. His sailing orders usually specified the route to be followed and might warn of areas where hostile cruisers or pirates were known to be operating. He also received directives dealing with cargo privileges, stowage, and wages, and was normally advised of his successor in the event of an emergency. Routine or petty voyages, especially those to the Caribbean under captains experienced in the sugar trade, were also conducted without supercargoes, as were slaving ventures, mainly because space was at a premium.

Rhode Island merchants also employed salaried agents. Some-times they sent them ahead to assemble a cargo in a particular port; and, despite their reluctance to institutionalize their activities, if the trading pattern became routine enough to warrant the innovation they stationed agents in ports regularly frequented, such as Canton or Havana. Long periods of residence gave these agents specialized knowledge of regional markets. They employed fleets of small craft to gather export cargoes and to distribute imported goods. Since shipments could be safely consigned to agents, supercargoes were needed only on unconventional voyages. From 1799 to 1803, Sul-livan Dorr, who later became a prosperous Providence entre-preneur, acted as agent for his father, a wealthy Boston merchant

[3] Weeden, "Early Oriental Commerce," 262.

engaged in the Cantonese fur trade. Edward Carrington, another young man who later joined the inner circle of Providence business families, also gained valuable experience in the Far East. He served a typical mercantile apprenticeship in the employ of a middling Providence trader, Samuel Butler. At the age of twenty-five, after a few modest ventures on his own account, Carrington became (in 1800) both a partner in and agent for an enterprise trading between Providence, Hamburg, and Havana. Two years later he was appointed United States Consul in Canton, a position that gave him special insights into Far Eastern commercial affairs and, as a private citizen, also allowed him to supplement his income by representing various American firms. When he relinquished these posts in 1811, he was able to form his own partnership. By 1818 his was the largest fleet owned in Providence.

Because Rhode Islanders placed a premium on flexibility they used factors more commonly than salaried agents, especially in those ports visited irregularly. Factors performed a variety of functions: they could facilitate the sale and purchase of cargoes, supply the latest commercial intelligence, and receive and forward correspondence between counting houses and supercargoes. They also bought and sold specie, discounted bills of exchange, and performed such sundry services as paying pilotage, anchorage, and consulate fees, clearing goods through customs, supplying provisions, and arranging for ship repairs. Too, if a supercargo arrived to find a market glutted, he could leave his wares in the hands of the commission agent and sail on to another port with a cargo more likely to yield a profit. This freed the vessel and trading goods, increased the return on fixed wage costs, and reduced the danger of desertion.

Correspondents supplied specialized financial services. Though such merchants both bought shipments outright and handled cargoes on commission, their most important function was to supply credit to mercantile houses large enough to deal on equal terms with them. In effect, correspondents provided reciprocal services by honoring drafts on each other. A Rhode Island merchant, anticipating a need for capital, might instruct his supercargo to draw on a London correspondent. Funds received in the course of the voyage were then remitted to London to insure continued supplies of credit. Since ten per cent damages were levied on protested paper, merchants were scrupulously careful to remain in good standing, and only in extreme cases did correspondents or their agents refuse to honor drafts.

The most successful Rhode Island merchants had developed a finely attuned sense of locale and timing. Whether they secured trading goods locally, or whether they assembled the typical New England cargo through a series of coasting voyages, they paid scrupulous attention to price, quality, and demand. Both from experience and from a well-organized system of commercial intelligence, traders developed a highly sophisticated understanding of the way the market operated in the dozens of ports with which they had regular dealings. By trading according to seasonal price variations, Narragansett Bay merchants acquired cargoes promising the greatest margin of profit, and they delivered their goods at the right place at the right time—when premium prices prevailed. And, because they understood the operation of the market so well, they could even afford to sell at a loss in one port merely to acquire the goods which experience had taught them could be traded extremely profitably somewhere else. Their methods were rough and ready, and occasionally they made costly miscalculations, but over the long haul their shrewd dealing paid handsome dividends.

The Rhode Island trader had also learned to hedge against disaster. To choose captains and supercargoes, agents and factors with care was not enough. Even the best of men can be undone by chance, and seafarer and gambler that he was, the merchant understood the need for protection against the unpredictable. His means was as old as merchant adventuring itself: he diversified. Though most merchants had a specialty, such as the Caribbean or European trades, they rarely pursued one interest to the exclusion of all others. In addition to protecting the merchant against sudden calamities in one branch of business, diversification also conferred flexibility of both mind and operation, and gave him the capacity to shift his effort from one field to another as conditions dictated. However, only the largest firms had the resources to engage simultaneously in many different types of commerce, and a specialty such as the Oriental trade required such enormous resources that only a handful of merchants were equipped to participate in it independently. Men of lesser substance, therefore, diversified in a second way—by adopting a system of joint ownership of vessels and by creating temporary alliances for particular ventures. Whether large or small, few craft were individually owned. Most had at least two owners and some had upwards of twenty. A variety of persons, ranging from blacksmiths to shipwrights and sometimes recruited from other towns or even from other states, joined merchants in such syndicates. Loss of a fractional share, perhaps a thirty-second part, in a two hundred-ton brig capitalized at $10,000 was unlikely to wipe out most investors. Joint trading ventures were also common and were formed by even the wealthiest merchants. They too appreciated that the loss of an Indiaman with a cargo worth as much as $300,000 was best spread over several counting houses.

For vessels and their equipment and for some trade goods the Narragansett Bay merchants continued to rely in part on Rhode Island itself. By 1790 the state had well-established shipbuilding, ropemaking, and rum distilling industries. It also had a handicraft iron industry producing everything from bolts to harpoons. Each had grown up as an ancillary to the maritime economy and each flourished in direct relation to the vigor of maritime trade. Each, therefore, like the merchant adventurers it served, appeared in 1790 to be on the verge of major growth and important profits. But appearances were not borne out, and as the decades of the new century unfolded each ancillary enterprise either sought sustenance in non-maritime ventures or died.

The iron industry felt the pinch first. Though pig iron and castings had figured prominently in the export trade after 1750, Rhode Island lacked the potential to become a major iron producer. Its ores were difficult to process, expensive to transport, limited in quantity, and inferior in quality. The trend was away from pig iron production, therefore, especially after competing European and American furnaces gained a marked edge in both quality and price.

Moreover, metal-working firms turned increasingly to imported bar iron for the raw materials they needed. By contrast, the market for anchors, bolts, chain, whale oil presses, and other types of hardware and equipment remained steady, but it lacked the capacity for growth sought by Rhode Island firms. The Brown family of Providence, who owned the largest integrated undertaking, the Hope Furnace at Scituate, responded to these conditions by gradually contracting their operations.[4] After the Revolution, they had no longer exported pig iron to London, and the once important iron trade with Newport and New York merchants had also disappeared. To be sure, the deterioration of international relations in the last decade of the eighteenth century brought cannon orders from both shipbuilders and the War Department, but munitions making was such an uncertain business that in 1806 the Browns sold out. Despite the temporary revival of cannon production during the War of 1812, the shift to non-maritime markets continued. According to a 1791 report,[5] Providence County alone had had one pig iron furnace and twelve or thirteen forges making bar iron from a mixture of black sand shipped in from the southern part of the state, pig ore, and scrap, but by 1810 the number of furnaces in the entire state had declined to nine and by 1819 only three were still operating.[6]

One reason was the decline in shipbuilding. If the 30,000 tons of new vessels added to Warren's fleet between 1790 and 1840 was indicative of Rhode Island demand, the industry should have flourished. Yet construction reached a peak in 1793, declined sharply in 1808, and, except in scattered years, remained depressed until whaling stimulated a temporary revival in the early 1830's. Shipyards were unusually busy after 1843, but the depression of 1857 halted construction and the industry had not recovered by 1860. Although vessels generally increased in size after 1790,

---

[4] Hedges, *The Browns*, 312–314; *Providence Gazette*, May 6, 1797.
[5] Field, *Rhode Island*, 3:333.
[6] *A Series of Tables of the Several Branches of American Manufactures . . .*, *1810* (Washington, 1813), 24–25; John C. Pease and John M. Niles, *A Gazetteer of the States of Connecticut and Rhode-Island* (Hartford, 1819), 311, 337, 344.

builders concentrated on schooners and sloops rather than on barks, brigs, and ships, and they built few steamboats. So long as timber resources lasted, craftsmen in the interior towns also built hundreds

TABLE 2

SHIPPING CONSTRUCTED AT RHODE ISLAND PORTS, 1790–1859[7]

(Tons by Admeasurement)

Ports	1790 to 1799	1800 to 1809	1810 to 1819	1820 to 1829	1830 to 1839	1840 to 1849	1850 to 1859	1790 to 1859
East Greenwich	1,294	976	575	91				2,936
Bristol	108	186	48	32	1,217	4,527	3,403	9,521
Newport	2,176	2,071	824	2,568	6,487	2,923	2,498	19,547
North Kingstown	101	957	959	2,239	339	44	20	4,659
North Providence	1,854	1,057			1,117			4,028
Providence	8,539	8,767	3,848	2,186	2,893	2,088	3,566	31,887
Warren	6,795	2,089	1,399	691	84	6,437	13,055	30,550
Westerly	1,048	1,039	534	797	109	34	458	4,019
Other	1,580	2,609	468	1,427	345	342	294	7,065
Rhode Island	23,495	19,751	8,655	10,031	12,591	16,395	23,294	114,212

of dinghies, skiffs, and whaleboats. As the table shows, Providence, Warren, and Newport were the chief shipbuilding centers.

[7] For data on shipbuilding, see Virginia Baker, Maritime History of Warren, typescript, in the Rhode Island Historical Society; Everett Barns, *History of Pawcatuck River Steamboats* (Westerly, 1932), 47–52; Carl C. Cutler, "A Brief Survey of the Early Shipping Industry in the Northern States," in *Publications of the Marine Historical Association*, 1:75–76 (March, 1932); G. M. Fessenden, *History of Warren . . . From the Earliest Times* (Providence, 1845), 116; Field, *Rhode Island*, 2:480–482; *History of Rhode Island, 1636–1878* (Philadelphia, 1878), 74; Schedule Five, Seventh Census of the United States, 1850, Rhode Island volumes, 13:81, in the Rhode Island Historical Society. See also, *Manufactures of the United States in 1860* (Washington, 1865), 545–551; Pease and Niles, *Gazetteer*, 336, 366, 378, 387. Table 2 is based on Work Projects Administration, comp., *Ship Registers and Enrollments of Providence, Rhode Island, 1773–1939* (vol. 1, pts. 1–2, Providence, 1941); Work Projects Administration, *Ship Licenses Issued . . . and Licenses on Enrollments Issued out of the Port of Providence, Rhode Island, 1793–1939* (vol. 2, Providence, 1941); Work Projects Administration, *Ship Registers and Enrollments of Newport, Rhode Island* (vol. 1, Providence, 1938–1941); Work Projects Administration, *Ship Licenses . . . and Licenses on Enrollments Issued out of the Port of Newport, Rhode Island, 1790–1939* (vol. 2, Providence, 1938–1941); Work Projects Administration, *Ships Registers and Enrollments . . . Issued out of the Port of Bristol–Warren, Rhode Island, 1773–1939* (Providence, 1941). Hereafter, these volumes

Since the Rhode Islanders had abandoned candlemaking and the processing of illuminating oils after the Revolution, these activities did not revive until Narragansett Bay ports re-entered the whaling business in the 1820's. Although they then added the production of combs and soap, all ancillaries to whaling remained unimportant. Even in 1840, they employed fewer than fifty workers. With the ensuing decline in whaling, factories turned increasingly to processing olive oil and animal fats, and by 1860 the manufacture of whale products had all but ceased.[8]

Rum distilling flourished until the drive against slavery closed its most lucrative market. Newport had operated twenty-two distilleries in 1769, but there were only fifteen rum and gin stills in all Rhode Island according to the census taken in 1810, two years after Congress had outlawed "blackbirding." Providence and Newport counties each had five stills, Bristol County four, and Kent County one. However, they produced over a million gallons of rum annually, sufficient at prevailing prices to buy a thousand slaves on the Guinea Coast. Though thirteen stills were reported in 1819, output had probably fallen to about 200,000 gallons, and in 1828, over the vigorous protests of Providence and Warren merchants, Congress injured the export trade still further by abolishing the drawback on molasses. Only four firms were producing in 1840, two in Providence and one each in Newport and Warren. To some extent, the growth of population gave distillers an expanding local market, but this advantage was partially offset by temperance propaganda and sumptuary laws, and, as compared to the slaving heyday, profits were small. By 1855 only one

are cited as *Ship Documents.* Since the abstracts are incomplete, Table 2 shows only the relative importance of shipbuilding in each port.

[8] *Statistics of the United States, Sixth Census, 1840* (Washington, 1841), 58–59; Schedule Five, Seventh Census of the United States, 1850, Rhode Island volumes, 1:4–5, 316–319; 2:153–157; 7:129–132, 225–227; 10:237–238; Edwin M. Snow, *Census of . . . Providence, 1855* (Providence, 1856) 40–41; Schedule Five, Eighth Census of the United States, 1860, Providence County, Rhode Island volumes, 1:245–248, 391–397, in the Rhode Island Historical Society. The volumes for the other four counties were not located. See also, *History of Rhode Island,* 74, 199; *Manufactures, 1860,* 545–551; Wilfred H.

Providence distillery, employing three workers but producing
400,000 gallons of rum annually, was all that remained of a once
thriving industry.[9]

Despite the enormous demand for sailcloth and the revival of
the state bounty on production in 1792, Rhode Island weavers
produced so little duck and canvas that shipowners obtained most
of their requirements from the Baltic. Providence merchants, con-
cluding apparently that even with a subsidy a sailcloth factory
could not earn the risk profits they expected, abandoned their plans
to enter the business. Instead, they urged Newport leaders to organize an undertaking, partly as a means of relieving the town's
chronic unemployment problem. The Newporters took this advice,
but according to an 1810 report high hemp prices and lack of capital soon forced them to close the factory. Although it was again reported in operation in 1819 it is doubtful that it stayed in business
much longer.[10]

Ropemakers did not merely attempt to meet local demand; they
aspired to enter the export trade. There were three ropewalks in
Providence in 1791 and probably as many more in each of the

Munro, *The History of Bristol: The Story of the Mount Hope Lands* (Providence, 1880), 370–371; Charles O. F. Thompson, *Sketches of Old Bristol* (Providence, 1942), 32, 89–90.

[9] Thomas Williams Bicknell, *The History of the State of Rhode Island and
Providence Plantations* (4 vols., New York, 1920), 3:832; *History of Rhode
Island*, 157, 199; *Manufactures, 1810*, p. 26; Pease and Niles, *Gazetteer*, 327, 363–
364; *Statistics, 1840*, p. 58; William R. Staples, *Annals of . . . Providence* (Providence, 1843), 626; Snow, *Census of Providence, 1855*, pp. 41–50; *Manufactures,
1860*, pp. 545–551; Schedule Five, Eighth Census of the United States, 1860,
Providence County, Rhode Island volumes, 1:607–609; Munro, *Bristol*, 246,
374–375; Thompson, *Sketches*, 3–4, 32, 89–90. See also, *American State Papers,
Finance*, 5:894–895, for a report that Providence merchants imported 856,512
gallons of molasses in 1827.

[10] Acts and Resolves, 27:77 (October, 1792), in the State Archives; *Providence Gazette*, January 26, 1793; Bayles, *Newport County*, 534, 537; George
G. Channing, *Early Recollections of Newport* (Newport, 1868), 144–145; Field,
Rhode Island, 3:334; Bicknell, *Rhode Island*, 3:832; William Ellery to Moses
Brown, December 5, 1791, quoted in Susan B. Franklin, "William Ellery, Signer
of the Declaration of Independence," in *Rhode Island History*, 13:16–17 (January, 1954); *American State Papers, Finance*, 2:428; Pease and Niles, *Gazetteer*,
353.

other major ports. Throughout the 1790's, ropemakers protested that the duty on hemp forced up the cost of raw materials and priced their products out of foreign markets. Yet the industry must have been expanding, for the census of 1810 reported that thirteen ropewalks produced 545 tons of rope valued at more than $100,000. In all probability, five of these undertakings were in Newport, four in Providence, and two each in Bristol and Warren. Output gradually contracted, especially after 1820, when ropemakers asserted that they needed greater tariff protection to retain even their domestic markets. By 1840, only nine ropewalks, employing a total of forty-five workers, remained. Of the five firms still in business a decade later, only one, a Warren enterprise, was a sizeable undertaking, and by 1860, there were but thirty-five ropemakers left in all Rhode Island to pass on their skills to a new generation.[11]

However, in 1790 the decline of the ancillaries, like the decline of the maritime economy they served, was in the future. To Rhode Island merchants, as to everyone else, it was not given to foresee. They could guess, of course, and some guessed with remarkable accuracy. Most traders changed with the times, therefore, not ahead of them. But an important number changed only after the times had left them behind or, in a few instances, not really at all. Although the growth of population made the Rhode Island market more valuable than it had been in the Colonial period, the habits of generations were long persisted in and Narragansett Bay merchants still expected to make most of their profits in interstate and especially in international trade. Trading patterns changed rapidly in detail—after all, this was part of the Rhode Island tradition—but they changed only slowly in general, and, despite the addition of two new trading areas (the Far East and South America), the principal trade was still with Europe and the Caribbean. Further,

[11] The discussion of the rope industry is based on Field, *Rhode Island*, 3:334; *History of Rhode Island*, 74, 199; *Manufactures, 1810*, p. 27; Pease and Niles, *Gazetteer*, 327, 353, 364; *Statistics, 1840*, p. 58; Schedule Five, Seventh Census of the United States, 1850, Rhode Island volumes, *passim*; *Manufactures, 1860*, pp. 545–551; *American State Papers, Finance*, 1:202, 351, 495–496; 5:894–895.

traditional Rhode Island methods of parleying goods into profits by simultaneous participation in several different kinds of venture kept the various trades as interdependent as formerly, and, superficially at least, the trading pattern remained as complex as it had ever been in the colonial heyday.

Europe was in 1790 and continued for about three more decades to be a most important trading area, though profitable commerce was unusually difficult throughout the period from the outbreak of the French Revolutionary wars in 1792 to the Treaty of Ghent in 1815.[12] As neutrals, until 1812, Narragansett Bay merchants benefited from the disruption of normal commercial channels, as well as from the increased European demand for American, Caribbean, and Oriental goods. But these advantages were offset by the quasi-war with France in 1799, by the breakdown of restraints on the Barbary pirates, and by both the French Continental System and the British Orders in Council. The Embargo of 1808 then halted all European trade, and the War of 1812 subjected transAtlantic commerce to still further difficulties.

On the whole, merchants tackled these problems successfully. When conditions permitted, they traded with three main European markets. From the Baltic, especially Denmark, Sweden, and Russia, they obtained naval stores as well as tallow, candles, iron, steel, and glass. England, France, Holland, and the Hanse ports were sources of manufactures, liquor, wines, nuts, cheese, salt, coal, and a variety of Oriental commodities. Southern Europe, particularly Portugal, Spain, and Gibraltar, supplied specie and such Mediter-

[12] The discussion of European trade is based on "Commerce of Rhode Island," *passim,* but especially pp. 411–428, 430–432, 434–441, 450–451, 453–456, 461–465, 472–473, 475–478; "List of American Vessels at Archangel, 1810–1811," in *The Essex Institute Historical Collections,* 68:378–384 (October, 1932); Field, *Rhode Island,* 2:456, 462, 464, 465–467, 469–470, 473, 475–476; Paul Francis Gleeson, "Attacks by Algerian Pirates Create Demand for American Navy," in *Rhode Island History,* 2:41–48 (April, 1943); Greene and Smith, *Journals,* 15–80, 127–143; Earl C. Tanner, Trade Between the Port of Providence and Latin America, 1800 to 1830 (doctoral thesis, typescript, Harvard University, 1951), especially pp. 20–27, 283; Tanner, "The Providence Federal Customhouse Papers as a Source of Maritime History since 1790," in *New England Quarterly,* 26:94–95 (March, 1953).

ranean specialities as currants, corks, baskets, and merino sheep. In
return, Rhode Island merchants shipped staves, provisions, tobacco,
sugar, rum, coffee, Oriental goods, and, occasionally, manufactures.
Vessels either loaded for Europe in Narragansett Bay harbors, or,
more frequently, carried domestic produce and re-exports to southern and Caribbean ports, where they obtained cargoes especially
suited to European markets.

Though rapidly changing conditions caused sharp annual fluctuations in the volume of trade, European commerce generally expanded until it reached its peak in 1806. The number of vessels
entering Providence from Europe rose from ten in 1800 to thirty
in 1806, and the duties collected increased from almost $39,000 to
nearly $108,000. The Baltic, Dutch, French, and Iberian trades
were chiefly significant. Commerce was generally depressed from
1808 to 1815, but shipowners discovered extraordinary opportunities in 1810, 1811, and 1813, when a lively trade with the Baltic
developed, and, even during the war with Great Britain, Rhode
Island vessels supplied flour to the British army in Portugal. They
returned from Iberian ports with cargoes of salt and specie.

With the restoration of peace in 1815, Narragansett Bay merchants resumed normal trade relations. Reciprocity treaties with
Great Britain and Sweden stimulated voyages to those countries
at the expense of trade with Russia, the Hanse ports, and France;
and Gibraltar began to rival Spain and Portugal as a supplier of
Mediterranean products. Twenty-six vessels arrived at Providence
from European ports in 1823, and importers paid some $86,000 in
duties in 1827. However, the volume of trade generally remained
below prewar levels, and beginning in 1829 it declined sharply.

Rhode Island's Far Eastern trade followed a similar pattern of
expansion and contraction.[13] Merchants had first entered the Ori-

---

[13] The discussion of the Far Eastern trade is based on "Affidavit Regarding *Ann
and Hope*," in *The American Neptune*, 21:73–75 (January, 1961); Carosso
and Leder, "Snow–Dorr Correspondence," 65–88; Lloyd G. Churchward, "Rhode
Island and the Australian Trade, 1792–1812," in *Rhode Island History*, 7:97–
104 (October, 1948); Clarkson A. Collins, 3rd., ed., "Pictures of Providence in
the Past, 1790–1820: The Reminiscenses of Walter R. Danforth," in *Rhode
Island History*, 11:26 (January, 1952); Corning, "Letters of Sullivan Dorr,"

ental trade in 1787, when the Providence firm of Brown and
Francis sent the ship *George Washington* on an exploratory voyage. She carried a mixed cargo—anchors, cordage, sailcloth, munitions, copper, rum, brandy, wine, cheese, and candles—valued at
$26,000. She returned eighteen months later with a cargo worth
almost $100,000, mainly in tea, but also including silks, china,
cottons, lacquerware, and spices. Encouraged by their success, and
benefiting from what their supercargo, Samuel Ward, had learned
about routes, markets, prices, commercial practices, and the special
problems involved in dealing with the Hong merchants in Canton,
Brown and Francis immediately prepared a second voyage. In
December, 1789, the *George Washington* again sailed for the
Orient. For more than a generation thereafter Narragansett Bay
ships carried on an extensive trade in Far Eastern waters.

Two ships sailed from Providence for the Orient in 1789, three
in 1792, two in 1794, another in 1798, and four in 1799. With the
exception of the war years, 1813 to 1815, and 1821, when no vessels arrived at Providence from the Far East, merchants pursued
the Oriental trade with regularity until an erratic decline began
in 1828. On the average, three Indiamen entered Providence an-

178–364; Corning, comp., "List of Ships arriving at the Port of Canton and
other Pacific Ports, 1799–1803," in *Essex Institute Historical Collections*, 78:329–
347 (October, 1942); Corning, "Sullivan Dorr (1778–1858): Biographical
Note," in *Rhode Island History*, 1:72 (July, 1942); Corning, "Sullivan Dorr,
An Early China Merchant," 158–175; Corning, "Sullivan Dorr, China Trader,"
75–90; Thomas Dunbabin, "New Light on the Earliest American Voyages to
Australia," in *The American Neptune*, 10:52–64 (January, 1950); Field, *Rhode
Island*, 2:445, 462–476, 478, 485–486; Robert W. Kenny, "Benjamin B. Carter,
Physician Extraordinary," in *Rhode Island History*, 16:99–104 (October, 1957);
Kenny, "*Ann and Hope*," 105–136; Kimball, *The East–India Trade of Provi-
dence*, 3–34; William Greene Roelker, "Captain Cornelius Soule," in *Rhode
Island History*, 5:115 (October, 1946); Tanner, "Customhouse Papers," 91–92;
Tanner, "South American Ports in the Foreign Commerce of Providence, 1800–
1830," in *Rhode Island History*, 16:70–73, 76 (July, 1957); Tanner, "The
Latin–American Trade of E. Carrington & Co., 1822," 33–44, 78–85; Tanner,
"The Voyage of the *Mercury*," 33–44, 65–79; Tanner, Providence and Latin
America, especially p. 222; Harriet Wood Weeden, "The Good Ship *Haidie*,"
in *Rhode Island History*, 17:57–61 (April, 1958); Weeden, "Early Oriental
Commerce," 236–278.

nually during the first three decades of the nineteenth century. In some years, notably 1803–1804, 1806, and 1817–1819, as many as six or seven vessels arrived. This produced sharp fluctuations in the volume of trade. Duties averaged some $123,000 annually, but they exceeded $200,000 in 1800, 1803, and 1810, and they rose above $300,000 in 1819 and again in 1822.

Cargoes destined for the Far East were sometimes assembled in Narragansett Bay warehouses, but more commonly Indiamen sailed via Europe, South America, or Australia, where goods were exchanged for cargoes commanding a ready sale in the Orient. Two or three years later, after a voyage of many thousands of miles, and after a complicated series of transactions in such ports as Pondicherry, Madras, Calcutta, Batavia, Botany Bay, and Canton, the great copper-bottomed, square-rigged ships, some of them exceeding nine hundred tons, lumbered into Narragansett Bay with their exotic cargoes. Other vessels rarely returned to Rhode Island ports. Instead, some plied the Amsterdam-Canton route; others were sold abroad after a few voyages; and still others gathered furs in the Pacific Northwest for sale in the China market, or entered the Chinese-South American metal trade.

Profits in Oriental commerce were on a grand scale. Cargoes were commonly valued at between $200,000 and $400,000, and net profits exceeding $100,000 were not unusual. The most spectacular voyage was one organized in 1804 by the DeWolf family of Bristol.[14] Encouraged by the profits James Phillips had earned on an expedition to Canton two years earlier, they acquired his brig *Juno* and placed it under the command of John DeWolf II, a young but experienced captain. They planned a typical DeWolf enterprise designed to wring many profits from a single three-legged voyage. The first was to be earned by trading a mixed cargo

[14] John DeWolf, *A Voyage to the North Pacific and a Journey through Siberia more than Half a Century Ago* (Cambridge, 1861), *passim*. According to Howe, *Mount Hope*, 135, the DeWolfs bought the *Juno* from Phillips for $7,600, but *Ships Documents, Bristol*, 143, and *Newport*, 1:355, report that the vessel was already owned by a DeWolf syndicate which, on March 18, 1801, registered it at Newport. This document was surrendered at Bristol on August 10, 1804.

for furs in the northern Pacific; the second by exchanging pelts for Oriental goods in Canton; the third by selling Chinese products in the American market. Though the venture did not proceed according to plan, when John returned to Bristol in 1808, he had crammed a lifetime of adventure into four brief years, and he had parlayed his employers' capital into a fortune.

Reaching Vancouver Island in April, 1805, John tried trading with the Kolosh Eskimos, but, impatient to gather a cargo, he soon pushed further north to New Archangel on the Gulf of Alaska. There he sold a third of his trading goods to the resident governor of the Russian-American Company, exchanged another third with Eskimos for sea otter pelts, and finally, in October, 1805, sold the *Juno* and the balance of its original cargo to Baron Nikolai Rezanov, a visiting company official. He received the equivalent of $68,000 made up of specie, a company draft, furs, and a forty-ton sloop. DeWolf loaded the sloop with pelts acquired since August (when he had sent a thousand sea otter skins to Canton via the *Mary* of Boston), and despatched her for China via Hawaii. Instead of accompanying this cargo, he wintered in Alaska, planning to cross the Pacific in the *Juno* as a passenger. But in June, 1806, when Rezanov showed no signs of departing, he hired a tiny brig and sailed for the Siberian port of Okhotsk. Delayed by a blizzard in the Kuriles, he wintered on the Kamchatka peninsula, and did not reach his destination until late in June, 1807. His taste for adventure still unsatisfied, John now set off across Siberia for the Baltic. The first American, and probably the first non-Russian to make such a journey, he reached St. Petersburg in October. There he learned that a duplicate of the draft on the Russian-American Company, payable in Spanish milled dollars, had already been cashed at a windfall premium of fifteen per cent. Cramer and Smith, the DeWolf Baltic agents, had reinvested the proceeds in a Russian iron and hemp cargo, which they had shipped to Bristol. Thus, when John DeWolf finally reported to his employers in April, 1808, the proceeds of this lengthy and complicated venture were already at work adding to the family fortune. In forty-two

months he returned a net profit exceeding $100,000 on an invest-
ment of only $35,000. The rate of return was over seventy per cent.

Rewarding though many Far Eastern ventures were, profits
were partly offset by extraordinarily damaging losses. The ship
Russell, owned by a Newport syndicate comprised of Gibbs and
Channing, George Champlin, Caleb Gardner, Peleg Clarke, James
Robinson, and William Wood, was captured off the coast of Java
by a French privateer in 1799, and another Newport ship, the
Semiramis, was wrecked off Vineyard Sound in 1804 with the loss
of most of its valuable cargo. The leading house in the trade before
1815, the Providence firm of Brown and Ives, lost the five hundred
and fifty ton ship *Ann and Hope* off Block Island in January,
1806, and a British sloop captured the firm's four hundred and
sixty-four ton ship *John Jay* a few days later. Though the *John
Jay* was eventually released after expensive litigation, the partners
faced the immediate prospect of a combined loss of almost half a
million dollars.

Because Oriental ventures required considerable capital, imposed
heavy risks, and demanded skilled management, only the largest
mercantile houses carried on a sustained trade. Apart from a few
syndicates which organized one or more voyages, a handful of
Providence and Newport merchants dominated the early trade,
and after 1815, Providence's two greatest firms, Brown and Ives
and Edward Carrington and Company, almost monopolized the
business. Yet if Far Eastern trade directly sustained only a few
ships, crews, and firms, it nevertheless poured hundreds of thousands of dollars in profits into the Rhode Island economy and was
a major source of venture capital.

If longevity, regularity, and volume—rather than value—be
the measures, the Caribbean trade dominated Rhode Island's maritime life.[15] There were two reasons. First, because the business

---

[15] The discussion of Caribbean trade is based on "Commerce of Rhode Island,"
409–411, 416–418, 423–424, 428–434, 441–452, 458–460, 465–471, 473;
Field, *Rhode Island,* 2:456, 462; Greene and Smith, *Journals,* especially 81–124,
144–211, 474–478, 486; Tanner, "Customhouse Papers," 90–91; Tanner,
Providence and Latin America, passim, and extracts from it published as "Caribbean Ports in the Foreign Commerce of Providence, 1790–1830," in *Rhode*

could be conducted in small craft, the Caribbean attracted men of small means. For some it served as a training ground, and many who became wealthy entrepreneurs started there, then went on to greater things. For those who remained petty merchants it was always the chief trading area. Second, because Rhode Island's own products were useless in direct commerce with many areas, the Caribbean trade served as an adjunct to other and more profitable ventures. It supplied highly prized trading goods and raw materials, and it also provided a market for many types of New England commodities that could not be disposed of elsewhere. Rum distilled from West Indian or Cuban molasses was the currency of the Guinea trade; the Caribbean was also a principal slave market. Vessels outward bound for Europe or the Orient unloaded American provisions, soap, candles, and lumber and goods derived from earlier foreign voyages. Inward bound they unloaded European textiles, wines, and naval stores, and Oriental goods. In each instance they acquired goods useful in further trade: molasses, sugar, rum, coffee, cocoa, spices, cigars, cotton, dyes, and lumber.

Though deeply affected after 1792 by the Anglo-French and Anglo-American conflicts, Rhode Island's Caribbean commerce sustained less damage, whether temporary or permanent, than any other branch of international trade. Throughout the period, the kaleidoscopic political and economic conditions in the Gulf of Mexico rigorously tested the skill, resourcefulness, and flexibility

---

Island History, 14:97–108 (October, 1955), and 15:11–20 (January, 1956). For protests against the proposed withdrawal of the molasses drawback privilege, see *American State Papers, Finance*, 5:877–878, 894–895.

Some petty merchant-shipowners, especially those operating from the minor ports of Pawcatuck, Narragansett, Wickford, East Greenwich, Warwick, and Portsmouth, entered the Caribbean trade via the fishing industry. Wickford in the early nineteenth century, for example, employed about six vessels and a hundred men in the Labrador fishery. They sold some of the catch, either dried or salted, directly to vessels sailing for the Mediterranean. Sometimes they carried the preserved fish to Italian ports themselves, returning with cargoes of fruit and other Southern European specialties. More often, however, they exchanged the catch in the West Indies for cargoes of molasses for the Narragansett Bay distilleries. See *History of Rhode Island*, 178, 190, 336; Henry E. Turner, *Reminiscences of East Greenwich* (n.p., 1892), 5.

of Narragansett Bay merchants. On the whole, they steered a successful course. Despite war, privateering, revolution, piracy, and commercial restrictions, the volume of business remained at a relatively high level. Merchants initiated or abandoned trade with particular Caribbean ports according to the exigencies of the moment. Surinam and Hispaniola supplied most of their molasses from 1790 to 1793; British possessions replaced them in importance between 1794 and 1809; and from 1810 onwards Cuba became their principal source of sugar products. From time to time they also imported cargoes from British Honduras, the Danish, Dutch, French, and Spanish West Indies, and from other minor ports.

Nevertheless, the volume of the Caribbean trade steadily contracted. The indirect trade to Europe, the Orient, and Guinea was reduced in proportion to the decline in Rhode Island's participation in those markets. The direct trade also suffered. Entries at Providence, which had averaged seventy-four annually from 1791 to 1796, declined to fewer than forty-eight per year between 1796 and 1815, and duties paid, which had averaged $85,000 annually from 1800 to 1807, fell to $67,500 per annum over the next eight years. Though merchants did re-enter the trade in force after 1815, they failed to restore volume even to its pre-Embargo level. A temporary revival began in 1826, but withdrawal of the molasses drawback privilege in the tariff of 1828 quickly reduced the sugar trade by making it cheaper to distill rum in Cuba than in Rhode Island. Between 1816 and 1830, an average of only forty-nine vessels entered Providence annually from the Caribbean, and between 1816 and 1825, the customshouse collected an average of only $70,000 in duties a year.

The South American trade was in many respects an extension of Caribbean commerce.[16] It, too, was especially dependent on flexibility and a willingness to circumvent trade restrictions. Portuguese, Spanish, and (later) national regulations had to be evaded or perverted, officials corrupted, and ports of call changed as the

---

[16] The discussion of South American trade is based on Greene and Smith, *Journals*, 81–124, 144–211; *Mathewson vs. Clarke*, 6 *Howard* 122 (1848); and the works by Tanner cited in note 15.

occasion demanded. South America also produced goods useful as adjuncts to other trades, and Rhode Island's participation was, therefore, most often indirect. Some vessels cleared Narragansett Bay ports with mixed cargoes of American manufacture, particularly textiles and flour, and other goods of European or Oriental origin. After exchanging these products for South American commodities, especially sugar, cocoa, coffee, beef, hides, wool, horsehair, feathers, and copper, they sailed for Europe, the Orient, or the sealing grounds of the Pacific Northwest. When they finally returned to Rhode Island, they were recorded as coming from trading areas other than South America. Many vessels entered South American commerce via Europe, especially by way of the Iberian ports or Amsterdam. Still others plied the Pacific Ocean routes between Canton or Batavia and the Chilean and Peruvian ports of Valparaiso and Callao. Beginning in 1811, when the struggle for Chilean independence broke out, lucrative gun-running opportunities also opened up. Profits from these varied ventures reached Rhode Island as trading goods or as specie and bills of exchange, even though the ships often returned from other areas or not at all.

Two features did distinguish the South American from the Caribbean trade. First, because the distances were greater and the risks higher, few petty merchants or beginners could participate. It was Nicholas Brown of the Providence Browns who, in 1785, first attempted to open the Brazilian trade; John Innes Clark of Clark and Nightingale who, in 1799, pioneered the Argentine trade with an exploratory voyage by the Providence frigate *Palmyra;* and the great Providence houses of Edward Carrington and Company and Nightingale and Jenckes which, after 1815, dominated the Chilean and Peruvian trades. Second, the trade was opened late. Even then, it was sporadic, small in volume, and lasted but a generation. Between 1811, when the first Providence ship arrived home with a Brazilian cargo (it was probably not the first to trade in Brazil), and 1831, when the direct trade ended, only twenty-five vessels entered Providence from Brazil and none entered in six of these twenty-one years. Between 1799 and 1816 only nine vessels entered Providence from the River Plate, and between 1817 and 1825, though the trade was relatively free of wartime difficulties, only nine more vessels arrived. In the entire period between 1790 and 1830 only three vessels entered Providence from the west coast ports. Though a remnant of the indirect trade probably persisted for a few more years, direct relations with the South American market had ended by 1831.

The decline that had become characteristic of the trade in each of Rhode Island's chief markets in the first three decades of the century persisted until, by 1860, Narragansett Bay vessels had all but disappeared from foreign ports.[17] The South American trade was over by 1831; the Oriental trade ended in 1841; and, though both the European and the Caribbean trades persisted, the volume was small and dwindling. An annual average of but thirty-seven vessels arrived at Providence from foreign ports in the 1830's, and between 1841 and 1856 the average fell to only twenty-one.

There were but three exceptions, all minor, to the general downward trend: the African commodity trade, the Canadian coal and lumber trade, and the Scottish iron trade. Some traffic in muskets, rum, tobacco, and provisions was carried on in African markets before 1830. This commerce increased slightly during the ensuing two decades. In average years, two or three cargoes of peanuts, palm oil, cam wood, ivory, and gold dust arrived at Providence, especially from Mozambique and Zanzibar. Before 1830, commerce with Canada was insignificant, largely because the economies of Rhode Island and British North America were competitive rather than complementary. There was significant commerce between the two areas only during the Embargo of 1808, when some Narragansett Bay merchants conducted a lively clandestine trade via the Maine coast. After 1830, when Canadian vessels were accorded equality of·treatment in American ports, coal shipped from Pictou and Sidney in Nova Scotia rose in demand, and lumber became a

[17] The discussion of trade from 1830 to 1860 is based on Field, *Rhode Island,* 2:484; Amos Perry, comp., *Rhode Island State Census, 1885* (Providence, 1887), 76–78; Tanner, "Customhouse Papers," 88–96; Tanner, Providence and Latin America, especially p. 222.

second important element in the trade. But, because these commodities were carried almost exclusively by Canadian vessels, Rhode Island merchants merely acted as local distributors, the profits were small, and the trade sustained few Narragansett Bay families. The volume of Scottish iron imported rose sharply in the early 1850's, but it too came in foreign rather than in Rhode Island bottoms, and the trade had no sooner developed than it declined.

The clearest reflection of the steady decline of Rhode Island as a center of international trade was in the volume of such business handled by Narragansett Bay customshouses. In the case of Providence, duties declined from a peak of more than $400,000 in 1804 to $100,000 in 1830, and to a mere $36,000 in 1860. The re-export trade also declined. For Rhode Island as a whole, the value of goods re-exported fell from over $1,500,000 in 1805 to $72,000 in 1830, and to less than $10,000 in 1860. Direct international trade in domestic products did not take the place of re-exports. In 1800, 1810, and 1820, more than $1,000,000 worth of Rhode Island goods entered directly into foreign commerce, but the volume declined to $280,000 in 1830 and to $221,000 in 1860.

Several factors were responsible for this abandonment of foreign commerce. In the world of the French Revolutionary and Napoleonic wars maritime operations could be carried on only at great risk. The quasi-war with France, the Barbary pirates, the British Orders in Council, the Berlin and Milan decrees, the Embargo, the Macon bills, and the War of 1812 exposed traders to a succession of impediments; the revolutions and intercolonial wars in the Caribbean and South America posed yet another set of hazards; and rapidly changing conditions made it impossible for even Narragansett Bay merchants to calculate the market. The restoration of peace in 1815 brought new and more serious difficulties, difficulties that could not be met by the traditional Rhode Island formula —aggressive opportunism. Competition from ports with richer hinterlands and better physical facilities, particularly New York, placed the Narragansett Bay traders at a disadvantage in the American market, and the steady institutionalization of world trade reduced the effectiveness of the dominant Rhode Island traits—

flexibility, timing, otherwise-mindedness, and individualism. This new trading world was no place for merchant adventurers. Risks were less now but so were profits. The majority of merchants, therefore, gradually withdrew and sought from other types of enterprise the speculative returns they had come to expect from foreign commerce.

Some refused to abandon the sea. Either because their range of choices was limited by physical and psychological factors or because they believed the solution to declining maritime profits lay in attack, not in retreat, these diehards retained their oceanic investments. The least adventurous turned to coasting, then to freighting. The more hardy—or foolhardly—turned to slaving, privateering, or whaling.

In the maritime heyday, coastal vessels had performed an integral function by gathering export cargoes and by distributing imported and local goods to American markets, but with the decline of foreign commerce most of this business passed to Boston and New York houses. Trade in domestic commodities was not immediately affected by these developments, but the steady nationalization of the economy, the coming of the railroad, and the rise of interior markets subjected the Narragansett Bay coasters to the same disadvantages encountered earlier by the foreign traders. Short of leaving the sea entirely, or venturing into high-risk enterprises, the domestic merchants had no alternative but to shift their vessels from trading into low-profit freighting voyages. They sought cargoes where they could, and though they carried vast quantities of raw materials and manufactured goods in and out of Narragansett Bay, they often had to sail in ballast. In the decade from 1843 to 1852, Providence recorded an average of 4,200 coastwise entries annually. The port also served as a gateway to the North Providence village of Pawtucket; in the typical year of 1852, some one hundred and forty coasters passed through Providence to reach the Seekonk River and the wharves at Pawtucket.[18] The rising volume of coastal freight notwithstanding, the carrying

[18] R. M. Bayles, ed., *History of Providence County* (2 vols., New York, 1891), 1:264–285; *The Providence Directory* (Providence, 1853), 343.

business lacked the excitement, variety, and financial rewards which had originally attracted merchants to international trade. From the very outset, therefore, many shipowners rejected transportation ventures as suitable outlets for their capital and talent. Instead, they sought other maritime alternatives.

Slaving, a highly speculative form of enterprise, met the classic Narragansett Bay requirements—low investments, high risks, rising demand, and speculative profits. Middling but ambitious merchants as well as the owners of small craft found the trade particularly attractive. The premium it placed on flexibility appealed especially. Moreover, traders could get financial support relatively easily and, because each voyage constituted a clearly defined venture which generally left no transactions dangling, both merchants and their backers could enter or abandon the trade at will. Despite the humanitarian and legislative drive against slaving, therefore, some merchants refused to withdraw from the Guinea trade.[19]

Rhode Island ports had virtually ceased to be slave markets after 1774, when the General Assembly had halted importations except from the West Indies. A decade later another law had provided for the gradual emancipation of slaves, and in 1787 the Assembly had forbidden Rhode Island citizens to carry slaves into foreign ports.

Restrictions were intensified after Rhode Island joined the Union. In 1794 Congress directed Americans to cease carrying slaves between foreign ports and made it a federal crime to violate

[19] The discussion of African trade is based on "Slave Trade in 1816," in *Rhode Island Historical Society Publications,* New series, 6:226–227 (January, 1899); Donnan, *Documents of the Slave Trade,* 3:346–404; Donnan, "The New England Slave Trade after the Revolution," in *New England Quarterly,* 3:251–278 (April, 1930); W. E. B. DuBois, *The Suppression of the African-Slave Trade, 1638–1870* (New York, 1954), especially pp. 27, 33–36, 70–150; Field, *Rhode Island,* 2:403–405, 476–478; Howe, *Mount Hope,* 87, 94, 97–133, 189–191, 201–213; M. A. DeWolfe Howe, *Bristol, Rhode Island: A Town Biography* (Cambridge, 1930), 64–88, 102–103; Irving Berdine Richman, *Rhode Island: A Study in Separatism* (Boston, 1905), 260–264; John R. Spears, *The American Slave-Trade* (New York, 1930), especially pp. 36–139; Tanner, "Customhouse Papers," 95–96; Tanner, Providence and Latin America, 222; Thompson, *Moses Brown,* 96–106, 175–202.

state laws against the slave trade. Convicted slavers forfeited their vessels and were fined $100 for each slave carried. Opponents of the trade, irked at the ineffectiveness of this law, sought more stringent penalties in 1800. John Brown, a member of the Rhode Island delegation in Congress, unsuccessfully defended the New England slaving interests. He argued that "we ought as . . . well enjoy that trade as to leave it wholly to others." Slaving, he contended, was beneficial in three ways. Negroes enjoyed better conditions in the New World than in Africa; the Treasury benefited from the collection of duties; and New England distilleries were kept in business by Guinea ventures. "Why," he protested, "should a heavy fine and imprisonment be made the penalty for carrying on a trade so advantageous?"[20] Brown's rationalizations notwithstanding, Congress stiffened the law by imposing prison terms and by increasing the fines. These restrictions failed to keep Rhode Islanders out of the traffic. As William Ellery, the Newport collector of customs, had observed in 1791, "an Ethiopian could as soon change his skin as a Newport merchant could be induced to change so lucrative a trade . . . for the slow profits of any manufactory."[21]

Rhode Islanders operated primarily on the Guinea Coast, although a few preferred Zanzibar and Mozambique, where slaves were higher in quality but could be obtained only by assuming the higher risks of extended voyages and larger investments. They disposed of their cargoes in the Caribbean and, to a lesser extent, in South America and the United States. Despite the prohibitions or restrictions imposed by British, French, and Spanish authorities, Narragansett Bay captains experienced little difficulty in smuggling cargoes into West Indian ports, especially after the outbreak of the French Revolutionary wars disrupted administration throughout the Caribbean. Havana became the prime slave market, partly because local officials elected—or could be bribed—to disregard Spanish edicts. The Rhode Islanders also traded in South American ports, chiefly Montevideo and Buenos Aires. North American

[20] *Annals of Congress,* 10:686–687 (April 26, 1800).
[21] Quoted in Richman, *Rhode Island,* 261.

markets continued to be unimportant until the early nineteenth century. Between 1790 and 1795, slave cargoes could be legally imported into two states only, Georgia and North Carolina, and between 1796 and 1798, into Georgia alone. South Carolina re-opened the trade in 1803. Over the ensuing four years Rhode Island firms were among the most active in the Charleston market, and after Congress closed the trade in 1808 they continued to smuggle shipments into the United States, often from nearby Cuban bases.

Because of the risks involved, merchants expected a net average return of twenty-five per cent on each voyage. Though slaves brought upwards of four times as much in New World markets as they cost on the African coast, various hidden expenses reduced profits substantially. Insurance premiums were high, fifteen to thirty per cent on typical ventures, and underwriters assumed liability only after a fifth of the Negroes had perished. Wages, ranging from $30 a month for captains to $8 for boys, and extending over voyages lasting anywhere from six to sixteen months, required a moderate investment, often by borrowing capital at high interest rates. Officers were normally entitled to purchase a per-centage of the slaves for themselves and to ship them free of charge. Other costs incurred by slavers included good conduct bonds, the vessel's bill of health, pilotage and wharfage fees, regis-tration papers, customs duties, bribes to officials, food and clothing for the slaves, and commissions if agents were employed to buy or sell cargoes. The total expenses of a single voyage often exceeded $15,000, all of which might be lost by misfortune or mismanage-ment. And sometimes the expenses of cleaning a slaver were so great that it was cheaper to dispose of it for whatever it would fetch rather than to fit it out for another venture.

All the major Rhode Island ports re-entered the slave trade after the Revolution. However, Providence houses gradually with-drew from "eastward" ventures, partly because the Abolition So-ciety, led by the influential Quaker merchant Moses Brown, waged an effective campaign against the traffic. Some eminent and respect-able firms, such as Clark and Nightingale, as well as lesser merchants and shipowners, notably Ebenezer Jenckes, Abijah Potter, Amasa Smith, and Cyprian Sterry, did trade on the Guinea coast, and doubtless other Providence men invested in syndicates operating from other Narragansett Bay ports, but the scale of Providence operations was modest and declining. Between 1803 and 1807 Providence vessels delivered less than five hundred and sixty slaves to the Charleston market, a tiny fraction of the total number supplied by Rhode Islanders. Warren merchants participated on approximately the same small scale, but, because the port itself was also minor, they were actually more dependent upon Guinea ventures than even Newporters, who had plunged back into slaving after the Revolution in a desperate attempt to rebuild the town's shattered economy.[22] An incomplete tabulation shows that two Newport vessels cleared for Africa in 1794, and seven in 1795. Over the next five years, the annual average rose to twelve, and no less than twenty-four departures were recorded in 1799. Between 1803 and 1807 Newport merchants shipped almost thirty-five hundred slaves to Charleston, about six times the number delivered by either Providence or Warren firms.

The scale of Newport's slaving operations might well have been larger but for William Ellery, the local customs collector, who kept a close watch for illicit ventures. Since his incorruptible administration extended as far north as Conimicut Point, Ellery also circumscribed the activities of the DeWolfs, Bristol's leading mercantile family. Never ones to submit meekly to damaging regulations, they fought back with unusual but effective stratagems.

The DeWolf star had begun its ascent in the mid-eighteenth century with the marriage of a young supercargo, Mark Anthony DeWolf, to the sister of his employer, Simeon Potter.[23] Through

[22] The firms of Gardner and Dean and Gibbs and Channing, as well as individual slavers, notably Nathaniel Briggs, Peleg Clarke, Clark and Reuben Booth, Caleb Gardner, William Gyles, Constant Taber, and John Topham, were active in the trade.

[23] The analysis of the DeWolfs which follows is based on "Slave Trade in 1816," 226–227; Allen Johnson and Dumas Malone, eds., *Dictionary of American Biography* (22 vols., New York, 1928–1944) 5:275; Donnan, *Documents of the Slave Trade*, 3: especially pp. 379–380, 388–393, 397; Donnan, "New

his wife's inheritance DeWolf acquired capital for operations as slaver, merchant, and privateer. Though Mark Anthony never became wealthy himself, one of his several sons, James, who had served a maritime apprenticeship during the Revolution, amassed an enormous fortune. James obtained his first command, a slaver, at nineteen. Thereafter his indifference to ethical niceties kept him in the traffic long after many Rhode Islanders had turned respectable, and after Guinea voyages had acquired the additional stigma of illegality. Apart from Levi, who proved too squeamish to follow the family tradition, and John, who abandoned slaving for farming as soon as his fortune was made, James had two other brothers, Charles and William, each of whom had the DeWolf touch of profitable opportunism. There were also assorted nephews, including John DeWolf of the *Juno*, the son of another brother, Simon, who had died at sea during the Revolution.

James DeWolf defended his "blackbirding" interests with extraordinary resourcefulness. In 1799, when Ellery libeled the DeWolf slave schooner, the *Lucy*, and the United States District Court at Providence ordered it auctioned, James retaliated by kidnapping Ellery's deputy just before the sale. This frustrated the plan to use the craft as a revenue cutter on Narragansett Bay, but even the unscrupulous James knew that he had won only a temporary respite. With a clever turn of opportunism, he and his brother John then embraced the Republican party. Jefferson soon rewarded their new found devotion to principle. By one of his early presidential acts, Bristol and Warren became a separate customs district and, over Ellery's indignant protests, he appointed Charles Collins, the *Lucy*'s captain, reputed part-owner of at least two other slavers,

England Slave Trade," especially pp. 257, 264, 266–267, 275; Howe, *Bristol*, especially pp. 31–116; Howe, *Mount Hope*, especially pp. 94–244; Munro, *Bristol*, 175–185, 274–279, 302–315, 322–325, 348–353, 366–372; Wilfred Harold Munro, *Tales of an Old Sea Port* (Princeton, 1917), 205–208; Calbraith B. Perry, *Charles D'Wolf of Guadaloupe, His Ancestors and Descendants* (New York, 1902), *passim*, but especially pp. 15–64; Charles O. F. Thompson, *Sketches of Old Bristol* (Providence, 1942), especially pp. 19-21, 98-123. For Kentucky interests, see *DeWolf vs. Johnson, et al.*, 10 *Wheaton* 367 (1825); for Cuban plantation investments, see *John E. Nichols vs. Mark A. DeWolf*, 1 *Rhode Island* 277 (1850).

and James' brother-in-law, collector. So long as Collins held office —twenty years—DeWolf slavers fitted out in Bristol as if the trade were legal. They posted good conduct bonds without question and changed ship registries at will. Armed with powers of attorney, DeWolf captains made nominal sales of vessels and cargoes to Spanish interests and thus operated with relative impunity. Collins, it seemed, was more the employee of the DeWolfs than of the United States.

This brilliant example of political chicanery guaranteed safety on Narragansett Bay, and "wash" sales to Spaniards provided protection on the high seas, but fluctuating markets in the Caribbean posed a third type of threat. James fashioned a typical DeWolf solution: he acquired Cuban sugar plantations. When prices were low in Havana, or when the risks of smuggling slaves into the United States were too high, DeWolf simply held his cargoes off the market. The Negroes were set to work raising sugar cane and converting it to molasses. This was then shipped to Bristol, distilled into the golden currency of the slave trade, and eventually invested to profitable advantage on the African coast.

James also knew how to squeeze great profits out of legitimate slaving voyages. Many of the thirty-nine hundred slaves shipped into Charleston in Bristol vessels between 1803 and 1807 were carried in DeWolf craft on consignment to the family's local brokerage house, DeWolf and Christian. Thus the DeWolfs kept sales commissions in the family, and if the firm took payment in a draft on New York, another DeWolf was in the northern city to cash it without the expense of paying collection fees to an agent.

Profitable though Guinea voyages were, James DeWolf was too shrewd to stay in slaving after the Congressional prohibition took effect in 1808. Like other Rhode Island merchants, James had always diversified his risks by engaging simultaneously in several different kinds of business, and he experienced no difficulty in shifting his effort to other profitable ventures. Not all Bristol traders followed this example. The most notable exception was James' nephew, George DeWolf.

Working in collusion with Charles Collins, who cleared vessels as before, George DeWolf dispatched slaver after slaver on illicit voyages. So long as his luck held the profits were fabulous. But in the years following the War of 1812, Congress enacted three additional restrictive measures. An Act of 1818 required a suspected slaver to prove her innocence; another adopted in 1819 encouraged informers by giving them half the value of a condemned vessel; and an 1820 statute made slaving a hanging crime. As a member of the United States Senate, James DeWolf relieved some of this pressure by securing an amendment to the Anglo-American treaty of 1819, which had provided for joint naval patrols of the African coast. By preventing British men-of-war from searching craft flying the American flag or American cruisers searching British vessels, the DeWolf amendment enabled slavers to escape by running up whatever colors—American, British, or Spanish—momentarily promised the greatest safety.

Bristol slavers also came under local pressure. In 1817, the DeWolfs had secured the Bristol postmastership for the Reverend Barnabas Bates, a Baptist pastor who had lost his living by turning Unitarian. Bates repaid them by supplying Ellery with information about illegal Bristol voyages. Over the next few years, the courts condemned nine Bristol craft as slavers. The DeWolfs breathed more easily when Ellery died in 1820, but their troubles were not over. President Monroe declined to reappoint Collins. Instead, he transferred Bates from the post office to the customshouse, a move that closed Bristol to slavers throughout the new collector's four-year term. James DeWolf did get his Senate colleagues to refuse confirmation of Bates' reappointment in 1824, but by that time Bristol merchants had probably withdrawn from the slave trade.

Privateering, like slaving, began as a lawful activity.[24] During the War of 1812 the diehard Rhode Islanders, especially the

[24] The discussion of privateering is based on Bayles, *Newport County*, 412–413; George Coggeshall, *History of the American Privateers, and Letters-of-Marque* (New York, 1861), *passim*, but especially pp. 6, 49, 65, 151, 319, 351,

Bristol men, seized on it as a profitable alternative to slaving, which was now piracy. Indeed, Bristol privateers operated so successfully that, even though it too became common piracy with the war's end, they refused to give it up.

Probably the most speculative of all lawful maritime enterprises, privateering was organized so as to spread the risks as widely as possible. Most vessels were jointly owned, and crews shared in the profits in lieu of wages. Owners usually took half the prize money; officers, sailors, and marines shared the balance according to rank and occupation. Special bonuses ranging up to fifty dollars were paid for being the first man to sight an enemy sail or to board a prize's deck, and the government paid a bounty of twenty dollars for each prisoner captured. In contrast to the Colonial and Revolutionary periods, when governments took half the prize money, during the War of 1812 it merely collected customs duties on those cargoes brought into American ports. On the average, this gave the Treasury a thirteen per cent share. Another two per cent had to be paid to the Hospital Fund for Seamen, and legal expenses incurred in condemnation proceedings reduced profits still further. Nevertheless, proceeds from a single cruise were sometimes enormous. Even a lowly cabin boy might earn as much in three months as he would normally earn in six years, and a captain's share might be sufficient for him to fit out a vessel of his own.

Small brigs or schooners, especially exslavers of proven speed and maneuverability, made the best privateers. In peacetime, such craft had carried crews of less than twenty, but when converted to armed cruisers, they had to accommodate upwards of a hundred men. Additional space had to be found for prisoners, weapons, ammunition, food, and water. The privateer's objective, of course, was not to destroy an enemy merchantman but rather to frighten

390, 456–460; Ralph M. Eastman, *Some Famous Privateers of New England* (Boston, 1928), especially pp. 1–7, 71–72; Field, *Rhode Island*, 2:431–432; Howe, *Bristol*, 90–101; Howe, *Mount Hope*, 165–187; Edgar Stanton Maclay, *A History of American Privateers* (New York, 1899), especially pp. 265–278, 438; Munro, *Bristol*, 302–315; Munro, *Tales of an Old Seaport*, 211–288. For Providence opposition to piracy in the Caribbean, see *Providence Gazette*, September 22, 1821; December 18, 1824.

it into submission. A prize crew then sailed her to the nearest friendly port. Toward the end of a successful cruise, therefore, a privateer might well be reduced to a skeleton crew.

Greed rather than patriotism probably explains the readiness of sailors and marines to endure the cramped conditions, harsh discipline, and grave dangers of privateering. Some expeditions failed outright or returned only trifling dividends, but a few were so lucrative that sailors fought for the privilege of signing on for cruises which, they fervently hoped, would make them independent for life.

The hundred and sixty-eight ton hermaphrodite brig *Yankee* came closest to fulfilling these hopes. She was partly owned by James DeWolf, who always defended his interests skilfully and, when the need arose, ferociously. For as long as he lived, he neither forgot nor forgave an injury. Partly out of anti-British sentiment— he had been imprisoned during the Revolution, and British cruisers had captured several of his vessels during the Napoleonic conflict— in 1812 he and his kinfolk declared war on British shipping. They fitted out eight of the nine privateers that operated from Bristol, and James himself invested in no less than six of them. Only the *Yankee* cruised successfully, but she captured forty vessels, including nine ships and twenty-five brigs, worth, with their cargoes, $5,000,000. James DeWolf, who owned a three-quarter share in the privateer, reaped a gross profit of about $1,500,000. Yet whatever else he was, James DeWolf was no miser. He spent $52,000 of his spoils on the four hundred ton cruiser *Chippewa* which he presented to the Navy, in the hope, one supposes, that it would destroy whatever enemy shipping eluded the *Yankee*.

By rights, the Treaty of Ghent should have halted privateering. But for Bristol folk the war had ended too soon. After all, the crews of the *Yankee* had spent about a million dollars in the little port. Understandably, people hankered for the glamor, excitement, and, most important, the high profits of wartime enterprise. To a certain extent illicit slaving ventures gratified their need, but the traffic grew steadily more dangerous. The chance to revive the port's flagging economy soon came when the outbreak of revolutions in Latin America created opportunities for mercenaries, and in the slaver, George DeWolf, Bristol had just the man to organize lucrative privateering voyages. It mattered little that the United States government expressly forbade Americans to outfit or serve in any vessel flying an insurgent flag. So long as a steady stream of specie flowed back to Bristol, investors conveniently overlooked the fact that what had been lawful during the War of 1812 was now piracy.

But the bubble eventually burst. As soon as word reached Bristol in June, 1825, that George's Cuban sugar crop had failed, confidence sagged, and when his London banker crashed in the fall to the amount of $700,000, creditors began closing in. Hope remained alive in Bristol into December, but George was making secret plans to escape. The people woke one morning to find George gone and Bristol tottering on the verge of ruin. Losses were staggering. Few residents had resisted the possibility of a steady twenty-five per cent return on investments. Cousin James, lacking his father's canniness, had borrowed and invested $250,000, and between them the townsfolk had lent George several hundred thousand more.

Bristol's prosperity collapsed overnight. Though A. T. and T. J. Usher bought up the DeWolf fleet and made a fortune in the Cuban molasses, Bristol onion, and carrying trades, many families faced bankruptcy. Some fled their creditors; others joined the stream of New Englanders migrating westward. The majority, however, hung on in Bristol hoping that some way would be found to repair the town's shattered economy, but a full decade elapsed before Bristol made up for the sudden loss of population, and the port never recovered.

For once, otherwise-mindedness and opportunism took a terrible toll. But in a special sense, Bristol's growth had been an aberration. Its economy, almost totally oriented as it was to the ocean, should have gone into decline with the onset of the maritime depression in 1808. Instead, the town went on growing apace. However, this was largely the work of one man, George DeWolf, and he was a maverick. Unlike his uncles James and John, George never served an apprenticeship to the sea. Thus he never experienced at first hand the fructifying trials and tribulations that were the basis of the successful Rhode Island entrepreneurial tradition. Nor is it without point that his uncles shunned his schemes. Had Bristol folk been less avaricious, they would have heeded this aloofness.

Fortunately for Bristol, the crisis did not completely destroy the port's resilience. James and John DeWolf preserved much of their capital intact; the Usher brothers built a prosperous shipping business; and a DeWolf protégé, Byron Diman, helped perpetuate the port's entrepreneurial leadership.[25] Of French Huguenot stock, Diman began his career as an apprentice to James DeWolf. Born too late (1795) to have had personal experience in his employer's slaving operations, Diman acquired his first sloop in 1822. Over the next half-century, he owned shares in at least twenty-one other vessels, mainly brigs and ships, which he employed in West Indian trade, coasting, freighting, and whaling. Like his mentor, he diversified into banking, insurance, and manufacturing, and he took an active part in state politics. Despite the staggering loss of hundreds of thousands of dollars in 1825, therefore, and the flight of dozens of families, Bristol's spirit was never entirely crushed.

By 1825, then, the two most lucrative alternatives to foreign trade—slaving and privateering—had become piracy and were too dangerous even for Rhode Islanders. Some shipowners now ventured into another line, whaling.[26] Though it met one Narragansett Bay requirement—high risks—it failed in all other respects. It

---

[25] Bicknell, *Rhode Island*, 4:385; Munro, *Bristol*, 377–378. For Diman's investments, see *Ship Documents, Bristol*, especially Abstracts 57, 67, 92, 119, 137, 142, 280, 289, 356, 364, 381, 383, 384, 402, 531, 533, 579, 628, 722, 786, 940, 956.

[26] The discussion of whaling is based on Fessenden, *Warren*, 104–105; Field, *Rhode Island*, 2:483–484; Elmo Paul Hohman, *The American Whaleman: A Study of Life and Labor in the Whaling Industry* (New York, 1928), *passim*; Emory R. Johnson, *et al.*, *History of Domestic and Foreign Commerce of the United States* (2 vols., Washington, D.C., 1915), 2:157–168; *One Hundred Years of the Savings Bank of Newport* (Newport, 1919), 25–27; Martha R. McPartland, *The History of East Greenwich . . . , 1677–1960* (East Greenwich, 1960), 182; Thompson, *Sketches*, 32, 89–90; Walter S. Tower, *A History of the American Whale Fishery* (*University of Pennsylvania Publications in Political Economy and Public Law*, no. 20, Philadelphia, 1907), especially pp. 122–125.

required large investments, placed almost no premium on flexibility
and opportunism, and, worst of all, rarely returned speculative
profits. A whaling syndicate stood to lose $30,000 to $50,000 on an
unlucky cruise. Worse, the rate of return over the long haul was
unusually low. On the average, sperm whalers earned about one
and a half per cent annually, right whalers about six and a half
per cent. Nevertheless, urged on by the desperate need to find outlets for maritime capital and talent, and encouraged by rising prices
and markets, after 1826 shipowners shifted into whaling in increasing numbers. The industry reached its peak in about 1843, then
declined. Partly because coal gas made inroads into the lighting oil
market, whaling failed to recover from the depression of 1857,
and by 1860 Rhode Islanders had almost completely abandoned
the industry.

Narragansett Bay whaling expeditions conformed to the practices commonly followed in the American industry. Ships rather
than brigs dominated the fleet. Some exceeded five hundred tons,
but they were usually about three hundred tons, employed a crew
of twenty-five, and represented an average investment of some
$40,000 in vessel and outfit. At first, the maritime depression forced
many unemployed sailors into whaling. But the wretched living
and working conditions made it so difficult to retain experienced
men that the industry grew increasingly dependent upon green
hands, many of whom were country boys with romantic notions
about the life at sea or immigrants signed on by fast-talking agents.
Under the stern tutelage of seasoned sailors—men of Yankee stock
continued to occupy most positions of responsibility and skill—
these motley crews gradually acquired a rough proficiency, and by
the time they reached the South Atlantic or Pacific whaling
grounds they could work the ship efficiently. The brutal discipline,
low earnings, and long, monotonous voyages, nevertheless, led to
frequent desertions.

Whaling, like privateering, was organized so as to spread the
risks among all participants. Owners and crews shared the profits
according to a commonly accepted scale. The owners (and most

vessels were owned by syndicates) took seventy per cent of the net proceeds. The officers and crew shared the balance. Most captains received an eighth share and could earn $6,000 on a successful four-year voyage. Ordinary seamen hoped for $300. Though crew members did not pay for their food, many sailors bought their outfits from the shipowner or agent on credit, and during the cruise they usually drew on the sea chest for additional supplies. These goods were often shoddy in quality and sold at exhorbitant prices. Crewmen could also get cash advances—usually at usurous rates—to spend at the various ports touched in the course of a voyage. These charges were deducted before the sailor received his share of the profits. Net earnings for even an experienced hand were often as low as $150, and in some cases, crewmen came ashore in debt to the owners. In effect, this profit-sharing system forced crews to assume heavy financial risks, but their compensation was substantially lower than what they would have earned as merchant seamen or as unskilled factory workers.

A few whalers had cleared Providence in the last decade of the eighteenth century, but whaling did not recapture its colonial importance until after 1820. Even then, Rhode Island was a minor American center. Newport led the revival with an exploratory voyage in 1816. Two more expeditions sailed in 1820. Thereafter, until 1856, Newport regularly sent vessels to the whaling grounds. Warren re-entered the industry in 1821 with the departure of the *Rosalie* for the Pacific. A second whaler cleared in 1825, and expeditions were regularly organized from 1828 to 1861. After a lapse of more than twenty-five years, in 1823 Providence shipowners returned to the whaling business, but they did not become regularly involved until 1830, and they abandoned whaling again in 1854. Bristol was the last of the ports to re-enter whaling and the first to withdraw. Syndicates organized their first two ventures in 1827 and their last in 1846. Indeed, by 1849, Bristol had so many idle vessels that several former whalers carried prospectors round Cape Horn to the California goldfields. Most of these craft were sold or abandoned on the Pacific coast.

TABLE 3

WHALING ACTIVITY OF RHODE ISLAND PORTS, 1825–1859

(Clearances, 1825–1839: Whalers Registered, 1840–1859)

(Annual Average)

Ports	1825 to 1829	1830 to 1834	1835 to 1839	1840 to 1844	1845 to 1849	1850 to 1854	1855 to 1859
Providence	0	1	1	5	7	2	1
Newport	1	2	4	11	7	5	4
Bristol	2	5	5	8	4	0	0
Warren	1	5	8	20	22	16	15
Rhode Island	4	13	18	44	40	23	20

As the table shows, Warren was the leading Narragansett Bay whaling center. In 1845, the industry absorbed over half the port's risk capital, or more than $450,000, and employed some 7,000 of its 9,000 tons of shipping. Less than a third of Newport's fleet, or eleven vessels totaling approximately 3,700 tons, and less than a fifth of Providence's fleet, or nine vessels totaling about 3,000 tons, were also engaged in whaling. In 1837, when Bristol was still active in the industry, its fleet had included nineteen whalers totaling almost 6,000 tons.

Most Rhode Islanders met the decline in foreign trading opportunities with characteristic spirit and imagination. Those with greatest perception and maneuverability left the sea altogether. Others, lacking the foresight, or the opportunity, or the will, shifted to freighting, slaving, privateering, piracy, and whaling in the effort to preserve the seafaring way of life. Though the Narragansett Bay fleet declined only temporarily after 1820, none of the alternatives to international commerce proved effective over the long haul. Despite the immense profits earned in some maritime activities, by 1860 circumstances had forced the abandonment of all except freighting and whaling, and they earned far less than the Rhode Islanders traditionally expected from oceanic undertakings. Step by step, as each profitable avenue closed, the maritime segment of the economy had declined until on the eve of the Civil War it absorbed only an insignificant fraction of the state's risk

TABLE 4

SHIPPING REGISTERED, ENROLLED, AND LICENSED AT RHODE ISLAND
CUSTOMS DISTRICTS, 1790–1860[27]

(Tons by Admeasurement)

Districts	1790	1800	1810	1820	1830	1840	1850	1860
Providence								
Registered		7,644	13,019	15,311	9,877	11,062	9,177	6,538
Other		2,145	2,845	5,265	4,523	5,548	7,544	13,041
Total	10,590	9,789	15,864	20,576	14,400	16,610	16,721	19,579
Newport								
Registered			8,910	7,468	4,880	5,529	5,644	6,671
Other			3.607	3,234	3,544	5,399	4,934	5,617
Total	6,600	9,000	12,517	10,702	8,424	10,928	10,578	12,288
Bristol								
Registered			6,646	6,611	6,655	8,894	11,247	8,399
Other			1,131	1,426	1,432	6,996	1,951	1,374
Total	2,200	6,598	7,777	8,037	8,087	15,890	13,198	9,773
Rhode Island								
Registered			28,575	29,390	21,412	25,485	26,068	21,608
Other			7,583	9,925	9,499	17,943	14,429	20,032
Total	19,390	25,387	36,158	39,315	30,911	43,428	40,497	41,640

capital, sustained only a small proportion of Rhode Island families, and was no longer a challenge.

The early burgeoning, then precipitous decline of the maritime economy completed the eclipse of Newport and abetted the emergence of Providence as the state's economic center of gravity. Already the principal port by 1790, Providence did not rest on its laurels. Far from abandoning their aggressive opportunism, or merely defending their newly acquired preëminence, Providence entrepreneurs let nothing impede their expansion. When silt threatened to choke the harbor they quickly organized a corporation to dredge ship channels,[28] and they plunged into international and

[27] Staples, *Annals of Providence*, 352; Perry, *Rhode Island Census, 1885*, p. 79. Data for Newport and Bristol in 1790 and 1800 are estimated.

[28] *Acts and Resolves*, January, 1790, pp. 3–5. See also, Joseph Stancliffe Davis, *Essays in the Earlier History of American Corporations* (2 vols., Cambridge,

interstate ventures with renewed vigor. At the same time that they were expanding their European, Caribbean, and re-export operations, Providence houses were also exploring the Oriental and South American trades. And they responded creatively when the Anglo-French conflict reduced maritime profits. Without hesitation, they began seeking substitutes. At what turned out to be precisely the right moment merchants diverted their main effort from shipping into land-based but equally rewarding forms of money making. But this adjustment was never permitted to jeopardize the northward movement of maritime supremacy from Newport to Providence. Once achieved, Providence's hegemony proved unassailable, and the port continued to surpass all other Rhode Island centers in both the volume and the profits of its maritime trade.

These successes were partly an outgrowth of Providence's location at the natural outlet of what was becoming a rich hinterland, but even this advantage did not go uncultivated. Providence leaders plunged into the development of a land transportation system

---

1917), 2:284–285; Field, *Rhode Island*, 2:457, 500–501; Charles Carroll, *Rhode Island: Three Centuries of Democracy* (3 vols., New York, 1932), 2:837; Thompson, *Moses Brown*, 245–246; Petitions Not Granted, October, 1849, in the State Archives. Following complaints, the legislature suspended the charter in October, 1794, but reversed itself early the following year, when it sought to assure other corporations, especially bridge and turnpike companies, that it would do nothing to impair the sanctity of charter rights. See Granted Petitions, 28: 139 (October, 1794), in the State Archives; *Providence Gazette*, February 7, 1795.

For a time, it also looked as if Providence's mercantile expansion would be checked by the growing shortage of space for wharves, warehouses, shipyards, and other facilities. Merchants then considered moving some of their operations to Wickford in North Kingstown. This port, although engaged in coasting, West Indian, and fishing ventures, was only partially developed but possessed the potential Providence entrepreneurs were seeking. The ice-free harbor could handle large ships engaged in foreign trade, there was no silting hazard, and there was plenty of land available for the various service facilities a vastly expanded maritime economy would require. Thus, there seemed to be nothing to prevent Wickford becoming a major commercial center. However, local property owners demanded much more than Providence merchants, especially Brown and Ives, were willing to pay. The negotiations then collapsed and Wickford failed to rise above the status of a minor port. See *History of Rhode Island*, 178, and J. R. Cole, *History of Washington and Kent Counties, Rhode Island* (New York, 1889), 83.

that gradually extended the hinterland eastward along the coastal plain and up the Blackstone Valley into southern and western Massachusetts, up the Pawtuxet Valley into eastern Connecticut, and along the western shore of Narragansett Bay into Washington County. This hinterland became one of the most highly industrialized areas in the United States, and most of the raw materials consumed and the manufactured goods produced passed through the port of Providence. Though most of these cargoes moved on consignment and in interstate rather than in international trade, Providence never lost its importance as a maritime center, and the mercantile community continued to profit from the vast volume of goods handled by the port's warehouses.

Newport, by contrast, failed to adjust successfully to the forces transforming maritime affairs. For a number of reasons, all uniquely local in character and origin, the town faced insuperable obstacles. Though Newport revived after the Revolution, the British occupation had inflicted such irreparable damage that the town's recovery soon lost momentum. The British had not only destroyed hundreds of houses but, more important, they had driven away Newport's capital and talent. Once gone, these risk funds and the entrepreneurial class that had managed them so successfully never returned. To be sure, the remaining merchants and shipowners did re-enter the European, Guinea, and Caribbean trades, and eventually they followed Providence houses into Oriental and South American ventures. But with the exceptions of the slave and molasses trades, their scale of operation was so modest that the town's population grew, on the average, by less than one per cent annually.

Two factors were chiefly responsible for Newport's decline. First, it was no longer favorably located for sustained commercial expansion. Unlike Providence, Newport had direct access only to the two sluggish agricultural and fishing communities of Middletown and Portsmouth, and any attempt to gain access to mainland markets was bound to collide with established interests. More important, the town's insular location impeded the development of turnpikes and railroads. Such a transportation system would have permitted merchants to capitalize on Newport's greatest asset, its accessible harbor, and might have made the town a major New England terminus.[29]

The second, and perhaps more important, factor in Newport's decline was the exodus of the entrepreneurial leadership that had made the town a great commercial center. The new generation of merchants lacked the vigor, resourcefulness, and determination one characteristic of the port's traders, and they did not display the same opportunism. Thus in 1799, at the height of the French crisis, when the government was considering various New England sites for a naval base, the mercantile community reacted with characteristic ambivalence and indecision. Some merchants extolled Newport's merits to the secretary of the navy, stressing, in particular, its accessibility, its sheltered, deep water anchorages, its suitability for ship construction, the availability of land for a marine hospital, and the abundance and cheapness of fresh provisions. But George Champlin, a leading merchant, argued that any advantages Newport might derive from the naval establishment "would be overbalanced by . . . many disagreeable circumstances" and recommended Fall River as a more suitable site.[30] Since the government soon abandoned its plans for a naval station, no damage resulted, but such attitudes pervaded Newport thinking throughout the Anglo-French conflict. They were especially symptomatic of Newport's timorous approach to the problems created by the Embargo and the closing of the slave trade in 1808, and by the outbreak of war with Great Britain four years later. Indeed, Newport residents were almost prostrate with fear that the British would again occupy the town, and this, together with the collapse of foreign trade, led to a second flight of capital and talent.

After the Treaty of Ghent, Newport proved incapable of rousing itself from its torpor. In 1819 an observer complained that mer-

[29] Mason, *Reminiscences*, 138–139. Dr. William Douglass had predicted Newport's demise as early as 1750. He observed that "Newport . . . is of easy and short Access, being near the Ocean, but for that Reason not so well situated for inland Consumption; Providence is about 30 miles farther up Narragansett–Bay inland, therefore in a few Years must be their principal Place of Trade." Quoted in Bridenbaugh, *Cities in Revolt*, 53.

[30] Mason, *Reminiscence*, 138–143, especially pp. 140–141.

chants had failed to divert their capital into the potentially valuable fishing industry.[31] Eventually they did turn to whaling and freighting, but these relatively unrewarding activities did not halt the drift of people away from the town. According to tradition, pupils were released from school˙ one day in 1829 to witness the raising of the first house to be built in Newport in fifteen years.[32]

Far from being a temporary phenomenon, the depression became chronic, and the town responded so lethargically to its problems that nearly a generation elapsed before anyone advanced major proposals for the revitalization of maritime affairs. In the early 1850's, a group of promoters organized the Atlantic and Mediterranean Banking and Navigation Company to operate a steamship service between Newport, Boston, and European ports.[33] Though the line never went into operation, the scheme was an ambitious one designed to stimulate various sectors of the Newport economy. A bank capitalized at $8,000,000 was to provide a profitable outlet for the town's idle funds and was to finance local con-

[31] Pease and Niles, *Gazetteer*, 350, 352, 354–355.

[32] Wilfred H. Munro, *Picturesque Rhode Island* (Providence, 1881), 51. For other comments on Newport's debility, see William Ellery to Moses Brown, December 5, 1791, quoted in Franklin, "William Ellery," 16–17; Richman, *Rhode Island*, 258–259; W. G. R[oelker]., "John Quincy Adams Admires Mr. John Brown's House," in *Rhode Island History*, 2:111 (October, 1943). Adam Hodgson, an English visitor to Newport in January, 1821, reported that he had seldom seen "a more desolate place . . . or one which exhibited more evident symptoms of decay. The wooden houses had either never been painted, or had lost their paint, and were going to ruin. A decent house here and there, seemed to indicate, that some residents of respectability still lingered behind; but the close habitations, with their small windows, and the narrow, dirty, and irregular streets, exhibited no trace of the attractions which once rendered this a summer resort for the planters from the South." Hodgson also noted that "a few young men dropped in, in the course of the evening, but I soon found, that, as usual, in declining sea-ports, they were *at a premium*." Adam Hodgson, *Letters from North America, Written during a Tour in the United States and Canada* (2 vols., London, 1824), 2:132–133. For similar comments by John Harriot, the Duke of La Rochefoucauld–Liancourt, Jacques Pierre Brissot de Warville, and Benjamin Waterhouse, see Munro, *Picturesque Rhode Island*, 51; Bayles, *Newport County*, 535; and Gertrude Selwyn Kimball, ed., *Pictures of Rhode Island in the Past, 1642–1833* (Providence, 1900), 115–116, 136, 170.

[33] See Petitions Not Granted, October, 1851; January, 1852; January, 1853; *Acts and Resolves*, January, 1854, pp. 298–301; *Petition and Magna Charta . . . Granted . . . to . . . "The Mediterranean Bank"* (New York, 1854), *passim*.

struction of eight steamships and their engines. Each vessel was to have but a single mast for the sole purpose of flying the "stars and spangled banner of the Union," and was to be suitable for conversion to an armed cruiser in wartime. By operating from Newport rather than from New York, fuel consumption would be reduced and the correspondingly larger volume of freight that could be carried would render government subsidies unnecessary. Then, concluded the promoters, the "destinies of Newport and Boston, PHOENIX-LIKE, RISING FROM THEIR ASHES, will be accomplished," and each would become not only independent of New York, "but equal with her in rights, wealth, and sovereignty." Impressive though the scheme may have seemed on paper, Newport investors were much too cautious to risk their remaining capital, and the charter obtained in 1854 lapsed for want of action. Since the corporation required capital far beyond the town's resources and would probably have proved unprofitable even if the funds could have been raised, this caution was undoubtedly justified. However, that such an improbable rehabilitation scheme should have been proposed was indicative of Newport's economic malaise. Ironically, the plan was not advanced by a local entrepreneur but by the French consul. In retrospect, Newport seems to have been the object of a cruel Gallic joke.

In a very real sense the death of Newport as a commercial center can be attributed to a failure of nerve. Of course, many of the circumstances destroying its economic vitality were beyond the control of business leaders. Nevertheless, they fought back half-heartedly. Indeed, each successive calamity seems to have gradually drained the town of its will to survive. Gone were the vigor, opportunism, and resourcefulness of earlier days, and the mercantile community timidly—almost absentmindedly—bowed to its fate. Newport became a sleepy shadow of its former self, and the only dreams worth dreaming were those conjuring up images of colonial preëminence.

CHAPTER THREE

Industrialization:
The Era of Experimentation

THE shrewdest Rhode Island merchants did not wait for the creeping paralysis that choked Newport. Nor did they resort to the stratagems that overnight crippled Bristol. Instead, they turned their wily talents to land-based ventures promising to yield the kind of profits they were accustomed to earning in seafaring enterprises. Some years before the Jeffersonian Embargo and the War of 1812 seriously depressed the maritime economy, they began moving into manufacturing. Using water as their source of power and the partnership as their form of organization, they rode the early crest of the industrial wave, at first tentatively, then confidently. Manufacturing soon replaced maritime activity as the dynamic element in the economy; and as the principal outlet for venture capital and the primary source of wealth, industrialization soon became the factor determining the locus and structure of economic power in Rhode Island.

The tiny state lacked the resources for heavy industry, but topographic and climatic conditions were ideal for lighter forms of manufacturing, especially for textile making. Power was readily available: narrow, swift-running streams, low waterfalls, and natural storage ponds abounded, particularly in the northern and western hill country. In many places it was sufficient merely to divert water into the mill race, and if a dam had to be built construction costs were low. Furthermore, the soft Rhode Island water did not require treatment before yarns and cloths could be washed or bleached, and dyes took easily. Finally, the Rhode Island climate was ideal for textile manufacturing. The high relative

71

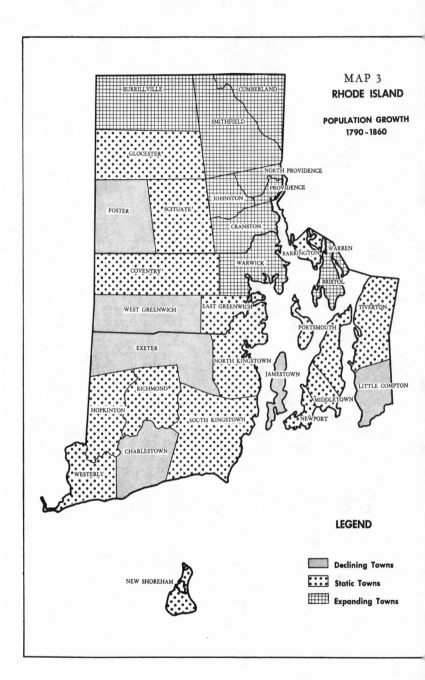

MAP 3
RHODE ISLAND

POPULATION GROWTH
1790-1860

BURRILLVILLE
CUMBERLAND
SMITHFIELD
GLOCESTER
NORTH PROVIDENCE
PROVIDENCE
JOHNSTON
FOSTER
SCITUATE
CRANSTON
WARREN
BARRINGTON
WARWICK
BRISTOL
COVENTRY
EAST GREENWICH
WEST GREENWICH
TIVERTON
PORTSMOUTH
EXETER
NORTH KINGSTOWN
JAMESTOWN
LITTLE COMPTON
RICHMOND
HOPKINTON
MIDDLETOWN
SOUTH KINGSTOWN
NEWPORT
CHARLESTOWN
WESTERLY

NEW SHOREHAM

LEGEND

Declining Towns
Static Towns
Expanding Towns

humidity kept fibers supple enough to be spun without breaking, and the comparatively even seasonal distribution of rainfall provided a steady flow of water for power and other purposes.

Social conditions also favored industrialization. The pioneer manufacturers benefited especially from an unusually congenial climate of public opinion. It manifested itself in what the *Providence Gazette* of August 8, 1789, called the "Spirit of Industry, and Zeal to promote Manufactures in this Town and its Vicinity . . . ," and in the general acceptance of the practice of employing women and children in factories. With Alexander Hamilton and other apologists for manufacturing, the majority of Rhode Islanders believed that work inculcated moral no less than economic virtues in the young. The oversupply of labor in many hill-country communities and, after 1808, in most ports, also facilitated the expansion of manufacturing capacity. Too, the early mill owners were able to draw on the mechanical aptitude and ingenuity of a large and traditionally opportunistic artisan class. Throughout the Colonial era these artisans had built in their homes and small workshops all manner of equipment both for the pioneer farmer and for the maritime trader; and they had turned the products of Rhode Island's stingy natural endowment, as well as imported raw materials, into the trade goods, so badly needed by the Narragansett Bay merchants. Cottage spinners and weavers, saw- and gristmillers, tanners, coopers, ironworkers, shoemakers, candle-makers, charcoal burners, and all manner of workers in wood had by 1800 come to constitute that reservoir of skill and experience essential to the successful launching of large scale industrial experimentation.

The mercantile community not only had the capital to exploit these advantages and to develop the local transportation facilities to service factories, it also had the managerial experience, market knowledge, and distribution organization to support the experiment. Equally important, it had a tradition of popular support for its objectives and of favorable relations with colonial and state government. Except for the conventional control of the extractive and processing segments of the economy (mining, farming, fish-

ing, and forestry), the state indulged in almost no public regulation. Furthermore, public officials almost without exception and by
long tradition operated on the premise that their purpose was to
support, not to check, Rhode Island's entrepreneurs.[1]

Despite the health problems caused by industrialization, the
legislature permitted manufacturers almost complete freedom of
action.[2] Slimy waste drained from tanneries and slaughterhouses

---

[1] During the Colonial period, the General Assembly had fixed gristmill fees to
protect the public from exploitation; it had required millers to open their dams
at particular seasons to enable fish to reach their spawning grounds; it had
legislated against "deceits and abuses by tanners, curriers, and shoemakers"; and
it had stipulated that certain commodities, particularly provisions and forest
products, meet specified standards of quality.

Many of these laws remained in effect after the Revolution, and the legislature
brought additional products, notably burnt lime, scythe stones, and whale oil,
within the scope of the inspection system. Goods condemned either because they
were inferior or because they were sold contrary to law were forfeited to the use
of the poor, and the lawbreakers were fined, the proceeds being shared by the in-
former and the needy in the community where the offence occurred. Congress
prohibited the export of all goods not inspected according to state law.

At various times after 1790, the General Assembly received petitions requesting changes in the inspection system—to extend its scope, to amend it in minor
details, or to exempt particular products or markets. According to complaints
published in the *Providence Gazette* on February 17, 1810, merchants engrossed
local markets, sometimes by intercepting wagons several miles from Providence.

The details of public regulation can be followed in Bartlett, *Rhode Island
Colonial Records*, 4:7–11; *Acts and Laws, 1767*, pp. 26–27; *Acts and Laws
Passed Since the Revision in 1767*, pp. 33–34; *Acts and Resolves*, August, 1784,
pp. 4, 15–16; October, 1784, pp. 7–8; June, 1785, pp. 24–25; August, 1785,
p. 18; *Annals of Congress*, 2:2266 (April 12, 1790); *Acts and Resolves*, September, 1790, pp. 15–17; Granted Petitions, 25:56 (October, 1790); *Acts and
Resolves*, February, 1792, pp. 30–32; June, 1792, pp. 18–19; February, 1797,
p. 27; May, 1797, pp. 24–25; *Public Laws, 1798*, pp. 509–527, 617–618; *Acts
and Resolves*, June, 1815, pp. 24–30; October, 1821, p. 42; *Public Laws, 1822*,
pp. 378–393, 422–423, 427, 472–478, 483–484; *Acts and Resolves*, January,
1823, p. 39; January, 1824, p. 20; June, 1825, pp. 54–56; June, 1826, pp. 16–
17; Miscellaneous Papers of the General Assembly, folder 10 (1826–1830), in
the State Archives; *Acts and Resolves*, January, 1830, pp. 20–22; January,
1831, pp. 33–41; June, 1831, p. 47; January, 1832, pp. 7–13; Petitions Not
Granted, January, 1833; *Public Laws, 1844*, pp. 440–463, 465–466; *Acts and
Resolves*, January, 1846, pp. 61–62; January, 1852, pp. 6–7; *Revised Statutes,
1857*, pp. 243–263.

[2] *Acts and Resolves*, May, 1772, pp. 8–11; October, 1802, pp. 9–11; October,
1843, pp. 72–74; January, 1851, pp. 18–19; Granted Charters, 7:47 (1820–

into stagnant, odiferous pools; pigs fed from the refuse in distillery cellars and yards; factory workers were crowded into unsanitary, teeming tenements, and they worked long hours under hazardous conditions; congested areas suffered from inadequate drainage facilities and from impure water supplies; and recurrent outbreaks of yellow fever endangered life. Yet the General Assembly did not authorize local authorities to regulate industrial nuisances until 1843. Even then, it merely empowered Providence to regulate steamboilers. Another eight years elapsed before town councils could zone slaughterhouses. Nor was the legislature perturbed by the high incidence of child labor or by unhealthy factory conditions. It took no action at all until after 1850, and even then the law was notoriously ineffective.

On the other hand, manufacturers received virtually no state assistance.[3] In colonial times, both local authorities and the General Assembly had encouraged certain industries. Towns granted land to gristmillers and weavers, and the legislature subsidized the manufacture of cloth and rope from locally grown flax, hemp, and wool. These and other techniques persisted after the Revolution. The legislature granted monopolies to a Smithfield marble works and a North Providence nailrod slitting mill in 1785 and

1823), in the State Archives; Miscellaneous Papers of the General Assembly, folder 13 (1841); folder 16 (1851); Petitions Not Granted, October, 1845; January, 1849; June, 1852 (in Outsize Petitions, box 2); *Providence Journal*, June 12, July 9, 21, 1858; Field, *Rhode Island*, 2:20–36, 41–42; Thompson, *Moses Brown*, 263–273. At common law, of course, aggrieved individuals could institute suits to abate nuisances and to secure compensation for damages suffered.

[3] *Acts and Laws, 1772*, pp. 23–24; *Acts and Resolves*, August, 1772, p. 37; June, 1774, pp. 30–31; August, 1774, pp. 78–79; August, 1785, pp. 4, 12; March, 1786, pp. 7, 12–13; Granted Petitions, 23:53 (1786–1787); *Acts and Resolves*, October, 1788, p. 11; June, 1792, pp. 6–7; October, 1792, pp. 9–10; February, 1793, pp. 17–18; June, 1796, p. 14; February, 1797, pp. 17–19; Granted Petitions, 37:122 (February, 1808); Petitions Not Granted, October, 1834.

See also, a letter from Moses Brown to John Dexter, July 2, 1791, quoted in Arthur H. Cole, ed., *Industrial and Commercial Correspondence of Alexander Hamilton* (Chicago, 1928), 74, in which he observed: "No Encouragement has been given [to manufactures] by any Laws of the State nor by any Donation of any Society or Individuals but Wholey began Carried on and thus far perfected at Private Expence."

1786; it authorized a nail factory to hold a $2,000 lottery in 1788; and it resumed subsidizing sailcloth production in 1792. The Assembly also exempted the newly constructed dam belonging to the first cotton mill from a directive to clear all obstructions on the Pawtucket River, and in 1796 it authorized the construction of a tidewater mill in Warwick, provided the undertaking did not impede the passage of lumber. But these measures had little impact on the process of industrialization, and it is notable that, with the exception of a lottery to stimulate coal mining, the legislature extended no further assistance in the nineteenth century. When a fire destroyed Hosea Humphrey's textile mill on the Woonasquatucket River in November, 1807, the Assembly rejected his request for a lottery, and it also refused to subsidize the establishment of the silk industry. Nor did the legislature exempt key factory workers from militia duty, a type of assistance commonly granted by other New England states. Manufacturers did not receive tax concessions either. Instead, the Assembly kept social services to the barest minimum. In this way the Rhode Islanders went for long periods without having to pay state property taxes at all.

Though private rather than public initiative determined the speed and direction of industrial growth, the state did make one significant contribution.[4] In the Colonial period, the Assembly had encouraged grist- and sawmilling enterprises by establishing procedures for settling disputes between millers, by allocating water supplies between competing users, and most important, by authorizing millers to overflow land upstream from their dams without first securing the permission of the property owners who would

[4] *Acts and Laws, 1767*, pp. 190–194; *Public Laws, 1798*, pp. 504–508; *Acts and Resolves*, October, 1835, p. 60; January, 1836, p. 49; June, 1838, pp. 38–41; Miscellaneous Papers of the General Assembly, folder 12 (1837); 1 *Rhode Island* 247 (1849); 2:211, 369 (1852); 4:55, 301 (1856); 5:299 (1858); 6:56 (1859).

Rhode Island industrialized rapidly as compared to Connecticut partly because it acted earlier to relax the laws requiring dams to be kept open to enable fish to reach their spawning grounds. These laws were burdensome, especially in summer, because they forced manufacturers to release water during the period when they needed all the storage capacity they could get.

be flowed out. In effect, the miller enjoyed the right of eminent domain. He paid an annual rent for the land he thus preëmpted and, if necessary, local courts fixed the compensation. By these means, the law made all mill sites useable. Farmers could refuse to sell or lease dam sites of course, but once they granted mill privileges they could not prevent exploitation of the water resources. The miller was restricted in only two ways: he was not entitled to flow out or otherwise injure an existing dam upstream, and he had to operate with due regard for the common law rights of users downstream. When textile manufacturing began, the pioneer industrialists secured these flowage privileges by the informal extension of the colonial law to analogous enterprises rather than by specific enactment. Nevertheless, the right was in no way diminished by this informality, and in 1837, when the General Assembly refused to restrict the scope of the statute to grist- and sawmillers, it indirectly sustained the underlying proposition—that industrialization served the public interest and that the needs of manufacturing took precedence over the property rights of farmers and other landowners.

Rhode Island's pioneer cotton manufactory was begun in 1789 by a merchant, Moses Brown of Providence, seeking to diversify his business interests. Shrewdly, in keeping with the mercantile tradition he personified, he selected the right man to direct his industrial experiments. After one false start with cumbersome machinery copied from jennies at the unsuccessful Beverly Mill in Massachusetts, Brown hired Samuel Slater, a young Englishman whose technical knowledge and managerial experience, acquired in the Derbyshire cotton industry, compensated for his lack of capital. Within a year, Slater had converted a Pawtucket mill on the Blackstone River in North Providence to the Arkwright system, and there, in December, 1790, cotton was spun by water power for the first time in America. Although the new process produced a yarn with a hard twist suitable for warps, thereby permitting the manufacture of pure cotton cloth instead of the traditional mixed fabric of linen and cotton, markets developed slowly and yarn production far exceeded demand.[5]

Slater was later admitted to partnership, but he never achieved equality of status with Moses Brown, whose financial backing was indispensable, or with William Almy, Brown's son-in-law, who managed the commercial side of the venture. Like many early in-

[5] The early growth of the cotton industry can be followed in *A Chronicle of Textile Machinery, 1824–1924: Issued to Commemorate the One Hundredth Anniversary of the Saco-Lowell Shops* (Boston, 1924), especially pp. 8–10; *Handbook of the Textile Industry of the United States* (New York, n.d.), especially pp. 23–24, 42–49; Noah J. Arnold, "The Valley of the Pawtuxet," in *The Narragansett Historical Register*, 6:222–259 (July, 1888), and his "Further Reminiscences of the Valley of the Pawtuxet River and its Branches," in *ibid.*, 7:233–280 (July, 1889); William R. Bagnall, *Samuel Slater and the Early Development of the Cotton Manufacture in the United States* (Middletown, 1890), *passim*; Bagnall, *The Textile Industries of the United States* (Cambridge, 1893), especially pp. 135–165, 213–219, 251–258, 276–279, 394–423, 433–457, 498–512, 524–535, 541–551, 594–597; Samuel Batchelder, *The Introduction and Early Progress of the Cotton Manufacture in the United States* (Boston, 1863), especially pp. 26–59; Orin Fowler, *History of Fall River* (Fall River, 1841), 29–32; Oliver Payson Fuller, *The History of Warwick* (Providence, 1875), 171–175, 189–192, 195, 203–205, 208–210, 225–242, 248–251, 264–265; Henry L. Greene, "The Lippitt Manufacturing Company," in *The Narragansett Historical Register*, 7:156–157 (April, 1889); Robert Grieve, *An Illustrated History of Pawtucket, Central Falls and Vicinity* (Pawtucket, 1897), 73–115 *passim*; S. S. Griswold, *An Historical Sketch of . . . Hopkinton* (Hope Valley, 1877); 56–65 *passim*; *History of Rhode Island*, 101–103, 106–107, 113–116, 120, 131, 138–139, 158, 163, 178–179, 185, 187–188, 234, 236, 259, 287–289, 304–305, 308–309, 327–328, 336–337, 342–343, 346–347, 356; James R. Irish, *Historical Sketch of . . . Richmond* (Hope Valley, 1877), 50–58; Francis Little, *Early American Textiles* (New York, 1931), 113–122; *North Providence Centennial* (Pawtucket, 1865), 75–85 *passim*; Frederick M. Peck and Henry H. Earl, *Fall River and its Industries* (New York and Fall River, 1877), 8–36; E. Richardson, *History of Woonsocket* (Woonsocket, 1876), 125–173; William B. Spencer, "A History of the North Branch of the Pawtuxet Valley," in *The Narragansett Historical Register*, 6:122–135 (April, 1888); Thomas Steere, *History of . . . Smithfield* (Providence, 1881), 75–78, 94–97, 99–100, 103, 106–111, 114–121, 129–134, 144; Thompson, *Moses Brown*, 203–233; Perry Walton, *The Story of Textiles* (Boston, 1912), 168–185, 199–200, 222–232, 246–247; Caroline F. Ware, *The Early New England Cotton Manufacture: A Study in Industrial Beginnings* (Cambridge, 1931), *passim*, but especially pp. 3–27; Samuel Webber, *Historical Sketch of . . . Cotton Manufacture in the United States* (New York, 1879), 7–62; George S. White, *Memoir of Samuel Slater* (Philadelphia, 1836), 234–236, 246, 249, 256–262, 302–303.

dustrialists, neither Brown nor Almy understood the mechanics of textile manufacturing. They left those mundane aspects of the enterprise to Slater, whom they regarded as little more than a hired technician.[6]

The industrial and business methods pioneered by Almy, Brown, and Slater established the cotton industry's early pattern of development. The partners increased efficiency, cultivated markets, and, in collusion with other manufacturers, maintained artificially high prices. They also campaigned for tariff protection against foreign producers, and, though Slater first refused to use American cotton because it was poorly cleaned, when Eli Whitney invented the cotton gin they called for national self-sufficiency in cotton production. The partnership earned a profit of $18,000 in the decade after 1793.[7]

Despite these technical and business accomplishments, the Rhode Island cotton industry developed so slowly that many years elapsed before a full-fledged factory system emerged. There were a number of reasons for this delay. Because Slater refused to share his industrial secrets and because the English government restricted the emigration of craftsmen and the export of machinery, mechanization of weaving lagged particularly. The difficulty of recruiting factory workers was another cause of delay. To some extent, this was directly attributable to the cotton weavers' vested interest in their craft. In the seventeenth century, the ability to make homespun yarn and cloth had been a necessary domestic accomplishment, especially in farming communities. Then, in the early eighteenth century, the rising affluence of the Rhode Islanders had given

[6] Federal Writers' Project, *Rhode Island: A Guide to the Smallest State* (Cambridge, 1937), 78–79. According to the *Pawtucket Chronicle*, "Mr. Slater was not exactly a generous man. He gave little to public institutions, and regarded not the appeals to private individuals. His object was gold; and no man was more indefatigible." Quoted in Leonard Bliss, Jr., *The History of Rehoboth* (Boston, 1836), 237. But compare White, *Slater*, 249–250, and Bagnall, *Textile Industries*, 336.

[7] Batchelder, *Cotton Manufacture*, 46; Field, *Rhode Island*, 3:333–334; Little, *Early American Textiles*, 116; Edwin M. Stone, *Mechanics' Festival* (Providence, 1860), 79–85; Ware, *Early New England Cotton Manufacture*, 44–45, 123–126; Webber, *Historical Sketch*, 18; White, *Slater*, 367.

itinerant weavers a market for their services, but increasingly, customers had turned to England for their needs. When the Revolution cut off the supply of imported fabric, cottage weaving revived and handicraft workers made a patriotic virtue of necessity. By 1790 they were producing many thousands of yards of woolen cloth, linen, and cotton goods in the Providence area, and the output of stockings, gloves, and fringe was also rising. These cottage weavers and knitters resented the development of factories, and, like farm workers, submitted reluctantly to factory regimentation.[8]

Partly because of technical lags and perhaps partly because cottagers resisted the factory system, the industry was slow to leave the putting out stage. Children performed the first task in their homes, loosening cotton fibers and removing dirt particles. The cleaned cotton was then sent to the mill, where other children spread it along the carding machines or tended the spinning frames. The coarse yarn they produced was distributed to cottage weavers scattered through the adjacent countryside. This system created many difficulties. Household workers could not be relied upon to complete their tasks on time, and cloth varied in quality from weaver to weaver. Moreover, the poor state of Rhode Island highways limited the number of workers who could be reached from any factory. Manufacturers solved these problems by installing hand looms in the mill, where they could exercise greater supervision, and by selling the surplus yarn outright. Almy and Brown, for example, organized retailers along the New England coast as far north as Portland and, in 1803, they dispatched Obadiah Brown, Moses' only son, to develop markets from New York southward. No change in this simple division of labor occurred until after the War of 1812, when the invention of the power loom and the introduction of cotton cleaning machinery extended the scope of the factory system.[9]

[8] The original Pawtucket mill was so exposed that in winter the water wheel froze each night. Since the workers refused to go into the race to clear the ice, Slater had to spend several hours each morning doing the job himself. White, *Slater*, 98; Field, *Rhode Island*, 3:343–345.

[9] Thomas Robinson Hazard, in *The Jonny-Cake Papers of "Shepherd Tom"* (Boston, 1915), xiii, 328, describes the difficulties of Rowland H. Hazard, an

Until the 1850's, managerial practices were modelled on those perfected in maritime ventures. The same joint-stock partnership was the commonest form of organization and partners exercised the same care in selecting business associates; they trained their sons to assume industrial responsibilities; and, occasionally, they cemented their industrial alliances by marriage. Conflicting interests, a potential source of friction, were usually avoided by each partner's agreeing to withdraw from all competing enterprises. Apart from silent members, each partner performed a specialized function. Some dealt with technical problems, others supervised particular phases of production, and still others served as business agents. These agents purchased raw materials, disposed of yarn and cloth, and recruited workers. Senior partners exercised general oversight and coördinated the various activities. Members received a salary or a commission for their services. The agent, for example, received a commission of two and a half per cent on all except local retail sales. Profits were usually divided at fairly long intervals or when the association was dissolved. In effect, partners earned both salaries for their labor and dividends on their capital. Some factories were family enterprises; others were operated by mechanics with outside financial backing; and still others were owned by investors who, since they lacked knowledge of the cotton industry, turned over the management to superintendents, an arrangement which a number of observers and commentators considered grossly inefficient.[10]

---

early woolen manufacturer, who rode throughout Washington County leaving rolls of carded wool at various homes to be spun into yarn. Sometimes he had to make as many as a dozen calls to collect yarn from delinquent spinners; after scouring and dyeing in the mill, it was put out to a second network of homes to be woven into cloth. For the cotton industry, see *North Providence Centennial*, 32–33; Steere, *History of Smithfield*, 132–133; White, *Slater*, 106; and Henry Bradshaw Fearon quoted in Kimball, *Pictures of Rhode Island in the Past*, 165–166.

[10] Louis McLane, *Report of the Secretary of the Treasury, 1832. Documents Relative to the Manufactures in the United States* (22 Congress, 1 session, *House Executive Document no. 308*, serial 222–223, 2 vols., Washington, 1833), 1: 928–929; Samuel Ogden, *Thoughts . . . on the Cotton Manufactures of this Country* (Providence, 1815), 22–23, 27.

At the outset, Rhode Island manufacturers were innovators. They preserved their industrial leadership by replacing obsolete plant and equipment, and by introducing new methods, machinery, and products. Slater had no sooner mechanized cotton spinning than Almy and Brown agreed to construct a mill to his specifications. Other manufacturers, who also began with mills originally built for other purposes, replaced their converted chocolate, grist, lumber, and fulling mills with larger, more efficient factories. A three-story stone factory was built in Warwick in 1808, and the Coventry Manufacturing Company operated a six-story stone and wooden mill in 1810. Perhaps only a quarter of the undertakings were large enough to utilize a thousand spindles, but a Warwick mill, owned by the Providence Manufacturing Company, operated twice that number. Still other manufacturers, as soon as their experimental ventures had proved successful, replaced their simple wing-style dams with storage reservoirs. Though some firms were timid about venturing into new processes, such as dyeing or weaving, Slater introduced sewing thread and stocking yarn to the American market, and others employed farm families to weave a variety of products ranging from sheeting and bedticking to checks and plaids.

Despite government restrictions, British equipment and technicians eventually facilitated the development of new methods and products. The Lyman Manufacturing Company, for example, which built a mill on the Woonasquatucket River in 1809, imported English spindles, employed an English-trained mechanic, Samuel Ogden, to construct equipment in his Providence machine shop, and in 1816 hired a Scottish-born machinist, William Gilmore, to copy the Scotch-style power loom.[11] John Slater, a Derbyshire millwright who emigrated to the United States in 1803,

[11] Lyman first employed one Blydenburg to develop power weaving but the attempt failed. According to one account, Lyman hired Gilmore only after Almy and Brown had refused to finance experimentation. A second account put the blame on Slater's son John, who, it reported, turned Gilmore away with the argument that economic conditions did not justify trying to develop power weaving. Compare Webber, *Historical Sketch*, 35; Field, *Rhode Island*, 3:348; Batchelder, *Cotton Manufacture*, 70; White, *Slater*, 389.

made other important contributions by supplying his brother Samuel with information about the latest English innovations, especially the spinning mule invented by Samuel Crompton in 1779 but not widely adopted in Lancashire factories until the early nineteenth century. In 1806, he joined Samuel in designing and managing the new Smithfield mill, one of the largest and most advanced factories in Rhode Island.[12]

Providence contributed significantly to the cotton industry's early expansion: it supplied most of the capital, the managers, and the technical knowledge. Providence entrepreneurs ventured much of the $134,000 invested in four mills which opened between 1806 and 1808; local mechanics and millwrights supplied the balance. Sometimes farmers exchanged mill privileges for factory shares but they rarely invested cash. This steady stream of Providence money flowing into the Blackstone and Pawtuxet valleys enabled merchants like the Almys, Browns, Carringtons, Jacksons, Masons, and Potters to tie hinterland communities to the city's expanding commercial and financial services, and stimulated regional economic growth. By creating a reservoir of skilled mechanics and operatives, Providence entrepreneurs shaped industrial development throughout southern New England. Employees or associates of Almy and Brown established at least eight early mills, and capital and artisans were sent to set up additional factories in Massachusetts and even in New Hampshire and New York. Except for James DeWolf's investment in the Arkwright Manufacturing Company in Coventry and Benjamin Hazard's small share in the Lyman mill in North Providence, neither Bristol nor Newport capital contributed to the rise of cotton manufacturing.[13]

Providence's technological superiority and its capital—and the control that went with it—were not always welcomed. Samuel

[12] Webber, *Historical Sketch*, 23.

[13] *Ibid.*, 21; Bagnall, *Textile Industries*, 150, 172, 183, 216, 219, 276–277, 368–369, 373, 404, 418, 442, 444, 502; Spencer, "Pawtuxet Valley," 132. See, however, Peck and Earl, *Fall River and Its Industries*, 11, for evidence of Warren, Tiverton, and Newport investments in the Troy Cotton and Woolen Manufactory and the Fall River Manufactory in 1813. See also, *History of Rhode Island*, 101.

Slater, whose employment practices and unwillingness to share his knowledge made him unpopular, provoked some of his employees to encourage construction of a rival mill. When it was completed in 1801, they demonstrated outside Slater's North Providence factory, hurling defiance at their former employer. In another case, Providence investors offered to finance the recovery of William Sprague, a Cranston farmer and sawmiller turned industrialist, whose mill was destroyed by fire in 1813. He rejected these offers, but his show of independence apparently worked him no injury. Despite generally low profits in the industry after 1815, and the loss of a second uninsured mill in 1816, this one valued at $25,000, Sprague purchased control of the Natick Mill in Warwick in 1821. When he died in 1836, he left a budding Rhode Island industrial empire to the management of two of his sons, Amasa and William, whom he had trained to succeed him.[14]

The significant shift of commercial capital into manufacturing began in 1804. This preceded the Jeffersonian Embargo and the War of 1812 by four and eight years respectively, and occurred before maritime operations reached their peak and when customs receipts were still growing rapidly. Though three spinning mills had gone into operation by 1795 and a fourth by 1801, nine factories opened between 1805 and 1807 and, to prevent the limited consumption of local handweavers from impeding this expansion, manufacturers extended yarn markets into the south as well as westward through up-state New York and Pennsylvania into Ohio, Kentucky, and Tennessee. Entrepreneurs planned their expansion long before the depression engulfed maritime endeavor. Thus when the embargo and the war halted British imports the Rhode Islanders had the manufacturing facilities, technical experience,

---

[14] Arnold, "Further Reminiscences," 248; Rhode Island Conference of Business Associations, comp., *Book of Rhode Island* (n.p., 1930), 201; Carroll, *Rhode Island*, 1:520–521; Bliss, *History of Rehoboth*, 236–237; Steere, *History of Smithfield*, 88–93; *Providence Gazette*, December 13, 1817. To a certain extent, Rhode Islanders were innovators by the force of circumstances rather than out of choice. The extraordinarily high incidence of fires in textile mills gave them many opportunities to replace obsolete equipment with the most up-to-date machinery available.

financial resources, and market connections to capitalize on the sudden shortage of foreign goods. They had 14,000 spindles in operation by 1809 and 31,000 by 1810, and their mills increased from 25 in 1810 to 38 in 1812.[15]

Rising domestic consumption, together with the suspension of British competition from 1808 to 1815, produced high earnings and capital appreciation. By encouraging competitors to resist cutting yarn prices when the export embargo lowered the cost of raw cotton, Almy, Brown, and Slater raised profit margins, and firms with large inventories of either raw materials or finished goods enjoyed windfall profits. One, the Coventry Company, distributed its first dividend in 1813, paying $1,000 per share, equal to twenty-six per cent over a seven year period. Although this was not a high return, most profits had been accumulated after 1811, when annual earnings ranging from twenty to thirty per cent were not uncommon. Property and share values also rose. During the five

---

[15] For customs receipts, see Perry, *Rhode Island State Census, 1885*, p. 76; for the extension of markets, see Ware, *Early New England Cotton Manufacture*, 28–29, 32–36, 42–43, 48–49, 55; and for industrial expansion, see *American State Papers, Finance*, 2:433, and White, *Slater*, 188. There has been considerable disagreement about the precise amount of growth in the early nineteenth century. Victor S. Clarke, *History of Manufactures in the United States* (3 vols., New York, 1929) 1:536, stated that more than fifty mills were under construction in New England in 1809, the majority of them in the Blackstone and Pawtucket [Pawtuxet?] valleys; Batchelder, *Cotton Manufacture*, 51, reported that ten mills were completed or under construction in Rhode Island between 1805 and 1807; J. Leander Bishop, *A History of American Manufactures from 1608 to 1860* (3 vols., Philadelphia, 1861–1868), 2:123, 132, 143, stated that three mills commenced operations in Rhode Island in 1808, that a total of seventeen were in business a year later, and that seven more were under construction; and John K. Pitman in a letter to Thomas Coles, November 8, 1809 [Zachariah Allen Papers, Rhode Island Historical Society, quoted in Joseph Brennan, *Social Conditions in Industrial Rhode Island: 1820–1860* (Washington, 1940), 4], reported sixteen cotton mills in operation in 1808 and seven more about to go into operation. At least sixteen had been constructed since 1804. However, *Manufactures, 1810*, pp. 23–24, said that there were fourteen mills in Kent County, thirteen in Providence County, and one in Washington County, a total of twenty-eight factories and 20,668 spindles. For data on hand spinning and weaving enterprises located in the cellar of the State House in Newport in the early 1790's, see Granted Petitions, 27:43 (June, 1792), and 29:57 (June, 1795), and Bagnall, *Textile Industries*, 169.

years after 1808 the Union Mill in Warwick increased in value
from $40,000 to $70,000, and between 1810 and 1812 the price
of shares in the Lippitt Mill in Warwick soared by over thirty-
three per cent.[16]

TABLE 5

THE RHODE ISLAND COTTON INDUSTRY, 1809–1812[17]

| Towns | MILLS | | SPINDLES | | | |
	1809	1812	1809	Actual 1810	1812	Potential 1812
Cranston	2	4		1,400	1,100	2,988
Johnston	2	2	896	2,400	1,382	2,700
Providence		1			540	1,250
North Providence	3	5	1,646	2,200	3,592	6,700
Cumberland	2	2	488	800	412	412
Smithfield	3	3	1,700	5,000	4,188	5,800
Warwick	6	9	5,894	10,400	10,757	17,856
Expanding Towns	18	26	10,624	22,200	21,971	37,706
Glocester		2			72	432
Scituate	2	3	1,584	5,000	2,688	4,000
East Greenwich	1		500	1,000		
Coventry	3	5	1,788	2,800	5,124	12,800
South Kingstown	1	1	200	500	408	408
Static Towns	7	11	4,072	9,300	8,292	17,640
Exeter, Declining Town		1			400	800
Rhode Island	25	38	14,696	31,500	30,663	56,146

Stimulated by high profits as well as by the transfer of capital
from the depressed maritime industry, cotton manufacturing expanded rapidly during the war. The number of mills almost
trebled and spinning capacity more than doubled. By 1815 nearly

[16] Ware, *Early New England Cotton Manufacture*, 44–45, 123–126, 315;
McLane's Report, 1:934–969 *passim*, but especially pp. 941–942, 944–946,
949–950, 953; Brennan, *Social Conditions*, 9.

[17] Albert Gallatin, "Manufactures," in *American State Papers, Finance*, 2:432–
433. Clive Day, "The Early Development of the American Cotton Manufacture,"
in *Quarterly Journal of Economics*, 39:464 (May, 1925), repeats the erroneous
total of thirty-three mills in operation in 1812 given by White, in *Slater*, 188.
Moses King, comp., in *King's Pocket-Book of Providence, R.I.* (Providence,
1882), 32, reported that there were seventeen mills in and around Providence in
1811 and five more under construction. Beyond Providence, but still within Rhode

three-fifths of southern New England's cotton factories were in Rhode Island. Many mills expanded their capacity. In 1810, only seven factories operated 1,000 or more spindles, but by 1815 this number had trebled and those utilizing 2,000 or more spindles had increased ninefold. The largest single mill—5,170 spindles—

TABLE 6

THE RHODE ISLAND COTTON INDUSTRY, NOVEMBER, 1815[18]

Towns	Mills	Spindles	Towns	Mills	Spindles
Cranston	8	6,322	Glocester	4	1,826
Johnston	4	3,034	Scituate	4	4,620
Providence	5	3,032	East Greenwich	2	1,428
North Providence	10	7,818	Coventry	10	10,358
Cumberland	10	4,884	North Kingstown	2	1,210
Smithfield	9	10,012	South Kingstown	1	420
Burrillville	4	1,056	Richmond	3	1,508
Warwick	11	15,610	Westerly	2	348
	—	—	Portsmouth	1	150
Expanding Towns	61	51,768	Tiverton	2	764
				—	—
Foster	2	700	Static Towns	31	22,632
West Greenwich	4	1,308			
Exeter	2	384			
	—	—		—	—
Declining Towns	8	2,392	Rhode Island	100	76,792

was that of Almy, Brown, and Slater located on the Branch River in Smithfield. The center of production, however, was on the Pawtuxet River, where a third of the state's mills, almost half the spindles, and over three-fifths of the largest mills were located.

Island, there were eight mills in operation and five others being built, a total of thirty-five. Bishop, in *American Manufactures*, 2:174, however, reported thirty-seven mills in 1811 and a spindle capacity of 56,257, of which only 32,786 were in operation. According to Zachariah Allen, there were thirty-six mills in Rhode Island on October 31, 1811. See Brennan, *Social Conditions*, 8. Many enterprises expanded rapidly in the years immediately preceding the outbreak of hostilities with Great Britain: one mill established with a capital of $20,000 in 1806, for example, utilized $56,000 in 1809. Perhaps six times as much cloth was woven by cottage weavers as by operatives in the mills. Compare *American State Papers, Finance*, 2:434, and *Manufactures, 1810*, pp. 23–24, for indications of the relative importance of the putting out system.

[18] *Transactions of the Rhode Island Society for the Encouragement of Domestic Industry*, 1863, pp. 73–75. Hereafter cited as *Transactions*. Both Field, *Rhode Island*, 3:351, and Batchelder, *Cotton Manufacture*, 58–59, gave 99 mills but reported 75,678 and 68,142 spindles respectively.

New construction also contributed to growth. In 1810, cotton manufacturing was carried on in only nine towns. By 1815, there were mills in twenty-one of Rhode Island's thirty-one towns, though many were small ventures, being operated by partnerships of farmers and mechanics. Over half the factories had less than 500 spindles and a tenth fewer than 200. Modest ventures were especially characteristic of Newport and Washington counties, where all except two of the thirteen mills were below average in size.

When peace returned in 1815, British cotton goods flooded the American market. This inundation rigorously tested the soundness of wartime growth and forced important changes in manufacturing methods. The protective tariff of 1816 eased the pressure on sheeting producers, but manufacturers of ginghams, the local specialty, could not compete with cheap British calicoes. Some mills failed outright; others had to change products.

Foreign competition also accelerated the introduction of power weaving, an innovation that lowered production costs, increased output, and extended the factory system to the only major segment of the industry still at the cottage stage of development. Since Gilmore did not patent his power loom and the consumption of hand weavers no longer restricted yarn production, spinning capacity increased substantially. Between 1809 and 1820, this and other improvements, especially the development of machine pickers, reduced hand labor by a quarter and halved weaving costs. Nevertheless, some manufacturers, including Samuel Slater, preferred the putting out system. His son, John, denied Gilmore permission to set up a loom in 1816, and though the Slaters began power weaving in 1823, they continued hand weaving for another four years. The Slaters reduced costs by distributing their yarn through contractors rather than directly to weavers, but their initial reaction to the power loom was symptomatic of a growing conservatism.[19]

Neither the tariff nor these technological improvements prevented a sharp postwar decline in earnings and property values. In the five years after 1813, the Union Mill's assets fell in value

[19] Massena Goodrich, *Historical Sketch of . . . Pawtucket* (Pawtucket, 1876), 66–67; Ware, *Early New England Cotton Manufacture*, 72, 74–75.

by almost a third, and a $7,000 share in another factory was auctioned for $750.[20] Such conditions forced consolidation and retrenchment throughout the industry. Successful manufacturers kept labor costs to a minimum. More than half the workers were children, and of the adults, nearly three-fifths were women. Although most firms gradually adjusted, some collapsed as soon as they felt the pressure of British competition. Others lingered until the general economic upheaval of 1819, which closed two-fifths of the mills. Yet, either because industrialists grumbled more from habit than from cause,[21] or because they misjudged conditions, or, more probably, because they sought to increase efficiency, they continued building mills. However, the closing of many old factories offset this new construction, and, though spindle capacity remained almost constant, the number of mills declined slightly.[22]

[20] *Semi-Centennial of the Providence Journal* (Providence, 1870), 15; *Mc-Lane's Report*, 1:929; *American State Papers, Finance*, 4:44–49; White, *Slater*, 215–216; Ware, *Early New England Cotton Manufacture*, 66–67, 127; Bishop, *American Manufactures*, 1:249–251; Fuller, *History of Warwick*, 171–173, 192, 228–229. Slater, a protectionist, argued that Rhode Island would suffer heavily if Congress allowed the cotton industry to languish. "Deprived of her manufactures, the State will have nothing left with which to maintain her usual exchanges with other States. The comparative sterility of her soil will not permit her to compete with them in agricultural products for exportation. There is now no *foreign carrying trade* to employ her shipping; her coasting trade will have been annihilated with her manufactures; and the poverty of the rural population of this and the contiguous States, now supplied with imported goods from her markets, would, in such a state of things, reduce her direct foreign trade for consumption to what it was before the adoption of the federal constitution." *McLane's Report*, 1:930.

[21] The State Archives contain numerous eighteenth and nineteenth century documents, especially petitions to the General Assembly, lamenting economic conditions. To read them, one would never suppose that some Rhode Island merchants were accumulating great wealth. Whether they reveal an ingrained business pessimism or merely a stratagem to discourage potential competitors is uncertain, but the latter explanation is the more likely one. See also, Ware, *Early New England Cotton Manufacture*, 126–127; Day, "American Cotton Manufacture," 466–468.

[22] Pease and Niles, *Gazetteer, passim* pp. 305–387. Compare a garbled table in the *Providence Journal*, June 19, 1876, purporting to show the situation in 1820. Henry Bradshaw Fearon, quoted in Kimball, *Pictures of Rhode Island in the Past*, 165, reported that there were thirteen cotton factories, six of them very large undertakings, in Pawtucket in 1817.

Once the depression had weeded out some of the inefficient producers and had forced others to reorganize, manufacturers resumed expansion. Recovery began in 1820 and the business revival quickly gathered momentum. In many respects, conditions favored industrial growth. Throughout the decade, both the rising level of prosperity and the rapid increase in population expanded the consumption of cotton goods, and consumers were forgetting their earlier distrust of American manufacturers. Moreover, British mill owners preferred Latin American markets. Working in conjunction with the protective tariff this change in the pattern of British trade gave United States producers a larger share of the growing domestic market.

Some Rhode Island manufacturers took full advantage of these opportunities. One group organized a reservoir company to manage the water resources of the Woonasquatucket River. The corporation derived its capital and operating funds by assessing participating factories, and it could enforce its demands by attaching the property of delinquent shareholders. Member mill owners were liable for the company's debts and, in recognition of the public character of the enterprise, the General Assembly extended the state's protection to the company's property. The reservoir, like the individually owned Greenville, Waterman, Sprague, Hawkins, and Bernon ponds in Smithfield, enabled mills to withstand long periods of drought and protected them against damaging floods. Between 1824 and 1860, seven more corporations were chartered to develop and conserve water resources in the Woonasquatucket, Moshassuck, Pawtuxet, Wenscott, and Blackstone valleys.[23]

Cotton manufacturers also turned increasingly to the services of the full-time professional manager. He helped revitalize the industry by introducing more efficient production methods and by diverting effort into specialty lines. The outstanding managers had organizing capacities of a high order, were receptive to new techniques of operation and distribution, and, when they enjoyed adequate financial backing, pushed forward with programs of modern-

[23] *Acts and Resolves*, January, 1824, pp. 30–34; Steere, *Smithfield*, 133–135; Peck and Earl, *Fall River and its Industries*, 26.

ization and integration. Some mechanized all processes from pick-
ing and carding to spinning, weaving, and fulling in a single mill;
others went still further by establishing bleaching, dyeing, and
printing departments; and the best mills had large machine shops
to repair damaged equipment, construct new machinery, and test
ideas. If his employers also created a mill village, a common practice during the decade, the manager became responsible for an
almost completely self-contained industrial community.

These developments raised the efficiency and increased the earnings of many mills, but because manufacturers had not participated
in the fundamental reorganization of the American cotton industry
that had been under way since the War of 1812, Rhode Island
derived less benefit from the favorable economic conditions of the
1820's than did northern New England. Beginning in 1813 with
the organization of the Boston Manufacturing Company of Waltham, Massachusetts, leadership in the cotton industry had passed
to a new breed of entrepreneur.[24] These Boston merchants, headed
by Francis C. Lowell, believed that cotton manufacturing could
be made immensely profitable by large scale operation, complete
mechanization, and integrated production. Using vast amounts of
capital, they exploited the costlier, more difficult New England
mill sites, particularly those on the Merrimack River in Massachusetts and New Hampshire and the Saco River in Maine. They
accompanied these engineering feats by constructing huge integrated mills in which all manufacturing processes, from cleaning
the raw cotton to finishing the cloth, were fully mechanized and
were carried on within a single complex of mills.

With few exceptions, Rhode Island manufacturers operated on
a much smaller scale. They mechanized and integrated more slowly
and less completely, and they failed to achieve the economies of
production, marketing, and financing obtained by their northern
competitors. Even as late as 1826, a decade after Gilmore had
introduced the Scotch power loom, only a third of the mills had
mechanized their weaving departments, and in 1832, at least a
tenth of the mills did no weaving at all. Throughout the 1820's,

[24] Ware, *Early New England Cotton Manufacture*, 60–64, 80–86.

therefore, sheeting mills lost business to the Lowell type of company. These mammoth competitors kept huge supplies of finished
goods on hand and could fill orders immediately. Most Rhode
Island firms could not adopt this practice because they lacked the
necessary capital. Instead, they converted to the production of high
quality specialty goods, lines that could be manufactured profitably
on a relatively small scale. This reorganization strengthened Rhode
Island's position in some markets, but inefficient management and
the slow adoption of power weaving left many manufacturers
vulnerable to fluctuations in consumer demand. The crisis of 1825
exposed some of these weaknesses, and the depression of 1829,
felt with unusual severity in Rhode Island, snuffed out perhaps
as many as a seventh of the firms and forced the remainder to
suspend or reduce production.

The inability or unwillingness to adopt the Lowell style of operation as well as the continued use of outmoded forms of production brought about a gradual decline in Rhode Island's status
within the American cotton industry. Though it remained a leading
producer—its spun almost a fifth of the nation's yarn and wove a
sixth of the cloth—Massachusetts, not Rhode Island, came to dominate the industry. According to an 1831 survey, the Bay State operated more than twice as many mills as did Rhode Island, spun
nearly half as much yarn, and manufactured more than twice as
much cloth. Nevertheless, Rhode Island ranked after Massachusetts
and before New Hampshire, Connecticut, New York, New Jersey,
and Pennsylvania in the number of mills, capital, and spindles employed, and after Massachusetts and Pennsylvania in the number
of looms and workers employed.[25] Moreover, by their own if not
by Lowell standards, Rhode Island manufacturers did operate
some very large factories. In 1832, five Warwick mills were each
capitalized at $100,000 or more, and four Smithfield factories had

[25] For statistical data, compare *Address of the Friends of Domestic Industry*
(Baltimore, 1831), 112; Timothy Pitkin, *A Statistical View of the Commerce
of the United States of America* (New Haven, 1835), 526; Field, *Rhode Island*,
3:353; Bishop, *American Manufactures*, 2:336. For the depression of 1829, see
Fuller, *History of Warwick*, 265; Goodrich, *Pawtucket*, 69–70; Ware, *Early
New England Cotton Manufacture*, 91; White, *Slater*, 244–248.

over $600,000 in capital between them. Too, thirty mills reported three thousand or more spindles as compared to only three such enterprises in 1820. But the typical unit, while larger than a decade earlier, remained a relatively small undertaking. Capital-

TABLE 7

THE RHODE ISLAND COTTON INDUSTRY, 1832[26]

Towns	Mills	Capital	Spindles	Looms	Employees
Cranston	7	$ 68,000	3,568	68	134
Johnston	4	177,000	7,550	206	297
Providence	4	284,000	10,197	244	360
North Providence	9	187,00	11,420	250	422
Cumberland	11	740,000	35,400	864	1,163
Smithfield	19	1,178,340	54,786	1,306	1,842
Burrillville	1	8,000	408		16
Warwick	13	1,136,300	50,086	1,301	1,813
Expanding Towns	68	3,778,640	173,415	4,239	6,047
Glocester	2	30,500	2,474	65	102
Scituate	8	455,500	18,884	487	690
East Greenwich	2	75,000	4,262	100	149
Coventry	13	483,000	23,551	638	1,035
North Kingstown	3	62,500	3,216	62	133
South Kingstown	1	Included in the Hopkinton summary, below			
Richmond	4	58,000	2,900	76	96
Hopkinton	4	60,000	3,000	80	100
Westerly	1	40,000	2,000	46	100
Newport	1	48,000			
Portsmouth	1	14,550	240		12
Static Towns	40	1,327,050	60,527	1,554	2,417
Foster	1	9,000	500	13	28
West Greenwich	5	8,500	720	16	28
Exeter	5	27,000	2,816	34	65
Declining Towns	11	44,500	4,036	63	121
Bleacheries	5	228,000			300
Print Works	2	212,000			186
Rhode Island	126	5,590,190	237,978	5,856	9,071

ized at less than $40,000, it operated only 1,000 spindles and 30 looms, and employed a mere 35 workers.

By the opening of the second quarter of the nineteenth century, then, cotton manufacturing had come to dominate the Rhode Is-

[26] *McLane's Report,* 1:970–976. Data on four of the five West Greenwich mills are included in the Coventry summary.

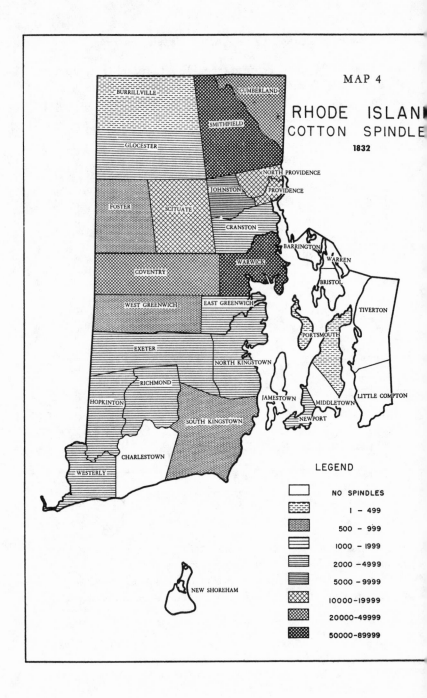

MAP 4

RHODE ISLAN
COTTON SPINDLE
1832

LEGEND

	NO SPINDLES
	1 – 499
	500 – 999
	1000 – 1999
	2000 –4999
	5000 – 9999
	10000–19999
	20000–49999
	50000–89999

land economy almost as completely as maritime activity had done during the preceding period. But, in keeping with their traditional practice, entrepreneurs had scrupulously avoided investing too heavily in any one branch of business. Instead, they continued spreading their risks over many types of venture in the conviction that losses suffered in one area could be counterbalanced by profits earned in another: to be sure, they put many thousands of dollars into the cotton industry, but they retained extensive interests in foreign and domestic trade, and they shifted additional resources into a variety of other types of manufacturing.

The woolen industry, which was eventually to become second in importance only to cotton manufacturing, was an early example of this pattern of diversification. But technical difficulties retarded development, and manufacturers made the mistake of trying to compete with English mills in the production of fine broadcloth.

Rowland Hazard, a well-to-do merchant, pioneered woolen manufacturing in Rhode Island. In 1804, he acquired full ownership of a water-powered carding mill established earlier that year by his partners, Joseph Congdon and John W. Knowles, at the South Kingstown village of Peace Dale on the Saugatucket River. Initially manufacturing was a subordinate Hazard interest and he expanded operations cautiously. Between 1804 and 1808 he was content to gain experience by distributing rolls of carded wool to cottage spinners in the district surrounding his mill and by developing yarn markets. But when international conditions began hampering his maritime ventures, especially his West Indian trading interests, Hazard shifted his main effort to manufacturing. First, he brought hand weavers into the mill, where they produced a kind of linsey consisting of a woolen weft woven on to a cotton warp. Next, he mechanized spinning. Then, in 1813 or 1814, he installed a power loom, invented by Thomas R. Williams of Newport, to weave saddle girths and other webbing. Though the scale of operations was unpretentious, the utilization of water power, the consolidation of all manufacturing processes from carding to finishing within a single mill, and the adoption of the principle of division of labor meant that the woolen industry achieved a fully developed factory system a year or two ahead of the cotton industry.[27]

The Providence Woolen Manufacturing Company—organized in 1812 by a group of cotton manufacturers that included Sullivan Dorr, Samuel G. Arnold, Joseph S. Martin, Daniel Lyman, and E. K. Randolph—attempted to integrate production on a much larger scale. Encouraged by rising prices produced by the wartime shortage of British cloth and by the availability of experienced workers from the west of England, the promoters hoped to capitalize upon an unusual business opportunity. They used the central portion of their stone mill for carding, the upper floors for spinning, and two wings for weaving. A steam engine built by Oliver Evans of Philadelphia operated shears which trimmed the nap raised by revolving brass wires. This was probably the first manufacturing application of steam power in America. The hand-woven broadcloths were then finished in a separate dyehouse. Despite the attractive, durable fabric produced, the postwar flood of British woolens drove the company from business. Shareholders lost $150,000.[28]

Technically, these efforts succeeded, but as business ventures they proved so disappointing that manufacturers proceeded cautiously. Though the number of mills increased from three in 1810[29] to twenty-four in 1819, most firms operated on a small scale, either

[27] Bagnall, *Textile Industries*, 280–305; Arthur Harrison Cole, *The American Wool Manufacture* (2 vols., Cambridge, 1926), 1:61–244 *passim*, but especially pp. 95, 117, 221; Cole, *History of Washington and Kent Counties*, 494–497; William Gammell, *Life and Services of Rowland Gibson Hazard* (Providence, 1888), 4–7; Royal C. Taft, *Some Notes upon the Introduction of Woolen Manufacture into the United States* (Providence, 1882), 39. For general developments, see *History of Rhode Island*, 295, 328, 342.

[28] Taft, *Woolen Manufacture*, 40–42. In the fall of 1810, the Providence Association of Mechanics and Manufacturers voted to invest in a woolen factory. See the journal of the Association, vol. 3 (October 8, 1810), in the Rhode Island Historical Society.

[29] Compare *Manufactures, 1810*, pp. 23–24; Albert Gallatin's report on manufacturing in *American State Papers, Finance*, 2:434, which listed two mills, one in Warwick employing 28 workers and capitalized at $9,000, the other in Portsmouth, a $3,000 undertaking; and Field, *Rhode Island*, 3:362, who reported

as carding, spinning, or fulling enterprises and only rarely as fully integrated undertakings. One of the largest mills, the Merino Factory in Johnston, made both cotton and woolen goods, but it employed a mere 280 spindles in its woolen business. Another, at Pawcatuck in Westerly, was described as an "extensive" four-story factory, though it measured only 64 by 36 feet in length and breadth. The industry located chiefly in the Blackstone-Pawtuxet towns of Cranston (three mills), Providence (two mills), and Warwick (two mills), and in the static southern towns of North Kingstown (two mills), South Kingstown (two mills), Hopkinton (three mills), and Portsmouth (two mills).[30]

In some respects, smallness was an asset. Throughout the post-war difficulties, and especially during the crisis of 1819, many ventures remained in business by relying on family members for most of their labor needs, and by not having to pay dividends. Some firms did fail, but losses were modest and other families took over, purchasing in confidence that they could operate more successfully.

In the 1820's, the Rhode Island woolen industry achieved a secure basis.[31] First, the crises of 1825 and 1829 eliminated more marginal producers; by 1832, fourteen of the twenty-four factories reported in 1819 were no longer operating. Of the eight towns affected, Hopkinton, Warwick, Cranston, and Providence bore the brunt of the consolidation movement. Second, the industry benefited from the general business expansion of the decade as well as from tariff protection and the diversion of British trade to Latin

---

twelve factories including, in all probability, carding and fulling mills. At most, factory production totaled about 15,000 yards of cloth annually, or only a tenth of cottage handicraft production.

[30] Pease and Niles, *Gazetteer*, 305–387 *passim*. Both South Kingstown mills were described as clothier's works. Johnston, Cumberland, and Burrillville among the expanding towns, Scituate, Richmond, and Westerly among the static towns, and Foster and Exeter among the declining towns each had one mill. Compare the imperfect census for 1820 in *American State Papers, Finance*, 4:44–49, which reported only two mills, both in Providence County. See also, *History of Rhode Island*, 143, 179–180, 288–289.

[31] Taft, *Woolen Manufacture*, 43; Amos Perry, *Memorial of Zachariah Allen, 1795–1882* (Cambridge, 1883), 47–48; Cole, *Wool Manufacture*, 1:148–153, 322.

American markets. These factors encouraged an inflow of capital for larger mills and improved equipment. Twelve new factories, most of them in North and South Kingstown, were in operation by 1832. Manufacturers improved carding machinery, experimented with the production of fine worsteds, and installed power

TABLE 8

THE RHODE ISLAND WOOLEN INDUSTRY, 1832[32]

Towns	Mills	Capital	Spindles	Looms	Cards	Workers
Johnston	1	$ 27,000			3	26
North Providence	1	94,000	600	21		67
Cumberland	1	6,500	240	12		15
Burrillville	1	15,000			2	12
Expanding Towns	4	142,500	840	33	5	120
Glocester	1	10,000			1	10
North Kingstown	6	47,000			14	80
South Kingstown	7	97,500	1,080	44	7	120
Westerly	1	18,000			2	26
Portsmouth	3	20,000				24
Static Towns	18	192,500	1,080	44	24	260
Rhode Island	22	335,000	1,920	77	29	380

looms to weave Negro kerseys for southern markets and broadcloth for other consumers.

The typical integrated mill was still a small venture. Capitalized at only about $9,000, it employed 17 workers, a third of whom were children, and operated two hundred spindles, a dozen looms, and two sets of carding machinery. The scale of operation was smallest in Washington County, where half the factories were capitalized at $5,000 or less, and largest in Providence County, where Zachariah Allen's North Providence broadcloth factory was capitalized at $94,000. But the woolen industry absorbed only a sixth of all the capital invested in textile manufacturing in Rhode Island and at least half the mills were engaged only in carding.

Rhode Island's pioneering rôle in the cotton and woolen industries gave it an initial advantage in the rapidly expanding field

[32] *McLane's Report*, 1:970–976. See also, White, *Slater*, 261.

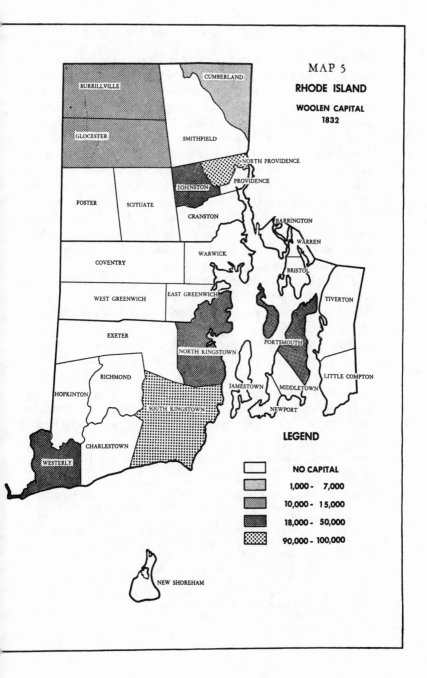

MAP 5

RHODE ISLAND

WOOLEN CAPITAL
1832

LEGEND

	NO CAPITAL
	1,000 - 7,000
	10,000 - 15,000
	18,000 - 50,000
	90,000 - 100,000

of manufacturing textile machinery and equipment.[33] Drawing on the artisan tradition, the early cotton manufacturers employed mechanics and blacksmiths to design and build machinery from imperfect descriptions of English inventions. By trial and error, craftsmen gradually became skilled in making and improving equipment. The Wilkinsons of Pawtucket secured much of the early business. They forged iron work, turned spindles and rollers on their lathes, and gradually expanded their markets from New England into the middle and southern states.[34] Before long, other Rhode Islanders entered the field and by 1810 there were at least twelve firms manufacturing machinery for sale. In addition, some mills produced equipment for their own use, and there were many self-employed metal and wood workers making simple items to the customer's order.

The expansion of American cotton and woolen production after 1810 created a burgeoning market for textile machinery. Rhode Island firms secured an important share of the business by improving spinning and weaving technology. John Thorpe, a Providence mechanic, patented a power loom in 1814, and he was later to secure eight other patents, including ones for separating ring and cap spinning frames, for netting and braiding machines, and, in 1828, for a spinning ring. Unlike the mule, the ring allowed spinning and twisting to be performed continuously and simultaneously. Formerly yarn was spun on the outward run and was twisted

---

[33] Rhode Island contributions to textile technology can be followed in *Commerce, Manufactures and Resources of . . . Providence* (n.p., 1882), 33; Batchelder, *Cotton Manufacture*, 81–82; Bicknell, *Rhode Island*, 4:141; *Book of Rhode Island*, 38, 165, 181; George Sweet Gibb, *The Saco-Lowell Shops: Textile Machinery Building in New England, 1813–1949* (Cambridge, 1950), 3–156 *passim*, but especially pp. 27–33; Goodrich, *Pawtucket*, 71–76; D. H. Greene, *History of . . . East Greenwich . . . 1677–1877* (Providence, 1877), 65; Robert Grieve, *Picturesque Narragansett* ([3d ed.], Providence, n.d.), 62; John L. Hays, *American Textile Machinery* (Cambridge, 1879), *passim; History of Rhode Island*, 143–144, 225, 304–305, 338; McPartland, *East Greenwich*, 216–217; *North Providence Centennial*, 33–34, 75–85 *passim;* John W. Oliver, *History of American Technology* (New York, 1956), 160; Steere, *History of Smithfield*, 120; Thompson, *Moses Brown*, 256–257; White, *Slater*, 243; *Manufactures, 1810*, p. 24; Pease and Niles, *Gazetteer*, 344.

[34] *North Providence Centennial*, 28–30.

on to the spindle on the inward run. William Gilmore succeeded in building a Scotch-style crank loom which many Rhode Island mills adopted, and he also introduced the Scotch dresser into the United States. It quickly came to be preferred to the one developed at Waltham. Thomas R. Williams of Newport invented the web loom adopted by the Hazards; in 1826 a Hopkinton firm began making kersey looms for the Peace Dale mill; and Job Manchester and Perez Peck of Coventry invented a bedticking loom. A Providence mechanic, John Brown,[35] invented a speeder in 1821. Though one of several different types of roving frames on the market, the Brown speeder gained widespread acceptance. A year later Asa Arnold of East Greenwich designed a differential speeder which was not to be superseded for half a century. A Pawtucket firm started by Larned Pitcher in 1813 introduced a geared cone speeder in 1823, and five years later the successor partnership of Larned Pitcher and James S. Brown[36] began the manufacture of self-acting spinning mules.

This ability to design and build improved equipment, the high quality of workmanship, and the central New England location gave Rhode Island textile machinery firms the capacity to capitalize on the opportunities created by the rapid expansion of cotton and woolen manufacturing. From their simple workshop origins these undertakings gradually lost their service characteristics. By the 1820's they operated as small but full-fledged industrial enterprises and formed a major though highly specialized segment of the base metal industry.

Other branches of the industry, as well as other craft or artisan oriented activities, were also profoundly affected, sometimes adversely, both by the rise of manufacturing and by the growth of the internal and external market. In scale and style of operation if not in total volume of business, the petty workshop ventures organized by blacksmiths and tinsmiths, copper and brass workers,

[35] No relation to the famous Providence family of the same name.
[36] James S. Brown was related neither to John Brown above nor to the Providence mercantile and industrial family. He replaced Gale in the Pitcher and Gale partnership.

generally changed very little. In 1785, these producers had de-scribed themselves as "artificers."[37] An apt title, it remained ap-propriate throughout the experimental phase of industrialization. Though they made a variety of articles ranging from wrought pewter and plows to door hinges and horseshoes, they directed their effort almost exclusively toward the satisfaction of local wants; they made most articles to order rather than in advance of demand; and they secured much of their business from repair work. In short, they operated service workshops rather than strictly manufacturing undertakings.

Some of the more skilful or ambitious of these base metal craftsmen did organize true industrial ventures. Though the arti-ficer aspect remained fundamental, these enterprises called for larger amounts of capital, greater managerial talents, and more complex marketing arrangements. Some or all of their business may still have been to the customer's order, but the types of arti-cles produced and the scale of production usually involved some division of labor and some degree of specialization. Moreover, their industrial enterprises sustained many workers and their fam-ilies. If operations were halted by panic or depression or if for other reasons the business failed, widespread distress could result.

Such undertakings were principally located in the Blackstone and Pawtuxet valleys and in Providence. There they had access to local iron and steel furnaces, to slitting and plating mills, and to im-ported supplies. The region also had numerous mill sites for op-erating triphammers and other machinery. This was also the area with the longest tradition in the iron business as well as the one with a New England reputation for the skill and ingenuity of its workers. The Wilkinson family of blacksmiths became especially well-known. At the end of the Revolution, Oziel Wilkinson and his sons had established themselves at Pawtucket, where they forged anchors, household articles, and farming tools. Before long, they attracted orders from distant customers. In 1794 they con-structed machinery for a canal near Boston and the iron work for

[37] Granted Petitions, 21:120 (1784–1785).

the draw in a bridge over the Charles River between Boston and Cambridge, and in 1804 they made the picks, shovels, and spades used in the construction of the Norfolk and Bristol Turnpike from Boston to Pawtucket. One of the five sons, Isaac, supervised the casting of cannon at the Providence "Cupola" during the War of 1812, and another, David, who was to succeed his father in 1815 and to extend the firm's operations into nail manufacturing, had earlier experimented with a steamboat and had invented a gauge and sliding lathe. Although few other Blackstone Valley iron undertakings diversified to this extent, enterprises in North Providence, Cumberland, and Smithfield became noted for the production of screws, nuts, bolts, muskets, edge tools, and, above all, textile machinery.[38]

But many craftsmen-proprietors of metal working ventures lacked the capital, the managerial skill, and, above all, the marketing experience that was the great strength of the Rhode Island merchant-industrialists. If they made the mistake of trying to expand too rapidly, and especially if they did so by selling on credit rather than for cash, they exposed themselves to considerable damage when the economy turned downward. Such was the case in 1829, when depression disrupted the industry, particularly in Pawtucket. Many firms failed, including the Wilkinsons and the large hardware house of Stephen Jenks and Sons, and some factories remained idle for several years. Nevertheless, Rhode Island had ten foundries and thirty machine shops in 1832. Together, they employed almost 1,250 men and represented an investment of over $800,000. In addition, there were several hundred petty ventures making simple articles ranging from reeds, bobbins, spools, pickers, shuttles, brushes, and temples for the textile industry to tacks, nails, utensils, firearms, shovels, plows, and tools for various other markets, local as well as external.[39]

[38] Field *Rhode Island*, 3:332, 371–375; White, *Slater*, 89, 258; *North Providence Centennial*, 75–85 *passim*.

[39] *McLane's Report*, 1:376; Field, *Rhode Island*, 3:373; Goodrich, *Pawtucket*, 70; Ware, *Early New England Cotton Manufacture*, 91; White, *Slater*, 244–248; *History of Rhode Island*, 228–229.

By all odds, the craft other than iron working to develop most significantly was the making of precious metal articles.[40] Jewelry making retained the artificer-workshop tradition long after manufacturers in other fields had introduced mechanization, the division of labor, and large scale production. The industry developed along two divergent paths. A minority of firms carried on in the tradition of Seril Dodge, a craftsman who had made fine quality silver buckles in a little Providence workshop at the time of the Revolution. Jabez Gorham, the most famous producer of this type, made gold and silver jewelry of superior quality. After serving the customary seven-year apprenticeship, Gorham in 1813 formed a partnership with four other journeymen. Dissatisfied with the prevailing system of disposing of finished articles to peddlers, Gorham began selling directly to Boston retailers. Most firms made less expensive jewelry, a craft Nehemiah Dodge had pioneered in Providence in 1794. These producers also sold in the external market—one firm, G. and A. Richmond, distributed its products as far south as New Orleans. By 1805, the industry employed some thirty artisans to make either fine jewelry or cheaper quality gold necklaces, rings, cases, knobs, chains, twists, keys, and seals. Since these craftsmen also trained apprentices, this concentrated production almost exclusively in Providence. The labor force rose to about 100 in 1810 and to 175 in 1815, but production almost ceased after the war, revived temporarily, then collapsed again during the depression of 1819. When manufacturing resumed in 1820, firms concentrated on the less expensive lines rather than on solid gold articles. By 1832 twenty-seven firms were in business, employing over 280 workers, almost half of them women. Aside from the use of foot-treadle lathes and drills, everything was made by hand.

[40] The discussion of the precious metal industry is based on Bicknell, *Rhode Island*, 3:841–842; *Book of Rhode Island*, 208; *Commerce, Manufactures and Resources of Providence*, 31, 78–81; William T. Davis, ed., *The New England States* (4 vols., Boston, n.d.), 4:2500–2517 *passim*; Field, *Rhode Island*, 3:377–380; Edmund C. Mayo, "Three Men in an Industrial Century: Jabez Gorham—John Gorham—Edward Holbrook," in *Rhode Island History*, 11:1–4 (January, 1952); *History of Rhode Island*, 264.

In the long run, some other crafts, most notably spinning and weaving, were adversely affected by the rise of manufacturing. Initially, however, industrialization increased the demand for handicraft skills even in textiles. A conservative estimate in 1810 placed household textile production at 1,230,000 yards of cotton, woolen, linen, and blended cloth annually, as well as many thousands of yards of web, lace, and fringe, and many thousands of pairs of stockings.[41] Though some textile employers brought handicraft workers into the mill, the majority continued to farm out raw materials and semi-finished textiles to cottage craftsmen until the invention of power-driven equipment (cleaning machinery, spinning mules, and looms), brought an end to the putting out system and displaced handicraft workers.

Most other craft and processing undertakings benefited from the rising demand resulting from population growth and the nationalization of the economy. According to the 1810 census, admittedly defective because many "people refused to give an account of their manufactured articles," or understated output fearing "that the returns were demanded with a view to taxing their industry," the Rhode Islanders turned out a wide variety of simple goods. They manufactured 100,000 woolen and almost 5,000 fur hats, as well as 7,000 straw bonnets, many thousands of pairs of shoes and gloves, and thousands of saddles, bridles, and trunks. The marshal also reported fifty-two tanneries, one leather dressing mill, one snuff mill, two bark mills, three flax seed oil mills, three paper mills, twenty-two gristmills, twenty-four fulling mills, twenty-eight sawmills, two sugar refineries, fourteen lime kilns, and several gin distilleries.[42] He might also have included cider presses, brick works, slaughterhouses, carriage and wagon workshops, tallow candle manufactories, furniture workshops, and cigar factories; a Cumberland marble works supplying the Worcester, Providence, and Boston markets; freestone quarries in Scituate and Johnston; hearthstone and whetstone quarries in Smithfield; and saltmaking in Barrington. Coal mining was soon to get underway in Ports-

[41] *Manufactures, 1810*, p. 23.
[42] *Ibid.*, 24–27.

mouth and granite quarrying in Westerly; Newport would be reported in 1827 to have a lace factory employing about 500 females; and five years later two comb factories would be employing a total of more than 150 workers.[43]

By the end of the third decade of the nineteenth century, then, the Rhode Islanders had completed the first phase of industrialization. Taking their lead from a coterie of shrewdly imaginative entrepreneurs, the Narragansett Bay merchants had contracted their maritime investments in order to establish or to expand their manufacturing ones. The industrial sector secured ample supplies of risk capital from this mercantile source; in time it secured additional funds from the reinvestment of manufacturing profits. Especially in the textile industry but also in the base and precious metals, the technology of production had made a comparable advance and all basic problems had been solved. A few factories in the cotton industry had achieved a notable scale of production, and in most phases of manufacturing the trend was toward fully mechanized, integrated production based on division of labor and specialization of product. The joint-stock partnership form of organization had proved well-suited to the era of experimentation, but in the drive to increase efficiency and earnings some mills had taken the additional step of hiring professional managers. Except on the commercial side, where certain marketing weaknesses persisted, manufacturing could no longer be regarded as a doubtful experiment. In short, though the Rhode Islanders had turned their backs on their traditional source of profits—the sea—they had effected the transition to an industrial economy swiftly and smoothly.

There were exceptions. The population grew no more rapidly after 1790—barely one per cent annually—than it had during the preceding period. In effect, industrialization had merely saved the tiny state from total collapse following the contraction of maritime activity, and it had not prevented substantial numbers of people emigrating. These consequences were not felt uniformly. Some

[43] Pease and Niles, *Gazetteer*, 305–389 *passim; McLane's Report*, 1:976; *Manufactures, 1860*, p. cii.

areas, particularly the manufacturing towns in the Blackstone-Pawtuxet region, as well as the maritime centers of Bristol and Warren on the eastern shore, grew rapidly. The annual rate for these ten expanding towns exceeded three per cent, and reflected the fundamental change in the configuration of economic power. By contrast, most towns, especially those in the south and west, contributed little or nothing to industrialization, and they grew even more slowly than the state. Ten towns actually declined in population, five remained virtually stationary, and the other six expanded almost imperceptibly.

Ever since the beginning of settlement, Narragansett Bay had threatened to become an economic backwater. For two hundred years the Rhode Islanders had averted this fate by ingenuity and imagination. By 1830, they had identified the state's industrial potential, but it remained to be seen whether manufacturing, already the dynamic element in the economy, could not merely arrest the outflow of native-born citizens but, more important, sustain a growth rate that would provide for the swelling tide of immigrants.

CHAPTER FOUR

Industrialization:
The Era of Expansion

MANUFACTURING more than lived up to expectations in the decades after 1830. By every measure—capital invested, factories in operation, workers employed, scale and volume of production—the industrial economy expanded prodigiously. By the Civil War, Rhode Island had over 174,000 inhabitants, an increase of more than 77,000 in thirty years, and almost 32,500 factory workers, an increase of nearly 16,000 in twenty years. Using steam instead of water as the source of power and the corporation instead of the partnership as the form of organization, the second generation of entrepreneurs plunged confidently, and Providence capitalists led the pack. Though the steam engine made industrialization feasible in many new areas, the Providence leaders had not wrested economic supremacy from Newport merely to abandon it on the first challenge. Once they achieved preëminence, they never relinquished control.

Steam power, which Samuel Slater pioneered in a large cotton mill he constructed at Providence in 1827,[1] accelerated industrialization and had other far-reaching consequences. First, every locality with cheap access to coal supplies was now a potential manufacturing site, which weakened the monopoly enjoyed by towns with water power. Steam power was particularly attractive to cotton manufacturers because it allowed them to locate mills along the

[1] Justitia [pseud.], *Strictures on Montgomery on the Cotton Manufactures of Great Britain and America* (Newburyport, 1841), 11. The Slater mill burned Schuykill coal. A powerful steam engine drove 10,500 spindles and equipment in a large machine shop employing about 70 workers.

coast—at Bristol, Warren, Fall River, and Newport, for example—where the humidity was particularly high. It also brought East Greenwich to prominence by making the unique qualities of its waters exploitable by the cloth printing industry, and though the Blackstone-Pawtuxet towns retained their manufacturing leadership, the growing use of steam engines by Fall River and other communities threatened to modify the configuration of economic power. But Providence, already the commercial capital, also took full advantage of changing conditions and by 1860 it had become the state's industrial capital as well.

Second, steam power had a marked impact on the economics of the textile industry. Machinery driven by an efficiently governed steam engine operated at a more constant and at a higher speed than that achieved in water-power mills. This improved the quality of yarn and cloth, increased productivity per unit of labor, and, except for the cost of fuel, reduced operating expenses. To a certain extent, the annual coal bill was offset by a reduction of transportation costs in those mills which secured their raw materials and shipped their finished products by water, and by the fact that they could stay in operation when droughts, floods, or frozen streams forced water mills to suspend production. Moreover, though Rhode Island steam mills were smaller than the mammoth factories in the Lowell system, some were large enough to secure similar economies of operation.

Third, the growing use of steam power brought a wholly new Rhode Island industry into being—the manufacture of steam engines; it raised the base metal industry to a prominent position in the state's economy; and it changed both the style and scale of production in the jewelry industry.

Finally, the adoption of steam power eventually reduced the flexibility of Rhode Island entrepreneurs. Traditionally, they had trimmed their sails to each shift in the economic breeze by re-allocating resources between different lines of business. Indeed, the rise of the cotton industry was a major example of this practice. However, manufacturing required large, fixed investments in buildings and machinery, and unlike ships, which could be diverted from one trade or port to another with ease and speed, factories could be converted from one product to another only slowly and at great expense. Though not a serious problem before the Civil War, it was potentially dangerous and eventually was to prove the major weakness in the Rhode Island economy.

To a lesser extent, the adoption of the corporate form of business organization also facilitated industrialization. Manufacturers in other eastern states had taken such a step a generation or more earlier, but Rhode Islanders proved exceedingly conservative on this question. The corporation did not replace the joint-stock partnership until the middle of the century and thus played no part in the state's first phase of industrial development and only a limited rôle in the second. To be sure, a group of Providence woolen manufacturers attempted to secure a charter in 1810,[2] but apart from a Smithfield limestone quarrying company incorporated in 1823,[3] the chartering of two reservoir companies the following year,[4] and an incidental grant to establish factories obtained by a coal mining company in 1825,[5] no further attempt was made to incorporate an exclusively manufacturing enterprise until 1827. In January of that year, the promoters of the Phoenix Company, probably a Providence iron working firm, asked to be incorporated.[6] Their petition

[2] They styled themselves the Smithfield Manufacturing Company. See House Journal, October 31, 1810, in the State Archives. The petition was not acted upon, perhaps because the promoters were of the wrong political stripe. According to Thomas Coles, some members of the Tammany Society and their Republican friends planned a $200,000 mill in Providence, but he had been informed that a charter would not be granted. See Coles to Jonathan Russell, October 31, 1810, in the Russell Papers, Special Collections, John Hay Library, Brown University. Earlier, in 1793, Providence merchants had discussed the possibility of establishing a joint-stock company to operate a proposed duck and twine factory. Whether they contemplated incorporating is not clear. See *Providence Gazette*, January 26, 1793.

[3] *Acts and Resolves*, June, 1823, pp. 57–59.

[4] *Ibid.*, January, 1824, pp. 30–34; May, 1824, pp. 21–24.

[5] *Ibid.*, May, 1825, pp. 46–48. Initially, the Rhode Island Coal Company had been denied perpetual succession. See Granted Charters, 3:34 (1805–1809).

[6] The petition has not been preserved, but action on it can be traced in the House Journal, vol. 23 (1826–1828, unpaged), and vol. 24, pp. 83, 203 (1829–1831).

became associated with a similar request submitted by the proprietors of the Providence Iron Foundry—Benjamin, Charles, Cyrus, Olney, and Paris Dyer, Samuel Slater, Joseph Tompkins, and David Wilkinson. It was a textile machinery venture dating back to the period following the War of 1812 and in 1827 it controlled property in both Providence and Freetown, Massachusetts. The petitioners sought permission to hold up to $500,000 worth of real and personal property, to engage in any type of business they chose, to force creditors to exhaust the corporation's assets before suing individual shareholders, and, by not providing for the right of the General Assembly to amend or repeal the charter, to place the company's affairs beyond the reach of future legislation. Even apart from the financial difficulties which were soon to engulf the partners, these provisions were sufficiently unusual to make the legislature hesitant about incorporating the enterprise.[7]

The House of Representatives referred these two petitions to a committee which, instead of acting on them immediately, drafted a general law defining the powers and duties of manufacturing corporations. It was not a general incorporation law. Rather, the legislature would continue to consider each application for a charter on its merits, but each corporation chartered would be subject to the general definition of rights and obligations. Thus the law would have extended customary powers to manufacturing corporations, including the right to corporate succession, to hold and convey property, to sue and be sued, to use a common seal, and to make by-laws. The measure also proposed rules to govern voting rights, stock assessments, and the disposition of delinquent shares, and it would have subjected corporations to all future legislative enactments. Authority to conduct banking or any type of manufacturing not specified in the charter was expressly denied, and corporations were to acquire no more real property than was necessary for the conduct of business. To strengthen the individual liability of share-

[7] Petitions Not Granted, June, 1827. See also, Cornelia C. Joy–Dyer, comp., *Some Records of the Dyer Family* (New York, 1884), 79–81; *Manufacturers' and Farmers' Journal*, May 18, 1831; Bagnall, *Samuel Slater*, 66–68; White, *Slater*, 216–217, 244–248.

holders, they were to be regarded as members of the corporation until an announcement of withdrawal had been published for three successive weeks. Creditors could attach a stockholder's property only after an execution against the corporation had been returned unsatisfied. The bill lay dormant for almost three years. Then it was indefinitely postponed and on the same day, June 22, 1830, the legislature also dismissed the two charter petitions.[8]

In the meantime, in June, 1828, the General Assembly had received a petition requesting incorporation of an East Greenwich cotton manufacturing venture. After a lengthy delay involving the submission of a fuller petition stating the reasons the owners considered they needed a charter, the legislature finally considered the request. Despite an undercurrent of opposition arising from fears that corporations would monopolize cotton manufacturing, the General Assembly granted the petition in January, 1829. However, the legislators made it clear that they had acted on the merits of the case and not out of any intention of granting charters indiscriminately. Moreover, the Assembly reserved the power to amend or repeal the charter, and, in the event of overdue debts, it insisted that creditors have the choice of proceeding against either the corporation or any individual stockholder. Therefore, though shares in the $100,000 venture were non-assessable, members were nevertheless subject to the same total liability as co-partners.[9]

The General Assembly was optimistic in supposing that it was possible to restrict the privilege of incorporation to a few excep-

[8] Miscellaneous Papers of the General Assembly, folder 10 (1826–1830); *Manufacturers' and Farmers' Journal*, November 12, 1827.

[9] Granted Charters, 10:17 (1828–1831). The initial request for incorporation was refused. See Petitions Not Granted, June, 1828; *Rhode Island American and Providence Gazette*, January 20, 1829; McPartland, *East Greenwich*, 219–220; *History of Rhode Island*, 121. Corporations generally and manufacturing corporations particularly evoked comparatively little opposition in Rhode Island. For a rare complaint, see *Providence Journal*, December 29, 1857, in which a manufacturer protested that corporations were poorly managed, grew too large too quickly, involved a danger of misrepresentation or fraud upon their shareholders by issuing only favorable reports of earnings, devoted too much energy to improving the minds of employees, and were assessed unfairly for taxation.

tional ventures. A steady stream of applications followed the grant to the East Greenwich Manufacturing Company, and over the ensuing ten years the legislature was to charter twenty-four manufacturing corporations and to deny not a single petition. However, the majority of businessmen continued to prefer the co-partnership to the corporation, a preference which persisted even after the Assembly liberalized corporate privileges in 1847.

The extremely conservative Rhode Island position on the incorporation question had its roots in a number of interrelated factors. First, the early corporations offered only one distinct advantage over the co-partnership—corporate succession. Unlike banks, which could be organized only with legislative sanction, or turnpikes, which required special authority to preëmpt private property for their rights of way, factories did not need public franchises. Although the joint-stock partnership was well-suited to the simple scale of operation used by the pioneer industrialists, some firms eventually had so many partners and some entrepreneurs had invested in so many ventures that enterprises were subjected to frequent reorganization. Corporate succession, an ideal solution to the managerial problems caused whenever partners died or withdrew, was the principal reason behind manufacturing incorporations before 1847.

Second, the early merchant-capitalists carried the trading tradition into their manufacturing enterprises. Had Almy and Brown sought a charter for their cotton spinning experiment, the corporate form of organization might have developed as an integral element in the process of industrialization, but they did not, and twenty years elapsed before any manufacturing venture sought to incorporate. By that time the legislature had chartered many banks and insurance companies and it had granted them limited liability, immunity from charter revision, and advantageous procedures for collecting debts. This led the public to associate the business corporation with special privileges, privileges which in the mercantile view threatened to jeopardize business integrity. The merchant-industrialists did not press the legislature for incorporation; they did not take advantage of the privilege of limited liability conferred on special partners in 1837;[10] and some corporations formed after the legislature enacted a limited liability law in 1847 specifically rejected the provision. Thus many manufacturers preferred the total liability of co-partners. This scotched any implication that they were the kind of men who operated so recklessly as to need to be able to evade their lawful debts.[11]

Third, the manufacturers who took the lead in applying for charters in the 1820's had industrial rather than mercantile backgrounds. The Slaters and Wilkinsons began their careers on the land, not on the sea: they were mechanics turned capitalists, not merchants turned industrialists. Thus they lacked the maritime frame of mind—particularly the sense of diversification, risk taking, and business integrity—bred into successive generations of Rhode Island traders, and they were less inhibited than merchant-entre-

[10] *Acts and Resolves,* January, 1837, pp. 14–17. George Curtis of Providence introduced the bill in November, 1836; the House adopted it by a vote of 46 to 14. Rural representatives cast most of the negative votes, but only two towns, Exeter and Middletown, cast both of their votes against the enactment. The other negative votes were cast by representatives from Burrillville, Cumberland, Foster, Scituate, Coventry, Warwick, West Greenwich, Charlestown, Richmond, and Bristol. House Journal, vol. 27 (1836–1838, unpaged). The Senate did not record its vote. A search of the extant town records shows no examples of limited co-partnerships; the *Providence Journal,* 1837–1851, reported only three, all in the late 1840's. See January 1, 1847; February 15, 1848; and October 28, 1848. Two were wool dealers, the other a printing firm. For examples of textile manufacturers who failed but later scrupulously repaid their debts, see *Book of Rhode Island,* 189, and Bicknell, *Rhode Island,* 4:381. For a typical general partnership formed in 1854 by William Cunliff and Amos N. Beckwith, see *William Cunliff vs. The Dyerville Manufacturing Company,* 7 *Rhode Island* 325 (1862).

[11] *Acts and Resolves,* June, 1847, pp. 30–37. The resolution for a general incorporation law was introduced on May 6, 1847; a narrower bill was reported by the House Committee on Corporations on June 22 and enacted into law within three days. Four memorials, containing 239 signatures (89 from Providence, 19 from Bristol, 97 from Newport, and 34 others, largely from North Providence and Woonsocket), were filed on June 23; they merely asked that the bill pass with whatever safeguards the General Assembly deemed advisable. See Granted Petitions, 70:9 (1847). Existing corporations were required to vote their acceptance of the statute in order to enjoy limited liability. See *New England Commercial Bank vs. Stockholders of the Newport Steam Factory,* 6 *Rhode Island* 154 (1859). For examples of corporations specifically rejecting limited liability, see *Acts and Resolves,* October, 1842, pp. 60–63; October, 1847, p. 67; June, 1853, pp. 181–183.

preneurs about resorting to the corporation as an appropriate way of organizing manufacturing ventures. It is not without point that the Wilkinsons failed in 1829; that the Dyers saved themselves only by liquidating their foundry holdings and by selling their interest in the steam cotton mill to Slater; that Slater himself would probably have gone under had not the Butlers, Browns, and Ives come to his rescue; and that the foundry was no longer in operation when the Assembly dismissed the charter petition in June, 1830. Despite the greater willingness of the artisan-capitalists to incorporate, the chartered manufacturing company did not become common until after 1847, or until leadership had passed to the second generation of industrialists—who had grown up in the manufacturing, not the mercantile tradition.

Legislative attitudes toward the corporation changed very slowly. The early companies were either charitable, religious, and educational institutions, or quasi-public utilities such as water, dredging, banking, insurance, and transportation ventures. Though the quasi-utilities were in business to make money, they received charters because the legislature recognized their public service function. Manufacturing enterprises could not qualify for charters as public utilities, but they could and did argue that there were other justifications for incorporating them.[12] The pioneer industrial companies were all new rather than established undertakings; they proposed to use new production methods, notably steam power, or to make

---

[12] Granted Charters, 10:17, 64, 76 (1828–1831); 11:49 (June, 1833). For dissatisfaction with the lack of perpetual succession in the general partnership, see *Manufacturers' and Farmers' Journal,* May 31, 1827, and for an early example (a church) of the importance of perpetual succession in petitioning to be incorporated, see Granted Petitions, 15:12 (1772).

Compare Oscar and Mary F. Handlin, "Origins of the American Business Corporation," in the *Journal of Economic History,* 5:1–23, but especially pp. 22–23 (May, 1945), who emphasized the social functions and quasi-public attributes of the corporation in Massachusetts, and Edwin Merrick Dodd, *American Business Corporations Until 1860* (Cambridge, 1954), 428–435, who surmised that the low capitalization of Rhode Island mills, the widespread satisfaction with the common-law joint-stock associations, and the pessimistic outlook for corporate charters containing limited liability probably explained the apparent Rhode Island disinterest in manufacturing corporations.

new products, such as flint glass; they obtained their capital by drawing on the savings of a large number of small shareholders; and they contended that such "doubtful experiments" would benefit from the privilege of corporate succession. The legislature considered these reasons valid and granted charters accordingly.

Significantly, most early manufacturing corporations failed within a few years. The attempt to establish the silk industry is a good illustration.[13] In 1835, Gamaliel Gay, a New York inventor of reeling machinery, appealed to the Rhode Island General Assembly to promote silk manufacturing. He offered to supply mulberry tree seeds, silk worm eggs, and a set of reeling and weaving machinery, and to initiate a number of females in each county into the mysteries of silk manufacture. In return, he asked permission to hold a lottery to cover his expenses and that the state subsidize the raising of mulberry trees and cocoons and the production of yarn and cloth. The legislature denied both requests, but it did incorporate Gay's Rhode-Island Silk Company, conferring the unusual privilege of limited liability on it. However, the charter was to be dormant until $60,000 had been subscribed, and if the corporation permitted its debts to exceed its capital, limited liability was to lapse automatically. A year later, complaining that this qualification had deterred investors, Gay reminded the General Assembly that governments had encouraged the silk industry since Roman times, and asserted that in the United States "the enterprise of individuals . . . had always been fostered and protected [by] bounties or [other] valuable privileges." It was unfair, he continued, to deny silk producers the same degree of limited liability enjoyed by all banks and insurance companies chartered before

[13] The analysis of the silk industry is based on the charters in *Acts and Resolves*, October, 1835, pp. 50–52; October, 1836, pp. 71–72; January, 1837, p. 58; January, 1838, p. 119; January, 1839, p. 52; on the requests for encouragement in Petitions Not Granted, October, 1834; January, 1836; January, 1839; May, 1839; on *Statistics, 1840*, pp. 58–61; and on the secondary accounts in L. P. Brockett, *The Silk Industry in America* (n.p., 1876), especially pp. 35–69; Field, *Rhode Island*, 3:367; Little, *Early American Textiles*, 150–155; William C. Wyckoff, *American Silk Manufacture* (New York, 1887), 31–32.

1818. The legislature removed the restriction in 1837, but share-holders did not raise sufficient capital to meet the charter require-ment, and the venture was forced to operate as the unincorporated Valentine Silk Company. Though the company displayed dozens of fabrics at an exhibition held at Albany, New York, in 1836, it is doubtful whether it ever manufactured more than sample cloths before it collapsed, with the loss of its entire capital, at the end of the decade.

Other silk manufacturing ventures also failed. In 1836 George W. Tyler secured a charter for the Scituate Silk Company, but it never went into operation. In the same year, four stockholders sought to revive the defunct Mount Hope Bank at Bristol. They proposed to double its capital and to invest $50,000 in a filature to provide employment for the families of the port's whalers and sailors. Without the support of the bank, claimed these promoters, the novel enterprise could never raise sufficient funds to go into operation. Nothing came of this petition. Another group brought forward its proposal in 1839. It asked to be incorporated as the Washington Silk Company and requested state assistance. The or-ganizers wanted a lottery to raise capital, a prohibition on the peddling of imported silk, and the right to sell their goods without paying the usual peddling fees. During the undertaking's formative stage, ran their argument, and until Congress gave the industry adequate protection, the company needed all the encouragement the General Assembly could give. When a legislative committee balked at these unusual requests, the promoters withdrew their charter petition to prevent its outright rejection.

Where novelty created special hazards, therefore, the legislature responded sympathetically even on the question of limited liability, though it did refuse to incorporate promoters who tied their schemes to banking privileges or who requested extraordinary con-cessions. But once the Assembly began granting charters, it ran the risk of creating privileged ventures—the very corporate monopolies it had feared initially. Before long, therefore, the legislature dis-regarded its avowed policy of chartering only exceptional firms and began incorporating all reasonable proposals, including ones for well-established, routine manufacturing enterprises.[14]

Besides the widespread application of steam power and the growing use of the corporate form, the period from 1830 to 1860 was also characterized by a change in the source of industrial venture capital. During the experimental phase, the cotton industry, in particular, and to a lesser extent the woolen industry, had drawn upon merchant-entrepreneurs for financial needs. With the decline of international trade, the stream of risk funds produced by maritime enterprise fell to a trickle, and by 1830 most mercantile houses had shifted their main resources out of oceanic enterprise. By that time, cotton manufacturers were earning and reinvesting profits on a scale large enough to supply most of their own needs. By 1840,

[14] The late development of the corporation does not seem to have reflected problems arising from formulating equitable principles of taxation. So long as the economy was simple and revenue needs slight, it was possible to retain pre-Revolutionary fiscal principles of taxing real property to the occupier. However, with the development of the joint-stock partnership and especially the industrial corporation, this rule began to create difficulties, not merely because of the danger of double taxation when realty and the shares which it represented were taxed separately, but also because it became increasingly hard to differentiate between real and personal property. Moreover, since the financial demands on the towns were rising in the early nineteenth century, the question soon arose: were they entitled to tax shares owned beyond their jurisdiction? Although the General Assembly began grappling with these problems as early as 1822, the situation was still confused as late as 1860; particularly unsettled was the determination of the ownership of personalty in the case of the industrial corporations. See *Revised Laws, 1822*, pp. 310–319, 437–438; *Acts and Resolves*, January, 1834, pp. 14–15; *Public Laws, 1844*, pp. 261–262; *Acts and Resolves*, June, 1847, pp. 30–37; January, 1849, pp. 8, 10; January, 1855, pp. 33–46; January, 1857, pp. 17–30; Field, *Rhode Island*, 3:235–253; Howard Kemble Stokes, *The Finances and Administration of Providence* (Baltimore, 1903), 265–271.

In 1860 the Rhode Island Supreme Court denied towns the right to tax cotton goods brought into the state to be printed, declaring that a community "the bulk of whose inhabitants derive their subsistence from manufacturing . . . is the last in which . . . the legislature should subject to a special tax personal property owned abroad, and brought here to be worked upon." See *Job W. Woodman, Collector vs. American Print Works*, 6 Rhode Island 470 (1860). See also, *American Bank vs. James Mumford, Collector* and *The Providence Institution For Savings vs. Marinus W. Gardiner, City Treasurer*, 4 *ibid.*, 478, 484 (1857), for two cases testing the right of the city of Providence to tax deposits in savings banks and surplus capital in commercial banks.

the industry was a producer rather than a consumer of capital. An increase in the tempo of industrial activity followed, and, after 1850, the woolen, base metal, and jewelry industries also commanded sufficient resources to finance their own expansion.

Though the growth of these secondary industries reduced the relative importance of cotton manufacturing, it retained its central position in the Rhode Island economy. In 1832, cotton manufacturing had absorbed almost $5,600,000 in capital and had employed nearly 9,100 workers. A generation later, on the eve of the Civil War, capital exceeded $12,000,000 and the labor force 15,700 workers. The scale of operation also showed a pronounced upward trend. In 1832, the largest single mill had been the Almy, Brown, and Slater factory in Smithfield, a $240,000 enterprise. By 1860, there were six firms in Providence County alone operating on at least that scale, and three were capitalized at $500,000 each.

The industry expanded at an irregular rate, and the weaknesses exposed in the 1820's continued to plague manufacturers in the next decade, when the rising cost of raw materials and the falling price of finished goods reduced profits. On the whole, the larger, more efficient mills adjusted successfully, but many firms, especially marginal ones, came under heavy pressure and some were already in difficulty long before the depression of 1837 halted production.

The factorage system of purchasing raw materials and marketing textile goods both contributed to and aggravated the business crisis. Most factors were located in Providence, the commercial center of the southern New England cotton industry, where, for a commission, they supplied every manufacturing need from raw cotton to dyestuffs and from coal to starch, then marketed the finished product. The system had obvious merits. The factor's specialized commercial knowledge was especially valuable to the small producer, and, by relieving professional managers of purchasing and marketing responsibilities, the factor freed them to concentrate on production problems. But the system also had decided disadvantages. It discouraged buyers from making direct cash purchases from the mill, and it perpetuated the system of credit sales.

Most goods were not sold for cash but for future payment. Discounts of four months were rare, six to ten months common, and eighteen months not extraordinary. Though manufacturers could borrow against these obligations, the discount rate varied with the supply of money, and bank accommodation was tightest when needed most. Since mill owners often lacked the liquid assets to meet demands from their own creditors, they were sensitive to the slightest economic fluctuations.

No solution to this problem had been devised before the depression. In 1826, as a means of bringing cash buyers to the state, the Rhode Island Society for the Encouragement of Domestic Industry proposed to establish a textile auction market at Providence, but the scheme had to be abandoned when the General Assembly refused to abolish the auctioneering tax. A decade later, manufactures from the Providence hinterland—northern Rhode Island, southern Massachusetts, and eastern Connecticut—turned to a second solution, a co-operative marketing organization. Located in Providence, the Rhode Island Cloth Hall Company extended credit to manufacturers based on the value of the goods they deposited for sale. Though the company distributed two dividends in the fiscal year ending in July, 1837, it suffered from weak management and attracted only a tenth of the capital it required. Hard hit by the general economic crisis, the cooperative failed in the first months of the depression.[15]

Despite these marketing problems and the difficulties experienced by individual producers, the cotton industry grew more rapidly during the 1830's than in any previous decade. Even after 1835, when the rate of expansion declined, efficient manufacturers, such as the Slaters, increased output and sales, and, once the depression of 1837 had spent itself, a minor boom ensued. One entrepreneur, Benjamin Cozzens, recouped two-thirds of a $150,000

[15] Petitions Not Granted, October, 1826; *Transactions*, 1857, pp. 75–76; Ware, *Early New England Cotton Manufacture*, 108–109, 176–178; *Acts and Resolves*, June, 1836, pp. 72–75; October, 1836, p. 85; October, 1837, p. 29. For a report on the emergence of jobbers who bought directly from manufacturers, and for a condemnation of the commission system, see *Providence Journal*, March 18, August 14, 1858.

investment in a single year.[16] By 1840, the number of mills had reached 226, an increase of 100 over 1832, capital and employment had each expanded by about forty per cent, and spindlage had more than doubled.

The finishing industry grew particularly rapidly. Though European immigrants had started printing Calcutta-style calicoes in Providence in 1794, large amounts of capital had not entered the printing business until after 1829, when manufacturers turned increasingly to calicoes as a substitute for ginghams. By 1832, two large printing establishments were in operation, one in North Providence, the other in Cranston. Together they were capitalized at over $200,000 and employed 186 workers. The tariff of 1833 stimulated further expansion. By 1840 the industry was so efficient that it could copy and undersell the newest French *de laines* within sixteen days of their appearance on the New York market. Bleaching, the other side of the finishing process, also made great strides. Five factories employing a total of 300 workers had been in operation in 1832. Over the next eight years, another ten bleaching and printing firms went into business, making seventeen in all by 1840. Eight finishing works were located in Providence, seven in the adjacent towns of Johnston and Cranston, and one each in Warwick and Tiverton.[17]

In 1840, therefore, as in 1832, cotton production was chiefly concentrated in northern Rhode Island. Seventy-nine of the one hundred new mills had been constructed in the rapidly expanding towns in the Blackstone-Pawtuxet region, which manufactured approximately four-fifths of the cotton goods produced in the state. Steam power played a major rôle in this growth, particularly in Providence, where, if the census can be accepted, the number of mills rose from four to thirty, capital quadrupled, yarn production increased sevenfold, and the labor force expanded more than six-

[16] Ware, *Early New England Cotton Manufacture,* 102; Fuller, *History of Warwick,* 174–175.
[17] *McLane's Report,* 1:976; *Statistics, 1840,* p. 59; Field, *Rhode Island,* 3:344–345, 353, 355; Fowler, *Fall River,* 31; Greene, *East Greenwich,* 62–63; *History of Rhode Island,* 161.

fold. This made the city Rhode Island's largest cotton manufacturing center. Steam power had also paved the way for industrialization in Bristol. Though the initial scale of operation was modest, cotton manufacturing did contribute to Bristol's steady economic recovery, and it brought about the first important shift of local resources from maritime to industrial ventures.

The principal concentration of mills was along the ribbon of discrete industrial communities stretching through the Blackstone

TABLE 9

COTTON MANUFACTURING IN THE BLACKSTONE AND BRANCH VALLEYS, 1844[18]

Villages	Population	Mills	Spindles	Looms	Employees		
					Females	Males	Total
Slatersville	1,200	4	12,000	350	212	108	320
Bernon	750	2	11,000	288	175	75	250
Woonsocket	4,000	18	40,825	978			890
Hamlet	250	2	5,832	120	67	74	141
Manville	700	2	12,000	300	80	150	230
Albion	400	2	8,500	206	115	102	217
Lonsdale	1,200	4	22,000	560	250	150	400
Valley Falls	1,500	5	22,340	627	276	205	481
Central Falls	1,307	7	19,714	425	284	240	524
Pawtucket	5,548	14	25,380	539			543
Total	16,855	60	179,591	4,393			3,996

Valley and its tributaries from northwestern Rhode Island to Pawtucket, five miles from Providence. In the extreme northwest, three mills were located on the Chepachet River in Glocester and Burrillville. The first major cotton manufacturing complex, comprising four large textile mills, was at Slatersville on the Branch River in Smithfield, some five miles west of its confluence with the Blackstone. Bernon, a slightly smaller center, was nearby. Woonsocket, Rhode Island's second largest cotton center, was located at the con-

[18] Compare Horace A. Keach, *Burrillville: As It Was and As It Is* (Providence, 1856), 118–121; *Facts and Estimates . . . of the . . . Providence and Worcester Rail Road* (Providence, 1844), 6–10 and the table facing p. 25; probably in error, Moore reported in the *Providence Almanac, 1844,* pp. 110, 112, that a Woonsocket calico printer employed 450 workers; and S. C. Newman, *A Numbering of the Inhabitants . . . and Other Information Relative to Woonsocket* (Woonsocket, 1846), 41, who reported 55,780 spindles, 1,323 looms, and 2,095 employees in Woonsocket.

fluence itself. Straddling both the Smithfield and Cumberland sides of the Blackstone Valley, and also located on two tributaries, the Mill and Peters rivers, Woonsocket had eighteen cotton mills and operated almost 41,000 spindles. Only a sixth of the factories operated fewer than 2,000 spindles. Two, the Hamlet and the Clinton, had over 5,000 each. Pawtucket, eleven miles downstream from Woonsocket, was the site of fourteen more mills and another 25,000 spindles. Scattered along the intervening stretch of river were six other industrial villages ranging in size from Hamlet, which had 250 inhabitants, to Central Falls, which had 1,500. These two communities, together with the others—Manville, Albion, Lonsdale, and Valley Falls—had twenty-two mills and over 92,000 spindles. In all, sixty mills and nearly 180,000 spindles operated along the valley between Slatersville and Pawtucket.

The relatively static towns expanded production at a slower rate than the Blackstone-Pawtuxet region towns and thus declined in status. Between 1832 and 1840, their mills fell from a third of the total to a fifth, and their share of capital, spindle capacity, and the labor force declined from a quarter to a fifth. The decline was more marked in some towns than in others. East Greenwich and Portsmouth halted production entirely, Scituate closed three of its eight factories, and Glocester reduced its labor force by almost a third. On the other hand, some towns expanded production rapidly and others began manufacturing for the first time. Newport, which constructed its first steam mill in 1832, achieved a significant shift in resources from maritime to industrial ventures, and by 1840 it ranked eighth in employment.

The Fall River section of Tiverton also derived considerable though lesser benefit from the introduction of steam power. Throughout the eighteenth century, Fall River had been part of the Narragansett Bay economy, and when industrialization got under way the area had remained in the Providence rather than the Boston sphere of influence. Providence County investors had supplied more than an eighth of the $304,000 ventured in five early Fall River cotton mills and an iron works, and when Job Durfee built a cotton mill there in 1811 he marketed his textile goods in

Providence. Two mills and 764 spindles were reported in Tiverton in 1815, but no cotton manufacturing was shown, probably through an oversight, in *McLane's Report* in 1832. In 1840, however, Tiv-

TABLE 10

THE RHODE ISLAND COTTON INDUSTRY, 1840[19]

Towns	Mills	Capital	Spindles	Employees	Value of Production
Bristol	1	$ 80,000	6,000	184	$ 99,178
Cranston	6	222,000	3,176	446	639,700
Johnston	21	272,000	86,000	585	330,500
Providence	30	1,449,000	76,554	2,025	1,287,290
North Providence	20	270,000	30,000	600	230,000
Cumberland	22	856,000	59,711	1,188	787,733
Smithfield	31	1,540,000	88,208	2,401	1,412,000
Burrillville	1	12,000	1,056	23	10,000
Warwick	29	1,128,000	73,074	1,946	967,000
Expanding Towns	161	5,829,000	423,779	9,398	5,763,401
Glocester	2	28,000	1,668	44	19,800
Scituate	11	324,000	19,654	552	259,500
Coventry	14	370,000	24,612	710	326,920
North Kingstown	5	45,500	5,756	134	45,200
South Kingstown	1	7,000	1,000	30	6,000
Richmond	6	60,500	7,038	178	72,900
Hopkinton	5	59,000	4,320	114	55,500
Westerly	2	46,000	2,536	80	34,271
Newport	4	397,000	20,290	580	212,000
Tiverton	7	99,000	1,600	115	270,750
Static Towns	57	1,435,000	88,474	2,537	1,302,841
Foster	1	4,000	624	25	5,250
West Greenwich	3	6,000	2,324	54	24,000
Exeter	4	50,000	3,016	72	21,000
Declining Towns	8	60,000	5,964	151	50,250
Rhode Island	226	7,324,000	518,217	12,086	7,116,492

[19] *Statistics, 1840*, p. 59. The table includes eight printing and dyeing works in Providence, five in Johnston, two in Cranston, and one each in Tiverton and Warwick. See Treasury Papers, 1820–1849 folder, in the State Archives, for 1836 data for mills on the southwest branch of the Pawtuxet River in Coventry. Ten factories having Providence agents (and, presumably, banking connections) were operating within two miles of the location of the proposed Coventry Bank. Only four mills utilized 2,000 spindles or more, and the average mill operated fewer spindles than in 1832. For later data, see Moore, *Providence Almanac, 1814*, p. 87, 101, 118–119; J. S. Buckingham, *America: Historical, Statistic, and Descriptive* (3 vols., London, [1841]), 3:497–502.

erton contained seven cotton factories, including a large finishing mill, operated 1,600 spindles, and employed 115 workers. Though the Old Colony railroad linked Boston to Fall River in 1846 and the area joined Massachusetts by a boundary adjustment in 1862, Fall River continued to have close ties with Providence.[20]

Throughout the early nineteenth century, the declining towns contributed little to the cotton industry. During the water power phase of development, their efforts had been hampered by the limited number of mill sites available, by their remoteness or inaccessibility, and by their lack of financial resources. These factors continued important after manufacturers had turned to steam power, in part because the scarcity of skilled workers and the general climate of economic stagnation deterred the inflow of capital. Some local leaders did construct a few small factories, but these towns were mainly important only as suppliers of unskilled labor.

All phases of the cotton industry expanded during the 1840's, but growth slowed considerably as compared to earlier decades, and in 1850 a severe economic crisis disrupted production. Consolidation and reorganization were the period's dominant characteristics. Spinning and weaving mills fell from 209 in 1840 to 158 in 1850, printing and dyeing works declined from seventeen to sixteen, and, though capital increased by a seventh and production by over a half, the labor force remained relatively constant. Wage cuts failed to offset foreign competition, and at least thirty-nine mills halted operations in 1850. Others, such as the Lippitt Manufacturing Company, operated only three days a week. Excluding finishing works, almost half the mills were capitalized at less than $25,000 each. A tenth utilized $100,000 or more. The four largest

---

[20] The 1828 tariff was especially important to the rise of the printing industry. Printing, in turn, stimulated the production of printing cloths. See *McLane's Report*, 1:930; White, *Slater*, 391–394. See also, Fowler, *Fall River*, 30–31; Walton, *Story of Textiles*, 222–229; Thomas Russell Smith, *The Cotton Textile Industry of Fall River, Massachusetts: A Study in Industrial Localization* (New York, 1944), 1–39 *passim*. However, *McLane's Report*, 1:69–76, 164–169, listed sixteen cotton factories in Troy (later Fall River), Massachusetts, including the Massoit Manufacturing Company, a mill operated by Brown and Ives and Holder Borden as tenants, and White, *Slater*, 234, reported ten cotton mills in the Fall River area in 1833, including a calico works employing nearly 300 workers.

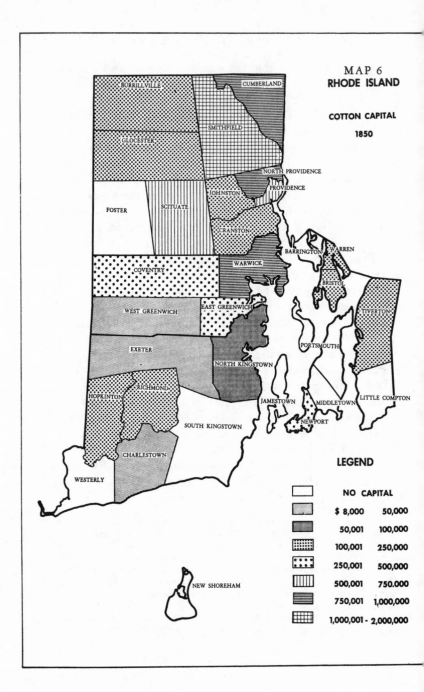

MAP 6
RHODE ISLAND

COTTON CAPITAL

1850

BURRILLVILLE

CUMBERLAND

SMITHFIELD

GLOCESTER

NORTH PROVIDENCE

PROVIDENCE

JOHNSTON

FOSTER

SCITUATE

CRANSTON

BARRINGTON

WARREN

WARWICK

BRISTOL

COVENTRY

TIVERTON

WEST GREENWICH

EAST GREENWICH

PORTSMOUTH

EXETER

NORTH KINGSTOWN

RICHMOND

HOPKINTON

JAMESTOWN

MIDDLETOWN

LITTLE COMPTON

NEWPORT

SOUTH KINGSTOWN

CHARLESTOWN

WESTERLY

LEGEND

	NO CAPITAL	
	$ 8,000	50,000
	50,001	100,000
	100,001	250,000
	250,001	500,000
	500,001	750,000
	750,001	1,000,000
	1,000,001 -	2,000,000

NEW SHOREHAM

TABLE 11

THE RHODE ISLAND COTTON INDUSTRY, 1850[21]

Towns	Mills	Capital	Employees	Value of Production
Bristol	2	$ 204,000	293	$ 178,384
Warren	1	125,000	126	110,000
Cranston	5	239,000	281	1,145,150
Johnston	10	235,400	391	739,665
Providence	8	731,800	1,138	668,225
North Providence	22	855,995	1,238	1,704,919
Cumberland	11	837,000	1,186	769,456
Smithfield	31	1,970,000	2,855	2,472,442
Burrillville	7	101,500	179	128,576
Warwick	9	964,500	1,104	1,538,878
Expanding Towns	106	6,264,195	8,791	9,455,695
Glocester	4	103,000	165	80,337
Scituate	14	560,960	775	432,608
East Greenwich	4	251,000	339	550,000
Coventry	10	334,000	599	276,558
North Kingstown	3	72,000	113	63,000
Richmond	7	199,200	336	209,055
Hopkinton	6	119,000	209	321,823
Newport	3	322,000	485	240,000
Tiverton	7	141,800	434	1,116,520
Static Towns	58	2,102,960	3,455	3,289,901
West Greenwich	5	31,000	76	54,630
Exeter	3	36,000	52	37,650
Charlestown	2	12,700	12	16,261
Declining Towns	10	79,700	140	108,541
Rhode Island	174	8,446,855	12,386	12,854,137

[21] Compiled from Schedule Five, Seventh Census of the United States, 1850, Rhode Island volumes, *passim*. Wherever the census takers recorded incomplete data, estimates have been supplied. For data on the Moshassuck Bleachery, see *History of Rhode Island*, 162–163, and for general accounts of the development of cotton manufacturing after 1830, see *ibid.*, 327–328, 342; Arnold, "Valley of the Pawtuxet," 226, 231, 241–259 *passim;* Bagnall, *Textile Industries*, 165, 257–258, 278–279, 381–382, 396, 399–403, 413–414, 436–439, 443, 447–451, 456–457, 530–532, 535, 551, 591, 596–597; Carroll, *Rhode Island*, 1:518, 520–522; 2:862–863; Field, *Rhode Island*, 3:354–357; Fuller, *History of Warwick*, 173–175, 195, 203–205, 210, 231–234, 249–253, 255–256, 265–266; Gibb, *The Saco-Lowell Shops*, 63–230 *passim;* Goodrich, *Pawtucket*, 82–95; Greene, *Providence Plantations*, 244–256 *passim;* Grieve, *Pawtucket*, 138–159, 162–164, 170–172; Irish, *Richmond*, 52–58; Munro, *Bristol*, 373–375; *Pawtucket Past and Present* (Pawtucket, 1917), 15–33 *passim;* Peck and Early, *Fall River and its*

ventures—the Slater steam mill in Providence, the Manville Mills in Cumberland, and two Smithfield undertakings, one owned by Henry Marchant and the other by the Lonsdale Company—together absorbed some $1,250,000, or more than the combined resources of the seventy-three smallest mills.

A few large producers also dominated the rapidly expanding finishing business. Growth reflected superior manufacturing techniques, competent management, and careful organization, and, in addition, the availability of large supplies of pure water for bleaching, dyeing, and printing. Except for a small Providence bonnet bleachery and two Johnston printing works, all sixteen factories used steam power. They were located on the Pawtuxet, Woonasquatucket, Moshassuck, Blackstone, and Taunton rivers, where they had easy access to coal supplies shipped in from Nova Scotia. Fourteen finishing mills operated in the Blackstone-Pawtuxet towns, and one each operated in East Greenwich and the Fall River section of Tiverton. The largest venture, the Clyde works in Warwick, was capitalized at $475,000, and processed more than $1,000,000 worth of cotton goods annually. A mill on the Woonasquatucket in North Providence operated on almost as large a scale; the Tiverton firm employed almost 300 workers and finished cloth valued at $875,000; and the A. and W. Sprague firm in Cranston had 200 employees and valued its production at $840,000. In all, these sixteen finishing mills had resources of $1,400,000 or almost a sixth of the funds invested in the cotton industry.

Following the consolidation and reorganization of the 1840's, cotton manufacturing resumed its rapid expansion. Despite the sharp recession of 1857, which closed many mills and reduced production in others,[22] the scale of operation increased substantially. Though the number of mills increased only slightly during the decade,

---

Industries, 37–62; Elizabeth A. Perry, *A Brief History of the Town of Glocester* (Providence, 1886), 67; Richardson, *Woonsocket,* 125–173 *passim;* Smith, *The Cotton Textile Industry of Fall River,* 40–47, 71–75; Spencer, "The North Branch of the Pawtuxet Valley," 125–126; Steere, *Smithfield,* 94–143 *passim;* Walton, *The Story of Textiles,* 247; Ware, *Early New England Cotton Manufacture,* 95–118, 143–160, 174–197.

[22] *Transactions,* 1857, pp. 77–81.

capital rose by over forty-three per cent, employment by more than twenty-six per cent, and ouput by almost sixty per cent. Since productivity increased almost three times as rapidly as wages, the industrialists benefited most. For example, in addition to distributing $680,000 in profits during the decade, the Lonsdale Company increased its undivided surplus by $500,000.[23]

This industrial growth was achieved in a variety of ways. In Washington County, manufacturers increased the output of old factories and constructed new mills; in Kent and Bristol counties

TABLE 12

THE RHODE ISLAND COTTON INDUSTRY, 1860[24]

Towns and Counties	Mills	Capital	Employees	Value of Production
Cranston	2	$ 225,000	579	$2,792,900
Johnston	11	202,000	452	408,580
Providence	15	1,093,800	1,730	1,835,400
North Providence	19	1,287,050	1,494	2,193,200
Cumberland	15	1,636,000	1,506	1,561,002
Smithfield	26	2,766,400	3,400	5,522,063
Burrillville	2	48,000	58	87,500
Glocester	1	40,000	68	44,720
Scituate	15	628,500	868	744,318
Providence County	106	7,926,750	10,155	15,189,683
Kent County	29	2,527,300	3,384	3,110,715
Newport County	10	435,400	547	454,780
Bristol County	3	395,000	530	408,000
Washington County	28	747,900	1,123	1,232,566
Rhode Island	176	12,032,350	15,739	20,395,744

they probably did no more than expand the capacity of existing factories; and in Providence County they closed some mills but increased production in others. The labor force declined sharply in Burrillville and Glocester, but in Cranston the expansion of the Sprague finishing operations offset the closing of three weaving mills and more than doubled employment. Almost 600 addi-

[23] Clarke, *History of Manufactures*, 1:553.

[24] Schedule Five, Eighth Census of the United States, 1860, Providence County volumes, *passim*. Where the census takers recorded incomplete data, estimates have been supplied. *Manufactures, 1860*, pp. 545–551; *Report on the Industrial Statistics of Rhode Island* (Providence, 1861), 20. For data on the Warren Manufacturing Company, see *History of Rhode Island*, 318.

tional jobs were created in Providence, notably by the new calico printing mill of Philip Allen and Sons, which hired 300 workers. In Newport County, where the number of mills rose from nine to ten and capital from $364,000 to $435,000, employment fell by almost twelve per cent and the value of production by over five per cent. The decline was probably a result of the relocation of the Globe Printing Company of Tiverton, which apparently shifted production from the Rhode Island to the Massachusetts side of Fall River.

The decade preceding the Civil War also saw a notable shift to the corporate style of industrial organization. Eight cotton enterprises, five of them steam factories, had been chartered in the 1830's and seven in the 1840's, but the legislature chartered twenty-seven in the 1850's, and by 1860 it had also incorporated twenty-three reservoir, finishing, and textile machinery undertakings. Though the unincorporated enterprise, whether owned by family members, partners, or shareholders, remained the typical business unit, the leading entrepreneurs were especially prone to incorporate. However, many chartered companies actually remained family or private joint-stock enterprises: they did not admit outside capital, or did so on only a very small scale. The histories of the Brown and Ives, Slater, and Sprague enterprises are illustrative.

Formed in 1796 by Nicholas Brown and Thomas Ives as the successor to a partnership which had also included George Benson, the great Providence house of Brown and Ives gradually abandoned its maritime interests in favor of industrial ones. For almost forty years the firm operated exclusively as a partnership, then joining forces with other powerful families in the inner circle of Providence entrepreneurial leadership—notably the Allens, Butlers, Carringtons, Duncans, and Goddards—it formed the Lonsdale, Blackstone, and Hope companies in 1834, 1841, and 1847 to manage its industrial holdings. By 1860, its mills, dispersed through northern Rhode Island and adjacent sections of Connecticut and Massachusetts, operated some 275,000 spindles.[25]

[25] *Acts and Resolves*, January, 1834, pp. 40–42; January, 1841, pp. 26–29; June, 1847, pp. 18–21; January, 1850, p. 44; *Book of Rhode Island*, 180; Carroll, *Rhode Island*, 2:863; *History of Rhode Island*, 163.

Samuel Slater, who was never admitted to this Providence cabal, gradually disassociated himself from his former partners, Almy and Brown. Though a member of the group that unsuccessfully petitioned for a charter for the Providence Iron Foundry in 1827, Slater did not incorporate his extensive textile properties in Rhode Island, Connecticut, Massachusetts, and New Hampshire. Following his death in 1835, however, his successors in the Providence steam mill did incorporate, though they left the Smithfield mills under partnership control.[26]

The Spragues incorporated in the 1850's. From its modest beginnings at Cranston in 1808, and with successive generations enlarging and diversifying operations, the family enterprise gradually acquired properties in Rhode Island, Connecticut, and Maine. In 1836, when control passed from William Sprague to the second generation, one son, Amasa, took charge of the bleaching, dyeing, and printing segment of the business, and another, William II, the spinning and weaving branch. Following the death of Amasa in 1844, and that of his brother in 1856, the third generation took possession. By 1859 the properties had been consolidated in three corporations with a potential capital of $2,000,000, but a conservative estimate placed the assets at twice that figure. The family operated some 300,000 spindles and twenty-eight printing presses.[27]

Commonly, then, as with the Spragues, who began manufacturing in 1808 and incorporated in 1854, or Brown and Ives, who formed their partnership in 1796 and incorporated in 1834, or the Chace family, who organized the Valley Falls Company in 1839 and did not incorporate it until 1853, private associations preceded corporations. Few manufacturing ventures, most notably the Atlantic DeLaine Company of Olneyville on the Woonaquatucket River in North Providence, began as chartered enterprises.

[26] *Acts and Resolves*, January, 1836, pp. 71–73. According to White, in *Slater*, 215, in 1817 he owned property in ten New England communities outside Rhode Island. For a brief history of the Knight mills, which operated between 1847 and 1912 as an unincorporated family enterprise, see Dodd, *American Business Corporations*, 431n.

[27] *Acts and Resolves*, June, 1854, pp. 46–49; May, 1858, pp. 37–38; May, 1859, pp. 21–23; Carroll, *Rhode Island*, 2:863; Field, *Rhode Island*, 3:316–317.

The typical Rhode Island mill by 1860 was still not incorporated and it was still a small enterprise. Even in Providence County, where the incidence of incorporation was relatively high, only one in every five mills was chartered. However, these corporations absorbed more than half the county's capital and employed almost half the workers, and of the county's seven largest undertakings four were chartered and a fifth, the Manville Mills, a $500,000 enterprise, was to incorporate in 1863. Only three of the county's twelve finishing works, including A. and W. Sprague (capitalized at $312,000) and the slightly smaller Providence Dyeing, Bleaching and Calendering Company, were chartered, though some fully integrated spinning and weaving corporations, such as the Lonsdale Company, also did bleaching and printing. The Allen and Woonasquatucket calico printing works were as large or larger ventures but were unincorporated. Of the ninety-six spinning and weaving factories in Providence County in 1860, over a third were capitalized at $25,000 or less, and four-fifths at $99,000 or less. The median mill was a $30,000 venture employing about 45 workers and producing $35,000 worth of goods annually. The situation was approximately the same in Kent County and, except that there were no very large mills, in Washington County. The typical unit was somewhat larger in Newport and Bristol counties, where manufacturers were more frequently incorporated and relied more commonly upon steam engines for their power requirements.

Over the entire seven decades from 1790 to 1860 the rise of the cotton industry in Rhode Island had yet another significant characteristic: it gave Providence entrepreneurs their most important opportunity to increase and consolidate the economic supremacy they had first achieved as traders. Though the city did not become a major cotton manufacturing center until the development of steam power, Providence risk capital, managerial ability, and technical knowledge were fundamental to the industrialization of the Blackstone-Pawtuxet region. After 1830, while simultaneously expanding production in the city and its hinterland, these entrepreneurs also reached out into neighboring states, and by 1855 they were as important to cotton manufacturing in eastern Connecticut, Rhode

Island, and southern Massachusetts as the Lawrences and Lowells were to northeastern Massachusetts and southern New Hampshire. At that time, Providence investors controlled at least eighty-four mills with a combined value exceeding $10,000,000, and their Rhode Island properties alone employed over 6,900 workers and contained more than 360,000 spindles. Significantly, the list included the Coddington mill in Newport which, in 1860, contained 11,000 spindles and 275 looms and employed 220 workers.[28] To be sure, residents of other Rhode Island towns also sent capital to those southern New England sites where it could be profitably employed, but they invested on a comparatively minor scale and they earned only a manufacturing profit. Providence, by contrast, through its factoring, banking, insurance, and transportation services, reaped many profits, and continued to expand as a commercial center despite the decline of the maritime economy.

At the same time that cotton manufacturing was becoming the outstanding source of Rhode Island wealth and, in some instances, was taking on the characteristics of big business, woolen manufacturing was developing into another though subordinate source of profit. In 1832 it had taken a mere 380 workers to operate the state's woolen mills; by 1860 the industry employed over 4,200 workers and was capitalized at almost $3,000,000.

Notable expansion occurred in the 1830's. The low earnings and business difficulties that had followed the Treaty of Ghent gave way in the late 1820's to higher profits. Large amounts of new capital then entered the industry to finance expansion of existing mills, install steam engines, and build steam mills at new locations. By 1836, Rhode Island was the sixth largest manufacturer in the Union, producing some two-fifths of the nation's linseys and smaller proportions of its broadcloths and satinets, and, by 1840, the industry was over twice as large as it had been in 1832.[29]

[28] Snow, *Census of Providence, 1855*, p. 55; Bayles, *Newport County*, 537.

[29] C. Benton and S. F. Barry, *A Statistical View . . . of the Principal Woolen Manufactories in . . . the United States* (Cambridge, 1837), 115–124; *Statistics, 1840*, pp. 58–61.

Edward Harris of Woonsocket and the Hazard family of Peace Dale contributed significantly to these developments. Harris, after gaining technical and managerial experience, first in his uncle's cotton mills at Albion and Valley Falls, then as agent for the Harris Lime Rock Company, ventured into manufacturing on his own account in 1832. Beginning with an initial investment of only $3,500, he acquired a share in a small Woonsocket satinet mill. Financial difficulties almost immediately forced him to return to his post as overseer of the Albion mills, but he increased his capital in the satinet factory and, in 1836, constructed a second and more efficient stone mill. By reinvesting profits in improved production methods, especially in power carders, Harris systematically established a reputation for his specialty, cassimeres, and within a decade had increased his capital tenfold. By 1844, he was employing 160 workers to tend 1,980 spindles and 49 looms, had opened a third mill, and was in the process of building a fourth capable of doubling his production, which already stood at $300,000 annually. In addition, he owned two large cotton mills containing a total of 10,000 spindles and earned additional profits by leasing them to other manufacturers.[30]

With some variations, the Hazards followed a similar path. After the death of their father in 1819, Isaac P. and Rowland G. Hazard had expanded the Peace Dale operations into the manufacture of cloth rather than webbing, enlarged spinning capacity, and, toward the end of the 1820's, had introduced new looms capable of weaving kersey cloths up to a yard in width. In the next decade poor health forced Rowland to winter in the South, but he turned misfortune to good account by expanding the firm's markets, especially in New Orleans. And, like Edward Harris, the Hazards reinvested their mounting profits in their own operations as well as in mills for lease to other manufacturers.[31]

To be sure, not all wool manufacturers were as successful as Harris or the Hazards. Zachariah Allen, who had been the largest producer in 1832, converted his North Providence mill to cotton

---

[30] *The National Cyclopedia of American Biography* (44 vols., New York, 1892–) 12:99; Bicknell, *Rhode Island*, 4:255–256.

[31] Gammell, *Hazard*, 6–8.

manufacturing in 1839, and the Union broadcloth mill, established at East Greenwich in 1836, failed under the pressure of foreign competition.[32] On the whole, however, growth was rapid.

Two significant changes in the geographical distribution of the industry occurred in the 1830's. First, manufacturers constructed many small mills beside streams in the western hill-country towns extending from Burrillville in the north to Westerly in the south. Second, other producers turned to the steam engine for their

TABLE 13

THE RHODE ISLAND WOOLEN INDUSTRY, 1836–1840[33]

Towns	Spinning Weaving 1836	and Mills 1840	Fulling Mills 1840	Capital 1840	Sets of Machinery 1836	Workers 1840	Value of Production 1840
Cranston			1	$ 2,000		2	$ 1,000
Providence	2	1	1	10,000	8		
North Providence	1		2	200	3		
Cumberland	1	1	2	32,800	2	68	74,000
Smithfield	1	1	10	90,000	1	190	120,000
Burrillville	3	2		3,000	6		
Warwick		2		14,000		30	76,000
	—	—	—		—	—	
Expanding Towns	8	7	16	152,000	20	290	271,000
Glocester	1				1		250
Scituate		1	1	5,000		10	5,000
East Greenwich		1	8	7,000			
Coventry	2	2	1	3,800	4	6	1,600
North Kingstown	4	4		19,000	8	68	59,600
South Kingstown	10	10	11	278,750	21	275	229,000
Richmond		3	2	43,000		56	58,648
Hopkinton	4	1		2,000	5	7	1,500
Westerly	4	4	2	46,800	7	57	78,360
Newport	1	2	1	70,000	6	85	75,691
Portsmouth	2	1	1	2,000	3	2	1,000
Tiverton	1	2		25,600	1	23	23,820
	—	—	—		—	—	
Static Towns	29	31	27	502,950	56	589	534,469
Foster			1	300		1	
Exeter	3	3	1	30,100	3	81	36,000
Charlestown	1				1		
	—	—	—		—	—	
Declining Towns	4	3	2	30,400	4	82	36,000
	—	—	—		—	—	
Rhode Island	41	41	45	685,350	80	961	841,469

[32] Taft, *Woolen Manufacture*, 43; Greene, *East Greenwich*, 62.

[33] *Statistics, 1840*, pp. 58–61; Benton and Barry, *Statistical View*, 115–124. See also, *History of Rhode Island*, 221, 288–289, 296, 342, 346–347.

power requirements and built factories at coastal locations, notably at East Greenwich, Providence, and Newport.[34] Though the Harris mill in Woonsocket was probably the largest single undertaking, the principal concentration of factories was in Washington County which, by 1840, contained three-fifths of the ventures, capital, and employees in the state. South Kingstown, the site of the Hazard operations, overshadowed the other twenty-two woolen manufacturing towns, accounting for two-fifths of the state's capital, nearly a third of its workers, and a quarter of its factories.

Despite occasional miscalculations, the woolen industry achieved a high rate of growth in the 1840's, and, significantly, leadership began to pass from southwestern to northern Rhode Island. Partly through the reinvestment of profits, and partly by drawing on the cotton industry for additional funds, woolen manufacturers increased their share of textile capital from nine per cent in 1840 to thirteen per cent in 1850, and their proportion of sales from ten to seventeen per cent. Growth was especially pronounced in the Blackstone-Pawtuxet region, which became the chief center of production and contained three of the five largest mills in the state.[35] Though woolen manufacturing was relatively unimportant in the economies of Cumberland and Smithfield, where two of these factories operated, it was the principal industry in Burrillville, which increased its mills from two in 1840 to eleven in 1850 and its capital from $3,000 to over $300,000.[36]

Throughout the period from 1824 to 1850, tariff policy significantly affected woolen manufacturers.[37] The tariffs of 1824 and 1828 protected woolens, but the high duties imposed on raw wool in

[34] Even as late as 1842, however, a Providence mill obtained its power from a windlass turned by oxen. See *A Sketch of the Mills of American Woolen Company* (Boston, 1901), 39.

[35] The organization and location of the woolen industry in 1850, including Table 14, is compiled from Schedule Five, Seventh Census of the United States, 1850, Rhode Island volumes, *passim*.

[36] A Burrillville mill built by the Sherman brothers took almost nine years to complete. *American Woolen Company*, 93. See also, *History of Rhode Island*, 179–180.

[37] Cole, *Wool Manufacture*, 1:297–349 *passim*; Gammell, *Hazard*, 7. For a proposed resolution (January, 1829) instructing the Rhode Island Congressional delegation to support a higher tariff on raw wool and woolen goods, see Miscel-

TABLE 14

THE RHODE ISLAND WOOLEN INDUSTRY, 1850[38]

Towns	Mills	Capital	Workers	Value of Production
Providence	2	$ 35,000	60	$ 40,000
North Providence	1	7,000	9	7,500
Cumberland	2	86,000	358	298,100
Smithfield	3	79,000	114	173,800
Burrillville	11	321,500	312	537,525
Warwick	2	23,000	120	154,000
Expanding Towns	21	551,500	973	1,210,925
Coventry	4	20,000	30	34,024
North Kingstown	5	55,500	83	180,600
South Kingstown	7	248,000	205	348,875
Richmond	2	47,000	40	65,080
Hopkinton	7	59,500	161	210,500
Westerly	2	75,000	250	300,000
Newport	1	18,000	50	50,000
Portsmouth	2	1,600	12	12,000
Tiverton	2	30,700	72	87,800
Static Towns	32	555,300	903	1,288,879
Exeter, Declining Town	4	32,000	67	72,040
Rhode Island	57	1,138,800	1,943	2,571,844

1828 offset this advantage. The steady reduction in protection prescribed in the 1833 tariff could have injured Rhode Islanders had they not reduced costs, increased efficiency, and improved quality. They installed new equipment, especially burr pickers, which permitted them to spin low cost Argentine wool, and better carding machinery, which enabled them to produce finer yarn and cloth. Efficient producers also increased the scale of production, especially for the Rhode Island specialties, satinets, cassimeres, and kerseys, and after 1841 capitalized on the restoration of protection to the 1832 level by introducing still better machinery and by using

laneous Papers of the General Assembly, folder 10 (1826–1830); see also, *ibid.*, folder 14 (1846–1848) for resolutions rejected in January, 1848, declaring existing tariff rates satisfactory.

[38] Data for the Elm Street Woolen Mill in Providence estimated. The value of production for Burrillville is probably too low since the Darius Law mill, capitalized at $11,000 and employing 23 workers, reportedly manufactured goods worth only $375. Charlestown's first woolen mill opened in 1831 but was soon converted to the manufacture of twine. A second mill began operating in 1845 but it too was eventually converted, in its case to cotton spinning. The mill was destroyed by fire in 1856. See *History of Rhode Island*, 96–97.

their technical resources to the best advantage. They also increased the variety of cloth patterns and experimented with new products, particularly plaids, tweeds, and carpet yarns. The Hazards, for example, converted to broadcloth production in 1847, but the timing was inauspicious. The Walker tariff of the previous year had reduced duties and, though most manufacturers were not adversely affected, the Hazard broadcloth venture proved unrewarding. However, with a notable show of entrepreneurial and industrial flexibility, the Hazard brothers immediately switched to the production of woolen shawls and escaped serious damage.

In the 1850's three factors working in combination—the rapid but locally disparate growth pattern, the enlarged scale of operation, and the slow down of the cotton industry's rate of expansion—increased the relative significance of woolen manufacturing both in the textile industry as a whole and as a factor in local economic development. With the single exception of the number of mills, which remained constant, every phase of the woolen industry, from capitalization to employment and production, more than doubled. By 1860, woolen manufacturing represented between a fifth and a quarter of the textile industry's effort.

Although the legislature chartered only three wooolen manufacturing corporations, one in 1833, a second in 1848, and a third in 1858,[39] by the Civil War the scale of operation, particularly in Providence County ventures, had reached the point at which incorporation was commonly sought by firms in other industries. Almost a third of the county's mills were capitalized at $100,000 or more, and two, one in Burrillville and another in Woonsocket, were valued at $225,000 and $500,000 respectively. Even the Hazard enterprise in South Kingstown could not match this rate of expansion. Moreover, the typical Washington County factory continued to be a relatively small undertaking. As a consequence, the dominant rôle of the arc of towns in the Blackstone-Pawtuxet region, which had begun to be apparent after 1840, was pronounced by 1860. Growth was especially rapid in Providence city, where the

[39] For charters of woolen manufacturing corporations, see *Acts and Resolves,* October, 1833, pp. 45–48; May, 1848, pp. 89–90; May, 1858, p. 40.

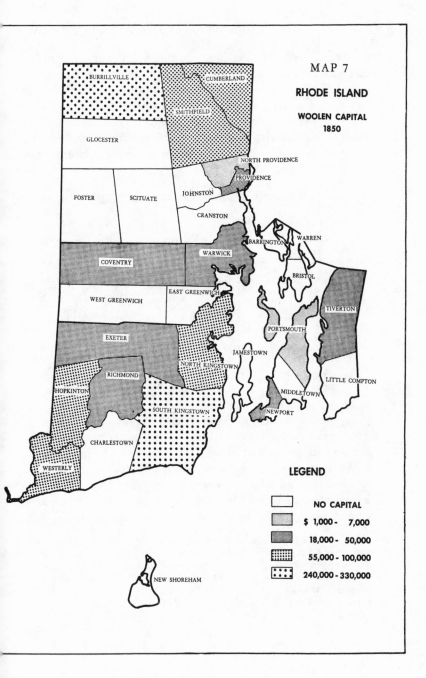

MAP 7

RHODE ISLAND

WOOLEN CAPITAL
1850

BURRILLVILLE

CUMBERLAND

SMITHFIELD

GLOCESTER

NORTH PROVIDENCE

PROVIDENCE

FOSTER   SCITUATE   JOHNSTON

CRANSTON

BARRINGTON   WARREN

COVENTRY   WARWICK

BRISTOL

EAST GREENWICH

WEST GREENWICH

TIVERTON

PORTSMOUTH

EXETER

JAMESTOWN

NORTH KINGSTOWN

LITTLE COMPTON

RICHMOND

HOPKINTON

MIDDLETOWN

SOUTH KINGSTOWN

NEWPORT

CHARLESTOWN

WESTERLY

LEGEND

NEW SHOREHAM

NO CAPITAL

$ 1,000 -   7,000

18,000 - 50,000

55,000 - 100,000

240,000 - 330,000

number of mills doubled, and capital, employment, and production grew respectively by seven, six, and almost fourteen times over. This laid the basis for a post-Civil War expansion which, by the end of the century, was to make Providence the center of the American worsted industry. But except in Burrillville, where woolen manufacturing was the dominant non-agricultural activity, the Providence County woolen industry merely reinforced the

TABLE 15

THE RHODE ISLAND WOOLEN INDUSTRY, 1860[40]

Towns and Counties	Mills	Capital	Workers	Value of Production
Cranston	1	$ 60,000	49	$ 72,000
Providence	4	260,500	382	550,000
North Providence	1	36,000	28	96,000
Cumberland	2	510,000	522	612,125
Smithfield	2	207,000	600	780,000
Burrillville	15	828,000	997	1,786,320
Glocester	1	9,000	18	24,000
Providence County	26	1,910,500	2,596	3,920,445
Kent County	5	68,500	97	184,800
Newport County	1	40,000	100	175,000
Washington County	25	980,000	1,411	2,563,560
Rhode Island	57	2,999,000	4,204	6,843,805

prior and stronger economic influence exerted by cotton manufacturing. The opposite was true of Washington County, where wool not cotton was the more important source of income, but except in South Kingstown and Westerly, economic growth was sluggish.

Woolen manufacturing, then, though it had played a minor rôle in Rhode Island's economic transformation before 1830, grew in importance, especially in particular localities. In some, notably Cumberland and Smithfield, where cotton manufacturing pre-

[40] Compiled from Schedule Five, Eighth Census of the United States, 1860, Providence County volumes, *passim*, and *Manufactures, 1860*, pp. 545–548. Only 11 mills operated during the 1857 depression; the industry utilized only twenty-five per cent of its capacity. *Transactions*, 1857, pp. 82–84. Burrillville had 22 mills in 1855; about 1,400 people in 260 families were dependents of the 750 operatives they employed. Keach, *Burrillville*, 160–161; *History of Rhode Island*, 92–93.

dominated, it was the major form of economic diversification; in others, especially Providence, which was a commercial as well as an industrial center, it was one of many manufacturing activities; and in still others, principally Burrillville, South Kingstown, Hopkinton, and Westerly, it was the chief factor in economic growth. Production, until 1840, was mainly concentrated in Washington County in the southwest; by 1860, it was dominated by factories in the Blackstone Valley and its tributaries, especially the Chepachet and Branch rivers in Burrillville in the northwest, where it significantly reinforced the region's rapid economic development.

The base metal industry also expanded prodigiously after 1830, and by 1860 it ranked alongside the woolen industry in importance. The dominant characteristics of these three decades, in this as in most other industries, were the adoption of the corporate form of organization; the mechanization of production; the use of steam power; the rise of large scale undertakings; the introduction of new products; and the emergence of Providence as the state's industrial center.

Wherever possible, metal working firms mechanized production. Many goods—especially heavy castings, sheet iron products, and copperware—were still made by hand, but most undertakings employed water or steam power to operate forging, cutting, and stamping machinery, to turn lathes and rollers, and to lift heavy weights. Although mechanization brought hundreds of unskilled workers, including women and children, into the industry and drove craftsmen out of particular fields, notably making horseshoes and nails, it also increased the demand for mechanics, blacksmiths, pattern makers, and other skilled artisans. The industry's success depended to a large extent upon their ability to design, construct, and maintain machinery and other equipment.

Steam was the principal source of power. Two factors were chiefly responsible. First, the growing shortage of water power at the very time that the industry was entering its phase of rapid expansion forced many firms to install steam engines. Second, the depression of 1829 broke up many Pawtucket firms. Though some were reorganized or moved to such other water power locations as Central Falls, many trip hammer operators moved to Providence, and there steam was the primary source of power.

The growing use of steam power created a new branch of the base metal industry, the manufacture of steam engines.[41] Joseph Brown had installed a steam pump to drain the Cranston iron ore pits in 1780 or 1781, and the Providence Woolen Manufacturing Company had used a steam engine in its finishing operations in 1812, but strong Rhode Island interest in the new source of power had not developed until after 1820. Even then mechanics had first experimented with marine rather than stationary engines. Robert

[41] The analysis of the steam engine industry is compiled from *Acts and Resolves,* October, 1826, pp. 41–44; May, 1856, pp. 94–97; Bicknell, *Rhode Island,* 4:223; John Hutchins Cady, *The Civic and Architectural Development of Providence, 1636–1950* (Providence, 1957), 85; Carroll, *Rhode Island,* 2:871; Alexis Caswell, *A Brief Memoir of John Barstow of Providence* (Albany, 1864), 3–11; *Commerce, Manufactures and Resources of Providence,* 40–42; Mary E. Corliss, *The Life and Work of George H. Corliss* (New York, 1930), *passim;* James Grant Wilson and John Fiske, eds., *Appletons' Cyclopedia of American Biography* (6 vols., New York, 1887–1889), 6:109; *Dictionary of American Biography,* 4:441; 18:520–521; Charles H. Dow, comp., *History of Steam Navigation Between New York and Providence from 1792 to 1877* (New York, 1877), 24–26; William A. Harris, *The Steam Engine: As It Was, and As It Is* (Providence, n.d.), *passim; History of Rhode Island,* 260; Robert Stowe Holding, *George Corliss of Rhode Island, 1817–1888* (New York, 1945), 8–11; Robert S. Holding, "George H. Corliss of Providence, Inventor," in *Rhode Island History,* 5:1–17 (January, 1946); King, *Pocket-Book of Providence,* 64; *National Cyclopedia of American Biography,* 10:394; *North Providence Centennial,* 28–29; Oliver, *American Technology,* 273; George G. Phillips, *The Early History of the Corliss Engine in the United States* (New York, 1902), 1–9; *Report on Steam Engines* (25 Congress, 3 session, *House Document no. 21,* serial 345, Washington, 1839), especially pp. 83–89; Staples, *Annals of Providence,* 626; Robert H. Thurston, *A History of the Growth of the Steam Engine* ([Centennial Edition], Ithaca, 1939), 280–281, 316–323, 501–506.

The extensive literature on steam engine technology notwithstanding, studies of the rôle of steam power in the development of the American economy are conspicuously absent. Data on the volume of steam engine business after 1840 compiled from Schedules Five, Seventh and Eighth Census of the United States, 1850 and 1860, Rhode Island and Providence County volumes, *passim; Transactions,* 1857, pp. 88–89; *Manufactures, 1860,* pp. 545–548; Thurston, *Gardner and Company vs. Charles T. James,* 6 Rhode Island 103 (1859).

L. Thurston, John Babcock, and Stephen T. Northam began constructing steamboats in 1821. Babcock, the designer of an engine which generated steam by injecting water into a hot boiler, tested this principle on a small ferry near Fall River, patented his idea in 1824, and in 1826 formed the Rhode Island Steam-Boat Company to link Providence and Newport. Despite initial difficulties with the engine he and Thurston built at Portsmouth for the steamer *Babcock*, he quickly perfected the design and commissioned a larger vessel, the *Rushlight*, in 1828. The *Rushlight* was built at Newport, its Babcock-type engine by James P. Allaire at New York. In the same year, a Pawcatuck firm built a steam ferry to operate between Westerly and Newport. It used a safety boiler system invented by a Providence physician, James A. Wadsworth, in which steam was generated in a series of pipes.

Rhode Island manufacturers soon turned to the construction of stationary engines. This shift reflected a sure appreciation of where Rhode Island's potential as a steam engine manufacturing center lay. The decline in Narragansett Bay shipbuilding gave the engine industry little hope of developing a profitable marine business, especially since New York and Philadelphia firms had already established a substantial lead in this field. On the other hand, Rhode Island's central location in southern New England gave the pioneer engine manufacturers access to a rapidly expanding industrial community. During the formative period, therefore, they built about eight times as many stationary as marine engines. Babcock and Thurston, the largest early engine making undertaking, constructed at least twenty-three stationary engines in its Providence foundry between 1825 and 1835. Engines ranging in size from four to a hundred horsepower were sold to factories in Boston, Newburyport, Fall River, Taunton, and Philadelphia as well as in Rhode Island itself. They were used to manufacture products as diverse as textiles, screws, and rum.

After 1835 Rhode Island factories turned increasingly to steam for their power needs. As a result, the engine building segment of the base metal industry boomed. Fairbanks, Clark and Company of Providence constructed a two-hundred horsepower engine for the Providence Dyeing, Bleaching and Calendering Company in 1836, and the Phoenix Iron Foundry built its own steam power plant a year later. By 1838 at least forty-two Rhode Island factories were entirely or partially dependent upon steam power. Providence firms operated half the engines. The rest were installed by undertakings in thirteen adjacent or coastal towns. Textile manufacturers operated twenty-three engines, metal working firms, ten, and rum distilleries, grist, saw, and dyewood grinding mills, a marble cutting works, a furniture factory, and a tobacco factory, the remainder. Four years later, in 1842, there were thirty-four steam engines in Providence alone, and their combined capacity exceeded nine hundred horsepower.

George H. Corliss became the most famous steam engine builder in Rhode Island. Born in New York State, he emigrated to Providence in 1844 hoping to secure financial backing for his design of a machine for sewing leather. Failing in this, he became a draftsman for the engine manufacturing firm of Fairbanks, Bancroft and Company. While there he conceived an improvement to the steam engine that was to make him as important to the technology of the nineteenth century as James Watt had been to the eighteenth. By connecting rotary valves to the steam and exhaust mechanisms and by regulating these valves with governors, Corliss revolutionized the reciprocating engine developed by Oliver Evans of Philadelphia. For the first time, manufacturers could operate machinery at a constant speed and could produce yarn and cloth of uniform texture. The Corliss engine's superior efficiency also reduced fuel costs and, because the machinery could be run at a higher speed, increased productivity.

Despite these advantages, manufacturers were slow to install Corliss engines. Corliss left Fairbanks, Bancroft and Company in 1848 to form his own partnership with John Barstow, a prominent Providence transportation and banking figure, and E. J. Nightingale. He completed his first engine that year, a two hundred and sixty horsepower machine for the Providence Dyeing, Bleaching and Calendering Company, and in 1849 secured a patent for his improvements. Litigation over patent rights[42] made many manufacturers apprehensive about installing Corliss engines. Others did so only on the unusual terms of setting an engine's price at a figure equal to the amount saved in fuel costs over an agreed period. Under the terms of one such contract, the James Mill at Newburyport paid Corliss almost $20,000.

By the Civil War, the manufacture of steam engines had become a major segment of the Rhode Island base metal industry. The Corliss Steam Engine Company, incorporated in 1856, employed 300 men in its large North Providence foundry where it made engines, boilers, shafting, and gears. A Providence enterprise owned by Thurston, Gardner and Company (formerly Thurston, Greene) employed 200 workers. Two other firms, both minor, the Cove Machine Company of Providence and a foundry in Washington County, also manufactured steam engines. By 1860 Rhode Islanders had captured a valuable share of the American steam engine market.[43]

[42] Corliss was especially involved in suits with Thurston, Greene and Company, successors to the Providence Steam Engine Company and assignees of Charles T. James' interests in the Frederick E. Sickel patents.

[43] Although the steam engine increased Rhode Island coal consumption enormously, local mines supplied only a fraction of the state's needs. The legislature had begun encouraging coal mining with lotteries and charters in 1808, and later it offered the privilege of limited liability. Nevertheless, the industry developed very slowly. By 1860, eleven companies had been incorporated, considerable sums had been expended in Cumberland and Portsmouth in driving shafts, constructing buildings, and installing pumps and other equipment, and Boston and New York capital had been attracted, yet only two mines were in operation. Together, they employed less than 90 men and produced only 31,000 tons of bituminous coal annually. Two factors were chiefly responsible for the failure of local mining companies. Coal deposits were both meager and expensive to exploit, and, more important, few mill owners learned how to burn Rhode Island coal efficiently. Instead, they preferred to import their supplies from Nova Scotia.

For developments between 1800 and 1860, see *Acts and Resolves*, May, 1808, pp. 16–17; February, 1809, pp. 13–17, 25–28; October, 1809, pp. 10, 34; June, 1811, p. 3; February, 1812, p. 18; June, 1812, pp. 10–11; October, 1812, p. 6; June, 1813, p. 6; May, 1825, pp. 46–48; January, 1827; p. 5; *An Enquiry into the Chymical Character . . . of Coal, Lately Discovered at Rhode Island* (Boston, 1808); Reports to the General Assembly, 7:36 (February 2, 1813); *ibid.*, addenda:4 (1824–1860); *Providence Journal*, July 27, 1826; Petitions Not Granted, January, 1829; *A Report . . . on the Memorial of the New England*

Though the majority of base metal firms were relatively small undertakings, some very large enterprises emerged after 1830.[44] Of the 142 firms in Providence County reported in the 1860 census, sixteen were capitalized at $50,000 or more. They accounted for almost three-quarters of the $4,100,000 invested in the Rhode Island industry. The largest firm was the American Screw Company of Providence. Capitalized at $1,000,000, it came into being through the merger of the Eagle and New England companies and employed 600 workers, half of them women. An affiliated venture, the Providence Iron Company, had a capital of $246,000 and employed another 200 workers. It had been organized by the

---

Coal Mining Company, for Encouragement from the State (n.p., 1838). The legislature rejected the latter report, including a recommendation that it lend the corporation $5,000 from United States funds deposited with the state. The committee justified state support with the argument that the mine would "reduce the price of fuel, [and] retain its cost within our own state." It "is the policy of all wise governments," concluded the report, "to encourage the development of hidden sources of wealth . . . and thereby promote the industry and increase and multiply the comforts of the people." See also, Miscellaneous Papers of the General Assembly, folder 13 (1841–1845); *Acts and Resolves*, October, 1835, pp. 50–52; January, 1838, p. 119; June, 1839, p. 36; June, 1840, pp. 3–4; George H. Ashley, *Rhode Island Coal* (Bulletin 615, United States Geological Survey, Washington, 1915), 8–11; Carroll, *Rhode Island*, 2:926; George Adams, *The Rhode Island Register . . . , 1853* (Boston, 1853), 107; Schedule Five, Seventh Census of the United States, 1850, Rhode Island volumes, 5:183–184; 10:301; *Manufactures, 1860,* pp. 545–548.

[44] The analysis of the base metal industry is based on *Acts and Resolves*, October, 1836, pp. 96–99; January, 1838, pp. 105–107; October, 1838, pp. 22–25; October, 1840, pp. 32–35; October, 1845, p. 56; October, 1845, p. 70; June, 1847, pp. 53–56; May, 1848, pp. 12–15; January, 1854, p. 301; May, 1860, pp. 17–18; Petitions Not Granted, May, 1848; June, 1851; 1 *Rhode Island* 312 (1850); *Statistics, 1840,* pp. 58–59; Schedules Five, Seventh and Eighth Census of the United States, 1850 and 1860, Rhode Island and Providence County volumes, *passim; Manufactures, 1860,* pp. 545–548; *Transactions,* 1857, pp. 88–89; *Report on Industrial Statistics, 1860,* p. 21; *Book of Rhode Island,* 184; *Commerce, Manufactures and Resources of Providence,* 34, 101; Davis, *The New England States,* 4:2528–2568 *passim; Dictionary of American Biography,* 3:143–144; *Facts and Estimates, 1844,* p. 9; Grieve, *Picturesque Narragansett,* 45; *History of Rhode Island,* 232–233; *Industrial Advantages of Providence* (Providence, 1889), 57, 59, 63, 114; Keach, *Burrillville,* 161–162; Moore, *Providence Almanac, 1844,* pp. 66–67; *North Providence Centennial,* 33–35, 51; J. G. Dudley, *A Paper on the Growth, Trade, and Manufacture of Cotton* (New York, 1853), 81–83; Peck and Earl, *Fall River and its Industries,* 25.

New England Screw Company to manufacture screw rods, but when the enterprise proved unsuccessful, the proprietors had incorporated it as a separate company and the factory had been converted to nail production. Apart from the Corliss Steam Engine Company and the Providence Machine Company, which were capitalized at $300,000 and $200,000 respectively, the other major undertakings were much smaller enterprises with resources ranging from $50,000 to $150,000. A number of factories, including the Cove Machine Company, Brown and Sharpe, and the Hope Iron Foundry in Providence, Fayles, Jencks and Sons in Central Falls, and the Union Butt Company in Cranston, were capitalized at less than $50,000 but also operated on a relatively large scale. In all, twenty-nine Providence County firms employed 35 or more workers and twelve employed 100 or more.

Base metal firms manufactured a wide variety of goods. As during the initial phase of industrialization, they made machinery, castings, edge tools, hinges, nuts, bolts, screws, nails, and agricultural implements, but, in some instances, such as the manufacture of builders' hardware and horseshoe nails, production methods were so different that for all practical purposes entirely new industries had come into being. Manufacturers also introduced a number of new lines, including gas burners, pipe, stoves, carpet sweepers, sewing machines, safes, cutlery, files, springs, valves, and rivets.

This diversity gave the industry a significance out of all proportion to the size of its capital or labor force. Since it geared production to staples, such as screws, hardware, and stoves, or to specialty lines, such as engines, sewing machines, and winches, it was not dependent upon a single market. Though deeply affected by general economic trends, therefore, and especially hard hit by the depressions of 1837 and 1857, the industry's broad interests gave it strength and resilience.

In certain respects, manufacturers of textile machinery did not enjoy this advantage. As suppliers to the notoriously erratic cotton and woolen industries, they assumed considerable risks. Moreover, a single invention could destroy the market for a particular piece of equipment, and in a field so specialized, firms encountered difficulty shifting production to new lines either within or outside the textile industry. Although most undertakings were so small that the failure of a single venture had a slight economic impact, their very smallness was an additional liability. For most of them lacked the resources to stay in business during extended depressions.

By 1860, the textile machinery industry consisted of 51 firms, absorbed more than $1,000,000 in capital, and employed almost 1,560 workers. This growth had been achieved in a variety of ways. Some ventures expanded by making technological contributions. In 1838, for example, James S. Brown of North Providence devised a metal boring machine which produced a particularly smoothly milled speeder tube. This facilitated the passage of the rover and increased spinning output. Brown's American speeder, a further improvement, followed in 1852, and by the Civil War he was employing 150 men and producing $100,000 worth of goods annually. The brothers-in-law David G. Fayles and Alvin Jencks of Central Falls built their business around Thorpe's spinning ring, which they perfected in 1845. Over the next fifteen years they expanded their labor force to 50 men and in 1860 valued their production at $45,000. The Phoenix Iron Foundry established its reputation by constructing the first American calico printing machines, by introducing a friction pulley, and by making gear wheels and calendering machinery. In 1860 it employed 100 workers and manufactured $75,000 worth of equipment. Alpheus Burges of Providence claimed to have pioneered the manufacture of industrial leather belting in the early 1830's. By the Civil War his family enterprise employed 18 men and did $60,000 worth of business annually.

Some firms expanded by manufacturing under license arrangements. Such was the case with Fayles and Jencks, which in 1833 began making Hubbard's rotary pump, and with Larned Pitcher and James S. Brown, which in 1840 began producing the Brown and Roberts spinning mule, an English invention.

Still other undertakings, particularly the older firms, based their expansion on engineering excellence. The Franklin Foundry and

TABLE 16

THE RHODE ISLAND BASE METAL INDUSTRY IN 1850 AND 1860[45]

(A) 1850

Towns	Firms	Capital	Employees	Value of Production
Bristol	5	$ 33,500	37	$ 81,400
Warren	5	11,900	17	20,432
Cranston	1	5,000	10	9,000
Johnston	1	2,150	3	2,300
Providence	25	474,000	2,022	1,426,900
North Providence	19	310,000	366	98,000
Cumberland	4	101,000	116	118,130
Smithfield	6	100,500	78	85,600
Burrillville	2	30,000	33	37,600
Warwick	4	12,600	16	17,500
Expanding Towns	72	1,080,650	2,698	1,896,862
Glocester	1	1,500	3	5,100
Scituate	2	5,500	9	6,600
Coventry	3	24,000	85	71,000
Richmond	1	5,000	13	10,476
Hopkinton	4	22,400	35	20,575
Westerly	2	2,800	6	22,024
Newport	2	14,000	12	13,000
Static Towns	15	75,200	163	148,775
Rhode Island	87	1,155,850	2,861	2,045,637

(B) 1860

Cranston	1	30,000	50	80,000
Johnston	1	3,000	3	1,600
Providence	94	2,977,000	3,131	4,019,594
North Providence	25	582,500	720	913,248
Cumberland	8	66,600	87	64,856
Smithfield	6	129,000	164	182,000
Burrillville	1	30,000	30	50,000
Glocester	1	5,000	8	6,000
Scituate	5	20,300	36	25,115
Providence County	142	3,843,400	4,229	5,342,413
Kent County	10	47,000	117	137,945
Bristol County	3	3,200	7	4,550
Newport County	9	67,750	187	186,276
Washington County	9	159,500	150	134,450
Rhode Island	173	4,120,850	4,690	5,805,634

[45] Compiled from Schedules Five, Seventh and Eighth Census of the United States, 1850 and 1860, Rhode Island and Providence County volumes, *passim.*

Machine Company had its origins as the Providence "Cupola" in 1800, incorporated in 1836, and by the Civil War had 250 workers engaged in the manufacture of cotton spinning and weaving equipment, calico printing machines, and castings valued at $225,000. The Providence Machine Company, another old firm, was almost as large. It was owned by Thomas J. Hill, who had moved from Pawtucket to Providence to manage the machine shop in the Slater steam mill following the 1829 Wilkinson failure. Hill was taken into partnership four years later, in 1834, when the firm divided its machinery and cotton manufacturing into separate enterprises. He bought out Slater's heirs in 1846, and by 1860 controlled a $200,000 undertaking with 175 employees and an output valued at $150,000.

Charles T. James, who was later to become a leading cotton manufacturer, played the rôle formerly taken by the Wilkinsons in extending the reputation for Rhode Island equipment. James learned the machinery business in the mid-1820's, and traveled from Maine to South Carolina, and from New Jersey to Indiana, constructing mills and supervising the installation of machinery. He is reputed to have erected or installed, between 1830 and 1851, more than thirty mills and some 300,000 spindles and 8,000 looms.

Like the base metals, the precious metals industry was dependent for its remarkable growth in the period 1830 to 1860 on technological improvement, developed skill, and reputation. It also, but to a lesser extent than base metals, sought the economies of large scale, mechanized production; and even more than base metals, it was concentrated in Providence. As during the formative stage of development, the majority of manufacturers produced the cheaper lines of gold-filled, gold-plated, or paste jewelry, but a few specialized in high quality work and silversmithing especially increased in importance.[46]

[46] The discussion of the precious metal industry is based on Bicknell, *Rhode Island*, 3:841–842; *Book of Rhode Island*, 208; *Commerce, Manufactures and Resources of Providence*, 31, 78–81; Davis, *The New England States*, 4:2500–2517; Field, *Rhode Island*, 3:373–381; *History of Rhode Island*, 165–166; Mayo, "Three Men in an Industrial Century," 4–5; *Statistics, 1840*, p. 59; Schedules Five, Seventh and Eighth Census of the United States, 1850 and 1860, Rhode Island

Jabez Gorham established the Rhode Island silver industry and his son John gave it a national reputation. Jabez had peddled his jewelry to Boston retailers. Convinced by these firms of the potential market for coin-silver articles, Gorham formed a partnership in 1831 with a young Boston silversmith, Henry L. Webster, and they began to make spoons, forks, thimbles, combs, and mugs. In 1847, when Jabez retired, management of the venture passed to his son John, who quickly manifested the typical traits of the Providence entrepreneur and proceeded to transform the industry. Dissatisfied with the prevailing style and scale of operation, he proposed to mechanize production while at the same time maintaining the firm's traditional standards of quality. Visits to the Springfield Arsenal and the Philadelphia Mint confirmed his belief that large scale, mechanized silversmithing was feasible, and when he returned to Providence he designed new equipment and installed a steam engine to operate it. Next, in 1852, he toured Europe to get additional ideas, visiting factories in Birmingham and Sheffield, the Woolwich Arsenal, and the London Mint, then crossing to the continent to inspect the work of silversmiths in Brussels and Paris. Gorham was particularly impressed by the superior craftsmanship and productivity of English workers. He realized that his expansion program would fail unless he increased the supply of artisans. To train additional apprentices he brought English silversmiths, diesinkers, and chasers to Providence to help the twelve journeymen he already employed as instructors. The Gorham enterprise was soon operating on a substantial scale and by the outbreak of the Civil War it was well on the way to becoming a national rather than a regional venture.

The manufacturers of plated and other cheaper lines of jewelry, a few of them very large enterprises, also raised the precious metal industry's importance. By 1850, the Warren partnership of Smith, Dee, and Eddy employed 90 people, a third of them women, Sackett, Davis and Company of Providence had a labor

and Providence County volumes, *passim; Transactions,* 1857, pp. 85–88; 1869, pp. 81–85. For an advertisement of steam for hire, see *Providence Journal,* February 15, 1848.

force of 80, and five other Providence firms each employed 25 or more workers. By the Civil War, Jabez Gorham and Son and Williams and Brown were the largest undertakings, employing 190 and 130 people respectively. However, the typical firm had only a dozen workers and was too small to operate its own power plant. This explains why the jewelry industry shifted from the east side of the Moshassuck and Providence rivers to what became the central Providence business district. There, small ventures

TABLE 17

THE RHODE ISLAND PRECIOUS METAL INDUSTRY IN 1850 AND 1860[47]

Towns	Firms		Capital		Employees		Value of Production	
	1850	1860	1850 $	1860	1850	1860	1850 $	1860
Warren	1		100,000		90		115,000	
Providence	57	82	499,200	1,450,900	594	1,871	1,182,875	3,015,725
North Providence		5		43,600		94		57,839
Smithfield		4		30,800		78		14,000
North Kingstown	1		15,000		20		40,000	
Rhode Island	59	91	614,200	1,525,300	704	2,043	1,337,875	3,087,564

could secure the economies of mechanized production by hiring power from a variety of sources ranging from cotton, planing, grist, and dyewood mills to iron foundries, and jewelry, stove, and nail factories. The system of hiring power also enabled many craftsmen to go into business for themselves. Between 1850 and 1860 the number of firms increased from fifty-nine to ninety-one and the labor force from some 700 to more than 2,000.

The precious metal working industry, then, passed through most of the stages of development already noted in the textile and base metal fields. Step by step, the workshop form of operation gradually disappeared as output increased, especially in the manufacture of the cheaper grades of articles. Though craftsmanship and the apprenticeship system retained their central importance, manufacturers relied increasingly upon unskilled workers for many phases of production, and wherever possible they installed power-driven machinery. Despite the size of the largest undertakings, no

[47] Compiled from Schedules Five, Seventh and Eighth Census of the United States, 1850 and 1860, Rhode Island and Providence County volumes, *passim*.

precious metal firm had taken the step of incorporating. Instead, like the majority of Rhode Island industrial ventures, they operated as partnerships or as family firms.

TABLE 18

RHODE ISLAND INDUSTRIAL CAPITAL, 1850[48]

Towns	Clothing	Maritime	Metals	Miscellaneous	Mining	Textiles	Woodworking	Total
Bristol	$ 11,100	$ 56,300	$ 35,700	$ 5,100	$	$ 204,400	$ 42,000	$ 354,600
Warren	14,850	75,837	118,600	13,200		125,000	2,500	349,987
Cranston	700		8,050	100	8,000	239,000	2,200	258,050
Johnston			3,650			235,400	5,600	244,650
Providence	172,975	174,500	973,200	307,843	20,300	769,300	130,400	2,548,518
North Providence			310,500	86,000		892,995	60	1,289,555
Cumberland			101,000	10,600	82,000	923,000	22,000	1,138,600
Smithfield	1,000		107,350	24,000	21,000	2,049,000	5,900	2,208,250
Burrillville	4,250		34,625	2,200		423,000	15,625	479,700
Warwick	1,400		13,400	5,400		989,500	15,400	1,025,100
Expanding Towns	206,275	306,637	1,706,075	454,443	131,300	6,850,595	241,685	9,897,010
Barrington				4,000	49,000			53,000
Glocester	1,200		3,800	3,000		103,000	23,860	134,860
Scituate			17,500	23,000		560,000	2,500	603,000
East Greenwich	8,375		3,100	2,300		251,000	6,000	270,775
Coventry	1,500		24,000	2,500	150	354,000	6,425	388,575
North Kingstown			15,000			127,500		142,500
South Kingstown			1,600	1,000		248,000	1,000	251,600
Richmond	400		5,500	3,000		246,200	4,800	259,900
Hopkinton			22,700	3,900		178,500	5,600	210,700
Westerly		2,500	2,800	3,800	4,500	75,000		88,600
Newport	800	37,000	12,000	10,300		340,000	16,000	416,100
Middletown								
Portsmouth		11,000		1,000	30,000	1,600		43,600
Tiverton			2,900	3,800	800	172,500	1,500	181,500
New Shoreham	1,025	500	250	4,500				6,275
Static Towns	13,300	51,000	111,150	66,100	84,450	2,657,300	67,685	3,050,985
Foster			2,200				4,300	6,500
West Greenwich						31,000	7,800	38,800
Exeter			1,900			68,000	4,800	74,700
Charlestown				2,000		12,700		14,700
Jamestown								
Little Compton			1,500	2,000				3,500
Declining Towns			5,600	4,000		111,700	16,900	138,200
Rhode Island	219,575	357,637	1,822,825	524,543	215,750	9,619,595	326,270	13,086,195

As the dynamic factor in the Rhode Island economy, industrialization exercised a rising influence on the rate of economic growth. Those communities which developed the most' extensive manufac-

[48] Compiled from Schedules Five, Seventh Census of the United States, 1850, Rhode Island volumes, *passim*. Footwear is included in clothing; shipbuilding,

turing interests also achieved the highest sustained rate of expansion. Throughout the first half of the nineteenth century, the leading industrial centers in the Blackstone and Pawtuxet valleys, namely Warwick, Providence, North Providence, Cumberland, and Smithfield, grew extremely rapidly. Though some of the towns which took up manufacturing on a large scale during the second phase of industrialization—Burrillville, East Greenwich, Hopkinton, Westerly, and Tiverton—exhibited comparable short term growth characteristics, others—North and South Kingstown, Newport, Bristol, and Warren—merely reversed the downward trend of economic activity or overcame extended periods of economic stagnation. In one case, that of Barrington, the establishment of the town's only industry, two brick works employing in 1850 a total of 120 workers, brought about a sharp increase in population. But some of the static and most of the declining towns developed no manufacturing interests at all, and the other communities in these two groups industrialized only to a very limited extent.

---

ropemaking, whaling, fishing, and such products of the sea as candles, soap, and oil are categorized as maritime; the metals category includes both base and precious metals, textile machinery, and, unlike Table 16, it extends to the capital employed by such artisans as blacksmiths and tinsmiths; the Providence gas works, capitalized at $150,000, food processing enterprises, carriage makers, and wheelwrights are among the more important classes of industrial capital categorized as miscellaneous; the mining category includes coal mining, lime burning, brickmaking, and stonecutting; cotton, woolen, and dyewood-grinding capital, but not capital employed in manufacturing textile machinery and equipment, are included in the textile category; where the census takers did not differentiate between gristmilling and sawmilling capital, the resources have been allocated in the woodworking category.

Many towns, especially those in the static and declining categories, understated their industrial effort by reporting only major enterprises. The owners of a Bristol sugar refinery even refused to divulge information about their operations. The total industrial capital invested in Rhode Island, therefore, was probably between five and ten per cent larger than reported. Because the 1860 census was probably more complete, the actual rate of industrial growth during the pre-Civil War decade (from $13,000,000 in capital in 1850 to almost $24,000,000 in 1860) was probably lower than the figures seem to indicate. Data for industrial employment substantiates this view. Even allowing for the rise in capital investment per worker, it is nevertheless significant that the labor force grew by only fifty-five per cent during the decade. Industrial capital, by contrast, grew by almost eighty-two per cent.

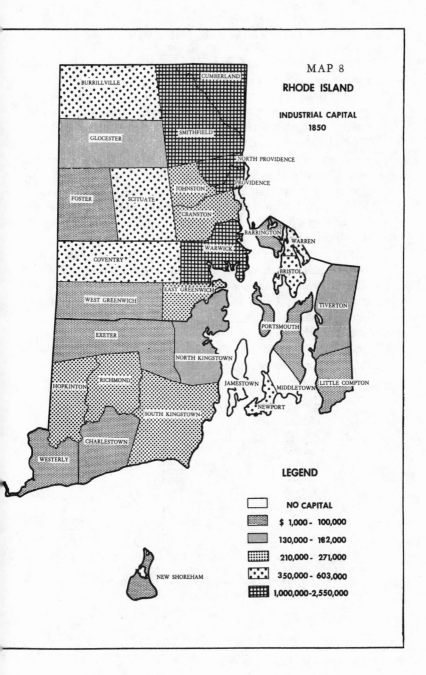

MAP 8

RHODE ISLAND

INDUSTRIAL CAPITAL
1850

BURRILLVILLE

CUMBERLAND

GLOCESTER

SMITHFIELD

NORTH PROVIDENCE

JOHNSTON

PROVIDENCE

FOSTER

SCITUATE

CRANSTON

BARRINGTON

WARREN

COVENTRY

WARWICK

BRISTOL

EAST GREENWICH

WEST GREENWICH

TIVERTON

EXETER

PORTSMOUTH

NORTH KINGSTOWN

JAMESTOWN

MIDDLETOWN

LITTLE COMPTON

HOPKINTON

RICHMOND

SOUTH KINGSTOWN

NEWPORT

CHARLESTOWN

WESTERLY

LEGEND

NO CAPITAL

$ 1,000 - 100,000

130,000 - 162,000

210,000 - 271,000

350,000 - 603,000

1,000,000-2,550,000

NEW SHOREHAM

They became the areas from which the expanding towns drew heavily for their labor supply.

But manufacturing was not the exclusive factor in the disparate growth rates exhibited by Rhode Island towns. For seafaring activities had stimulated expansion in the maritime centers until 1808 and, in the case of Bristol, until 1825, and the relatively stable agricultural and fishing communities of Middletown and New Shoreham did not industrialize, yet they grew more rapidly than many towns that did. The explanation lies in the rich soils of Middletown, which made for agricultural prosperity, and in the isolation of New Shoreham, which impeded emigration to the mainland. After 1840, Cranston's population increased more rapidly than did its manufacturing interests. Actually, the town's northeastern region became Providence's first suburb, and by 1860 adjacent areas of Johnston and North Providence had also become dormitories of the city. The Providence hinterland was developing into an urban continuum.

Despite the drag on economic development caused by the negligible amount of manufacturing carried on in some areas, the Rhode Island population increased more than two-and-a-half times as

TABLE 19

THE PRINCIPAL OCCUPATIONS OF RHODE ISLANDERS, 1860[49]

Occupation	Number	Percentage
Manufacturing	22,857	36.6
Agriculture	10,616	17.0
Services	9,176	14.5
Laborers	7,483	12.0
Commerce	4,990	8.2
Trades	4,031	6.5
Maritime	1,747	2.8
Transportation	1,192	1.9
Mining	316	0.5
Total	62,399	100.0

[49] *Population of the United States in 1860; Compiled from the Original Returns of the Eighth Census* (Washington, 1864), 656–657. Compare *Manufactures, 1860*, pp. 549–551, and the table of manufacturing employment in Mayer, *Economic Development and Population Growth*, 38.

rapidly during the era of industrial expansion as during the experimental phase of industrial development. The dominant rôle of industrialization in this growth can be judged from the census of 1860. By one reckoning, more than half the labor force worked in factories, and by another, more than a third. Manufacturing employed twice as many workers as farming, the second sector of the economy, and the disparity would be even more pronounced if those unclassified laborers who were really industrial workers were added to the manufacturing total. The services, including professional people and such others as laundresses and domestics, sustained approximately a seventh of the workers; commerce, primarily retailing, less than a tenth; and the trades, mainly construction, about a fifteenth. Significantly, maritime ventures, including shipbuilding, employed fewer than three per cent.

It was no mean achievement for the Rhode Islanders to have shifted so much of their effort from the sea to the land, from oceanic to manufacturing ventures. But in one sense, they had been too successful. Although the rapid growth of population led to such a sharp increase in demand for agricultural products and hence in land values that in 1860 Rhode Island farms were valued at over $19,500,000 as compared to $23,800,000 invested in industrial undertakings, the economy was seriously unbalanced.[50] Over half the manufacturing capital was absorbed by the cotton industry alone, and over four-fifths by textiles and metals. Much of the remainder was invested in petty enterprises, especially in the processing of food and other materials for local sale. In the long run, industrialization had reduced rather than increased economic diversification, and it had been at the expense of flexibility.

Overspecialization was especially pronounced at the local level. Most towns had only one principal source of employment other than farming. In the majority of Blackstone and Pawtuxet valley

[50] *Agriculture of the United States in 1860; Compiled from the Original Returns of the Eighth Census* (Washington, 1864), 126.

localities it was cotton manufacturing or, in the case of Burrillville, woolen manufacturing. Some coal was mined in Cumberland. Smithfield made scythes, Burrillville edge tools, Johnston chemicals, Cranston carpet sweepers, North Providence steam engines, and Scituate wooden combs. But many of these undertakings were relatively small, employed only a tiny fraction of the total industrial labor force, and, in some villages, were the sole source of employment. The level of diversification was even lower in other parts of the state. According to the 1850 census of Washington County, a jurisdiction with almost 16,500 inhabitants, less than 120 people were employed in industrial ventures outside of textile manufacturing, and over 40 of them were employed by just three firms. The majority of undertakings were petty—sawmilling, blacksmithing, tanning, shoe repairing, and harnessmaking—and could hardly be regarded as industrial enterprises at all. Comparable conditions prevailed in Newport County, where the overwhelming majority of non-textile firms were handicraft or service undertakings such as bakeries, tinshops, and grist and planing mills. The only notable exceptions were two rope walks, two fish oil works, a candle factory, a cooperage, a stone cutting works, and a coal mine. The latter enterprise employed 40 workers, but no other firm had more than ten employees and the typical undertaking was a two man operation.

Bristol County, which covered an area of only twenty-six square miles, developed a seemingly diversified economy. Though cotton manufacturing was easily the largest industry, it was not of overshadowing importance. At least a quarter of the firms were auxiliary to maritime activity, and a tenth—a saw mill, a hardware factory, two brick works, a clothing factory, a jewelry factory, and a sugar refinery—were substantial enterprises employing from 20 to 90 workers. But diversification did not automatically guarantee prosperity or economic growth. The sugar refinery excepted, all the larger non-textile ventures went out of business after 1850, and by the Civil War the Bristol County economy had only three props—farming, maritime enterprises, and cotton manufacturing.

Providence fared by far the best of all Rhode Island localities. The city both was the leading Rhode Island industrial center and had the best balanced manufacturing economy. Four factors were chiefly responsible for the concentration of activity in this relatively small area. First, the superior financial resources and banking facilities available in and around Providence, and the willingness to invest venture capital in promising undertakings, attracted many firms to the region. Second, the location of several steam engine works in the area enabled manufacturers to secure service and technical advice, and to adopt improvements as soon as they became available. Moreover, many firms installed larger engines than they required, and, by means of shafting and belting, supplied power to enterprises that could not afford to operate engines of their own. Arrangements of this kind were possible only in a heavily industrialized urban center such as Providence. There had to be a heavy demand for power, and buildings had to be both large and close together to permit many firms to obtain their power from a single source. Third, Providence became the hub of the Rhode Island transportation network. Manufacturers in and around the city not only enjoyed advantages in securing their raw materials, but they also had cheap and efficient access to expanding regional and national markets. Fourth, after a certain point in Providence's economic development (perhaps immediately after the depression of 1829), the city became the leading base metal working center. Thereafter, so long as economic conditions remained approximately the same, the Providence region generated the conditions most conducive to industrial expansion. The city attracted a disproportionately large share of the Rhode Island business. It became the place to which skilled workers, inventors, and capital gravitated.

Diversification was the logical result. In addition to its extensive cotton, wool, iron, jewelry, silver, and brass industries, Providence also manufactured large quantities of clothing (especially men's wear), hats, leather and rubber footwear, and, on a smaller scale, cigars, wagons, and carriages. Marble and stone cutting works, printing and bookbinding establishments, dyewood mills, distilleries, breweries, shipyards, rope walks, and leather working establishments were other sources of wealth. The city also had a large number of service undertakings, including blacksmithing, woodworking, and food processing enterprises, and a gas works.

Moreover, Providence never abandoned its commercial functions. Entrepreneurs drastically reduced their maritime investments, but they expended considerable money and effort developing profitable economic relations with the growing hinterland area. In this way, the city gradually expanded its rôle as the industrial and commercial capital of Rhode Island until it became the metropolitan center of southern New England.

CHAPTER FIVE

The Making of a Metropolis

WHEN Rhode Island declared its independence from Great Britain, international trade dominated Narragansett Bay life and Newport dominated the maritime economy. Eighty-five years later, on the eve of the Civil War, Rhode Islanders looked to manufacturing instead of to the sea for their livelihood and to Providence instead of to Newport for their economic leadership. Though both were important, neither accident nor necessity was chiefly responsible for the change. It was ambition. Providence entrepreneurs were not content merely to occupy the vacuum left by Newport's failure of nerve and concomitant demise as a center of maritime activity. As eager as they were to wring all they could from oceanic trade and as successful as they were in the endeavor, Providence leaders had no intention of contenting themselves with or of committing themselves irrevocably to the sea. Instead, they exploited the geographical advantages conferred upon them by the industrial trend (a trend they themselves started and abetted at every turn); and they capitalized upon every opportunity to make their city the economic center of an ever-widening hinterland. By 1850 they had developed the transportation and financial services that made a reality of the regional control they had been seeking. Providence had become, in the classic sense, a metropolis.

The creation of the transportation network well exemplifies this theme. Indeed, Providence entrepreneurs so clearly recognized the significance of transportation as an instrument for extending, consolidating, and protecting their economic influence that Rhode Island's transportation history is almost exclusively the story of the effort to expand the Providence hinterland. Except for the sailing packet industry, which was already thriving in colonial times, transporting people or things as a business was not organized until the last decade of the eighteenth century. Prior to the Revolution, both the local separatist spirit and the general maritime tradition inclined towns to be uncooperative even in building and maintaining roads. But the low volume of export staples to be freighted from the interior made highway construction far from urgent anyway. It was the increase in travel between northern New England and the Middle Atlantic region, the spread of settlement into isolated country areas, the ambition to bring the economies of eastern Connecticut and southwestern Massachusetts into the Rhode Island orbit, and the industrialization of the river valleys that rendered an efficient transportation system imperative.[1]

Providence business leaders strengthened their hand at each stage of technological advance. Turnpike roads and sailing packets first laid the basis of an integrated transportation network. Toll highways extended interior markets, provided access to new industrial communities, and linked Rhode Island to the major Massachusetts and Connecticut commercial centers. Sailing packets both complemented and, over certain routes, particularly to Long Island Sound, competed with turnpikes. Then, in the 1820's, steamboats drove sailing packets out of the passenger business and a canal threatened turnpike interests in the northeast. Finally, and within a decade, railways revolutionized transportation, forcing steampackets out of the lucrative branches of the carrying trade and, eventually, putting the canal and all except the feeder toll roads out of business. Whether moving by packet, stagecoach, wagon, canal barge, or railway car, most passengers and freight had to pass through Providence, the hub of transportation in Rhode Island.

Between the Revolution and 1825, the period of greatest activity, sailing packet operations were an integral part of Rhode Island's bustling maritime commerce. Besides linking the major and minor

[1] Merchant-manufacturers, in particular, demanded an efficient transportation system. Overland freight moved so slowly that early in December, 1803, Almy and Brown could only advise their consignees in Hartford, some seventy miles distant, that a shipment of yarn they were sending might be expected to arrive "in the course of the winter." See Edward C. Kirkland, *A History of American Economic Life* (New York, 1932), 305.

Narragansett Bay ports, packets shuttled between Providence or Newport and coastal communities from Boston to Baltimore and, conditions permitting, such interior ports as Hartford and Albany. They carried passengers, freight, commercial intelligence, and counting-house instructions, collected export cargoes, distributed imported goods, and, after 1789, strengthened the growing national spirit. Speedy, maneuverable sloops and schooners of seventy-five to a hundred tons were principally employed because they were too small to pay pilotage and docking fees. By 1825, eighteen such craft operated regularly on the Providence-Newport-New York run, eleven traded with Philadelphia, and six, including the brig *Mount Hope,* sailed to Baltimore.[2]

These packet lines, whether owned by Rhode Islanders or by other Americans, eventually forced the relocation of Providence's maritime facilities. Upon the contraction of foreign trade, India Point on the Seekonk River, which had been the base for Oriental and other international ventures, declined. Activity then came to be concentrated on the Providence River, where docks and warehouses were constructed to meet the packet industry's expanding requirements. Convoys of coaches, ranging up to twenty in number, daily lurched and swayed along the Boston and Providence postroad to connect with the New York packets, and by 1829 more than three hundred stages, other than those in local service, arrived at or departed from Providence each week.[3]

Though steamboats regularly plied between New York and Albany as early as 1807, Rhode Islanders did not see their first steamer until 1817, when the *Firefly* arrived from New York to establish a service between Providence and Newport.[4] But this experiment lasted only four months since, except under the most favorable conditions, the cumbersome *Firefly* could not compete with sailing packets. Four years elapsed before a second steamboat, the *Fulton,* arrived. Despite the stormy waters off Point Judith at the entrance to Block Island Sound, a regular semiweekly service

[2] Carroll, *Rhode Island,* 2:824–825, 832; Field, *Rhode Island,* 2:506–509.
[3] Dow, *History of Steam Navigation,* 8, 10.
[4] *Providence Gazette,* May 31, 1817.

between Providence, Newport, and New York went into operation in 1821.

Sailing packet owners, fearing the loss of business, immediately protested. In 1822, they petitioned the General Assembly for relief, complaining that the steamboat monopoly granted Robert Fulton by the New York legislature plainly contravened both constitutional and republican principles by discriminating against vessels owned in other states. They asked that Rhode Island impose a fifty cent levy on each steamer passenger ticket sold. When the Assembly rejected this request, packet owners fought the steamboats by improving service and by cutting rates, but neither technique more than deferred steamboat supremacy. Steamer companies, whether chartered in New York or Rhode Island, soon preëmpted both passenger and express traffic, leaving the less lucrative bulk and heavy freight business to the sailing packets.[5]

Steamboat owners had no sooner driven the sailing packets from the passenger business, than they too began struggling among themselves over the spoils.[6] In 1831 one line offered passage from Providence to New York, including meals, for $6. A competitor immediately countered with a deck passage fare of only $3. Rivalry also reduced the traveling time between the two ports. Though a twenty-hour passage had been usual in 1825, a decade later some trips took as little as eleven hours.

Upon the opening of the Providence and Boston railroad in 1835, the transportation pattern again changed. To be sure, it was to be many years before passengers could travel by train from Boston to New York, but railroad companies intensified competition within the packet industry by operating their own steamers or by making alliances with particular steamboat lines. Railroads also changed the traffic load, forcing steamboat companies to raise their

[5] Petitions Not Granted, May, 1823; *Providence Gazette*, May 14, 17, June 18, 1823; Dow, *History of Steam Navigation*, 9–13, 16. See also, Miscellaneous Papers of the General Assembly, folder 9 (1821–1825), for a report of a Scituate town meeting in September, 1822, urging that New York steamboats be barred from Rhode Island waters.

[6] Dow, *History of Steam Navigation*, 9–16, 18–21; *Acts and Resolves*, October, 1837, pp. 42–44.

investments substantially and to make their operations more flexible. Only very large and costly vessels, such as the five hundred and seventy-six ton *Narragansett*, could accommodate the hundreds of Boston passengers carried on a single train, and beginning in 1837, when the railway inaugurated services from Providence to Stonington, travelers between Boston and New York had the choice of transferring to steamers in either Rhode Island or Connecticut.

Earnings were so low throughout the decade of intense railroad competition from 1835 to 1845 that most packet enterprises encountered serious difficulties. When the Atlantic Steamboat Company placed the *Richmond* in service in 1837, the Boston railway canceled all special trains so that passengers arriving from New York on the *Richmond* would face a nine-hour delay in Providence if they missed the regular Boston connection. By 1840 this tactic forced the *Richmond* out of service. Though some other companies were not immediately bankrupted by such methods, most steamers were driven into the freighting business, and in 1848 the railroads shifted their terminals from the Providence waterfront to a newly constructed union station. Thereafter, train schedules paid little heed to steamer operations.

A notable exception occurred in 1851, when William P. Williams and Benjamin Buffum organized the Commercial Steamboat Company as a freight line to New York. The railroads then slashed rates and the steamboat company retaliated by entering the passenger business. Though freight charges to New York fell from eight to two cents a cubic foot and passenger fares to fifty cents, the steamer enterprise prospered. Forced to compromise, the railroads abandoned freight competition. In return, the steamer company withdrew its passenger vessels. By 1855, the company was operating a daily freight service to New York and, by 1858, it was despatching two and sometimes three steamers daily. However, completion of the Old Colony railroad from Boston to Fall River in 1846 had opened a superior train-steamer freight route to New York and eventually, this reduced the significance of Providence as a through freight traffic center.[7]

[7] Field, *Rhode Island*, 2:515–517.

Turnpike companies either succumbed, as had the packets, to railroad competition or were bought out by state and local authorities. In the interim transitional phase of Rhode Island's development into an industrialized society, they provided an essential service. Initially, promoters sought commercial rather than industrial ends and were especially interested in extending markets into new territory. Later, turnpikes became increasingly significant in the flow of raw materials and finished goods to and from Rhode Island factories. While shareholders expected a reasonable return on turnpike investments, they anticipated additional benefits as merchants or manufacturers, and they cast themselves in the rôle of public benefactors.

The first of forty-six toll road corporations, the Glocester West Turnpike Company, received a charter in February, 1794. Its organizers clearly perceived the beneficial effects of rebuilding and maintaining the road from the Chepachet Bridge in Glocester to the Connecticut line. The "mercantile . . . community will find an advantage," they argued, "as it cannot fail to extend . . . trade and create a preference for Rhode Island markets throughout an extensive tract of back country. Nor can the agricultural part expect less benefits, for it is evident that the value of their productions and even of their farms will appreciate in the same ratio as facility is given to the transportation of their produce to market, and the mere traveller whether for business or pleasure, while he cheerfully contributes to defray the expense, will partake of the general joy resulting from a measure so well calculated to advance the interests of society at large."[8]

Similar arguments later supported the extension of this toll road to Providence. The promoters then contended that "our roads should be of safe, easy, and pleasant passage. Not merely because we should thereby induce travellers . . . to take their route this way rather than to pass round our State" but because "our principal towns are the natural market for the country around. . . . In the

[8] Granted Charters, 1:24 (1790–1800); *Acts and Resolves*, February, 1794, pp. 9–11; October, 1794, pp. 3, 15–16; February, 1800, p. 11; June, 1800, p. 4; October, 1800, p. 13.

present condition of our roads people in the interior carry their produce to market and supply themselves with imported goods at Boston, Norwich, Hartford, and even New York . . . rather than pass over roads so crooked, rough, and unimproved as ours."[9]

In 1794, Providence merchants also proposed spending $600 of their own money and $10,000 raised by lottery to reconstruct the highway passing through Johnston, Scituate, Foster, and Coventry to Norwich, Connecticut. They too saw the turnpike as an instrument of economic aggrandizement. The road was to revert to public ownership as soon as the proprietors recovered their capital plus a six per cent return on the investment.[10]

A legislative committee investigating alternate routes from Providence to Douglas, Massachusetts, had the same clear appreciation of the relationship between the transportation system and economic growth. It acknowledged that one route would pass through an undeveloped region containing valuable stands of shipbuilding timber, but, it concluded, such "is not the material object. . . . The benefit to be derived to the community is from the abundant produce of that extensive and fertile country lying beyond the northerly line of this State; and which from the expense and inconvenience of travelling bad roads to our market, now go to add to the opulence and respectability of . . . Boston, although the latter is a day or two journey further than Providence. The State therefore is deprived of this wealth, and in great measure too, only from a want of enterprise to make a good road to the distance of about sixteen miles."[11]

Toll road construction was also a recognized method of defending existing economic interests. For, as the promoters of the Louisquissett turnpike from Providence to northern Smithfield argued,

[9] Granted Charters, 2:42 (1801–1805); *Acts and Resolves*, June, 1804, pp. 22–25.

[10] *Acts and Resolves*, October, 1794, pp. 13–15; February, 1799, p. 8; February, 1800, p. 11; October, 1800, p. 3; February, 1801, p. 20; October, Second Session, 1803, p. 35; February, 1805, pp. 6–7.

[11] Granted Charters, 2:48 (1801–1805). See also, *Acts and Resolves*, February, 1805, pp. 26–28; October, 1806, p. 11; June, 1807, p. 9; October, 1808, pp. 22–24.

unless a road were built "there is reason to apprehend that the produce of the neigboring [*sic*] States, which has heretofore in great quantities been brought to our seaports for sale, will be diverted to other markets."[12]

In granting charters containing such privileges as corporate succession, eminent domain, tax exemptions, lotteries, and the right to take stone, gravel, and timber from adjacent public land, the General Assembly acknowledged the assertions of larger service to the community reiterated in these petitions, and though it regulated tolls and required companies to give free passage to certain users, it permitted turnpike proprietors a generous twelve per cent return on their capital before turning toll roads into freeways.[13]

Beginning in 1807, when Providence and Pawtucket textile manufacturers built a turnpike to serve both the industrial and the mercantile communities, toll roads became increasingly important to industrialization. Thus the names of the pioneer manufacturing families, such as Almy, Allen, Brown, Slater, and Wilkinson, figured prominently in the lists of turnpike incorporators, and routes were frequently described in relation to particular factories. The Hazards obtained one of the last turnpike charters in 1842. The road was to run from their mills at Peace Dale to the Narragansett Pier and was probably intended to give them an alternative to the Stonington railroad, whose discriminatory policies Rowland G. Hazard assailed. Sometimes, however, as in the Woonasquatucket River road between the North Providence villages of Manton and Centerdale, the distance was too short to

[12] Granted Charters, 2:2 (1801–1805); *Acts and Resolves*, October, 1805, pp. 23–26; June, 1807, p. 10.

[13] The turnpikes are listed in Joshua M. Addeman, *Index to the Acts and Resolves, 1863–1873* (Providence, 1875), but the routes and powers granted must be followed in the session laws themselves. Some companies were permitted to recoup their entire investment plus a twelve per cent return on capital. For individual histories see Frederic J. Wood, *The Turnpikes of New England* (Boston, 1919), 287–327; and *History of Rhode Island*, 31. See also, Thompson, *Moses Brown*, 254–256. For a measure prohibiting turnpikes, railroads, or bridge corporations from holding land in fee, for life or for lives, or for a term of years, or for any use other than that specified in the charter, see *Acts and Resolves*, January, 1840, p. 47. The statute was not designed to apply to any company chartered before the date of its passage.

warrant a toll road. In such cases, manufacturers raised funds by public subscription and themselves contributed generously.[14]

Providence was the chief beneficiary of toll road construction. Eighteen companies proposed to give direct access to the city, twenty others to construct through adjacent parts of Providence County, and still others to intersect the city routes in Kent and Washington counties. Although perhaps only half the corporations actually went into operation, those that did passed through the northern and western rather than the southern and eastern segments of the state. Thus the major routes radiated northeastward from Providence to Pawtucket to join the Boston turnpike; northward through Cumberland and Smithfield into western Massachusetts, and westward and southward across the breadth of Rhode Island into eastern Connecticut. In addition to freight, thousands of passengers were carried annually over the Boston and Providence turnpike to connect with New York packets, or after 1820, across the state via Providence and Pawcatuck to make ferry connections at Stonington or New London.[15]

As the large number of dormant corporations attest, turnpikes proved doubtful investments. For if traffic rarely fufilled expectations, construction costs usually exceeded them, and in the few instances of lucrative toll roads, the properties reverted to the state. Partly because of these financial uncertainties, and partly because of the search for other modes of transportation, applications for

[14] *Acts and Resolves*, June, 1807, pp. 19–23; October, 1842, pp. 44–46; Frank C. Angell, *Annals of Centerdale in the Town of North Providence* (Central Falls, 1909), 45–48. See also, *Acts and Resolves*, January, 1825, pp. 25–27, for authority granted to James DeWolf, proprietor of the Arkwright mills in Coventry, to erect a toll gate at the bridge over the north branch of the Pawtuxet River; Journal of the Providence Association of Mechanics and Manfacturers, vol. 3 (July 14, 1806), for additional evidence of the rôle of turnpikes in opening up markets for manufactures; and Granted Charters, 5:44 (July, 1815), for a petition from the Providence Manufacturing Company. See also, White, *Slater*, 239, for a statement that Slater held some $40,000 in turnpike stocks. The Hazard toll road was not built.

[15] The legislature chartered three turnpikes to run northeastward from Providence; they were the Providence and Boston, the Providence and Pawtucket, and the Pawtucket and Providence East. See *Acts and Resolves*, October, 1800, pp. 29–34; June, 1807, pp. 19–23; Granted Charters, 5:44 (June, 1815); *Acts and Resolves*, May, 1816, pp. 41–46; October, 1825, pp. 55–60.

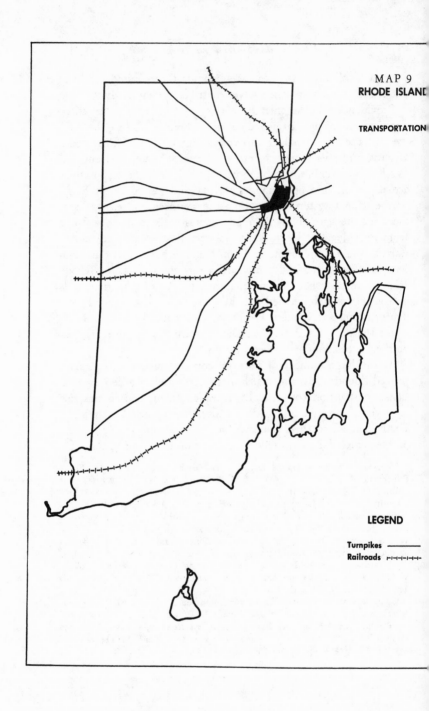

MAP 9
RHODE ISLAND

TRANSPORTATION

LEGEND

Turnpikes ————
Railroads ┝━┿━┿━┿━┿┥

turnpike franchises declined after 1830. The most successful road was the Providence and Pawtucket turnpike, which earned over $56,000 between 1809 and 1830 on an outlay of only $7,000 in capital, maintenance, and other operating costs. But these high profits prompted the state to take over the property in 1833. Public operation was even more lucrative, a net income of $40,000 being earned in the 1835–1836 fiscal year. This contrasted sharply with the Pawtucket and Providence East, a parallel turnpike whose shares fell from $50 to $16 when earnings failed to reach anticipated levels. Railroad construction sounded the death knell of both these toll roads in 1835, and a like fate befell the Providence and Pawcatuck two years later, when the Stonington line opened. Railways also put an end to the staging houses which had sprung up at such points as Hopkinton City.[16] To a lesser extent, canal construction also jeopardized turnpike investments.

A scheme for a canal between Providence and the upper Connecticut Valley was first proposed in 1796.[17] Grandiose in concept,

[16] Compare "Investigator," [pseud.], *Attempted Speculation of Lemuel H. Arnold and James F. Simons* (Providence, 1831) *passim; Examination of Certain Charges Against Lemuel H. Arnold* (Providence, 1831), *passim;* Griswold, *Hopkinton,* 55; Field, *Rhode Island,* 2:543–544; *History of Rhode Island,* 143. For the overburdening of the Providence and Norwich during the War of 1812, and for data on the low earnings of the Powdermill turnpike leading out of Providence to connect with the Glocester toll road to Connecticut, see Granted Charters, 5:16, 39 (1814–1817).

[17] The analysis of the Blackstone Canal which follows is based on Granted Charters, 1:46 (February, 1796); *Acts and Resolves,* February, 1796, pp. 15–21; June, 1823, pp. 28–39; January, 1826, pp. 37–41; May, 1827, pp. 58–60; *Providence Gazette,* April 27, May 18, June 1, 1822; January 8, March 1, 1823; April 30, 1825. See also, Davis, *Eighteenth Century Business Corporations,* 2:176; William Greene Roelker, "The Providence Plantations Canal," in *Rhode Island History,* 5:19–25, 54–56 (January and April, 1946); Field, *Rhode Island,* 2:497–500; Haley, *Lower Blackstone River Valley,* 153–158; *History of Rhode Island,* 32. The petitioners supporting canal construction in the 1820's were careful to remind the General Assembly that the scheme would do for Providence and Rhode Island what the Erie Canal was doing for New York. Two groups opposed construction: mill owners on the Blackstone River who feared that their water privileges would be injured, and residents of East Greenwich who feared intensified competition in agricultural produce shipped to the Providence market from the Worcester area. See Granted Charters, 8:11–13 (1823–1825).

the project reflected the soaring ambition of Providence merchants. They planned nothing less than the diversion of northwestern New England trade from Springfield, and of Worcester trade from Boston. Everyone, especially residents of interior Massachusetts, was to benefit. Cheap transportation of farm produce, lumber, firewood, lime, and stone would create larger, more profitable markets; canal towns would obtain cheaper imported goods; and the growth of manufacturing would stimulate employment. Eager to see these expectations realized, the General Assembly empowered the Providence-Plantations Canal Company to dig a channel northward from Providence along the Blackstone Valley. After seventy years, prescribed toll rates were to be subject to legislative review and the state entitled to a perpetual quarter-share of net profits. The privilege was to lapse if the promoters failed to complete the canal by 1811. And lapse it did. For despite John Brown's willingness to invest $40,000, Massachusetts refused to grant the enterprise a charter.

The resistance of Massachusetts interests delayed canal construction for a generation and limited the project's scope. Neither Middlesex Canal proprietors nor Boston and Springfield merchants deferred to Providence ambition until 1824, when they concluded that the waterway no longer threatened them. Promoted chiefly by Nicholas Brown, Edward Carrington, and Thomas P. Ives, the canal was to terminate not above Springfield in the Connecticut Valley but at Worcester. The waters of the Blackstone were apportioned among competing interests, particularly those acquired by manufacturers since 1796. Canal property was to be tax free for eight years. Four feet deep, forty-five feet wide, and over forty-four miles long, the canal with its forty-nine locks was completed in July, 1828. Some twenty horse-drawn freight barges, each of twenty to thirty tons capacity, and one passenger packet, sufficed to meet all traffic requirements.

From the outset, lack of foresight, inefficiency, and rapid obsolescence made the enterprise unprofitable. Instead of acquiring all riparian rights the corporation merely secured joint use. This embroiled the company in disputes over its management of water resources, deprived it of revenues from the sale of water to manufacturers, and aggravated problems of slack water navigation. Barges stranded frequently, sometimes for weeks, making freight deliveries, at best, uncertain. Defective planning also hurt the venture. Ironically, the promoters underestimated their capital requirements and turned away many would-be investors. Later, when construction costs proved higher than anticipated, additional funds could not be raised and the engineers had to condone shoddy work. Operating costs then soared. To obtain additional working capital, the promoters organized the Blackstone Canal Bank, but three years later, in 1834, when it became clear that the canal company would fail, the legislature authorized the bank to distribute its canal stock to its own shareholders and to retire from the transportation experiment.[18]

These difficulties brought the canal corporation to the point of collapse as early as 1835, but the actual demise did not come for another decade. Even then, legal entanglements delayed dissolution for another two years. In May, 1841, claiming an $11,000 loss from flood damage and an adverse legal decision, and asserting the dissipation of some $700,000 since 1825, the corporation threatened to abandon its property. Manufacturers interested in water privileges along the canal immediately protested. Three years later and again in 1846 the corporation sought to halt operations to facilitate construction of the Providence and Worcester railroad. Manufacturers once more protested, arguing that the corporation should not be permitted to abandon its property without first compensating mill owners, who, it was claimed, had public-spiritedly allowed the company to preëmpt their water rights. Finally, in 1849, after eight years of agitation, and after the railroad had been in operation for two years, the legislature author-

---

[18] W. G. Roelker and C. A. Collins, 3rd., *One Hundred Fifty Years of Providence Washington Insurance Company, 1799–1949* (Providence, 1949), 59–65; *The Hundredth Milestone: . . . the Blackstone Canal National Bank* (no imprint), 4–10.

ized the corporation to disband under rules carefully safeguard-
ing the interests of all parties.[19]

Although the Blackstone Canal failed to meet expectations, for
more than a decade it served Providence's expanding needs. Entrepreneurs extended their sway over the rapidly developing communities to the north and reached into Massachusetts in search of
markets and investments. Even the canal's failure testified to the
city's strength: the financing of the Worcester railway, despite the
loss of more than $700,000 in the canal venture, demonstrated
both Providence's capital reserves and its economic resilience.

Because Rhode Island straddled the sea-level overland route between Boston and New York, its railroads developed as integral
parts of a New England rather than a purely state-wide transportation system. Nevertheless, routes and policies had local repercus-
sions and, as in the earlier turnpike, packet, and canal phases,
Providence made itself indispensable to regional communications.

After several false starts, the first railway, from Boston to Providence, opened in 1835. Rhode Island first authorized the Massachusetts Board of Internal Improvements to construct a line but
it withdrew the franchise when the board failed to act.[20] Then, in
1831, the legislature incorporated private Massachusetts promoters
as the Providence and Boston Railroad Company. They too gave
up their privilege, largely because Rhode Island imposed impossible conditions. Though the legislature originally authorized a
capital of $500,000, a regional monopoly, branch line privileges,
and valuable tax concessions, it later required the company to purchase the Providence and Pawtucket turnpike and to compensate
the Pawtucket and the Providence East Turnpike Company for an-

[19] Petitions Not Granted, May, 1841; January, 1844; January, June, October,
1846; June, 1847; *Acts and Resolves*, January, 1849, pp. 60–67. Three other
canals were proposed but not built: one was to improve the Pawcatuck River for
lumber shippers, the second to link Narragansett and Boston bays via the East
River, the third to cut a ferry channel through Conanicut Island to facilitate
travel between Newport and the Stonington Railroad in Washington County.
Petitions Not Granted, January, 1827; *Providence Gazette*, November 7, 1818;
Acts and Resolves, January, 1854, pp. 296–298.

[20] Granted Charters, 10:9 (1828–1831); *Acts and Resolves*, May, 1828, p. 39;
June, 1828, pp. 42–45; June, 1831, p. 64.

ticipated loss of revenue, revoked the branch line grant, regulated
rates, and reserved the right to purchase the railway itself. Subsequent concessions modified these provisions insufficiently to satisfy
the promoters and the corporation never went into business.[21] Instead, another company, organized by leading Providence entrepreneurs, notably Nicholas Brown, Edward Carrington, Moses
Brown Ives, and Thomas Poynton Ives, built the short eastern rail
outlet in 1835. From its terminal at India Point it crossed the
Seekonk River to join a line from Boston. Significantly, the charter
said nothing about rate regulation or public ownership.[22]

A second road, commonly known as the Stonington line and the
Providence to Pawcatuck section of the Boston-New York route, was
chartered in 1832 and completed five years later. Various legislative restrictions limited the company's freedom of action. The chief
of these set a maximum annual return on capital, barred any in-
vestor from voting more than a quarter of the stock, reserved a
proportion of the shares for subscription by Rhode Island citizens,
and authorized the state to purchase up to a thousand shares and
to appoint one director. The railway established its terminal on
the southwestern shore of Providence harbor; passengers arriving
at India Point from Boston could either transfer to the Stonington
railroad by ferry, or complete the journey to New York by steam
packet. Since each railway operated a steamer service, rivalry be-

[21] Granted Charters, 11:9 (June, 1831); *Acts and Resolves*, October, 1831,
pp. 77–78; January, 1832, pp. 45–48; January, 1833, pp. 41–42. The legislature denied the corporation a monopoly of routes between Providence and Massachusetts, and refused to allow it a ten year period of grace before rate regulation became effective. See Petitions Not Granted, June, 1833.

[22] *Acts and Resolves*, May, 1834, pp. 35–43; January, 1835, pp. 28–30; October, 1842, pp. 68–69; June, 1853, pp. 170–172; Field, *Rhode Island*, 2:546;
Greene, *Providence Plantations*, 133–134; *History of Rhode Island*, 32. Although forbidden to do so, the railroad operated steamboats between Providence
and New York. See Granted Petitions, 62:43 (October, 1836); Reports to the
General Assembly, 10:2 (June 23, 1837); and, for ten memorials of protest
containing a total of nearly a thousand names, Petitions Not Granted, March,
1842. In 1853 the legislature authorized the Boston and Providence to acquire
up to ten per cent of the stock of the Providence and Plainfield Railroad, a
company which tried but failed to get a charter not subject to legislative amendment. See Granted Charters, 15:89½ (June, 1846).

came so intense by 1842 that the legislature had to require the Boston and Providence line to give unrestricted access and accommodation at its wharves to passengers and freight passing to and from the south.[23]

The Stonington line encountered political difficulties even before it opened, and financial problems arose soon after. Complaints about the acquisition of the right of way led to a provision that in appeals from condemnation proceedings, the railroad had to pay all court costs if it lost, its own costs if it won. The Assembly also required the company to erect fences along its route, made it liable for damages caused by fires started by its locomotives, and revoked the power to build branch lines. Financial difficulties also plagued the line's operations. Neither freight nor passenger traffic met expectations, in part because the company operated steamboats in competition with its own trains, and the railway could not service its bonds. Second and third mortgagors controlled the property until the corporation redeemed the road in 1843.[24]

Providence secured in 1847 a third rail outlet, the Providence and Worcester line, which was almost wholly owned by Rhode Islanders. As a replacement for the Blackstone Canal, the railway stimulated economic growth throughout the northeastern region, especially after the Boston line built a branch to Pawtucket and after the union station opened in Providence. These improvements gave Blackstone Valley communities rail connections with Boston, Worcester, Stonington, and, later, Fall River and Hartford.[25]

[23] *Acts and Resolves*, June, 1832, pp. 66–67; June, 1833, pp. 10–12; January, 1840, pp. 83–84; January, 1841, pp. 8–10; October, 1842, pp. 68–69.

[24] *Acts and Resolves*, January, 1836, p. 26; June, 1836, pp. 3–6; June, 1840, p. 24; Reports to the General Assembly, 9:91 (January, 1836); Petitions Not Granted, June, 1837; October, December, 1840; June, 1842; Greene, *Providence Plantations*, 134–135; *History of Rhode Island*, 32.

[25] *Acts and Resolves*, January, 1837, pp. 78–84; May, 1844, pp. 34–42; January, 1846, pp. 43–44; *Facts and Estimates of the Providence and Worcester Rail Road, passim.* High construction costs reduced earnings below the anticipated ten per cent per annum and, by the mid-1850's, halved stock values. See *Providence Journal*, April 9, 1855. The Worcester line enjoyed the unusual privilege of being able to take land for its right of way before paying damages or even instituting condemnation proceedings. An earlier proposal for a northern

Three other railroads gave access to Providence. Two, the Providence, Warren and Bristol, and the Fall River, Warren and Providence, completed in 1855 and 1860 respectively, served the eastern shore. The third, the Providence, Hartford and Fishkill, served eastern Connecticut. Fearing that a proposed northern line from Woonsocket to Connecticut would, like the Norwich and Worcester road, divert business from Providence, city leaders threw their support behind the Fishkill route which, they contended, would "increase the commerce of our ports, . . . accommodate and permanently benefit a great portion of our people, . . . and . . . create at the centre of the business of the State, a market for our manufactures and our commerce, which must largely increase the numbers and prosperity of our people." Trains were running between Providence and Hartford by 1854, but the company's failure to construct into the Hudson Valley soon plunged the line into bankruptcy. When the corporation defaulted on its obligations in 1857 and 1858, the city of Providence, which had invested $468,000 in the railroad, appointed trustees to take possession of the property and to operate the line in the interests of the bondholders.[26]

Only two other companies chartered during the period from 1830 to 1860 went into operation. One, projected to link Providence to Springfield via the Woonasquatucket Valley, actually terminated at Pascoag in Burrillville, and because the Civil War delayed construction, did not open until 1873.[27] The second, char-

outlet had been to convert the Pawtucket and Providence East Turnpike to a railroad and to extend its route up the Blackstone and Branch valleys into Connecticut. See *Acts and Resolves,* January, 1837, pp. 78–84.

[26] *Acts and Resolves,* August, 1850, pp. 6–18; October, 1850, pp. 7–18; May, 1856, pp. 106–117; Petitions Not Granted, June, 1846; January, 1848; *Providence Journal,* December 1, 1846; Greene, *Providence Plantations,* 138. Promoters of the Bristol line solicited stock subscriptions on a house to house basis, but voters divided on the question of authorizing the town to invest in the railroad. See *Byron Diman vs. The Providence, Warren, and Bristol Railroad Company,* 5 *Rhode Island* 130 (1858); Petitions Not Granted, June, 1852. The northern Woonsocket line received a charter but the corporation did not go into business. See also, Keach, *Burrillville,* 69–70.

[27] *Acts and Resolves,* January, 1857, pp. 62–75; Greene, *Providence Plantations,* 136–137.

tered in 1846 to link Newport to Fall River, attempted to capitalize upon Newport's accessibility. Its promoters envisioned an all-
weather rail terminus which would serve New England even in
what its promoters called "that dangerous season." They hoped
to stimulate economic expansion, partly by making the railroad an
additional reason for establishing a naval base for Newport. But
service did not begin until 1864 and then only after Newport and
Middletown had acquired the right of way as an inducement to
construction.[28]

In all, promoters submitted twenty-one railroad charter petitions between 1830 and 1860. Of the seventeen corporations created, only six had their lines operating when the Civil War broke
out. All served Providence. Two ran down the eastern shore of
Narragansett Bay to Warren and Fall River, the others ran to
Boston, Worcester, Hartford, and Stonington. Just as Providence
had earlier dominated packet, turnpike, and canal transportation,
so it became the hub of the Rhode Island railway system, occupy-
ing the center of a web of interests spun out in every direction and
drawing more and more southern New England communities into
its economic orbit.

Railroad regulation, a major political issue after 1835, was
largely a regional question, the clamor for rate equalization and
non-discriminatory policies being loudest in Washington County,
an area served only by the Stonington line. Opposition to controls
was strongest in Providence. As a major railroad junction, Providence benefited from both rate wars and discriminatory tariff
schedules, whereas Washington County, which expected to derive
great benefits from railroad construction, partly blamed its slow
rate of industrialization on railroad practices. Moreover, as heavy
investors in railway securities, the city of Providence and its residents were more likely to resist regulation than were people with
no proprietary interest in the transportation system.

In chartering railways the legislature imposed restraints with
one hand and dispensed assistance with the other. Provisions restricting earnings, requiring annual legislative reports, limiting

[28] *Acts and Resolves*, May, 1846, pp. 80–91; January, 1860, pp. 192–193;
May, 1860, pp. 28–32; Petitions Not Granted, June, 1846.

stock voting rights, or reserving shares for Rhode Island residents, were balanced by tax exemptions, gifts of land, investment of public funds, grants of monopolies, or authorizations to operate steamboats. This pattern grew out of the colonial tradition of regulating and encouraging ferry, wharf, bridge, mill, and factory proprietors, and of placing public welfare above private profit. To a limited extent, it also reflected suspicion of particular types of economic activity.

Since railroads were monopolies by nature as well as by legislative fiat, they were particularly susceptible to popular criticism. All inherited the general stigma attached to business corporations, a legacy of the English past, and those controlled by Boston or New York entrepreneurs were doubly suspect for fear that outside interests would take precedence over commonwealth.

Legislative restrictions, first imposed on the Stonington line and then extended to the railroad industry generally, focused initially on public safety, then on railroad discrimination. Warning devices —bells on locomotives and signals at level crossings—were required almost immediately, and later the Assembly enacted the principles of Campbell's Law, making common carriers liable in cases of wrongful or negligent death. Finally, attention shifted from safety to equality. In 1839 the legislature outlawed discrimination between inhabitants of the several states, making rates proportional to distance and equal treatment of connecting steamboats the standard of acceptable conduct. Neither this law nor the commission appointed to implement it satisfied railroad critics.[29]

Dissatisfaction mounted throughout the 1840's. Rowland G. Hazard, the prominent South Kingstown manufacturer, advanced one remedy in an essay, "Relations of Railroad Corporations to the Public," published in Hunt's *Merchants' Magazine* in December, 1849. Hazard contended that common carrier law could not bring about impartial railroad practices, for the "unprincipled autocrat

[29] *Acts and Resolves,* January, 1838, pp. 103–104; June, 1839, pp. 23–24; October, 1853, pp. 257–258; January, 1857, p. 9. Before the adoption of Lord Campbell's Act, common carriers were liable only in cases of injury. For an attempt to alter liability, see Miscellaneous Papers of the General Assembly, folder 19 (1855–1856), and for other examples of proposed safety legislation, see *ibid.,* folder 20 (1857–1858).

of Wall Street, with his plotting, subtle advisers" and "soulless
. . . corporation" could be restrained neither by competition nor
by moral obligation. Possessed of unlimited power, railways could
plunder the public, dominate regional economies and particular
businesses, and even humble legislators and judges. Since they
were created for public rather than for private benefit, railroads
should not discriminate against any region or class of users. Instead, they should behave as if they were competitive by making
terminal competition determine rates for intermediate points.[30]

Beginning in 1850, Hazard's views were supported by charges
of oppressive and vindicative discrimination. The Stonington line,
it was alleged, rewarded its friends and punished its enemies, and
deprived Washington County of the benefits of being on the main
route between Boston and New York. The railroad commissioners
dismissed these complaints in October, 1851, finding that rate dis-
crepancies resulted from economic necessity rather than from discrimination, and that railroads incurred proportionately higher
costs over short distances than over long ones. However, the commissioners did question the special treatment accorded some connecting stage coach lines, and in 1852 the legislature outlawed
such discrimination.[31]

Rhode Island's first comprehensive regulatory statute, adopted
in 1855, fell far short of equalizing freight and passenger rates.
In the debate on the bill, Hazard accused the Stonington road of
manipulating rates so as to monopolize the through freight business to New York, of punishing those who dared to prefer damage
claims against it, and of political chicanery. He feared the road's
power to control the legislature and pack the judiciary, thereby
destroying "even the hope of legal . . . relief." In such circum-

[30] Rowland Gibson Hazard, *Economics and Politics: A Series of Papers Upon
Public Questions* (Cambridge, 1889), *passim*, pp. 32–43.

[31] See Petitions Not Granted, in Special Railroad folder (1850–1856), for
fourteen petitions submitted in June, 1850, and January, 1851; *Acts and Resolves*, October, 1851, pp. 78–88; January, 1852, pp. 5–6. For the repeal of the
anti-discrimination statute, perhaps because 112 Hopkinton residents complained
that the law deprived them of railroad connections, see *ibid.*, January, 1853, p.
262.

stances, he thought, there could be no remedy "but one fearful to contemplate . . . revolution."[32] Other critics, including the majority of the railroad commissioners, also concluded that lines were more interested in profits than in community welfare. They noted that it was cheaper to ship coal from Providence to Worcester than to Woonsocket, and that rates were lower from Providence to Boston than from Boston to Providence. The minority dissented, contending that rates were intrinsically reasonable. Railroads had either to match prices for coal delivered via Norwich or not haul it at all. The choice was simple: competitive rate schedules or bankruptcy.[33]

Although the legislature refused to enact Hazard's program in its entirety, it conceded that abuses existed and that they should be corrected. The Assembly outlawed free passes and granted shippers the right to recover damages in cases of unwarranted delay. It also required railroads to furnish reasonable passenger and freight facilities, to transfer goods from one line to another free of charge, and to obtain legislative approval before abandoning any depot. But it refused to regulate rates.[34]

The transportation business gave Providence entrepreneurs an early and particularly effective instrument of regional aggrandize-

[32] Hazard, *Economics and Politics*, 44–54, 63–73. Hazard was speaking in favor of the equalization bill first proposed in 1851. See also, Petitions Not Granted, January, 1851, in Special Railroad folder (1850–1856). For the commissioners' report on Hazard's charges, see Reports to the General Assembly, 12:89–91 (October, 1851).

[33] *Acts and Resolves*, May, 1854, pp. 147–151; *Report of the Railroad Commissioners, January, 1854* (Providence, 1854), 3–8. See also, Petitions Not Granted, in Special Railroad folder (1850–1856), for an undated petition from Isaac Saunders and eight others expressing alarm at reports of unjust discrimination; and Miscellaneous Papers of the General Assembly, folder 18 (1853–1854), for a proposed investigation of alleged railroad wrongdoing.

[34] *Acts and Resolves*, January, 1855, pp. 13–16. For two earlier drafts and remonstrances in favor of regulation, one in January, 1854, the other undated but referred to the House Committee on Corporations on February 17, 1855, see Petitions Not Granted, in Special Railroad folder (1850–1856). For Hazard's speech on the bill, see Hazard, *Economics and Politics*, 74–114; and for South Kingstown and Woonsocket petitions, dated January, 1855, supporting Hazard, see Petitions Not Granted, in Special Railroad folder (1850–1856). A Richmond

ment. Radiating from the city like the spokes of a wheel, the communication system, with its successive packet, turnpike, canal, and railway components, channeled an ever richer hinterland trade through Providence warehouses. By exploiting the city's natural advantage as a convenient transfer point for freight and passengers moving along the busy route between Boston and New York; by drawing the products of eastern Connecticut and southwestern Massachusetts down to Providence rather than to other ports; by exchanging these commodities for imported goods; and by making the city the staging point for the raw materials and finished products of the emerging industrial communities—in short, by making Providence indispensable to producers and consumers throughout an expanding area—Providence leaders realized their ambitions. The city became, as they intended it should, the trade center of southern New England.

Providence emerged as the financial capital of Rhode Island at much the same time as it became the state's transportation, commercial, and industrial capital. Nor was the unbroken record of financial growth fortuitous. The entrepreneurs who built the city's banking institutions guarded their corporate reputations just as jealously as they defended their reputations as private businessmen. They raised banking capital from profits earned in trading and manufacturing ventures, then integrated their operations. But

---

town meeting complained that the Stonington line had tried to coerce one of the town's representatives, Abial S. Kenyon, into opposing the statute. See Petitions Not Granted, May, 1855, in *ibid.*, and, for the committee's rejection of the charge, Miscellaneous Papers of the General Assembly, folder 19 (1855–1856).

The statute also made roads liable for the safety of all goods they delivered in Rhode Island; it applied even in those cases where damage occurred on lines other than those controlled by the deliverer, including those operating outside the state. For six petitions, dated May, 1855, and January, 1856, protesting this section of the act, see Petitions Not Granted, in Special Railroad folder (1850–1856). For William L. Baker's characterization of Hazard's views as "contemptible humbug," see *Providence Journal*, June 20, 1855. For a later attempt to prevent railroads charging more for the short haul than for the long haul, see Miscellaneous Papers of the General Assembly, folder 20 (1857–1858).

such arrangements were only as strong as the weakest link, which they determined would not be their banks.

From their modest late eighteenth century beginnings, banking institutions quickly became indispensable to all phases of business life. After a relatively slow start, banks increased rapidly in number as well as in size. Throughout, they both reflected and abetted the expansion of the Rhode Island economy. Organized at the outset to serve the mercantile and agricultural communities, banks eventually became thoroughly involved in transportation and industrial developments.

Incorporation of commercial banks proceeded at an irregular rate. In general, requests for charters increased during the upswing in the business pendulum but declined or ceased entirely during the downswing. Growth was especially cautious during the formative period. Only two banks were operating by the beginning of 1800, one in Providence, the other in Newport. Although the legislature incorporated two additional banks that year, another in 1801, and eight more between 1803 and 1805, the maritime depression then discouraged further applications. Another corporation was formed in 1809 and three more toward the end of the War of 1812, but the postwar recession quickly halted expansion. Then, late in 1817, as the business boom gathered momentum, the legislature began receiving a trickle of petitions which, early the next year, became a flood. In the brief span of less than two years, the Assembly authorized nineteen new banks. This equalled the number that it had chartered over the preceding twenty-six years. However, the Panic of 1819 abruptly checked this growth. Business no sooner revived in 1821 than promoters resumed their pressure for a further expansion of the banking system. By 1824 the Assembly had created another seventeen banks. Although the sharp business crisis of 1825 put an end to new requests for charters, the lull was only temporary and five additional banks came into existence between 1826 and 1828. A further period of quiescence ensued until the effects of the depression of 1829 had worn off. The legislature resumed chartering banks in 1831; by 1836 it had created eleven more corporations. This upsurge was followed by the Panic of 1837 and by an extended period of economic sluggishness. No further banks were created for a decade. Then, for the first time in twenty-five years, there was a rush to incorporate. Between 1850 and 1856 the General Assembly granted forty-five petitions, more than were issued over the entire thirty years from 1790 to 1820. However, the Panic of 1857 quickly dampened enthusiasm and no further banks were chartered until 1861. In all, the legislature received 146 applications. Although it denied 31 of them, it granted charters to 115 syndicates. Most banks went into business and, in 1860, 91 were still in operation.

From the outset, banks formed an uneven pattern of geographical distribution. More than a fifth of the towns made no effort to organize banking corporations. Almost half the institutions located in the four major seaports. Providence businessmen formed thirty-six banks and obtained two more through relocation; Newport, Bristol, and Warren secured nine, seven, and three charters, respectively. More important, the ten rapidly expanding towns obtained seventy-two charters, the sixteen relatively static communities obtained thirty-nine, and the six declining towns obtained only two.

Local differences existed not only in the number of banks but also in the size of their resources. This disparity became increasingly pronounced. Though bank capital generally ranged from $50,000 in rural institutions to $130,000 in many urban houses, most Providence banks operated on a much larger scale. By 1860 the typical Providence bank was four times as large as its country counterpart, and the combined resources of the two largest houses in the city exceeded the combined capital of twenty-four other banks located in fourteen separate towns. Because the ten rapidly expanding communities accounted for more than three-quarters of Rhode Island's banking capital, therefore, they enjoyed a marked economic advantage in the amount of funds available for commercial and industrial development as well as for routine day-to-day transactions.

TABLE 20

THE DISTRIBUTION OF BANKING CAPITAL, 1800-1860[35]

$

(000's omitted)

Towns	1800	1810	1820	1830	1840	1850	1860
Bristol	80	220	458	437	385	317	317
Warren		73	85	205	245	275	401
Cranston			25	25	25	25	120
Johnston				50	50		
Providence	322	822	1,472	3,516	6,867	8,466	15,208
North Providence			110	304	137	309	642
Cumberland				131	150	293	923
Smithfield		50	84	240	295	194	200
Burrillville			5	37	35		60
Warwick			60	133	163	75	163
Expanding Towns	402	1,165	2,299	5,078	8,352	9,954	18,034
Glocester			8	38	38	38	50
Scituate			14	16	40	40	56
East Greenwich		50	60	66	82	82	123
Coventry			10	20	30	55	150
North Kingstown		50	66	95	125	125	125
South Kingstown			39	50	150	200	320
Richmond							50
Hopkinton						10	75
Westerly	50	54	115	117	220	250	540
Newport	100	350	545	545	730	680	855
Tiverton					100	200	
Fall River							400
Static Towns	150	504	857	947	1,515	1,680	2,744
Foster				40	80	60	
Exeter					21	21	36
Charlestown							50
Declining Towns				40	101	81	86
Rhode Island	552	1,669	3,156	6,065	9,968	11,715	20,864

[35] The table and preceding analysis are based on the archival collection of Petitions, both Granted and Not Granted, and on the returns published in the *Acts and Resolves*, especially October, 1810, p. 24; May, 1820, p. 48; October, 1830, p. 72; June, 1840, p. 14; in *Abstract Exhibiting the Condition of the Banks in Rhode Island, 1850* (Providence, 1850), 5–50; and in *Banks Throughout the Union* (36 Congress, 1 session, *House Executive Document no. 49*, serial 1050, Washington, 1860), 75–78. Since West Greenwich, Barrington, Portsmouth, New Shoreham, Jamestown, Middletown, and Little Compton failed to organize banks, they have been eliminated from Table 20. Though West Greenwich promoters applied for four charters, the legislature granted only one;

Rhode Island developed one major and several minor financial centers. Providence, which by 1860 had three times more capital per resident than any other town, quickly emerged as the state's preëminent banking community. This was the logical outcome of the leading rôle played by the city's entrepreneurs in maritime, industrial, and transportation affairs, and reflected the willingness of hinterland residents to transact their banking business in the city. Except for Woonsocket, which eventually became a secondary banking center serving the northern region's textile manufacturers, Providence dominated the financial life of the Blackstone-Pawtuxet community. Lesser banking centers also developed in Bristol-Warren,[36] Fall River, Newport, and Westerly.

Providence was the first Rhode Island town to organize a bank.[37] After an unsuccessful attempt to create a banking house immediately after the Revolution, business leaders again took up the question in 1791, when John and Moses Brown asserted that a bank would discourage both capital and youth from leaving Providence. Though not unmindful of the potential profits to be earned in banking, they stressed service rather than financial gain in asking to be incorporated as the Providence Bank. They be-

the corporation did not go into business. New Shoreham groups submitted petitions for two charters. The General Assembly incorporated one bank; it, too, never advanced beyond the planning stage. The statistics of capital in 1800 are estimated.

[36] Seemingly, between 1800 and 1820 Bristol had more banking resources per inhabitant than Providence did. This was deceptive. Unlike Providence banks, most Bristol institutions rested on stock notes rather than on specie or its equivalent.

[37] Field, *Rhode Island*, 3:261–262; *Acts and Resolves*, October, 1791, pp. 11–16; February, 1807, pp. 5–6; Hope F. Kane and W. G. Roelker, "Notes and Documents: The Founding of the Providence Bank," in *Rhode Island Historical Society Collections*, 34:113–128 (October, 1941); William Greene Roelker, "The Merger of the Two Oldest Banks in Providence," in *Rhode Island History*, 4:107–114 (October, 1945); *The Centennial of the Providence National Bank, 1891* (Providence, n.d.), especially pp. 41–43; *Providence Gazette*, June 18, August 13, September 10, October 8, 15, 1791; December 5, 12, 1795; January 9, 1796; Thompson, *Moses Brown*, 246–254. The corporation took over the Providence branch of the second Bank of the United States in November, 1835. See *Book of Rhode Island*, 258.

lieved that it would promote punctuality in contracts, increase the medium of trade, prevent the export of specie, and facilitate payment of public as well as private obligations. The bank would also furnish vaults for the storage of valuables. The following year, in 1792, and practically without amendment, the General Assembly ratified the charter the Browns and their allies, the Ives, submitted. Apart from requiring directors and officials to abide by whatever regulations the stockholders laid down, the legislature imposed virtually no restrictions. On the other hand, it did give generous assistance. Limited liability encouraged cautious investors to buy stock, and, to ensure adequate working funds, the Assembly authorized the national and state governments as well as the Bank of the United States to subscribe to the bank's initial capital of $250,000. More important, as compensation for making its own paper redeemable in specie on demand, the legislature permitted the corporation to attach real property as soon as an obligation became ten days overdue. A writ of attachment was automatically available merely on presentation of evidence substantiating the existence of an unpaid debt. Since realty was a prerequisite for admission to the rank of freeman in Rhode Island, a status conferring both political and legal rights, the bank's ability to go directly to real property without first attaching personalty represented an important safeguard. This privilege became even more useful in 1807, when the legislature abolished the waiting period by granting the bank immediate resort to a debtor's realty.

Events proved these inducements to investment unnecessary. The first stock offering was so heavily oversubscribed that the organizers had to parcel out shares among 138 applicants. Holdings averaged $4,000 each. Neither this stock distribution, nor a voting system giving small shareholders a disproportionately strong voice in management, threatened the position of the original promoters, and the Ives family retained control throughout the first century of the bank's history. The public service concept of the corporation's functions notwithstanding, from the outset the institution earned high profits. Stock values quickly rose to premium levels and dividends ranged from six to ten per cent annually during the first decade of business. Thus the Browns and Ives, who at much the same time were pioneering three other important fields—Oriental trade, cotton manufacturing, and turnpike roads—were also instrumental in establishing the first Rhode Island bank. Moreover, the general pattern of corporate rights and duties they established set the pattern followed by Newport merchants in 1795 when they organized the state's second banking house.[38]

New principles were introduced as the banking system developed. Six of the twelve banks chartered between 1800 and 1809 served communities outside the major seaports. This dispersion of banking facilities was the first of four significant innovations. Arguing that Providence and Newport were too distant to meet local needs, and that they wished to promote agricultural and mechanical interests rather than mercantile ones, a group organized the Washington Bank in Westerly in 1800. Four years later, following complaints that existing institutions refused to lend on the security of farm land, another group formed the Rhode Island Union Bank. Though the legislature did not reserve a fixed proportion of the bank's capital for the exclusive use of the agricultural community, a common rule in other New England states, it did vest sole management in Newport County residents. However, since the bank established its office in Newport, and since the town's leading merchants figured prominently among the incorporators and directors, it is doubtful that the bank was actually established to serve agricultural interests.[39]

In 1800 the legislature set aside half the stock in the Bristol Bank for purchase by the Bristol Insurance Company. Thereafter,

[38] *Acts and Resolves*, October, 1795, pp. 11–16; Davis, *Eighteenth Century Business Corporations*, 2:99, 104. Operating with a much smaller capital than the Providence Bank, the Newport enjoyed immediate resort to the bank process and until 1800 earned an average of eight per cent annually.

[39] *Acts and Resolves*, June, 1800, pp. 14–19; June, 1804, pp. 11–16. Opponents narrowly defeated the first attempt to incorporate the Rhode Island Union Bank. Only Portsmouth representatives unanimously supported the proposal, perhaps because Newport and Middletown interests opposed the creation of a competitor for the Bank of Rhode Island. Washington County and the town of Providence also supported the charter application. See House Journal, March 2, 1804.

insurance companies often invested in seaport banks, and the same mercantile interests usually controlled affiliated banking and underwriting houses.[40]

The legislature liberalized the terms of stock subscription in many banks chartered after 1799. Unlike the Providence Bank, which required full payment in specie or funded United States securities within nine months, installments on Exchange Bank stock could be postponed indefinitely, and Farmer's Exchange Bank shares could be purchased with the deposit of a single dollar.[41]

The General Assembly strengthened corporate power over shareholders and fixed managerial responsibility. Newport Bank stock was automatically pledged for delinquent installment payments, and only fully paid up shares were transferable. Rhode Island Union Bank directors became personally liable for all corporate debts if they reduced capital before honoring outstanding obligations; Bristol Commercial Bank officers could not sit on the board of any other bank; and, to qualify for office, Smithfield Union Bank directors had to own a prescribed minimum of shares.[42]

These restrictions strengthened the banking system, but they guaranteed neither capable management nor honest operation, and a major though local crisis occurred in 1809. For twenty years capital had accumulated steadily and profits had met expectations. Then, without warning, the Farmer's Exchange Bank of Glocester

[40] *Acts and Resolves,* June, 1800, pp. 19–23; October, 1803, pp. 9–13.

[41] *Ibid.,* February, 1801, pp. 11–15; October, 1801, p. 3; February, 1804, pp. 11–16.

[42] *Ibid.,* October, 1803, pp. 9–13; June, 1804, pp. 11–16; February, 1805, pp. 13–17; February, 1809, pp. 6–10. The Smithfield Union later relocated at Woonsocket in Cumberland. See *ibid.,* May, 1848, p. 102. The General Assembly rejected a provision in the draft charter of the Bristol Commercial permitting the state to acquire up to a third of the bank's stock. The charter had a life of only eight years. This was the only banking corporation not created in perpetuity. The bank's organizers encountered considerable difficulty in securing a charter. The General Assembly incorporated them by a very narrow majority. Opposition was concentrated in the country towns in Providence County and in scattered rural areas in Washington and Newport counties. Amendments in 1811 and 1813 first extended the life of the corporation to thirty years, then removed the time limit entirely. See Granted Charters, 3:53 (1805–1809); 4:16, 57 (1810–1814); House Journal, November 4, 1808.

collapsed, ruining hundreds of New England families. Since its incorporation in 1804, the bank had been managed honestly, if incompetently, by a group of inexperienced farmers. Four years later, in 1808, they sold out to Andrew Dexter, Jr., who controlled a number of rural New England banks as well as the Boston Exchange Office, an early clearing house. Dexter no sooner assumed control of the Glocester institution than he began borrowing heavily to get paper currency to sell to speculators. Public suspicion barely developed before the bank failed with Dexter owing it $800,000 in unsecured loans and with no specie to redeem $600,000 in notes that were circulating. It was the first American banking failure.[43]

The legislature reacted swiftly but ineffectually. It regulated circulation of out-of-state bills, prohibited banks from issuing notes of less than $50 payable outside Rhode Island, made directors personally liable if they permitted bank debts to exceed capital, and required banks to report regularly on their activities and condition. Though this was an important early step toward public control, these regulations fell far short of providing adequate protection for the public.[44]

The first bank reports showed urban institutions to be sounder than rural ones. Those in Providence maintained adequate specie reserves but many country banks, especially the Washington of Westerly, the Narragansett of North Kingstown, and the Rhode Island Central of East Greenwich, issued up to six times as much paper as they had specie with which to redeem it. Urban banks not only attracted more deposits than rural institutions but they also followed more conservative lending policies. Providence houses discounted only five times as much paper as they had specie; some other institutions permitted ratios to rise to as high as ten to one.[45]

[43] *Acts and Resolves*, February, 1809, pp. 36–37; March, 1809, pp. 9–18; March, 1809, p. 21; May, 1809, p. 17; October, 1819, p. 37. See also, Bray Hammond, *Banks and Politics in America from the Revolution to the Civil War* (Princeton, 1957), 172–176.

[44] *Acts and Resolves*, October, 1809, pp. 22–30.

[45] *Public Laws, 1810*, pp. 126–129.

For a time, the legislature created no more banks but toward the end of the War of 1812 it resumed issuing charters and in the seventeen months preceding the Panic of 1819 it incorporated seventeen institutions. More than half of them were country houses. Some were probably organized for speculative purposes, or as an outlet for mercantile capital idled by the Embargo of 1808 and the War of 1812. Promoters advanced various reasons in support of incorporation. Residents of the North Kingstown port of Wickford argued that they needed a local bank because other institutions were too distant to serve as the "hook of silver" their fishing industry needed. North Kingstown, because of its "command of [an extensive] back country, its central situation in the county, and seconded by the active energy of her citizens," they boasted, "cannot fail of becoming equal, if not superior to any [locality] in the State. A town under these prospects, we think ought to have the same favours . . . as others whose advantages in business are far inferior." Other bank promoters substituted manufacturing for commerce or fishing as the segment of the economy most needing encouragement. Organizers of the Franklin Bank in Glocester explained that a new institution would facilitate economic adjustments—presumably, the damage caused by the collapse of the Farmer's Exchange Bank. Supporters of the Freemen's Bank of Bristol claimed that they could solve a pressing local problem—the high price of bank securities. A third banking house, they asserted, would provide another outlet for venture capital produced by the sale of stock in the second Bank of the United States. Newport faced an entirely different problem. According to promoters of the Merchants Bank, so much banking capital was invested in public securities that insufficient risk money remained to satisfy local requirements. If this was true, Newport's three banks not only reflected the pessimistic mood prevailing in local business circles but also, by the cautious investment policies they followed, the banks compounded the economic difficulties the town had been suffering for a generation.[46]

[46] Granted Charters, 3:1 (1805–1809); 5:56, 70 (1814–1817); 6:5, 6, 8 (1818–1819).

Neither the rapidity of the financial expansion, nor the creation of rural institutions, jeopardized the inherent soundness of the banking system. Since many of the new corporations had too little time before the depression of 1819 to overextend themselves, or did not actually go into business until the crisis had run its course, only the older banks were really tested. They stood up well during the panic.[47]

Four factors, namely conservative banking policies, the pressure of public opinion, the currency redemption system, and abolition of the bank process privilege, gave Rhode Island houses their early strength. Most bankers, especially those in maritime communities, took the long view, preferring soundness and long term growth to quick profits. Since they invested heavily in mercantile or, increasingly, in industrial loans, the relatively meager call funds at their disposal obliged them to behave cautiously. Discount rates on industrial paper normally ran at about twelve per cent but ranged as high as thirty-six per cent during crises. But over the long haul, the favorable balance of trade drew coin to Rhode Island, thereby allowing banks to convert their profits to specie and their stock notes to real capital.[48] Moreover, the restraining legislation of 1809, making directors personally liable for all debts if they permitted liabilities to exceed assets, encouraged bankers to meet expanding needs not by extending credit imprudently but rather by organizing additional banks. Thus banking operations, whether measured by currency circulated, loans granted, or bills discounted, generally expanded more slowly than did authorized capital.

Second, the latent popular suspicion of financial corporations strengthened these inherently conservative tendencies. Critics, especially from those rural areas which had failed to organize banks, advocated the taxation of capital, sometimes, they argued, as an act of natural no less than divine justice, sometimes to finance pub-

[47] The Rhode Island banking system also survived the earlier crisis of August, 1814, which damaged all banks outside New England. See Field, *Rhode Island*, 3:284.
[48] *Ibid.*, 289.

lic education, and sometimes in payment for the special privileges banks enjoyed. The banking question also divided parties, the Democrats asserting in 1812 that if the Federalists had their way, "merchants would be gratified with . . . banks in abundance."[49]

In 1805, over the protests of Providence, Bristol, and Newport representatives, the Assembly imposed a small annual capital levy. However, when most institutions failed to comply, the legislature repealed the statute, but in 1822 it imposed a new and higher tax, the constitutionality of which the courts sustained. Relying on the sanctity of contracts principle laid down in the Dartmouth College case, bankers asserted that their charters guaranteed them unqualified enjoyment of profits, and that a capital levy destroyed the tax-free status of benevolent and charitable institutions investing in bank stock. They also claimed that it was morally wrong to tax both capital and shares. Such burdens, bankers asserted, were denounced in the Declaration of Independence. Speaking through Chief Justice John Marshall, the Supreme Court of the United States rejected these arguments. A charter's silence about taxation, declared the court, no more precluded a future levy than the grant of land by the state placed it beyond the reach of taxation.[50]

Before 1822 the possibility of taxation checked banking policies likely to arouse public hostility; after 1822 the rising tax rate indirectly strengthened the banking system by forcing a sounder specie basis and by discouraging incorporation for speculative purposes. Most rural banks established with stock notes rather than specie usually reported large capital resources so that they could issue correspondingly large quantities of paper money. But as tax costs rose, the penalty for maintaining fictitious capital also in-

[49] Petitions Not Granted, 36:30, 94 (May, 1804, June, 1805); 40:68 (May, 1812); *Providence Gazette*, February 22, 1812; House Journal, June 14, 1806; Miscellaneous Papers of the General Assembly, folder 8 (August 25, 1807, June, 1818).

[50] Petitions Not Granted, 36:93 (June, 1805); October, 1826; *Acts and Resolves*, January, 1822, pp. 34–36; May, 1826, pp. 39–40; June, 1826, p. 33; *Providence Bank vs. Alpheus Billings and Thomas G. Pittman*, 4 *Peters* 514 (1830); *Providence Gazette*, November 9, 1822; Joseph K. Angell, *An Essay on the Right of a State to Tax a Body Corporate* (Boston, 1827).

creased. The state levy therefore encouraged banking houses to reduce capital to realistic levels and to maintain more adequate specie reserves with which to redeem their currency.[51]

Third, the New England Bank, an early regional clearing house organized in Boston in 1813, discouraged irresponsible practices, especially excessive note circulation, by discounting currency and other paper at the cost of sending it home for redemption. As soon as the scheme went into operation, Narragansett Bay banks retired a third of their bills and exchange rates between Boston and Rhode Island fell sharply. The Suffolk Bank of Boston took over the system in 1819, agreeing to redeem the bills of participating banks without charge, provided each house maintained $5,000 on permanent deposit. The Merchants Bank of Providence, acting as the system's Rhode Island agent, provided a statewide clearing house service between urban and rural banks. Institutions in the same town were expected to settle their own accounts. The Suffolk system facilitated the transaction of banking business throughout the Narragansett Bay region, exerted pressure on member banks to maintain adequate specie reserves, and protected the community from unscrupulous practices. Four maverick rural institutions—the Cranston, Fall River Union, Kent, and Village—refused to join the "Holy Alliance," as they branded the Suffolk system, mainly because the higher standards of behavior it imposed deprived them of the windfall profits they had formerly obtained by buying up their own depreciated paper currency.[52]

Finally, virtual abolition of the bank process privilege in 1818 both reflected and added to the growing strength of Rhode Island institutions. By that time, the older banks had accumulated sufficient reserves to deal with all eventualities except a general suspension of specie payments. Having learned the safe limits of operation, they no longer needed to be able to realize on their debts

[51] For examples, see *Acts and Resolves*, June, 1826, p. 23; May, 1830, pp. 39–40; May, 1831, pp. 34–35.
[52] Field, *Rhode Island*, 3:284–286, 320–321; Hammond, *Banks and Politics*, 549–556; Wilfred S. Lake, "The End of the Suffolk System," in *Journal of Economic History*, 7:183–207 (November, 1947).

more rapidly than other creditors. Under the revised system, banks enjoyed immediate resort to real property, but writs of attachment could be obtained only after notice and a full hearing. This change denied them the speedy system of recovery formerly protecting their interests and thus forced them into cautious, self-reliant policies. It also eased some of the hardship experienced by debtors during and after the crisis of 1819.[53]

The resilience demonstrated during the depression of 1819 encouraged so much complacency in financial and political circles that between 1820 and 1836 the Assembly permitted the banking system to expand very rapidly.[54] Although the legislature refused charters to twenty-one groups of applicants, it did incorporate thirty-three other syndicates. This doubled the number of banks in operation. Capital, loans, and circulation approximately trebled during the sixteen-year period. Since merchants were contracting international trade and manufacturers were consolidating earlier growth, the banking system then threatened to outstrip need.

A succession of local crises and an official investigation of financial conditions confirmed suspicions that many banks were organized for speculative purposes. In 1818 promoters of the New England Pacific Bank of Smithfield obtained a charter to sell it to out-of-state interests, and in 1825 the failure of George DeWolf threatened all five Bristol banks. When they called in their loans to the backers of DeWolf's "blackbirding" and piracy ventures, they sent a wave of bankruptcies through the town and barely escaped ruin themselves. New Englanders refused Bristol bank

---

[53] Field, *Rhode Island*, 3:264–271, 291; Rhode Island Records, 1817–1820 volume, 104; Petitions Not Granted, May, 1820; *Acts and Resolves*, February, 1818, pp. 110–114. Misgivings as to the constitutionality of the repealing statute followed the Dartmouth College decision and the General Assembly restored the privilege in 1822. However, no banks chartered after 1818 received the bank process privilege.

[54] The discussion of banking expansion between 1820 and 1836 is based on *Acts and Resolves*, January, 1823, pp. 24–29; *Report* [on] *Banking Capital* (Providence, 1826), 3–40; *Acts and Resolves*, June, 1829, pp. 29–32; October, 1829, pp. 54–56; October, 1833, p. 74; May, 1835, pp. 36–37; May, 1837, p. 48; Granted Charters, 7:68 (1820–1823); Field, *Rhode Island*, 3:290–291, 293–294, 296–297; Howe, *Mount Hope*, 232–233.

notes, and James DeWolf saved his Mount Hope Bank only by advancing it the specie it needed. In all, the banks lost $210,000. It was small consolation that the General Assembly granted them tax relief by authorizing a reduction in capital.

In 1826, Benjamin Hazard of Newport presided over a legislative investigation of the banking system. He reported that most institutions were organized with stock notes rather than with specie or public securities; that rather than adding to the supply of "real" capital they merely diluted the specie backing of paper currency; and that potentially they were politically dangerous. Though the legislature rejected all pending petitions for new banks or for increases in capital, it resumed issuing charters the following year.

Some of Hazard's misgivings were then confirmed. The Burrillville Bank, which had been organized in 1818, barely escaped some New York manipulators who intended to flood Rhode Island with paper money. Thus weakened, the institution experienced a series of difficulties culminating in the suspension of specie payments in 1832. Another crisis developed in Pawtucket, where the Farmers and Mechanics Bank was managed with scandalous incompetence. Organized in 1823 by a syndicate headed by Abraham Wilkinson, the bank served the specialized needs of the local textile and related base metal industries. Resting as it did on this as yet precarious facet of the economy, the bank was unusually vulnerable to fluctuations in the business cycle. Foolhardy administration aggravated this weakness. The bank loaned considerably more than its total resources, maintained only token reserves of quick assets, and, though on the verge of collapse, continued borrowing from other banks and endorsing paper for its customers. This accommodation did not save the Wilkinsons, the Albion and Valley Falls companies, or Stephen Jenks and Sons during the crisis of 1829, and when they failed they carried the bank down with them.

These weaknesses revived demands for remedial legislation. They had already led to the reimposition of bank taxation as well as to modification of the bank process privilege, and in 1831 the legislature not only increased the annual tax but it also levied a bonus as the price of incorporation. Too, it first contracted and then entirely withdrew the privilege of limited liability, and it subjected all banks to future general laws. The national debate over the Bank of the United States reinforced popular suspicion of banking corporations, especially of their privileged status.[55]

These misgivings culminated in 1836 in the appointment of a commission to investigate complaints that banks were charging more than the legal six per cent interest rate. Thomas W. Dorr, the son of the prominent Providence merchant-manufacturer, and later to become famous as the leader of the popular revolution known as the Dorr War, led the campaign for public regulation. Although the commissioners—Dorr himself, cashier George Curtis of the Exchange Bank, and attorney Samuel Y. Atwell—uncovered no glaring defects in the banking system, they did substantiate the usury allegations. In various ways banks forced up interest rates to as high as eighteen per cent annually. They made loans payable at distant points and then charged exchange on the paper; they antedated notes; and they discounted paper in the currency of other banks so that borrowers had to pay exchange commissions. These techniques were so lucrative that only four of Rhode Island's sixty-one banks paid dividends of less than six per cent annually. By 1835 undivided profits had exceeded $300,000. No wonder two Providence houses, the Union and the Weybosset, had sought to increase their capital to $1,000,000 and $500,000 respectively.[56]

---

[55] Compare *Acts and Resolves*, October, 1814, pp. 31–34; January, 1823, pp. 34–38; and June, 1827, pp. 4–8, for typical charter amendments. The General Assembly generally gave small shareholders a disproportionately large voice in management. For examples, see the Eagle Bank of Providence in Granted Charters, 6:12 (1818–1819), and the Bristol Union Bank in Miscellaneous Papers of the General Assembly, folder 9 (1821–1825). See also, *ibid.*, folder 11 (1831–1835), for a proposal that all charters granted before May 1, 1831, expire on July 1, 1834. The resolution was withdrawn on June 24, 1834. The legal effect of the amendments to the liability clauses in charters remained clouded even in 1860. See *Providence Journal*, February 13, 1860.

[56] *Acts and Resolves*, January, 1836, pp. 62–63; Petitions Not Granted, January, 1825; October, 1832; *Report* [on] *the Banks in this State* (Providence, 1836), 3–34.

Despite the general soundness of the banking system and the willingness of the public to pay usurous interest rates, Dorr and his colleagues recommended reform. In 1836 the Assembly codified the existing laws and added some new principles, thereby enacting the first comprehensive American banking statute.[57] It stipulated that no bank be chartered with less than $50,000 in capital, that no business be transacted before shareholders subscribed $25,000, that capital be fully paid up within one year of incorporation, and that local residents receive preferential treatment in the allocation of shares. No bank could reduce capital, shift location, or establish branches without legislative approval. The Assembly also confirmed the six per cent interest rate, established a scale of exchange rates for all points in the United States, and threatened usurous banks with charter forfeiture. Finally, the Assembly created a permanent banking commission to supervise new institutions, receive the semiannual bank reports, and investigate complaints of mismanagement or malpractice. In serious cases, the commissioners could request the Supreme Court to enjoin a bank from transacting business.

Though these regulations provided some safeguards, they fell short of being adequate. Failure to enact a general incorporation law perpetuated legislative log rolling, and the lack of reserve requirements and a safety fund system permitted isolated cases of incompetence or fraud to jeopardize the reputation of all Rhode Island banks. Of course, the Assembly may have considered the Suffolk redemption system adequate, but the failure to specify a particular day for bank reports allowed specie to be shifted from institution to institution to create a false impression. Nor did the

---

[57] *Acts and Resolves*, June, 1836, pp. 62–70; Field, *Rhode Island*, 3:300–302. For an earlier bill (1831), see Miscellaneous Papers of the General Assembly, folder 11 (1831–1835). It proposed that banks recover debts in the same way as other creditors, that interest rates, either directly or indirectly, not exceed six per cent per annum, that all banks report on the same day twice each year, that the reports show all debts due the bank from shareholders and directors or from all partnerships in which they were interested, and that no bank do business at any place except the one specified in its charter. Finally, no bank was to issue any note, bill, draft, or other instrument payable at a future day or bearing interest.

legislature require banks to support local enterprise. Nothing prevented them sending their capital to Providence or New York, as the Mount Vernon of Foster, the Lime Rock of Smithfield, or the Exchange of Newport had done before 1836, and other banks lent large sums to their own officials. In effect, these institutions served a few individual enterprises rather than the public at large. Usually, the directors channeled such funds into the mercantile and industrial ventures in which they had investments, but occasionally, as in the Merchants Bank of Providence, they used the capital to discount privately at usurous interest rates. Before these defects could be remedied, the 1837 panic tested both the regulatory legislation and the banking system.[58]

Though the origins of the crisis lay beyond Rhode Island, local banks were deeply affected by the succession of events culminating in the suspension of specie payments on May 11, 1837. Several institutions were already in trouble before the depression's onset, and others remained weak for some years after the crisis ended, but all escaped serious damage. At the outset, banks purchased gold on the open market. Then, as the depression intensified, bullion flowed out of the state. Throughout, the commissioners required weekly reports from each institution, and the General Assembly alleviated public distress by permitting banks to issue one-year post notes bearing between five and six per cent interest. They had to accept their own bills for deposit at five per cent interest. In October, the legislature limited loans, discounts, and circulation but reduced the interest rate on bills deposited to allow banks to earn a profit on such transactions. Holders of paper currency received priority over all other creditors. Conditions slowly improved over the winter of 1837. Manufacturers and merchants recovered markets for their goods and services, employment increased, and the outflow of specie first declined, then stopped. By the spring of 1838 the tide began to turn; by August the banking system had sufficient reserves to resume specie payments. Though

[58] *Acts and Resolves*, January 1837, pp. 89–92; Petitions Not Granted, December, 1825; January, 1828; October, 1832; Field, *Rhode Island*, 3:300–302, 308.

a minor recession again drove banks off gold in October, 1839, Rhode Island came through both crises without the failure of a single bank.[59]

This achievement revived complacency. The legislature relaxed its restrictions even before the depression had run its course. Then, in June, 1842, it replaced the banking commission with an *ad hoc* committee system. In view of the commission's effectiveness during the crisis, as well as the cases of fraud and mismanagement it had uncovered, its abolition was a backward step which deprived the public of a reasonable measure of protection.[60]

Even so, cautious restraint characterized banking history during the decade following the depression. The legislature dismissed three out of a total of five charter applications, twice refused to authorize a general increase in banking capital, rejected a proposal for a state-supervised currency, and in 1851 refused to charter a Providence clearing house. Only one new bank went into operation between 1837 and 1849. Most corporations expanded operations relatively slowly, and some institutions even voluntarily reduced capital. Thus the banking system expanded at the slowest rate in its history; for the first time population grew more rapidly than did banking capital. Except in a few towns, per capita banking resources declined.[61]

[59] *Acts and Resolves*, May, 1837, pp. 47–48; June, 1837, pp. 42–43; October, 1837, pp. 70–72; Field, *Rhode Island*, 3:305–306. Newport investors continued sending capital to New York. See *Providence Journal*, December 18, 1860.

[60] *Acts and Resolves*, June, 1842, p. 10; January, 1843, pp. 3–4. The conservative reaction to Dorr's leadership of the popular revolution was partly responsible for the abolition of the commission.

[61] *Acts and Resolves*, May, 1839, pp. 42–43; June, 1839, p. 28; October, 1839, pp. 53–54; January, 1840, pp. 53–54; Petitions Not Granted, January, 1838; October, 1839; January, 1851; June, 1852; Reports to the General Assembly, 10:43 (May, 1839); Treasury Papers, October, 1839; Miscellaneous Papers of the General Assembly, folder 13 (1841–1845); folder 14 (1846–1848). The co-partners Otis A. and Joseph B. Wheelock were providing an unincorporated clearing house service to Providence banks as early as 1842. See *Providence Journal*, November 4, 1842. Six towns—North Providence, Cumberland, Coventry, South Kingstown, Exeter, and Tiverton—increased their per capita resources, but the growth was more apparent than real in Exeter since the town lost population in the 1840's.

The phase of financial consolidation eventually gave way to a period of spectacular growth. Between 1850 and 1856, the General Assembly chartered forty-five banks. The formation of these new institutions, together with the expansion of many long-established banks, forced up Rhode Island's banking capital from less than $12,000,000 in 1850 to almost $21,000,000 in 1860. Providence secured seventeen charters, and eight Providence banks, including four newly created ones, each received authority to raise $1,000,000 in capital. By the Civil War, the American and the Commerce exceeded this figure, and nineteen Providence banks, each with resources exceeding $300,000, were the largest in Rhode Island. Even the city's two smallest institutions, the Atlas and the Mercantile, were larger than most country banks. In all, Providence houses controlled almost three-quarters of Rhode Island's banking capital. Rapid though less significant growth also occurred in Cranston, North Providence, Cumberland, Coventry, South Kingstown, and Fall River.

As the depression of 1857 showed, however, this expansion had been at the expense of safety. Some banks had over-reached themselves by sending their note issues out of the state; others had raised circulation to preposterous levels; and still others had purchased railroad securities with bills of credit that were then circulated in western states. Many institutions loaned large sums to their officers or to ventures in which their directors were interested, and many of the most powerful manufacturers, including the Browns, Ives, Knights, Smiths, and Spragues, operated their banks as integral parts of their complex business empires. Other institutions, such as the Globe, which was the fiscal agent for the Stonington railroad, were tied to a single enterprise or served a single industry, and the legislature even permitted three Providence banks, the Blackstone Canal, the American, and the Phoenix, to organize the What Cheer Company, a real estate venture. It also chartered the Atlantic and Mediterranean Banking and Navigation Company, a grandiose Newport enterprise proposing to conduct a banking house, to build and own steamships, and to operate an international transportation service. Certain mercantile practices, particularly the method of selling on time discounts, also weakened the banking system. This tied up working capital in unpaid debts and exposed manufacturers, factors, and bankers to possible damage. Some of the expansion, of course, reflected growing needs, particularly in manufacturing, where larger payrolls required banks to increase their circulation and where burgeoning production forced up discounts from some $14,000,000 in 1850 to almost $29,000,000 in 1856. Though the legislature revived the banking commission in January, 1857, it had delayed action too long. The regulatory agency had curbed only the worst excesses when Rhode Island felt the full force of the depression.[62]

The economic crisis gathered momentum in the summer of 1857. First, New York houses began recalling loans to meet their own obligations. Though many Rhode Island industrialists were creditors in the south and west, funds came home too slowly to stave off collapse. Discount rates soared to prohibitive levels, manufacturers closed their mills or cut back production, unemployment rose, and at the end of September banks suspended specie payments. Five country banks went into receivership. Two houses, the Fall River and the North Kingstown Farmers, succumbed to out-of-state manipulators, and three, the South County, Hopkinton, and Rhode Island Central, located in South Kingstown, Westerly, and East Greenwich respectively, crumbled under the economic pressure. Their speculations in western land securities had left them with virtually no specie with which to redeem their currency.[63] The Providence Board of Trade urged the General Assembly to circulate state-guaranteed bills of credit, but, when the tide turned in January, 1858, and banks resumed specie payments, the scheme became unnecessary.[64]

[62] *Acts and Resolves*, January, 1857, pp. 3–7. For two earlier attempts to revive the banking commission, see Miscellaneous Papers of the General Assembly, folder 19 (1855–1856). See also, Field, *Rhode Island*, 3:289–290, 308–309.

[63] *Report of the Bank Commissioners of Rhode Island, January, 1858* (Providence, 1858), 3–8; *The Bank Commissioners vs. The Rhode Island Central Bank*, 5 *Rhode Island* 12 (1857); *Providence Journal*, August 28, 1857.

[64] Field, *Rhode Island*, 3:309–311.

Rhode Island learned little from its tardy revival of the banking commission. The legislature again abolished the regulatory body as soon as the depression had run its course. It did restrict the debts and circulation of the weakest banks but it lifted this check from the Exchange, Phoenix Village, and Franklin as soon as they complained that the law would reduce their profits and encourage them to move to Providence. Thus the banking system soon resumed its pattern of freewheeling expansion, and by the time of the Civil War most corporations had extended their operations to the charter limits.[65]

Initial promises of community service rather than private profit notwithstanding, commercial banking became a lucrative business. Many institutions served the private interests of their owners rather than the public welfare. The General Assembly must bear some of the responsibility. From the outset it pursued a lenient policy as compared to Connecticut and Massachusetts, which granted narrower corporate privileges, imposed heavier taxes, and instituted rigorous inspection at an earlier date. All but one Rhode Island bank was chartered in perpetuity; the General Assembly even failed to reserve the power of amendment or revocation until 1818; and the distinction of creating the first banking commission and passing the first comprehensive regulatory legislation is a dubious honor in view of the agency's brief life and the statute's serious omissions. From the outset, the Assembly established a maximum interest rate of six per cent, but it did not regulate exchange rates until 1837, and it left discount rates to move with market conditions. Thus bank earnings generally exceeded the legal rate for loans. Early dividends ranged from six to ten per cent annually; they averaged nearly seven per cent between 1837 and 1860. But during the latter period, banking houses also increased their undistributed profits from some $470,000 to over $1,175,000.[66]

[65] *Acts and Resolves*, January, 1858, pp. 15–24; Granted Petitions, 64:33–35 (January, 1859).
[66] Field, *Rhode Island*, 3:302, 320–321.

These earnings partially explain the rapid expansion of banking activity. Between 1800 and 1860 the number of banks rose from two to ninety-one and capital increased from approximately $550,000 to almost $21,000,000. Between 1809 and 1860 circulation increased from $435,000 to almost $3,775,000, and loans and discounts increased from barely $2,137,000 to over $25,000,000. Deposits showed a corresponding increase, rising from less than $550,000 in 1809 to over $3,700,000 in 1860. However, specie reserves remained small. They totaled only $410,000 in 1809, declined to $243,000 in 1837, and never exceeded $657,000, the figure reached in 1858.[67]

Much of the expansion occurred in Providence. By the Civil War, over two-fifths of the state's banks and almost three-quarters of its banking resources were located in the city. This concentration not only reflected the importance of Providence as a commercial, industrial, and transportation center, it also reflected the steady inflow of risk money from southern New England. As the managerial center for much of the manufacturing and other economic activity of a region extending into eastern Connecticut and southern Massachusetts, Providence was the logical place to which such funds gravitated. High demand, attractive profits, and safety of capital were traditional Providence inducements. Though occasionally forced to suspend specie payments, no Providence house failed or withdrew from business. No wonder many country banks invested their capital in the city or even sought permission to relocate there. The most notable example was the Farmers and Mechanics Bank of Pawtucket. When it was reorganized as the Phoenix Bank (having arisen from the symbolical ashes of the Wilkinson failure), it moved to Providence, where it became one of the largest and most successful of the city's banking houses. Capital entering the Providence money market had a snowballing effect. It enlarged the city's capacity to serve the financial needs of a growing hinterland region; it increased the profits of banking; and, magnet like, it attracted still more investment capital from outside the city.

67 *Ibid.*

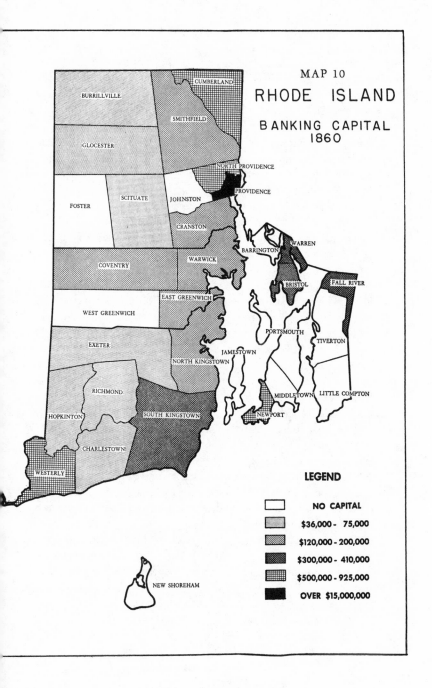

MAP 10

RHODE ISLAND

BANKING CAPITAL
1860

CUMBERLAND

BURRILLVILLE

SMITHFIELD

GLOCESTER

NORTH PROVIDENCE

FOSTER   SCITUATE   JOHNSTON   PROVIDENCE

CRANSTON

BARRINGTON   WARREN

COVENTRY   WARWICK

BRISTOL   FALL RIVER

EAST GREENWICH

WEST GREENWICH   PORTSMOUTH   TIVERTON

EXETER   JAMESTOWN

NORTH KINGSTOWN

RICHMOND   MIDDLETOWN   LITTLE COMPTON

HOPKINTON   SOUTH KINGSTOWN   NEWPORT

CHARLESTOWN

WESTERLY

LEGEND

☐	NO CAPITAL
	$36,000 - 75,000
	$120,000 - 200,000
	$300,000 - 410,000
	$500,000 - 925,000
■	OVER $15,000,000

NEW SHOREHAM

On a considerably smaller scale, savings institutions had a some-what comparable effect by consolidating thousands of small invest-ments into a few large funds. Formed primarily to protect factory workers, seamen, and especially whalers from the various tempta-tions to squander their wages, savings banks located in the chief centers of employment. The geographical concentration char-acteristic of commercial banking, therefore, was less pronounced. Of the twenty-one institutions operating in 1860, Providence had four, Pawtucket and Woonsocket each had three, Newport, War-ren, and South Kingstown each had two, and Fall River, Bristol, Warwick, East Greenwich, and Westerly each had one. Almost two-thirds of the towns, including all the declining communities and most of the relatively static ones, failed to organize local savings banks.

Expansion occurred chiefly in the decade preceding the Civil War. The legislature chartered fifteen institutions between 1850 and 1860; deposits rose from less than $1,500,000 to over $9,160,000. By 1856, the Providence Institution for Savings had more deposits than all seven banks in the system had had six years earlier. But except for another Providence bank, the People's, and the Newport, Fall River, and Pawtucket, where deposits ranged from $422,000 to $750,000, most savings institutions were rela-tively small.[68]

The first savings bank, organized in Newport in June, 1819, established the pattern of corporate rights and duties followed in other charters. The legislature fixed the scale of operations by limiting the bank's resources. Except for seamen, no individual could deposit more than $100 a day. Corporations could not be-come depositors at all. In effect, the bank operated on a mutual principle, having neither capital nor shareholders. It invested in public securities, commercial bank stock, and real estate mortgages, paying depositors five per cent annually for the use of their money and prorating surplus profits among depositors every three years.

[68] *Abstract* [of] *the Condition of Institutions for Savings, 1850* (Providence, 1850), 3–13; *Rhode Island Register, 1856*, pp. 48–50; *Banks Throughout the Union*, 75–78.

Funds on fixed deposit could be withdrawn only at stated intervals of three months. Later charters prohibited loans to bank officers, permitted a much larger scale of operation, reduced the minimum sum that could be accepted for deposit, and broadened the types of securities that could be purchased. Because savings banks were few in number and small in size, before 1850 their influence on economic growth and financial stability was both minor and localized. Conditions changed fundamentally over the next decade.[69]

In 1854 the legislature lifted most investment restrictions by permitting banks to hold all types of collateral, including personal notes secured by government bonds, commercial bank stock, railroad paper, or real estate. A bank could invest up to half its resources in individual notes. Since deposits rose fivefold in the 1850's, the sharp increase in risk capital stimulated growth in all segments of the economy. Many banks invested their funds prudently, but some were prone to speculate and, on the whole, the expansion intensified the general economic weaknesses of the period. Their purchases of commercial bank stock contributed to the rise in commercial discounts and circulation; their speculation in western securities accelerated the outflow of capital; and their loans to merchants and manufacturers abetted the over-extension of credit that culminated in the explosion of the economic bubble in 1857. Though all savings institutions survived, they had established some potentially dangerous practices, the full implications of which were not to become apparent until after the Civil War.[70]

If banking provided entrepreneurs with a profitable outlet for venture capital and a system of supporting their varied business interests, insurance gave them a method of protecting these enterprises. Providence capitalists, in particular, whether acting as investors concerned for the safety of their resources or as citizens

---

[69] *Savings Banks of Newport,* 9, 13–25, 34, 43–48; *Acts and Resolves,* June 1819, pp. 28–37. For examples, see *ibid.,* January, 1836, pp. 24–25; October, 1841, pp. 51–52; August, 1850, pp. 24–26; May, 1855, pp. 46–51. For the Senate's refusal to permit the Citizens Savings Institution of Woonsocket to make personal loans, see Petitions Not Granted, January, 1854.

[70] *Acts and Resolves,* January, 1854, pp. 259–260; January, 1855, p. 9; *Banks Throughout the Union,* 75–78.

dedicated to making their town a metropolis, quickly appreciated the essential rôle that underwriting could play in the realization of their ambitions.

Operating both as traders and as underwriters, Narrangansett Bay merchants had begun insuring each others' voyages as early as the mid-eighteenth century.[71] Though they were to formalize their underwriting operations after the Revolution and to adjust the kinds of risks they insured according to the changing pattern of economic activity, they continued to regard the underwriting business as an adjunct to their primary investments rather than as a separate field of enterprise, and, following the pattern established in both transportation and commercial banking, insurance houses came to be concentrated almost exclusively in Providence. They issued either marine or fire policies, sometimes both, and used either the stock or the mutual form of organization. A few companies protected farmers against horse thieves[72] but none issued life insurance or, so far as is known, underwrote railroad freight shipments.

Reflecting the maritime source of most Rhode Island wealth, all but one of the early companies specialized in marine risks. Commonly, they began as informal syndicates, then incorporated. Since they came into being during an unusually difficult period for oceanic trade, most proved unrewarding. Some quickly disbanded, others lingered on into the whaling era, and a few, adjusting successfully to changing conditions, were still vigorous in 1860.

The Providence Insurance Company, formed in 1799, became the most successful early underwriter.[73] Some of its stockholders had previously participated in syndicates organized by a local in-

[71] For examples, see Hedges, *The Browns*, 10; H. W. Georgi, "The Beginnings of Insurance in Providence," in *Publications of the Rhode Island Historical Society*, New series, 3:180–182 (October, 1895); Greene, *Providence Plantations*, 348.

[72] For their activities as private protective associations, see *Providence Gazette*, August 17, 1793; February 10, 1798; February 21, 1801; January 26, 1805. For a representative charter, see *Acts and Resolves*, February, 1819, pp. 23–38.

[73] *Acts and Resolves*, February, 1799, pp. 3–7; Roelker and Collins, *Providence Washington Insurance Company*, 10–28; Davis, *Eighteenth Century Business Corporations*, 2:244; Granted Charters, 3:57 (1805–1809); 4:55 (1810–1814).

surance broker, John Mason. In one such venture, thirty-two individuals and firms had agreed to underwrite a West Indian voyage by the brig *Murfree*. They charged the owners a premium of twenty per cent, plus a surcharge of five per cent for each port entered in addition to Tobago. If the brig returned safely, the syndicate stood to earn a handsome profit, but as the high rates indicated, it was a gamble in which the partners also stood to lose heavily. They guarded against this possibility by limiting individual liability to the amount of risk each assumed, a principle they carried over to the corporation. Expressing its willingness to "give encouragement to every institution which promises to advance the interest of commerce," the General Assembly incorporated some of these former partners as the Providence Insurance Company. It authorized the corporation to insure vessels, cargoes, lives, and buildings, but it prohibited the underwriting of any slaving venture. The shareholders obtained limited liability. Like other early underwriting companies, the firm allied itself with a banking affiliate, in its case the Providence Bank. In point of fact, it was the underwriting agency of the continually expanding Brown and Ives mercantile empire.

Such affiliations were the product of mutual convenience. Until the decline of international trade, ships and cargoes were the principal risks assumed. Premiums were normally paid by note rather than by cash, the obligation being redeemed out of profits at the end of each voyage. In effect, insurance companies earned two profits, one as underwriters, the other by lending merchants the premium money. For traders, this arrangement had the advantage of freeing mercantile capital for maritime ventures. However, since many trading voyages lasted several years, most insurance companies had a great deal of money tied up in premium notes, and during any given period, they had sufficient resources to underwrite only a limited number of undertakings. Moreover, their business was spasmodic rather than continuous: they issued policies and paid out claims at irregular intervals. It was to their advantage, therefore, to invest in bank stock and to reduce their operating expenses by turning over such routine matters as collecting premium notes or meeting claims to their banking affiliates.

Though the Providence Insurance Company earned high profits initially, a series of extraordinary losses coupled with the general contraction of maritime activity eventually forced a reduction of capital from $150,000 in 1809 to $75,000 in 1813, and to less than $63,000 in 1817.

Some of the partners in the *Murfree* syndicate of 1798 had not invested in the Providence Insurance Company. Instead, they had planned a banking and underwriting organization of their own, made up of the Exchange Bank and the Washington Insurance Company. The Browns, hoping to thwart this challenge to their profits, and believing that the multiplication of banks would impair the reputation of Rhode Island paper in Boston and New York, then offered to allow the rival faction to buy into the Providence Bank. They argued that one large institution could circulate more paper with greater safety and less expense than could two small ones and complained that the public had been denied the opportunity to invest in the proposed Exchange Bank. Richard Jackson, spokesman for the interlopers, replied that a second house "would facilitate and ultimately advance the trade and manufacturing of the town." Though the Browns and their allies wielded considerable political influence, as Federalists they suffered from the rising Republican tide and failed to prevent the charters being granted.[74]

The Washington Insurance Company enjoyed a brief period of striking success. It paid a dividend of fifty per cent on its capital during its second year of operation, and in 1803 it opened an agency in New London to solicit additional business. But like other underwriting firms, the Washington suffered so much from the ensuing decline in trade and the rising incidence of claims that in 1813 it reduced its capital from $110,000 to $60,000.[75]

Thus time and common adversity narrowed the gulf separating the Brown and Jackson factions. This reconciliation led to merger

[74] *Acts and Resolves*, February, 1800, pp. 17–19; Granted Charters, 2:5 (1801–1805); Roelker and Collins, *Providence Washington Insurance Company*, 29–41; Greene, *Providence Plantations*, 347–348; Field, *Rhode Island*, 3:276–277.

[75] Greene, *Providence Plantations*, 347; *Acts and Resolves*, February, 1813, pp. 33–34.

discussions in 1815, and five years later the Providence-Washington Insurance Company went into business. Capitalized at $132,000, the company retained substantial investments in the Providence and Exchange banks, but the steady withdrawal of Narragansett Bay merchants from oceanic ventures dictated fundamental changes in other aspects of its affairs. Shrewdly, as always, the company's directors secured authority to enter the fire insurance field, a step which saved the firm when other marine companies were forced to withdraw from business.[76]

Such was the fate of the Newport Insurance Company. Incorporated in 1799, it had begun fifteen years earlier as a syndicate in which sixteen members shared profits and losses according to the amount of risk each assumed in any particular trading venture. Though the corporation was set up to have shareholders and a minimum capital of $100,000, it actually operated on the old basis with a syndicate of twelve merchants placing $12,000 in the Bank of Rhode Island as a fund from which to pay losses. After five years they abandoned this arrangement as unsatisfactory. The company had insured almost $3,374,000 worth of property and had paid out over $145,000 in claims but it had earned only five per cent on its outlay. It then invested its capital in the newly formed Rhode Island Union Bank in the hope that the affiliation would prove mutually profitable. These expectations failed to materialize. The Napoleonic Wars, the Embargo of 1808, and the War of 1812 successively hampered the marine underwriting business. Following heavy losses, the company halved the par value of its stock, reduced its capital to $50,000, and, apparently, withdrew from business in the early 1830's.[77]

The legislature chartered nineteen other marine underwriting companies between 1800 and 1831, but only one was still in business in 1860. One of the unsuccessful firms, the Bristol which

---

[76] *Acts and Resolves,* February, 1818, pp. 47–51; February, 1820, pp. 6–11; and the secondary works cited in note 74.

[77] *Acts and Resolves,* February, 1799, pp. 13–17; February, 1809, pp. 3–4; Davis, *Eighteenth Century Business Corporations,* 2:244; Mason, *Reminiscences of Newport,* 174–177; Greene, *Providence Plantations,* 346–347.

James DeWolf and his confederates organized in 1800, lasted only three years. Despite the company's avowed purpose of promoting "the honest, industrious merchant," it insured illicit ventures, including slavers and their cargoes, charging fifteen per cent on the vessels and over eighteen per cent on the slaves. Another, the Marine of Providence, operated between 1805 and 1807 as an unincorporated partnership and claimed to have prevented the flight of business to other states, but its activities were severely circumscribed by the embargo and the war. Reorganized as the Union in 1815, the company, like the Peace, Commercial, Marine, and Bristol Marine, which were also formed to exploit the anticipated postwar trade revival, went out of business when its profits failed to meet expectations. The Warren had a longer and more successful history. Chartered in 1800, it operated until 1844, paying an average dividend of fourteen per cent annually. Although the American was still active when the Civil War broke out, it had not been formed until 1831, and thereby escaped the difficulties encountered by the earlier firms. Significantly, in 1860 marine risks constituted less than a quarter of its business.[78]

After a lapse of seventeen years in which no additional marine insurance companies were formed, the Assembly chartered the Roger Williams in 1848, and by 1860 there were a total of six companies, including the Providence-Washington, in operation. All had their headquarters in Providence. Because of the steady improvement in the safety of navigation, marine premiums averaged only six per cent. About $6,000,000 worth of policies were in effect at the time.[79]

[78] *Acts and Resolves*, February, 1800, pp. 20–24. For the Bristol Company's rates, see Howe, *Mount Hope*, 110. See also, Granted Charters, 3:26 (1805–1809); 5:19, 21, 22 (1814–1817); 7:21 (1820–1823). In 1801 the legislature denied the Warren Insurance Company the privilege of recovering debts by the bank process, but reversed itself the following year. See Granted Charters, 2:4, 14 (1801–1805). For dividends, see Fessenden, *History of Warren*, 105. For the charter of the American Insurance Company, see *Acts and Resolves*, June, 1831, pp. 32–36.

[79] The charters are indexed in Addeman, *Index to the Acts and Resolves*, xii–xiv. For data on each firm, see *Abstract of Insurance Companies, 1860* (Providence, 1860), 5–21.

Reflecting the general economic trend away from oceanic ventures, Rhode Island underwriters gradually shifted their main effort until by the Civil War they were transacting approximately ten times as much fire as marine business. The pioneer company, the Providence Mutual, formed in 1800, could insure property up to a maximum value of $1,500, and for a maximum term of seven years. Premiums were forty cents for each $100 of ordinary coverage, but special rates applied to dangerous risks such as distilleries, paintworks, and tar, tallow, and hemp warehouses. Members secured each other by notes payable with interest. When a policy expired, the company simply collected the note, deducted its compensation for any losses it had incurred on other property, and returned the balance. Though the firm established agencies in Taunton, New Bedford, and Nantucket contrary to the restriction that it operate only within Rhode Island, the Assembly confirmed its charter in 1821, and the company went on to become the largest fire underwriting association in the state.[80]

Fire insurance companies derived considerable benefit from the work of volunteer fire engine companies and mutual protection societies. The Providence Mutual Fire Society, for example, organized a fire fighting service and required its members to equip themselves with buckets, axes, and ropes. It played an important part in containing a conflagration which in January, 1801, threatened to destroy the town's mercantile section. Although the fire was eventually brought under control, estimates of damage ranged from $160,000 to $200,000.[81]

Despite the obvious need for underwriting organizations, the fire insurance business developed very slowly. The Columbian of Providence was formed in 1818 but went out of business almost immediately, perhaps because it failed to obtain limited liability. Apart from the Providence-Washington, which became a fire under-

[80] *Acts and Resolves*, October, 1800, pp. 16–28; February, 1821, pp. 17–28.

[81] For the articles of the Providence Mutual Fire Society, see *Rhode Island History*, 2:58 (April, 1943); for the society's activities, see Robert Morton Hazelton, "Moses Brown on Fire-Fighting," in *ibid.*, 4:80–83 (July, 1945); Thompson, *Moses Brown*, 278–280; and for a request that members be exempt from militia duty, see Petitions Not Granted, vol. 33, part 2, p. 87 (June, 1801).

writing firm in 1820, and the American, which was incorporated in 1831, no other fire insurance company was chartered until the North Providence industrialist, Zachariah Allen, organized the Manufacturers Mutual in 1835. The new firm grew out of widespread dissatisfaction with the high rates mill owners had to pay for insurance protection. Conscious of the fire hazard, Allen had built his woolen mill with unusually thick floors, he had specified that the shingles be set in mortar, and he had established his own fire fighting company. Yet underwriters classified his factory like all other industrial buildings as a dangerous risk and charged accordingly. Allen then convinced other manufacturers that an industrial mutual company would better serve their needs. By using prominent industrialists to solicit business throughout the northern section of the state, the company took only eight days to obtain applications to insure property valued at $1,000,000, the sum specified in the charter before the company could begin operating. Rates varied according to risk, and no policy could exceed $15,000 or extend for more than one year. As the firm acquired experience it lowered premiums. Members saved over sixty per cent on their first policies as compared to former costs, and within a quarter-century rates declined from $2.50 per $100 insured to a mere thirty cents. Although the company doubled its business within the first two years, its outlook was so conservative that in 1860 it had only $3,000,000 worth of policies in effect.[82]

Between 1848 and 1860, the legislature chartered twenty-six additional stock and mutual fire insurance companies. However, some never advanced beyond the organizational stage, some did so only after 1860, and some went out of business within a few years. Thus only eight stock and eleven mutual companies, including four that had been chartered before 1848, were operating in 1860. Since all

[82] *Acts and Resolves*, October, 1835, pp. 61–67; *The Factory Mutuals, 1835–1935: Being Primarily a History of the Manufacturers Mutual Fire Insurance Company, the Original of the Factory Mutual Companies, During its First One Hundred Years* (Providence, 1935), 31–63 *passim*; John Bainbridge, *Biography of an Idea: The Story of Mutual Fire and Casualty Insurance* (Garden City, 1952), *passim*, but especially pp. 92–113. For the Columbian, see Granted Charters, 6:3 (1818–1819), and *Acts and Resolves*, February, 1818, pp. 17–21.

except two mutual firms, the Farmers of East Greenwich and the Pawtucket, had their headquarters in Providence, city companies wrote over ninety-two per cent of the $65,000,000 worth of fire policies issued by Rhode Island underwriters. The Providence Mutual, with almost $13,000,000 worth of policies in 1860, was the largest firm, and the Atlantic, with almost $8,500,000, and the American and the Providence-Washington, each with over $5,000,000, were the other major underwriters. Because local firms competed with thirty-five agencies operated by out-of-state companies, the Providence monopoly was more apparent then real. Most mutual companies had few assets other than their premium notes, but stock companies owned large blocks of shares in Providence banks. The Merchants, for example, acquired a quarter interest in the Bank of Commerce, and between them insurance companies owned over $1,165,000 worth of bank stock, or almost a tenth of the total.[83]

The state began regulating insurance companies during the decade before the Civil War. Apart from license and premium fees, first required in 1822, out-of-state underwriters were not regulated until 1854, when the legislature required agents to submit detailed annual reports, insisted that only companies capitalized at a minimum of $100,000 operate Rhode Island agencies, and ordered underwriters to pledge no more than a tenth of their resources to a single risk. Rhode Island companies also paid taxes and reported to a Board of Insurance Commissioners, but their activities were otherwise unregulated until 1859, when the board received visitation powers. It could enjoin operations or, in cases where an insurance company's activities threatened the public interest, appoint receivers. The failure of the Trident Mutual in 1858 brought about these regulations. The company had gone into business with only a fraction of its capital reserve paid in. It invested about a third of its funds in depreciated securities issued by the Indianapolis and Cincinnati, and the Providence, Hartford, and Fishkill railroads. Unable to realize on these assets when called upon to meet losses on the policies it had written, the com-

[83] For conditions in 1860, see *Abstract of Insurance Companies, 1860*, pp. 5–21.

pany defaulted on its obligations with heavy damage both to itself and to its policy holders.[84]

In the insurance business, then, private marine insurance syndicates and later joint-stock corporations had developed in each of the major Narragansett Bay ports. On the whole, these ventures proved so disappointing that few marine underwriting companies had been chartered after 1816, all except the Providence firms had withdrawn from business, and underwriters had begun specializing in fire risks. This trend not only occurred at the same time that the Rhode Island economy was becoming oriented to the land rather than to the sea, but when all the ports except Providence were suffering from the steady contraction of oceanic opportunities. Thus, as each marine insurance company in Newport, Warren, and Bristol closed its doors, the remaining business passed to Providence firms and agencies, and when the residential and industrial fire insurance business developed, Providence alone had the capital, the underwriting organization and experience, and the commercial connections throughout the state to capitalize on expanding opportunities. By 1860, therefore, Providence had made itself a regional insurance center serving the marine and fire underwriting needs of eastern Connecticut, southern Massachusetts, and all Rhode Island.

At each stage in the shift from a mercantile to an industrial economy and in the geographical relocation of power, the developing transportation network had served to draw more and more business to Providence at the expense of its southern rival, Newport. At much the same time, ever increasing amounts of risk capital had flowed to Providence as the emerging financial center of the southern New England textile industry, and, even before the maritime economy had gone into serious decline, Providence had secured a virtual monopoly of the underwriting business.

[84] *Acts and Resolves*, January, 1822, pp. 34–36; October, 1854, pp. 13–18; *Revised Laws, 1857*, pp. 300–304; *Acts and Resolves*, January, 1859, pp. 21–24; *Abstract of Insurance Companies, 1858* (Providence, 1858), 12–13. For protests against regulation, see Petitions Not Granted, January, May, 1856, and *Providence Journal*, June 4, 1855. For data on insurance corporations chartered outside Rhode Island, see *Abstract of Insurance Companies, 1860*, pp. 22–75.

Providence could certainly take pride in this achievement, especially in view of the dissipation of hundreds of thousands of dollars in the 1801 fire, the great hurricane of 1815, and the Blackstone Canal venture. But the emergence of Providence as the metropolis of southern New England produced two unexpected results. By integrating transportation, banking, and underwriting enterprises as a method of stimulating economic growth, particularly in manufacturing, entrepreneurs gradually lost the flexibility that had once been their great strength. And eventually, as the economy matured, they found that Rhode Island could no longer produce the risk profits to which they had become accustomed. In the pre-Civil War decades, therefore, opportunists began investing their burgeoning capital outside the state. Though such ventures benefited the recipient areas and produced profits for Rhode Island entrepreneurs, the outflow of capital diverted funds from Rhode Island enterprises and, in particular, reduced the capacity to solve the state's most fundamental economic problem, its over-specialization in a few narrow industrial fields.

CHAPTER SIX

Society and Politics

PARADOXICALLY, Rhode Islanders seem to have been both revolutionaries and conservatives. The first Americans to declare their independence from Great Britain, they were the last to replace their colonial charter by a constitution of their own making. Slater, the creator of the factory system and an early user of steam power, refused to mechanize weaving until a decade after Gilmore had introduced the power loom, and despite their rôle as pioneer industrialists, Rhode Island manufacturers lagged a full generation behind other New Englanders in adopting the corporate form of business organization. Brown University was one of the first American colleges to dethrone the classics in favor of a utilitarian curriculum, and it even introduced short courses for the calico printing and jewelry industries.[1] Yet public education lagged in Rhode Island, popular opposition to child labor was notoriously weak, and there was little enthusiasm for an industrial code to protect adult workers. However, the same Rhode Islanders who seemed so indifferent to social problems were also among the first Americans to abolish capital punishment and to give married women control of their own property.[2]

The distinction between receptiveness to some kinds of change and not to others is an artificial one. On the whole, the Rhode Islanders responded to changing circumstances with characteristic pragmatism. Some merchants certainly abandoned the slave trade out of principle, but most did so out of economic necessity—when

[1] Brennan, *Social Conditions*, 104–106.
[2] Caroline H. Dall, *Woman's Rights Under the Law* (Boston, 1861), 124–125. For an attempt to give married women equality with men in holding, conveying, and devising real property, see Petitions Not Granted, January, 1854.

the risks outweighed the profits. The head rather than the heart prevailed in many other instances. Child labor persisted as long as employers considered the system profitable, and manufacturers opposed reform not through blind conservatism but through fear of a reduction in earnings. And the same industrialists who voted against higher school and poor law taxes operated schools for their workers, gave land and buildings for workhouses, endowed universities and hospitals, and financed the temperance movement.

Whether directly or indirectly, profoundly or slightly, all Rhode Island communities were affected by the reorientation of economic life. Some towns, especially those in the dynamically expanding Blackstone-Pawtuxet region, bore the brunt of the economic revolution; others, the relatively static localities in the southern and western segments of the state, were more affected by the relocation of economic power than by the change in their own primary source of wealth; and still others, the declining towns, were mainly affected by the increasing difficulty in providing livelihoods for their inhabitants.

The disparities between towns can be gauged, in part, by the amount and rate of population growth.[3] The most significant increase in the number of Rhode Islanders occurred in the eight northern industrial communities, which constituted the Blackstone-Pawtuxet region. They had approximately 20,000 residents in 1790, or not much more than a quarter of the state's 68,800 inhabitants. Expanding decade by decade, by 1860 they contained over 108,000 people, or almost two-thirds of the 174,600 residents of Rhode Island. During the transitional phase in the shift from the maritime to the industrial orientation, from 1790 to 1820, the

[3] The demographic analysis is based on *Compendium of the Seventh Census of the United States, 1850* (Washington, 1854), 118; Newman, *Woonsocket*, 36–39; C. W. Parsons, *Notice of the History of Population in the State of Rhode Island* (n.p., 1859), 5–7; Edwin M. Snow, *Report upon the Census of Rhode Island, 1865* (Providence, 1867), l–lxiii, 4–27; Snow, *Census of Providence, 1855*, pp. 5, 12–20, 26–31; *Sixth Report . . . of the Births, Marriages and Deaths . . . 1858* (Providence, 1859), 44. The number of foreign born rose from 1,110, or barely one per cent of the total population in 1830, to more than 23,000, or over sixteen per cent in 1850, and to more than 37,000, or over twenty-one per cent in 1860.

TABLE 21

THE POPULATION OF RHODE ISLAND, 1790–1860[4]

Towns	1790	1800	1810	1820	1830	1840	1850	1860
Bristol	1,406	1,678	2,693	3,197	3,034	3,490	4,616	5,271
Warren	1,122	1,473	1,775	1,806	1,800	2,437	3,103	2,636
Cranston	1,877	1,644	2,161	2,274	2,652	2,902	4,311	7,500
Johnston	1,320	1,364	1,516	1,542	2,115	2,477	2,937	3,440
Providence	6,380	7,614	10,071	11,767	16,836	23,171	41,513	50,666
North Providence	1,071	1,067	1,758	2,420	3,503	4,207	7,680	11,818
Cumberland	1,964	2,056	2,110	2,653	3,675	5,225	6,661	8,339
Smithfield	3,171	3,120	3,828	4,678	6,857	9,534	11,500	13,283
Burrillville			1,834	2,164	2,196	1,982	3,538	4,140
Warwick	2,493	2,532	3,757	3,643	5,529	6,726	7,740	8,916
Expanding Towns	20,804	22,548	31,503	36,144	48,197	62,151	93,599	116,009
Barrington	683	650	604	634	612	549	795	1,000
Glocester	4,025	4,009	2,310	2,504	2,521	2,304	2,872	2,427
Scituate	2,315	2,523	2,568	2,834	3,993	4,090	4,582	4,251
East Greenwich	1,824	1,775	1,530	1,519	1,591	1,591	2,358	2,882
Coventry	2,477	2,423	2,928	3,139	3,851	3,433	3,620	4,247
North Kingstown	2,907	2,794	2,957	3,007	3,036	2,909	2,971	3,104
South Kingstown	4,131	3,438	3,560	3,723	3,663	3,717	3,807	4,717
Richmond	1,760	1,368	1,330	1,423	1,363	1,361	1,784	1,964
Hopkinton	2,462	2,276	1,774	1,821	1,777	1,726	2,477	2,738
Westerly	2,298	2,329	1,911	1,972	1,915	1,912	2,763	3,470
Newport	6,716	6,739	7,907	7,319	8,010	8,333	9,563	10,508
Middletown	840	913	976	949	915	891	830	1,012
Portsmouth	1,560	1,684	1,795	1,645	1,727	1,706	1,833	2,048
Tiverton	2,453	2,717	2,837	2,875	2,905	3,183	4,699	1,927
Fall River								3,377
New Shoreham	682	714	722	955	1,185	1,069	1,262	1,320
Static Towns	37,133	36,352	35,709	36,319	39,064	38,692	46,216	50,992
Foster	2,268	2,457	2,613	2,900	2,672	2,181	1,932	1,935
West Greenwich	2,054	1,757	1,619	1,927	1,817	1,415	1,350	1,258
Exeter	2,495	2,476	2,256	2,581	2,383	1,776	1,634	1,741
Charlestown	2,022	1,454	1,174	1,160	1,284	923	994	981
Jamestown	507	501	504	448	415	365	358	400
Little Compton	1,542	1,577	1,553	1,580	1,378	1,327	1,462	1,304
Declining Towns	10,888	10,222	9,719	10,596	9,949	7,987	7,730	7,619
Rhode Island	68,825	69,122	76,931	83,059	97,210	108,830	147,545	174,620

[4] Burrillville was set off from Glocester in 1806, and Fall River from Tiverton in 1856. The 1891–1892 and all subsequent editions of the *Manual of Rhode Island* give erroneous totals of 3,657 and 1,383 for Cumberland and Exeter in 1830 respectively. The *Fifth Census of the United States, 1830* (Washington, 1832), 24–25, gives 3,675 and 2,383, and a state total of 97,199.

static, not the expanding towns, contained the larger number of people. The two groups became approximately equal in size (about 36,000 people each) in 1820, and over the next decade the Blackstone-Pawtuxet region forged ahead. Its margin exceeded 4,000 people by 1830 and 57,000 people by 1860. But this crescent-shaped group of towns extending from Warwick through Providence to Burrillville actually constituted the nucleus of a much larger economic area. It included all of Providence and Kent counties and, after the collapse of the maritime economy, all of Bristol County. In 1790 these three northern counties contained 36,450 people, or barely half the total population of the state. Seventy years later, in 1860, they contained over 134,000 people, or almost four-fifths of the population. Washington County in the southwestern part of the state had some 18,000 people in 1790. It declined during the next generation, then, with the expansion of manufacturing, gradually recovered. Nevertheless, the revival was so modest that by the Civil War it had gained less than 650 people as compared to its 1790 total. Newport County was more successful. Its population increased from almost 14,300 to nearly 21,900, an increase of almost 7,600. However, considering the time span involved, seven decades, the record was not impressive. Moreover, Newport was the only large town in the entire southern half of the state, and its population on the eve of the Civil War, some 10,500, compared most unfavorably with Providence's 50,666. Newport was smaller than even North Providence and Smithfield. Indeed, seven of the eight towns with 5,000 or more inhabitants were in northern Rhode Island.

The concentration of population in the northern half of the state and especially in and around Providence, both reflected and abetted the region's rapid economic growth. This regional market, which was already fairly substantial by contemporary American standards when Rhode Island entered the Union, cushioned Providence merchants when the hazards of international trade forced them to contract their maritime operations. The region also had the physical attributes which merchant-entrepreneurs could exploit when they gradually diversified out of maritime activities and into in-

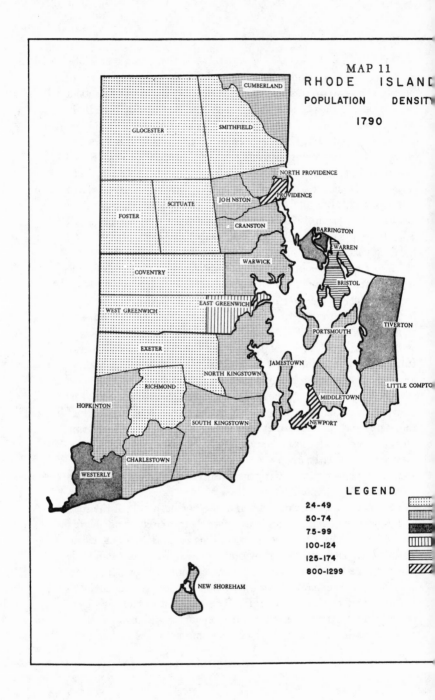

MAP 11
RHODE ISLAND
POPULATION DENSITY
1790

LEGEND

24-49
50-74
75-99
100-124
125-174
800-1299

dustrial ones. It also had a firmly established craft tradition as well as a substantial labor pool on which the pioneer textile manufacturers could draw. By 1860, Providence and its satellite towns of Cranston, Johnston, and North Providence had grown so rapidly that they constituted a market of nearly 75,000 people. Including East Providence and Pawtucket across the border in Massachusetts, there were probably about 100,000 consumers within a ten mile radius of the center of the city. With the exception of Bristol and Warren, which grew rapidly until the maritime boom abruptly ended, and the industrialized Fall River section of Tiverton, no other towns came close to matching this dynamic growth, and no other region provided such a large concentration of population. At best, other communities managed merely to provide sufficient employment to allow them to retain their natural increase of population; at worst, they lost residents to the thriving manufacturing centers or to other states. Over the entire seventy year span, the industrial towns achieved an average population growth of more than six per cent annually. North Providence, the most successful community, increased its population by some fourteen per cent annually. The relatively static western and southern towns, by contrast, achieved an average gain of only a half of one per cent annually, and the declining towns lost, on the average, four out of each thousand of their residents each year. Significantly, during the era of industrial expansion, from 1840 to 1860, even the static towns registered impressive population gains. Had they not done so, many of them, including Barrington and almost every town in Washington County, would have fallen into the declining category.

Since industrialization and urbanization generally went hand in hand, only a limited area of Rhode Island actually lost its rural character. This was true even of some parts of the Blackstone and Pawtuxet valleys. In Cumberland, Smithfield, and especially in Burrillville, for example, large areas remained in farmland or in forest, and even in the river valleys themselves the mill communities were separated from each other by green countryside. On the other hand, many regions seemingly unaffected by the industrial revolution actually contained urban enclaves such as Peace Dale in

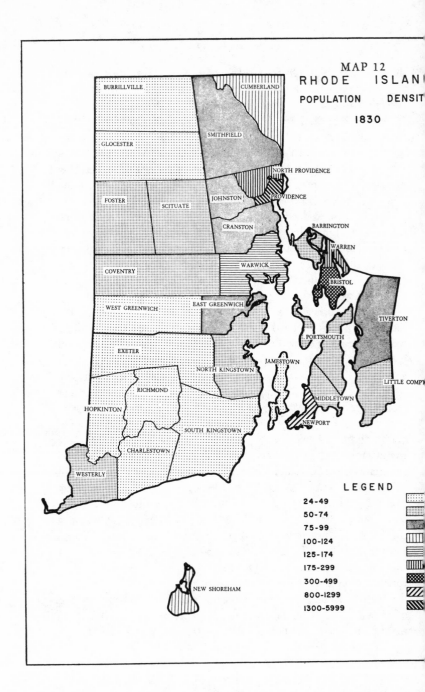

MAP 12
RHODE ISLAN
POPULATION DENSIT
1830

BURRILLVILLE

CUMBERLAND

SMITHFIELD

GLOCESTER

NORTH PROVIDENCE

FOSTER

SCITUATE

JOHNSTON

PROVIDENCE

CRANSTON

BARRINGTON

WARREN

WARWICK

BRISTOL

COVENTRY

WEST GREENWICH

EAST GREENWICH

TIVERTON

EXETER

PORTSMOUTH

JAMESTOWN

NORTH KINGSTOWN

LITTLE COMPT

RICHMOND

HOPKINTON

MIDDLETOWN

NEWPORT

SOUTH KINGSTOWN

CHARLESTOWN

WESTERLY

NEW SHOREHAM

LEGEND

24-49
50-74
75-99
100-124
125-174
175-299
300-499
800-1299
1300-5999

TABLE 22

THE RATE OF POPULATION GROWTH, 1790–1860[5]

Towns	1790 to 1800 %	1800 to 1810 %	1810 to 1820 %	1820 to 1830 %	1830 to 1840 %	1840 to 1850 %	1850 to 1860 %	1790 to 1860 %	Rate per Annum
Bristol	19	61	19	− 5	15	32	14	275	3.9
Warren	31	21	2	0	35	27	− 15	135	1.9
Cranston	− 12	31	5	17	9	49	74	305	4.4
Johnston	3	11	2	37	17	19	17	168	2.7
Providence	19	32	17	43	38	79	22	694	6.9
North Providence	0	65	38	45	20	83	54	1,004	14.3
Cumberland	5	8	20	39	42	28	25	325	4.6
Smithfield	− 2	23	22	47	39	21	16	319	4.6
Burrillville			18	2	− 10	79	17		2.5
Warwick	2	48	− 3	52	22	15	15	257	3.9
Expanding Towns	8	40	15	33	29	41	24	458	6.5
Barrington	− 5	− 7	5	− 4	− 10	45	26	46	0.7
Glocester	0		8	1	− 9	25	− 16		0.1
Scituate	9	2	10	41	2	12	− 7	84	1.2
East Greenwich	− 3	− 14	− 1	5	− 5	56	22	58	0.8
Coventry	− 2	21	7	23	− 11	5	17	71	1.0
North Kingstown	− 4	6	2	1	− 4	2	5	6	0.0
South Kingstown	− 17	4	5	− 2	2	2	24	14	0.2
Richmond	− 22	− 3	7	− 4	0	31	10	12	0.2
Hopkinton	− 8	− 22	3	− 2	− 3	44	11	11	0.2
Westerly	1	− 18	3	− 3	0	45	26	51	0.7
Newport	0	17	− 7	9	4	15	10	89	1.3
Middletown	9	7	− 3	− 4	− 3	− 7	22	20	0.3
Portsmouth	8	7	− 8	5	− 1	7	12	38	0.5
Tiverton	11	4	1	1	10	48	13	112	1.6
New Shoreham	5	1	32	24	− 10	18	5	94	1.3
Static Towns	− 2	− 2	2	7	0	20	10	37	0.5
Foster	8	6	11	− 8	− 18	− 11	0	− 15	− 0.2
West Greenwich	− 1	− 8	19	− 6	− 22	− 5	− 7	− 39	− 0.6
Exeter	− 1	− 9	14	− 8	− 26	− 8	7	− 30	− 0.4
Charlestown	− 28	− 19	− 1	11	− 28	8	− 1	− 51	− 0.7
Jamestown	− 1	1	− 11	− 7	− 12	− 2	12	− 21	− 0.3
Little Compton	2	− 2	2	− 13	− 4	10	− 11	− 15	− 0.2
Declining Towns	− 6	− 5	8	− 4	− 21	− 3	− 1	− 30	− 0.4
Rhode Island	0	11	8	17	12	36	18	154	2.2

[5] The Fall River section of Tiverton probably grew rapidly enough to be classified as an expanding town. Glocester, North Kingstown, South Kingstown, Richmond, Hopkinton, Middletown, and, perhaps, Portsmouth occupied a middle position between the declining and the static towns. Barrington, East Greenwich, and Westerly fell into this intermediate category before 1840 but grew out of it over the next two decades. Between 1810 and 1860, Burrillville grew by one hundred and twenty-six per cent, Glocester by six per cent. The annual Glocester rate is based on an estimate for the 1790–1860 span; the Burrillville rate is based on the 1810–1860 span only; and the Tiverton rate, for 1850–1860 and for 1790–1860, considers Tiverton and Fall River one jurisdiction.

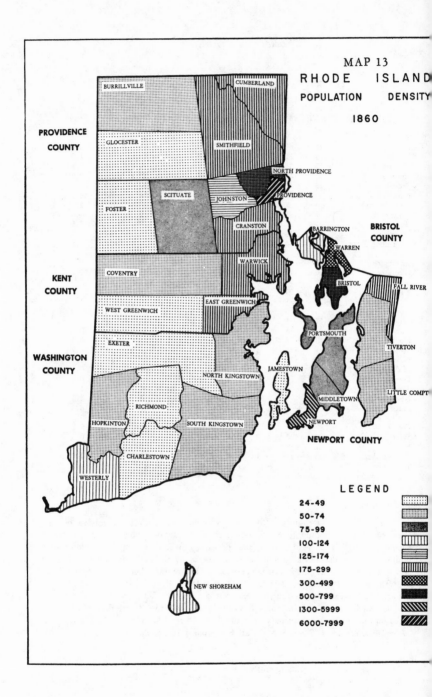

MAP 13

RHODE ISLAND

POPULATION DENSITY

1860

PROVIDENCE COUNTY

BRISTOL COUNTY

KENT COUNTY

WASHINGTON COUNTY

NEWPORT COUNTY

BURRILLVILLE

CUMBERLAND

GLOCESTER

SMITHFIELD

NORTH PROVIDENCE

SCITUATE

JOHNSTON

PROVIDENCE

FOSTER

CRANSTON

BARRINGTON

WARREN

WARWICK

BRISTOL

COVENTRY

FALL RIVER

WEST GREENWICH

EAST GREENWICH

PORTSMOUTH

EXETER

TIVERTON

JAMESTOWN

NORTH KINGSTOWN

MIDDLETOWN

LITTLE COMPT

RICHMOND

NEWPORT

HOPKINTON

SOUTH KINGSTOWN

CHARLESTOWN

WESTERLY

NEW SHOREHAM

LEGEND

24-49	
50-74	
75-99	
100-124	
125-174	
175-299	
300-499	
500-799	
1300-5999	
6000-7999	

South Kingstown, Fall River in Tiverton, and Pawcatuck and White Rock in Westerly. By definition, Rhode Island was the most densely settled and most urbanized American state, but only Newport, Fall River, Bristol, Warren, Providence, Pawtucket, and Woonsocket were true urban centers, and, even on the eve of the Civil War, twenty-three of Rhode Island's thirty-two towns retained their rural classification. These qualifications aside, industrialization did produce fundamental differences in population density as between northern Rhode Island and the southern and western regions of the state.

These differences were particularly noticeable between the expanding, static, and declining towns. On the average, in 1860 the expanding towns had a population density of almost 380 persons per square mile. Density ranged from 72 persons per square mile in Burrillville to over 7,560 in Providence. The median town, Cranston, had a density of 223 persons per square mile. On the average, the static towns had a population density of 95; individual towns ranged from a density of 43 for Glocester to 1,323 for Newport; Middletown, the median community, had a density of 75. On the average, the declining towns had a population density of 33; individual towns ranged from a density of 24 for West Greenwich to 59 for Little Compton; Exeter, the median town, had a density of 29. By American, and even by New England standards, Rhode Island was certainly closely settled, but it would be a mistake to conclude that the entire area had become, or was even in the process of becoming, urbanized.[6]

Though all towns in the state both gained and lost people, differences in growth rates generally reflected disparities in geographical mobility. On balance, the rapidly expanding towns retained a high proportion of their native-born residents and, at the same time, attracted a net gain of immigrants, whether from other Rhode Island communities, from other New England towns, or from foreign countries. By the Civil War, locally-born residents constituted between a quarter and two-fifths of the populations of

[6] The expanding towns had 84 persons per square mile in 1790 and 158 in 1830; the static towns, 64 and 72; the declining towns, 47 and 43.

these communities. Depending upon location within the state, among the relatively static towns, locally-born residents made up from four- to nine-tenths of the inhabitants. Thus much of the growth in these communities depended upon natural increase. The declining towns had a particularly high population turnover and retained a fairly low proportion of their locally-born residents.

Intrastate migration was especially high among the rapidly expanding towns. With the exception of Warwick, they followed the Providence pattern, where in 1855 every seventh resident (6,750 people) was an intrastate immigrant. More than a third of them came from neighboring industrial communities, but almost a thousand had emigrated from the county's western hill country; nearly 1,200 came from Kent County; over 900 from Newport County; and about 600 each from Bristol and Washington counties. There were three migration patterns discernible among the relatively static communities. Some isolated towns, such as New Shoreham and Jamestown, attracted practically no intrastate migrants; others, such as the two Kingstowns, reported about a fifth of their residents to be natives of other Rhode Island communities. And still others, such as Richmond and Barrington, which grew fairly rapidly after 1840, depended heavily upon intrastate migrants for their expansion. The declining towns also attracted many people, mainly because of the shortage of farm land. But these semidepressed rural areas were notoriously unsuccessful in holding migrant families, and there was a steady population turnover.

Interstate migration also contributed to the high rate of population mobility. By 1860, more than 45,000 Rhode Islanders were living in other states, principally Massachusetts and Connecticut. This outflow was partially counterbalanced by the influx of some 27,000 American-born migrants, mainly from southern New England. Thus, Rhode Island incurred a net loss of more than 18,000 native-born residents. In general, commercial and manufacturing communities attracted more newcomers than did rural ones, but interstate migrants constituted more than a fifth of the total population only in Providence, Newport, and Little Compton. Though the proportion was only slightly smaller in such industrial or border towns as Westerly, Cranston, North Providence, Cumberland, Smithfield, and Barrington, there were twelve jurisdictions where fewer than a tenth of the inhabitants had emigrated from other American states. In Jamestown and New Shoreham the proportion was less than five per hundred.

The high rate of foreign immigration more than offset Rhode Island's net interstate loss of population. Although the influx was numerically inconsequential until after 1830, foreign immigrants accounted for about half the state's increase in the 1850's, and by the Civil War they constituted more than a fifth of the population. Partly because of the higher immigrant birth rate, their segment expanded more rapidly than the native one, so that by 1865 there were almost 28,000 native-born children of immigrant parents. The birth rate among Irish and French Canadian families was between two and three times higher than that among English, Scottish, Welsh, or German families, and since the Irish made up more than two-thirds of the immigrant population, they quickly became a substantial minority group.

Foreign immigrants comprised up to a third of the population in the rapidly expanding towns, about a fifth in the semi-industrialized static towns, and less than a twentieth in the static and declining towns in rural areas. The foreign-born were also unevenly distributed within particular towns. As early as 1846, before the great tide of immigration reached Rhode Island, immigrant families constituted as many as a third of the inhabitants of some Cumberland mill villages but only a tenth in others, and a decade later, when every fourth resident of Providence was an immigrant, the foreign-born were mainly crowded into the first, third, and fifth wards. In general, the Irish remained unskilled laborers owning little personal property and virtually no real property, but others, particularly the English and Scottish immigrants, were often skilled craftsmen, many of whom rose to positions of affluence and responsibility.

Though less easy to measure, the economic revolution deeply affected Rhode Island's social and political structure. With the collapse of the household system of production, a landless class of factory workers came into being, a class for whose health and safety many mill owners showed little concern. Despite the efforts of labor leaders to win better conditions, the trade union movement had already collapsed before the great flood of foreign immigration raised insuperable obstacles to effective collective bargaining. Though legislative action brought some results, gains proved more illusory than real. Thus, Rhode Island's child labor, illiteracy, and education problems were only partially solved by 1860, and adult workers lacked even the rudimentary protection extended to children. The legislature's failure to deal effectively with industrial problems, its willingness to leave responsibility for alleviating poverty to the towns, and its tardy adaptation of the judicial system to changing social and economic conditions reflected a general lack of interest in reform.

Native-born workers constituted the chief source of industrial labor until the second quarter of the nineteenth century and thus bore the initial impact of the economic revolution. Although the small number of factories kept the demand for mill workers at a low level during the first fifteen years of industrialization, employers found it difficult to regiment cottage spinners and weavers within the factory system. The rapid expansion of the textile industry after 1804 not only aggravated this problem but also created a new one, a shortage of skilled workers. Over the long haul, however, changing social and economic conditions gradually increased the supply. Many mill laborers came from rural areas, having given up the struggle to eke out an existence from the stony soil. Their problems were compounded by the rising competition of farmers in the trans-Appalachian west and by the subdivision of farms under the intestacy law into units too small to be worked efficiently. The maritime depression and the influx of European and Canadian immigrants after 1830 also enlarged the labor pool. Too, the mechanization of production eased pressure indirectly, by reducing the demand for skilled handicraft workers.[7]

[7] Pioneer manufacturers struggled to overcome the general Jeffersonian opposition to industrialization and urbanization. It took many years to allay the widely held suspicion that factories degraded moral integrity in the worker, employer, and community alike. Even as late as 1835, White felt constrained to devote an

Nevertheless, employers had to devise ways to attract and retain factory operatives. Newspaper advertisements recruited mill hands, and agents scoured rural New England for others. Since Rhode Island manufacturers generally followed the so-called Slater system of employing entire families, including children,[8] agents generally promised more than steady work at good wages. Some manufacturers stressed the mill's proximity to a free school or to a meeting house, and others, notably the Allens, Hazards, and Slaters, took the logical step of providing these and other facilities in a company-owned mill village. A model factory community, such as that established at Peace Dale by the Hazards, might include tenements, a store, a church, a school, and a library.[9]

Paternalism, a striking characteristic of such communities, strengthened the employer's control over his labor force and provided an additional source of profit. Many manufacturers required their workers to trade only in the company store or to live only in mill-owned tenements. Since dismissal from the factory usually included eviction from mill housing and sometimes the loss of residence requirements for poor relief, the employer exercised considerable influence. Some manufacturers also subjected their employees to political pressures, used the pulpit to exhort mill hands to practice hard work, honesty, thrift, and sobriety, and established savings banks to encourage adherence to these pastoral

---

entire chapter (IV) of his *Memoir of Samuel Slater* to demonstrating the "Moral Influence of Manufacturing Establishments." See also, George Cabot to Alexander Hamilton, September 6, 1791, quoted in Cole, *Hamilton Correspondence*, 62; Ware, *Early New England Cotton Manufacture*, 216; White, *Slater*, 127; Paul H. Douglas, *American Apprenticeship and Industrial Education* (New York, 1921), 59; Gammell, *Hazard*, 5.

[8] In 1816, for example, twenty-five Slater employees were drawn from four families and a further thirty-one from nine families. See Ware, *Early New England Cotton Manufacture*, 199. See also, *ibid.*, 22–23, 29–30, 212; Edith Abbott, "A Study of the Early History of Child Labor in America," in *American Journal of Sociology*, 14:28 (July, 1908); [Thomas R. Hazard], *Facts for the Laboring Man* (Newport, 1840), 24; *Massachusetts Senate Document no. 21*, 1868, p. 25.

[9] *Rhode Island American*, April 18, 1828; *Manufacturers' and Farmers' Journal*, August 13, 1835; Staples, *Annals of Providence*, 532; White, *Slater*, 107–108, 117; John Ker Towles, "Factory Legislation of Rhode Island," in *American Economic Association Quarterly*, 3d series, 9:14 (1908).

teachings. Some mill owners operated taverns to supplement their income, but most tried to keep carousing to a minimum. A few prohibited taverns in company villages or prodded local authorities into denying liquor licenses to particular districts.[10]

Though many employers were paternalistic on matters of morality, education, temperance, and thrift, working conditions in most early textile factories reflected a general indifference to the workers' health, safety, comfort, and convenience. Mills were usually cold and drafty in winter, hot and humid in summer, and dusty, noisy, and cramped throughout the year. Except for two brief respites for breakfast and dinner, the typical factory operated from sunrise to sunset, and tardy workers were usually penalized by the loss of a quarter-day's wages. A few mills operated longer hours, but most overseers preferred to avoid the higher heating and lighting costs. Indeed, considerations of economy, not humanity, reduced the working week from seventy-eight hours in the 1840's to sixty-nine hours in the 1850's.[11]

[10] Edith Abbott, *Women in Industry: A Study in American Economic History* (New York, 1919), 272–273; Cole, *Wool Manufacture*, 1:242; John R. Commons, *et al.*, *A Documentary History of American Industrial Society* (10 vols., Cleveland, 1910–1911), 7:50; Fuller, *History of Warwick*, 179; *Manufacturers' and Farmers' Journal*, July 5, 1827; Ogden, *Thoughts*, 11–12, 20; *Pawtucket Chronicle*, August 1, 1829; Peck and Earl, *Fall River and Its Industries*, 20, 28–29; Steere, *History of Smithfield*, 129; John H. Stiness, "A Century of Lotteries in Rhode Island, 1744–1844," *Rhode Island Historical Tracts*, 2d series, 3:65 (1896); Walton, *Story of Textiles*, 174; Ware, *Early New England Cotton Manufacture*, 30, 51, 245, 248; Francis Wayland, *The Elements of Political Economy* (Boston, 1837), 294; White, *Slater*, 117–118, 125–128, 133, 215, 224–225, 229–230.

[11] Grieve, *History of Pawtucket*, 98; Thomas R. Hazard, *Miscellaneous Essays and Letters* (Philadelphia, 1883), 123; Seth Luther, *An Address to the Working-Men of New-England* (Boston, 1832), 18, 21; *New England Artisan*, January 26, February 16, March 22, 1832; Peck and Earl, *Fall River and Its Industries*, 28; *Providence Gazette*, March 24, 1845; *Providence Journal*, February 28, May 5, 1853; [Welcome Sayles], *Report of the Commission Appointed to Ascertain the Number, Ages, Hours of Labor, and Opportunity for Education of Children* (Providence, 1853), 3–8; Ware, *Early New England Cotton Manufacture*, 30, 249. In 1855 a Fall River factory owner openly declared that he regarded his workers as so much machinery to be replaced whenever they became old and useless. See *Massachusetts Senate Document no. 21, 1868*, p. 23.

Despite the low cost of living, even by early nineteenth century standards, real wage levels permitted workers few luxuries. Before 1812 capable cottage woolen spinners earned as little as seventy-five cents for a six day week, and youths employed in the early cotton mills received only forty-two cents weekly, plus board and lodging. Though wage rates rose steadily after 1820, especially for skilled mechanics and craftsmen, the typical textile mill family, comprising two adults and four children, earned less than $8 a week. Even though rent, light, heat, staples, and clothing were cheap, necessities absorbed the bulk of family income. Before the Civil War wages rose to $7 a week for a male textile factory worker and $11 for a journeyman jeweler, but except for salaried overseers, wages lagged behind mill profits and productivity. And unemployment always threatened. Though steam power reduced the frequency of layoffs caused by periodic shortages of water to drive mill machinery, the pattern of boom and depression, as in 1819, 1829, 1837, 1850, and 1857, produced widespread hardship among workers.[12]

With tacit public approval, Rhode Island mill owners continued employing children long after most American manufacturers had discontinued the practice. In the industrial view, economic no less than moral necessity justified child labor. Thus Samuel Slater deliberately decided against becoming a woolen manufacturer be-

[12] Buckingham, *America*, 3:497–502; Henry Bradshaw Fearon, quoted in Kimball, *Pictures of Rhode Island in the Past*, 165; Federal Writer's Project, *Rhode Island*, 80; Fuller, *History of Warwick*, 227; Edward B. Hall, *Sermons* (Boston, 1867), 26; Hazard, *Facts for the Laboring Man*, 16; Hazard, *Jonny-Cake Papers*, 22; Keach, *Burrillville*, 161; *McLane's Report*, 1:970–974; *Manufacturers' and Farmers' Journal*, June 7, 1824; *Manufactures, 1860*, p. x; *North Providence Centennial*, 32–33; Ogden, *Thoughts*, 20; *Republican Herald*, October 8, 1836; July 4, 1846; Schedules Five, Seventh and Eighth Census of the United States, 1850 and 1860, Rhode Island and Providence County volumes, *passim*; *Transactions*, 1857, pp. 87–89; Walton, *Story of Textiles*, 174; Ware, *Early New England Cotton Manufacture*, 29–30, 72–76, 117, 238–239, 244, 260–261, 269–271, 307; White, *Slater*, 340. See also, *James W. Sweet vs. Jenkins and Man*, 1 *Rhode Island* 147 (1840), a case in which evidence was presented to the court to demonstrate that a skilled mechanic received wages of less than $1.50 a day.

cause the industry depended too heavily upon adult male workers, and many mill owners sought to escape both the heavy capital investment required by the installation of new equipment and the high labor costs involved in the employment of adults. Instead, they continued to operate simple but obsolete machinery which could be tended by children. In 1824 some 2,500 children, ranging in age from seven to fourteen, worked in Rhode Island textile mills, and in 1831 cotton factories employed almost 3,475 children under twelve years of age, or three quarters of all the children reported working in American cotton mills.[13]

The traditional Rhode Island suspicion of idleness encouraged manufacturers to hire children in the belief that work conferred positive moral, social, and economic benefits upon child, parent, and employer alike. Thus the local press defended the system with the argument that "honest labor is much better than the most romantic indolence," and even though one visitor to Slater's mill thought that tending machinery dulled the spirit, "the misery [of] an overflowing and underemployed population" was even more fearful. It was better to be overworked, asserted one editor, than "to pine in sloth, rags, and wretchedness."[14]

Both the child labor system and working conditions evoked occasional splutterings of social criticism. Critics condemned the physical and mental consequences of overworking children in noisy,

[13] Abbott, "Child Labor in America," *passim*, but especially pp. 28–31, 34–35; Bagnall, *Textile Industries*, 159; Cole, *Hamilton Correspondence*, 77; Douglas, *American Apprenticeship*, 57; Federal Writers' Project, *Rhode Island*, 246; Grieve, *History of Pawtucket*, 98; Luther, *Address*, 18, 21; *McLane's Report*, 1:976; *Manufacturers' and Farmers' Journal*, January 26, 1824; January 17, 1828; *New England Artisan*, March 22, 1832; Pitkin, *A Statistical View, 1835*, p. 526; [Elisha R. Potter], *Report of the Commissioner of Public Schools* (Providence, 1852), in *Acts and Resolves*, January, 1852, *passim; Providence Patriot*, May 30, 1829; [Josiah Quincy], "Account of Journey of Josiah Quincy," in *Proceedings of the Massachusetts Historical Society*, 2d series, 4:124 (Boston, 1887–1889); Snow, *Census of Providence, 1855*, p. 32–36; Snow, *Census of Rhode Island, 1865*, pp. lxxiv–lxxxi, 39–44; Walton, *Story of Textiles*, 174; Ware, *Early New England Cotton Manufacture*, 64, 210–211, 236–237.

[14] *Rhode Island American*, March 21, 1828; Quincy, "Journey," 124. The *Providence Patriot*, May 30, 1829, observed with satisfaction that factory children had little free time "to spend in idleness or vicious amusement."

dark, dusty, and badly ventilated mills, or denounced their limited educational opportunities.[15] Seth Luther, the most prominent New England labor leader, protested against corporal punishment for minor infractions of factory rules or as a stimulus to greater effort. Some alleged that neither girls nor even deaf and dumb children escaped the overseer's lash or his brass-studded leather strap, and Thomas Man reported that some manufacturers "lost sight of the human beings who operated their machines, and . . . too often mistook injustice and cruelty for order and discipline. I know of one," he wrote, "who was in the habit of flogging the children . . . out of sheer wantonness. Many of the mill owners were of the loosest morals, and the factory girl was fortunate who preserved her honor and her position."[16] There were few safeguards against these abuses. As the father of a young girl employed in Slater's Smithfield mill found, the politically dominated system of justice favored employers. He sought damages from an overseer whom, he alleged, "beat, bruised, pinched, choked and pushed" his daughter. Though he obtained a favorable verdict, the court awarded him only token damages—ten cents. Determined to secure redress, the outraged father appealed the award. He obtained the maximum damages permitted by the law, but it amounted to a mere twenty dollars.[17]

Beginning in 1824 with a strike in the Pawtucket cotton industry and ending a decade later with a similar dispute at Woonsocket,

[15] Commons, *Documentary History*, 5:195–199. One critic argued that "no nation has ever yet pushed its manufactures to any great extent without introducing and continuing a very alarming quantity of misery and disease." See John Bristed, *The Resources of the United States of America* (New York, 1818), 54. Rowland Hazard, in *Economics and Politics*, 253, contended that "justice to the community, as well as the common sentiment of humanity, demands that minors should be protected from the excessive toil that stints their intellectual growth." See also, Henry Barnard, *Journal of the Rhode Island Institute of Instruction* (Providence, 1846), 1:34; White, *Slater*, 126–128; *Acts and Resolves*, June, 1851, p. 30; *History of Rhode Island*, 160.

[16] Luther, *Address*, 18; *New England Artisan*, March 29, 1832; Massachusetts Bureau of the Statistics of Labor, *Report of 1870* (Boston, 1870), 122; Thomas Man, *Picture of Woonsocket* ([Providence], 1835), 15–16.

[17] *Republican Herald*, February 20, 1833.

dissatisfaction with industrial conditions provoked sporadic outbursts of protest. Though higher wages and shorter hours constituted the chief issues in contention between workers and employers,[18] the labor movement quickly absorbed the prevailing reform currents. By the early 1830's, when the Providence branch of the New England Association of Farmers, Mechanics and Other Workingmen became labor's chief spokesman, employees demanded redress of both political and social grievances without simultaneously losing sight of their more immediate objective of improved working conditions. They wanted extra pay for overtime work, restrictions on the employment of women and children, and the legalization of trade unions, but they also urged the abolition of monopolies, of imprisonment for debt, and of religious legislation. The workers also appealed for a reduction of legal fees, the establishment of manhood suffrage, the direct election of public officials, and free public education.[19] Applauding the refusal of Taunton mill hands to work by candlelight, delegates to a Providence meeting in the fall of 1831 declared that if "it would be a public benefit . . . to work fifteen hours, we ought to do it," but "if ten hours work per day is a public benefit our employers ought to be satisfied, notwithstanding it be to their disadvantage."[20] To deprive mill children of educational opportunities was as cruel as it was unjust, argued delegates to a Boston convention three months later, for it sacrificed their "dearest interests . . . to the cupidity and avarice of their employers." Ignorance would ultimately prostrate the workers' "liberties at the shrine of a powerful aristocracy."[21] Already,

[18] Towles, "Factory Legislation," 59; *Providence Patriot*, March 7, 1832. See also, Norman Ware, *The Industrial Worker, 1840–1860* (New York, 1924), *passim*.

[19] J. R. Commons, *et al.*, *History of Labour in the United States* (2 vols., New York, 1918), 1:318–325; G. E. McNeil, ed., *The Labor Movement* (Boston, 1887), 77–78; *Newport Mercury*, October 5, 1833; *Republican Herald*, October 19, 1833; *Providence Patriot*, October 26, 1833. See also, *Republican Herald*, November 10, 1849, for the assertion that "factory life . . . is little better than slavery."

[20] *Providence Patriot*, October 1, 15, 1831. See also, *Providence Journal*, October 25, 1831.

[21] Grieve, *History of Pawtucket*, 99.

asserted Thomas Man, the factory system had deprived workers of liberty of thought, speech, and body, and he supposed that operatives must imagine themselves to be brutish inhabitants of "the lower regions."[22]

A series of factors worked against the early trade union movement. Though the General Assembly did enact a lien law to protect mechanics in January, 1834, this was its only notable concession.[23] The large labor pool formed the chief obstacle to effective action, for it allowed employers to disrupt trade unionism either by dismissing workers for sending delegates to regional conventions or by blacklisting labor leaders and their supporters. Mill owners also used their political influence to frustrate union activity, as when the Woonsocket school committee refused to allow the workers to meet in the school house to elect representatives.[24] Economic conditions also militated against collective bargaining. The ever-present fear of unemployment, particularly following the recession of 1829, made many workers unwilling to jeopardize their jobs. Moreover, the chronic jealousy between cottage and factory weavers, and the mutual suspicion between native- and foreign-born workers imposed additional strains upon trade unionism. Finally, because labor leaders involved the movement in the reform issues of the Jacksonian era, they dissipated working class effort by failing to concentrate upon the narrower goal of improving factory conditions. Thus the early Rhode Island labor movement was short-lived. Union activity was already declining when the depression of 1837 brought about its collapse, and for all practical purposes it did not revive until after the Civil War.[25]

[22] Man, *Picture of Woonsocket*, 16.

[23] *Acts and Resolves*, January, 1834, pp. 30–34. For an attempt to extend the scope of the statute, see Petitions Not Granted, January, 1857, and for an extension, see *Acts and Resolves*, January, 1859, p. 305.

[24] Luther, *Address*, 23; *New England Artisan*, February 22, 1832. For typical anti-trade union points of view, see two works by Francis Wayland: *Elements of Political Economy*, 117, and *Limitations on Human Responsibilities* (Boston, 1849), 105, 112. See also, White, *Slater*, 337–339; and Hazard, *Economics and Politics*, 253.

[25] *Providence Journal*, November 25, 1827; Commons, *Documentary History*, 6:196; Charles R. Crow, "Utopian Socialism in Rhode Island, 1845–1850," in

The cause of public education suffered from these trade union weaknesses as well as from the popular indifference to child labor. Reformers had also to battle the apathy of some religious sects. Traditionally, the Baptists showed little sympathy for learning. Unlike the Congregationalists, who demanded an educated clergy, at best, the Baptists were indifferent to education; at worst, they were openly hostile. Though their leaders eventually tried to remove this stigma, especially after 1820, the ingrained suspicion of education nevertheless lingered for many years. As a consequence, the school system developed much more slowly in Rhode Island than in either Massachusetts or Connecticut.[26]

The General Assembly did not even authorize towns to establish schools until 1800. But neither the legislators nor the Providence Association of Mechanics and Manufacturers, the chief advocate of public instruction, thought children should be in school rather than in factories. The legislature merely hoped that citizens would eventually "rival in knowledge and morals the most refined and enlightened in the nation."[27] Though many communities did open schools, only Providence established a permanent educational system, and though some children attended private academies or the Sunday and evening schools provided by paternalistic employers, many went untutored.[28] In 1824 the Assembly rejected a plan

Rhode Island History, 18:20–26 (January, 1959); Federal Writers' Project, *Rhode Island*, 81–82; Ware, *The Industrial Worker, passim*, but especially p. xx. Significantly, Ware devotes virtually no attention to the Rhode Island labor movement after 1840.

[26] For a discussion of the general difficulties, especially the religious ones, encountered by the school reformers, see George E. Horr, "The Baptists," in William W. Fenn, *et al.*, *The Religious History of New England* (Cambridge, 1917), 168; Keach, *Burrillville*, 131, 141–142; William Howe Tolman, *History of Higher Education in Rhode Island* (Washington, 1894), 23–24; F. and H. L. Wayland, *A Memoir of the Life and Labors of Francis Wayland* (2 vols., New York, 1867), 2:235; Edwin M. Stone, *The Life and Recollections of John Howland* (Providence, 1857), 136–148. See also, *Providence Journal*, June 8, 1839.

[27] Charles Carroll, *Public Education in Rhode Island* (Providence, 1918), 77–81, 298–300; Henry Barnard, *Report on the Condition and Improvement of the Public Schools of Rhode Island* (Providence, 1846), 100–101.

[28] According to Thomas B. Stockwell, ed., *A History of Public Education in Rhode Island from 1636 to 1876* (Providence, 1876), 21, the initial effort to

requiring employers to educate child workers.[29] Another four years
elapsed before the legislature began making a token annual grant
of $10,000 to local school authorities. Significantly, it raised these
funds from such sources as license fees rather than from property
taxes. Towns could supplement the state grants, but parents had
to assume the major educational cost and schooling remained
voluntary. Though poor families could get fees remitted, many
parents were too proud to acknowledge their distress or too desti-
tute to forego the meager income their children earned.[30] Thus the
Children's Friends Society, organized by Seth Luther in 1836 to
oppose child labor and promote public schools, won little support.[31]

In 1840 the General Assembly prohibited the employment of
children unless they attended school three months annually, but
in the absence of an inspection system, most manufacturers and
parents ignored the law.[32] Since taxpayers balked at financing education, in 1845 the Assembly omitted the compulsory provision
for factory children from the school law codification.[33] For a

---

establish public education was "virtually defeated by simple non-enforcement."
Newport, for example, took no action under the act of 1800, and though Simeon
Potter, wishing to promote Newport's revival, deeded the town property for a
school as early as 1795, almost twenty years elapsed before instruction began.
See Carroll, *Public Education*, 47–49. See also, *ibid.*, 41–46, 50–72, 300–302.

[29] Towles, "Factory Legislation," 14. For other attempts (in 1818, 1821, and
in the constitutional convention of 1824) to establish public schools and, especially, to require that factory children obtain a rudimentary education, see
Carroll, *Public Education*, 82–83, 333.

[30] *Acts and Resolves*, January, 1828, p. 9; *Providence Patriot*, February 8,
1828; Carroll, *Public Education*, 72–77, 85–106, 148, 302–303, 333–345;
Elizabeth A. Perry, *A Brief History of . . . Glocester* (Providence, 1886), 78.

[31] Luther, *Address*, 21; *Providence Journal*, November 5, 1836; Federal
Writers' Project, *Rhode Island*, 80.

[32] *Acts and Resolves*, January, 1840, p. 92; *Providence Journal*, November 5,
1838; February 4, October 30, 1839; *Manufacturers' and Farmers' Journal*,
January 27, 1840; [Henry Barnard], *Report of the Commissioner of the Public
Schools of Rhode Island, 1845* (Providence, 1845), 37; [E. R. Potter], *ibid.*,
1851, in *Acts and Resolves*, January, 1851, appendix, pp. 113, 117; January, 1852,
appendix, p. 28; Carroll, *Public Education*, 120, 134; Francis Wayland, *Thanksgiving Discourse* (Providence, 1843), especially p. 24.

[33] *Acts and Resolves*, June, 1845, appendix; Rowland Hazard, *Address before
the Washington County Association for the Improvement of Public Schools*
(Providence, 1845), 7; *Republican Herald*, March 18, 1848; Carroll, *Public
Education*, 114.

decade, all efforts to revive the statute or to regulate working conditions failed.[34]

The General Assembly re-examined the child labor question in 1851, when it appointed Welcome Sayles to study factory conditions. He reported that some 1,850 children under fifteen years of age were employed. Almost forty per cent of them were under twelve; nearly five per cent were under nine. In some cotton mills they worked seventy-eight hours a week, and in two highly mechanized Providence hardware factories some children worked on the night shift. Sayles emphasized the adverse physical effects of these conditions, and also observed that many youthful workers had received their only schooling in Ireland. Some members of the legislative committee that considered this report protested that nearly 10,000 children were "chained to the wheel by poor or exacting parents." How were such youngsters, asked these critics, "with their physical frames undeveloped, their minds uncultivated, their moral nature undisciplined, or worse than undisciplined, to become considerate, virtuous, law abiding citizens?"[35]

The Assembly enacted regulatory legislation in 1853,[36] but the general public remained indifferent to the child labor problem, and most employers, taking their lead from the Providence stove maker, A. C. Barstow, opposed restrictions. Instead of requiring the education of factory children and appointing inspectors to enforce the law, as Sayles had urged, the legislature merely barred the employment of children and youths on night shifts or for more than

[34] Petitions Not Granted, May, 1851, January, 1852; Miscellaneous Papers of the General Assembly, folder 12 (1836–1840), folder 16 (1851); *Manufacturers' and Farmers' Journal*, January 13, 1845; October 28, 1847; February 7, 1848; October 30, 1851; February 2, 1852; *Providence Journal*, November 2, 1849; February 1, 1850.

[35] Reports to the General Assembly, 13:5 (1853); *Sayles' Report*, 3–8.

[36] *Acts and Resolves*, January, 1853, pp. 245–246; *Manufacturers' and Farmers' Journal*, February 5, May 12, 1852; February 29, 1853; *Providence Journal*, February 24, 25, 28, 1853; *Providence Evening Post*, February 3, 24, 25, March 3, 9, 1853; [E. R. Potter], *Report of the Commissioner of Public Schools, 1853*, in *Acts and Resolves*, January, 1853, appendix *passim*; Ware, *The Industrial Worker*, 160. For two attempts to get the ten hour day for all, see Petitions Not Granted, February, 1852, in Outsize Petitions, boxes 1 and 2.

eleven hours a day. The law did not apply to slaughterhouses or to non-industrial undertakings. Though the Assembly revived the compulsory educational requirement in 1854,[37] it refused to extend the eleven hour day to workers under nineteen.[38] The public continued to believe that the virtues of regular employment outweighed the possible dangers of overwork,[39] the same economic pressures that had made the earlier legislation a broken reed persisted, and the Irish and Canadian immigrants, who constituted the bulk of the labor force after 1850, feared that blacklisting or eviction would follow if they protested. As a result, the employment of children was probably as extensive in 1883 as it had been before the Civil War.[40]

Foreign immigration also raised the incidence of illiteracy, especially in industrial areas.[41] In 1855, Providence had 2,660 illiterate residents. Every ninth youth and every fifth adult of foreign parentage could neither read nor write. Persons of American descent, by contrast, even in the older age category, were rarely illiterate. Overwhelmingly, it was the Irish who lacked education. Of the 10,181 illiterate Rhode Islanders reported in 1865, 7,313 were of Irish extraction, and every fourth Irishman over fifteen years of age was unlettered. Among English-born immigrants, some of whom were undoubtedly from Irish families who had first migrated to the Lancashire cotton industry, the ratio was one illiterate in

[37] *Acts and Resolves,* January, 1854, pp. 262–263. See also, *Providence Journal,* February 25, 1854; *Revised Statutes, 1857,* pp. 326–330.

[38] Petitions Not Granted, September, 1853. See also, *Manufacturers' and Farmers' Journal,* November 7, 1853; Stockwell, *Public Education,* 84.

[39] See Miscellaneous Papers of the General Assembly, folder 19, (1855–1856), for a bill to punish idleness.

[40] In 1883, Rhode Island had a higher illiteracy rate than any other northern state. See Carroll, *Public Education,* 200–201. See also [Robert Allyn], *Report of the Commissioner of Public Schools, 1857,* in *Acts and Resolves,* January, 1857, appendix, pp. 13, 18.

[41] Carroll, *Public Education,* 127, 159; Keach, *Burrillville,* 88; Luther, *Address,* 21; *New England Artisan,* May 3, 1832; *Sixth Census of the United States, 1840* (Washington, 1841), 52–55; Snow, *Census of Providence, 1855,* pp. 32–36; Snow, *Census of Rhode Island, 1865,* pp. 39–44; Stockwell, *Public Education,* 179; Towles, "Factory Legislation," 20–21.

twenty, and among native-born white residents it was only one in seventy-eight. Irish illiteracy reflected a combination of factors: the inability of parochial schools to cope with the annual deluge of immigrant children, parental fears that public schools would corrupt faith, and economic necessity.[42]

Illiteracy served as a major barrier to the social, economic, and political advancement of such ethnic groups as the Irish. It limited their job opportunities, kept them in the ranks of the poorly paid, unskilled workers, and exposed them to discrimination and exploitation by employers, merchants, money lenders, and politicians. The political system discriminated against naturalized citizens, and even their native-born children could not vote freely.

The prevalence and intensity of ethnic and religious conflict rose sharply in the second quarter of the nineteenth century. It had many causes and took numerous forms. Irish immigrants were commonly blamed for most outbreaks of lawlessness. Their indifference to trade unionism and their displacement of native-born workers made them especially unpopular. With the introduction of the power loom Irish Catholics replaced Ulster hand weavers, thereby reviving traditional antagonisms. Immigrant labor predominated in canal and railroad construction projects, the Portsmouth coal industry, and the building of Fort Adams at Newport, but some employers refused to hire Irish workers. In 1833, Francis Wayland, the Baptist President of Brown University, believed the alien influx to be a clever Popish plot to subvert Rhode Island institutions, and, in the 1850's, Providence Protestants so feared that Catholics would appropriate public funds for parochial schools that they abandoned the system of electing the members of the school committee.[43]

[42] The first two Catholic schools in Providence did not open until 1851 and 1855. Large numbers of Catholic children withdrew from the public schools in 1852 and 1853. See Carroll, *Public Education*, 155; *Report of the Commissioner of Public Schools, 1857*, p. 15.

[43] Rowland Tappen Berthoff, *British Immigrants in Industrial America, 1790–1950* (Cambridge, 1953), *passim*; Ray Allen Billington, *The Protestant Crusade, 1800–1860: A Study of the Origins of American Nativism* (New York, 1938), *passim*, but especially pp. 32–48, 53–70, 166–185, 238–256, 322–338; William Byrne, *et al.*, *History of the Catholic Church in New England* (2 vols.,

Many Rhode Islanders considered that the verdict in the famous Gordon murder trial of 1844 was a travesty of justice and that the bench had allowed racial prejudice to influence its decision. The Gordon brothers, two Irish immigrants, were charged with the murder of the industrialist Amasa Sprague, who had opposed the licensing of their tavern. When Sprague's mutilated body was discovered, the Gordons were immediately suspected and, though the evidence against them was flimsy and circumstantial, they were brought to trial. The court found John Gordon guilty and sentenced him to death, but it released his brother. Coming as it did so soon after the Dorr War, in which the opponents of reform had deliberately appealed to nativist, Protestant prejudices, the trial seemed to many to have been a mockery of justice. Though the reaction to Gordon's execution contributed eight years later, in 1852, to the abolition of capital punishment, the case left bitter memories in the Irish community.[44]

On the other hand, goodwill prevailed in some quarters. David Wilkinson, the North Providence industrialist and Quaker con-

Boston, 1899), 1:380, 410; Carroll, *Public Education*, 276, 390–391; Carroll, *Rhode Island*, 2:1147–1153; *Christian Watchman* (Boston), January 17, August 15, 1834; April 8, 1835; Fuller, *History of Warwick*, 201; Alexander Griswold, *A Brief Exposition of Some of the Errors and Corruptions of the Church of Rome* (Boston, 1834), *passim*; Keach, *Burrillville*, 87–88; Luther, *Address*, 20; John H. McKenna, *The Centenary Story of Old St. Mary's, Pawtucket, 1829–1929* (Providence, 1929), 12–14, 23–24; *North Providence Centennial*, 72; *Providence Daily Post*, February 28, 1854; *Providence Journal*, March 25, 1851; Turner, *Reminiscences of East Greenwich*, 4; Ware, *Early New England Cotton Manufacture*, 232; T. T. Waterman, *Lecture on the Christmas Festival* (Providence, 1835), *passim*; Francis Wayland, *Occasional Discourses* (Boston, 1833), 53, 55. For two general discussions, see Field, *Rhode Island*, 2:especially pp. 93–104, 114–122, 137–150, 164–212; and Thomas F. Cullen, *The Catholic Church in Rhode Island* (North Providence, 1936), *passim*, especially pp. 77–126, 219–345.

[44] George Potter, *To the Golden Door: The Story of the Irish in Ireland and America* (Boston, 1960), 441–446; Zechariah Chafee, Jr., "Weathering the Panic of '73: An Episode in Rhode Island Business History," in *Proceedings of the Massachusetts Historical Society*, 66:271 (Boston, 1942); *State vs. John Gordon*, 1 *Rhode Island* 179 (1844); *Acts and Resolves*, January, 1852, pp. 12–13. See also, *Providence Daily Post*, October 27, 1855, for the murder trial of Mary Flanagan. The case had striking parallels with the Gordon case.

vert to Episcopalianism, donated land for Pawtucket's first Catholic Church. Providence permitted Catholics to celebrate Mass in the Old Town House, and in other communities services were occasionally held in taverns or in Quaker homes. Many Protestants applauded the temperance efforts of Bishop William Tyler and the Irish Capuchin, Father Theobald Mathew.[45] Though Democrats Philip Allen and William Sprague cultivated Irish support, they regarded their workers as so many sheep to be herded to the polls, and they showed little interest in social or economic reform. Indeed, they behaved like feudal seigneurs, counting their employees' political support as one of the allegiances sealed in the labor contract.[46]

Since naturalized citizens could vote only if they held a minimum of real property, the refusal to sell land to Catholic immigrants prevented them from acquiring political rights, and the acute shortage of land in such urban centers as Providence enabled Protestants to impede church construction by discriminating against Catholic buyers. This forced Catholics to resort to dummy purchasers in order to acquire realty, but when sellers discovered the deception they sometimes offered substantial and tempting premiums to recover the property. Naturalized citizens could buy land so long as they could find someone who was willing to sell, but aliens could hold or convey real estate only with the express permission of the General Assembly or, later, the probate courts. An attempt to repeal the law in 1847 failed. But even if Catholics did acquire land for a church, as they did in Providence, they had still to raise funds for construction. The Reverend R. D. Woodley, pastor of the Providence Catholic community, sought to obtain funds through the sale of lottery tickets, the method usually practiced by Protestant churches, but the legislature denied him

[45] Cullen, *The Catholic Church*, 77; James Fitton, *Sketches of the Establishment of the Church of New England* (Boston, 1872), 222; Frances Morehouse, "The Irish Migrations of the 'Forties," in *American Historical Review*, 33:579–592 (April, 1928); *Republican Herald*, September 22, 1849; Wayland, *Memoir*, 2:58.

[46] Munro, *Picturesque Rhode Island*, 175; Cullen, *The Catholic Church*, 111.

permission to do so, and after 1830 neither Protestant nor Catholic congregations secured authority to hold lotteries.[47]

A particularly significant manifestation of religious animosity occurred in 1834 in a bill regulating religious corporations. Had it passed, it would have frustrated the practice of Catholicism in Rhode Island. The bill comprised four main sections. First, except for maintenance and insurance, no members, pews, shares, nor other property in the church could be subjected to compulsory assessment. Second, no religious corporation could take, receive, or hold any property or beneficial interest by devise or bequest unless the transfer occurred at least a full year before the donor's death. Third, pastors were to be elected by their congregations. Fourth, no church, as distinct from a locally governed society or congregation, could hold property, and over and above the building and lot, the maximum was set at $10,000 in realty and $20,000 in personalty. It is possible, but unlikely, that the bill was innocently drafted by a Protestant. Even the seemingly innocuous fourth section would have created difficulties for the Catholic Church by forcing the Boston diocese to relinquish legal control of all its property in Rhode Island in favor of the individual congregation. In effect, the bill struck a blow at the very roots of episcopal authority.[48]

These sporadic outbursts of bigotry reached their climax in the pre-Civil War decade and probably explain the late incorporation of the Catholic Church in Rhode Island. Despite the rapid increase in communicants and the organization of industrial parishes, the church hierarchy was apparently unwilling until 1869 to risk denial of an application for incorporation of the diocese of Rhode

[47] *Ibid.*, 78; *Providence Gazette*, March 10, 1798; Granted Petitions, 64:16 (January, June, 1839); Petitions Not Granted, June, 1830; May, 1846; Miscellaneous Papers of the General Assembly, folder 14 (1846–1848); *Acts and Resolves*, January, 1853, p. 293. For a general discussion see Ware, *Early New England Cotton Manufacture*, 229–235.

[48] Miscellaneous Papers of the General Assembly, folder 11 (1831–1835). See also, *Manufacturers' and Farmers' Journal*, January 19, 1835, and *Public Laws, 1844*, p. 431, for a law taxing religious and educational property held by unincorporated societies, and restricting the amount of realty a church could hold.

Island. By that time, the favorable public reaction to the Irish immigrant community's patriotism during the Civil War had somewhat tempered religious animosity. Too, many second generation citizens had reached voting age and were beginning to exert some political influence.[49]

But religious and ethnic antagonisms, while chiefly manifested between Protestants and Catholics, or between native and foreign-born workers, also occurred within particular religious denominations. The anti-Masonic movement split Protestants into bitterly opposed factions in the early 1830's, and French Canadians held themselves aloof from the Irish, partly in their determination to maintain their cultural and linguistic individuality, but also because they considered the Irish boorishly inferior. And county jealousies brought from the Old Country rent the Irish community. Nor were the Irish particularly fond of the Yankee priests who were generally their first Rhode Island pastors. As converts to Catholicism, many of these spiritual advisors were sharply critical of Irish religious laxity, of their propensity for trouble making, of their intemperance, and of their brawling ways.[50]

Serious social dislocation followed the rapid spread of industrialization and urbanization, particularly in the second quarter of

[49] *Acts and Resolves*, January, 1869, pp. 221–222. Note, however, that three parishes, two in Woonsocket and one in Providence, were separately incorporated earlier. See *ibid.*, January, 1864, p. 221; January, 1866, pp. 298, 300. See also, Cullen, *The Catholic Church*, 129–131.

[50] For anti-Masonic legislation, see *Acts and Resolves*, October, 1831, p. 90; January, 1832, p. 51; August, 1832, p. 5; June, 1833, p. 26; January, 1834, p. 55; May, 1834, p. 44; January, 1835, p. 20; January, 1842, p. 36. For anti-Masonic literature and investigations, see John Quincy Adams, *Letters Addressed to William L. Stone . . . and Benjamin Cowell* (Providence, 1833); Richard Rush, John Quincy Adams, William Wirt, *et al.*, *A Portrait of Masonry and Anti-masonry* (Providence, 1832); *An Investigation into Freemasonry by a Joint Committee of the Legislature of Massachusetts* (Boston, 1834), especially appendices D, E, and F, pp. 39–52; *Proceedings of the Rhode-Island Anti-Masonic State-Convention, September 14, 1831* (Providence, 1831); B. F. Hallett, George Turner, *et al.*, *Notes of a Legislative Investigation into Masonry . . . before a Committee of The General Assembly of Rhode Island . . . Between December 7, 1831, and January 7, 1832* (Boston, 1832). For additional data on ethnic and religious conflict, see Man, *Picture of Woonsocket*, 32; *Providence Journal*, July 6, 1850, November 3, 1851; Field, *Rhode Island*, 1:325–329; Henry Jackson, *An Account of the Churches in Rhode-Island* (Providence, 1854), 100–102.

the nineteenth century. The public was generally content to blame the Irish for the rising crime rate and for the rowdyism and lawlessness reputed to have taken root in Pawtucket, Lippitt, Phoenix, Crompton, Natick, and other mill villages. Catholic leaders, lay as well as clerical, struggled to counteract this criticism by organizing parishes in the new manufacturing centers, but Whig newspapers, especially the *Providence Journal*, the chief spokesman for anti-Catholic sentiment, undermined these pastoral influences. In many mill communities the *Journal's* vicious indictments of the Irish, whom it compared unfavorably to the Negro, goaded immigrants into occasional frenzies of hooliganism and petty rioting, and, incidentally, strengthened the Irish identification with the Democratic party.[51]

The *Journal* also helped to stampede voters into the Know-Nothing camp. Nativist sentiment gathered momentum during and after the depression of 1850. In the summer of 1854, Governor William A. Hoppin, a Whig, acquiesced in the formation of several quasi-private armed companies of "Guards of Liberty." Early the following spring, in March, 1855, popular animosity turned against the Sisters of Mercy Convent in Providence, where, it was alleged, a young woman was being held against her will. Tempers flared among the crowd which milled around the convent gates; Bishop Bernhard O'Reilly feared the outbreak of a serious disturbance; and for a few days it seemed as if the crowd intended to put the convent under siege. In the end, however, the defenders, onlookers, and protesters, growing tired of picketing, drifted away. Though Hoppin, running on the Whig and Know-Nothing tickets, scored a resounding victory in the April election, the legislature resisted the temptation to exploit anti-Catholic sentiment and it took no more drastic action than to deny state courts the authority to naturalize aliens. The Whigs, having capitalized on this religious and ethnic bigotry in order to discredit the Democrats, soon aban-

[51] Barnard, *Report on the Public Schools*, 1846, p. 73; Jackson, *The Churches of Rhode Island*, 56; Keach, *Burrillville*, 72; Peck and Earl, *Fall River and its Industries*, 32–33; *Providence Journal*, March 30, November 3, 1851; February 24, 1853; Richardson, *History of Woonsocket*, 93–94; Stone, *Mechanics' Festival*, 34.

doned their nativist crusade in favor of a campaign against slavery. Rhode Island thus escaped the violence which characterized the Know-Nothing era in Massachusetts, New York, and Maryland.[52]

But not even the *Journal* could indict the Irish for an earlier manifestation of social dislocation, the rioting which had broken out in the fall of 1831, when some drunken sailors invaded the Providence Negro district. For three days the authorities struggled vainly to control the rioting mobs roaming the streets. When they eventually restored order, at least eight Negro shanties had been torn down and a number of people had been killed. This brief, seemingly purposeless explosion evoked two different reactions. To some observers the mob violence showed that the town council lacked the authority to deal effectively with modern problems. They urged the incorporation of Providence as a city. To others, the reign of terror gave further proof of "Demon Rum's" evil consequences. To these reformers, prohibition rather than the reorganization of local government seemed the proper solution.[53]

Temperance agitation had been slowly gaining strength since the beginning of the century.[54] Though a desire to supervise ap-

[52] *Acts and Resolves*, January, 1855, p. 11; Beaman, *Historical Address*, 215; Byrne, *Catholic Church in New England*, 1:376; Field, *Rhode Island*, 1:365–367; Thomas R. Hazard, *A Constitutional Manual for the National American Party* (Providence, 1856), 24; Petitions Not Granted, February, 1855; *Providence Journal*, January 30, 1851, June 22, 1853, June 5, 6, 1855; *Providence Daily Post*, March 20, 23, July 31, 1854; Charles Stickney, "Know-Nothingism in Rhode Island," in *Publications of the Rhode Island Historical Society*, New series, 1:243–257 (January, 1894).

[53] *Acts and Resolves*, January, 1830, p. 31–39; Irving H. Bartlett, *From Slave to Citizen: The Story of the Negro in Rhode Island* (Providence, 1954), 27–33; Richard M. Bayles, ed., *History of Providence County* (2 vols., New York, 1891), 1:199–201; Carroll, *Public Education*, 157–158; Field, *Rhode Island*, 1:320–321; *Providence Journal*, September 26, 1831; *Providence Patriot*, September 28, 1831; Wayland, *Occasional Discourses*, 358.

[54] For the temperance movement, see *Acts and Resolves*, October, 1817, pp. 25–26; January, 1824, p. 47; May, 1825, p. 55; June, 1826, p. 34; October, 1826, p. 32; January, 1830, p. 63; June, 1835, p. 4; June, 1838, p. 29; January, 1841, p. 73; January, 1843, p. 54; January, 1845, p. 93; May, 1852, pp. 3–17; June, 1852, pp. 118–119; Brennan, *Social Conditions*, 74–75, 80–87, 123–124; Carroll, *Rhode Island*, 2:648–649, 1101; Cole, *History of Washington and Kent Counties*, 581; *History of Rhode Island*, 53; *Joel Fletcher vs. Rhode Island*,

prentices unduly addicted to nocturnal revelling was one reason for the formation of the Providence Association of Mechanics and Manufacturers at the end of the eighteenth century, the crusade against alcohol did not gain momentum until after the War of 1812, when many Protestant ministers, resident as well as itinerant, took up the prohibition cause. During the 1820's, some mill towns, notably Pawtucket, organized campaigns against both drunkenness and sabbath breaking. The temperance movement attracted many manufacturers, especially after delegates convened in Providence in 1828 to form a state organization. Some mill owners retained their taverns as business investments, but others followed the example of Zachariah Allen and Rowland G. Hazard, who encouraged temperance taverns and groceries, lectured their employees on the virtues of abstinence, and organized cold-water Fourth of July celebrations. Despite occasional mob attacks on such temperance journals as the Pawtucket *Battle Axe*, a chain of prohibition societies soon linked Rhode Island localities. Organizers claimed striking successes even in notoriously bibulous Washington County.

Cheap New England rum, Irish immigration, and monotonous working conditions in Rhode Island mills posed almost insuperable obstacles to the enforcement of the local option and statewide prohibition laws enacted between 1838 and 1852. In many factory villages the tavern was the chief recreational center, and even in Providence, where libraries, theaters, and a variety of social and religious organizations provided alternatives to tippling houses, the incidence of drunkenness rose fivefold after prohibition took effect in 1852. Many Newporters saw the sumptuary laws as a threat to the town's growing resort business, and throughout the state authorities lacked the funds to enforce prohibition.

The recurring economic crises accompanying industrialization made poor relief another major social problem.[55] Throughout, local

5 *Howard* 504 (1846); Keach, *Burrillville*, 57–58, 60–61, 187–188; *Republican Herald*, July 12, 1845; Stone, *Mechanics' Festival*, 34.

[55] The discussion of poor relief is based on *Public Laws, 1798*, pp. 357–358; *1817–1818*, pp. 255–256; *1822*, p. 279; *Acts and Resolves*, June, 1847, pp. 27–28; June, 1851, pp. 4–5, 22–25, 50; Reports to the General Assembly, 1847–1852; Miscellaneous Papers of the General Assembly, folder 14 (1846–1848);

authorities remained responsible for their own poor and preoccupied with determining questions of eligibility. Whenever possible, paupers were returned to the towns where they were legal residents. The common objective was to provide minimal assistance at minimal cost. Towns farmed out paupers to contractors, auctioned others off, and apprenticed orphans. Increasingly after 1840, however, a few communities cared for the poor on farms or in workhouses, and some voted small pensions to induce undesirables to "keep off the town."

The care of indigents changed only slowly. The traditional identification of poverty with sin remained so strong, and misunderstanding of its causes so widespread, that in 1850 an investigation lumped the sane and insane poor together in a single frame of reference. Thomas R. Hazard, the Peace Dale industrialist appointed to examine the system, roundly condemned the inhuman exploitation of indigents, especially the auction system, but he made no recommendations for fundamental reform, and the General Assembly contented itself with making only minor changes in the law. Though it began subsidizing private asylums, particularly the Butler Hospital in Providence, it merely prohibited the worst abuses identified by Hazard, notably corporal punishment, solitary confinement, and the use of chains to restrain the insane.

Despite the local concern with residence qualifications, the poor law did not impede population mobility. The high rate of intra-

---

Brennan, *Social Conditions*, 140–146; Margaret Creech, *Three Centuries of Poor Law Administration: A Study of Legislation in Rhode Island* (Chicago, 1936), *passim*, but especially pp. 111–133, 164–205, 253–257, 276–283, 323–325; Henry J. Crepeau, *Rhode Island: A History of Child Welfare Planning* (Washington, 1941), *passim*, but especially pp. 4–7, 20–23, 29–33, 46–50, 93–102, 107–109, 121–129, 188–192, 205, 215–220, 289–291, 304, 310–316; Field, *Rhode Island*, 3: especially pp. 402–410, 419–422; Glocester Town Meeting and Town Council Minute Books; Hall, *Sermons*, 35; Thomas R. Hazard, *Report on the Poor and Insane in Rhode Island* (Providence, 1851), *passim*, but especially pp. 64–65, 85–87, 91–92; Keach, *Burrillville*, 164; Anne Royall, quoted in Kimball, *Pictures of Rhode Island in the Past*, 171. Slater is supposed to have told President Jackson that he was glad that he was not a pauper in America "where they are put up at auction to the lowest bidder." See White, *Slater*, 264. For the status of apprentices, see *Public Laws, 1844*, pp. 277–279; Douglas, *American Apprenticeship*, 59.

state migration, especially from the western and southern rural areas to the industrialized Blackstone-Pawtuxet communities, shows the ease of establishing new legal residence.[56] Families with good work records and no history of indigence found a ready welcome. However, foreign immigrants burdened many manufacturing towns since they could not be returned to their homelands. The Assembly did require ship captains to submit passenger lists to local authorities, a principle later applied to the railroads, but it made no effort to subsidize poor relief or to assume any obligation to care for the indigent.

The inadequacies of this system reflected the same parsimony which retarded public education and made a farce of the child labor and prohibition laws. Since only property owners could vote to levy or spend taxes, public officials were frequently hampered by a lack of funds. Indeed, in the quarter century after 1824, at the very time when the problems created by industrialization were becoming acute, farmers, manufacturers, and other taxpayers successfully opposed the expansion of most forms of public welfare. Thus restricted, the state easily met its fiscal needs from such sources as license fees rather than from taxes levied directly on property.[57] Paupers, in particular, had to rely on the grudging charity of town councils or private benevolence, and officials everywhere found it impossible to cope with the fundamental causes of poverty or with such other social problems as prostitution.

The judicial system was also slow to adjust to Rhode Island's rapidly changing needs, and the judiciary remained subservient to the legislature until after 1843.[58] The central problem lay in the

[56] Brennan, *Social Conditions*, 141, asserts that Rhode Island's residence requirement—one year without becoming a public charge—was among the most stringent in the Union. On the contrary, it was liberal as compared to Connecticut's requirement of six years, adopted in 1792. See *Connecticut Public Acts and Resolves*, May, 1792, p. 378.

[57] Field, *Rhode Island*, 3:240–242, 254; Stokes, *Finances and Administration of Providence*, 256n.

[58] The analysis of the judicial system is based on *Acts and Resolves*, January, 1827, p. 13; Amasa M. Eaton, "The Development of the Judicial System in Rhode Island," in *Yale Law Journal*, 14:148–170 (January, 1905); Field, *Rhode Island*, 3:89–169, but especially p. 120; Abraham Payne, *Reminiscences*

General Assembly's right under the Charter to alter or reverse
judicial decisions, and in the scope of its original jurisdiction. Supreme Court judges could sit in the legislature until 1780 and
judges of the Court of Common Pleas until 1833, and even in
the 1840's judges refused to publish their opinions because, so
they claimed, justice would be better served by oral decisions.
Practicing before such a court must have been, at best, hazardous,
the more so because judges were political appointees. Many so
lacked formal legal training that they were embarrassed by the
1827 requirement to instruct juries on points of law. Jurisdiction,
in particular, lagged behind social and economic change. Rhode
Island courts could not entertain bills to redeem property before
1798; they could not hear petitions to foreclose a mortgage until
1822; and they did not secure jurisdiction over trusts created by
assignments for the benefit of creditors until after the depression
of 1829. Courts could not hear suits dealing with trusts, liquida-
tions, or forfeiture of turnpike, railroad, or bank charters until
the mid-1830's, and the Supreme Court secured full equity jurisdiction in fraud cases only in 1841. This tardy extension of jurisdiction, the generally inferior caliber of the judiciary, and the
costly delays resulting from inept, careless decisions of the courts
of common pleas, made many litigants prefer to have their cases
heard before federal courts. Especially in equity and commercial
suits, one party commonly established residence in Massachusetts
or Connecticut in order to secure federal jurisdiction on grounds
of diversity of citizenship.

Modernization of the General Assembly's part in the judicial
system became especially urgent. Ever since the mid-seventeenth
century, it had acted both as a legislative body and as a court of
law. Its jurisdiction over insolvency cases illustrates the problems

of the Rhode Island Bar (Providence, 1885), 9–10; *Manufacturers' and Farmers'
Journal*, January 8, 1827, September 28, October 10, 1829. For an earlier proposal (1818) to bar members of the General Assembly from holding judicial
office, see Miscellaneous Papers of the General Assembly, folder 8 (1809–1820).
For resolutions passed by Cranston, Smithfield, Burrillville, Scituate, and West
Greenwich town meetings protesting the judicial reorganization of 1827, see *ibid.*,
folder 10 (1826–1830).

inherent in such an arrangement.[59] During the depression brought on by the Anglo-French crisis in the middle of the eighteenth century, the General Assembly granted a stay of execution on all debts. Until 1827 debtors could petition the legislature for the benefit of this Act of June, 1756. In effect, petitioners asked the General Assembly to institute bankruptcy proceedings. This kept the debtor out of prison so long as action was pending before either the legislature or the courts, and gave him a respite, sometimes lasting several years, in which to recoup his fortunes. In this way, the statute eased economic hardship, but population growth, industrialization, and the mounting severity and frequency of recessions made it impossible for the General Assembly to cope with the rising flood of insolvency petitions. In 1827, therefore, it relinquished jurisdiction to the courts.

Paradoxically, though Rhode Island did respond to the growing humanitarian spirit of the early nineteenth century by steadily mitigating the savagery of criminal punishments[60] and though no court imposed the death sentence after the Gordon murder case

[59] The analysis of the insolvency and debtor laws is based on Rhode Island Colonial Records, 1746–1757, pp. 492–495; *Acts and Resolves*, June, 1756, pp. 24–29; June, 1819, pp. 6–7; June, 1820, pp. 18, 23; January, 1826, p. 31; January, 1828, p. 52; May, 1828, p. 51; the petitions for bankruptcy and/or release from debtors' prison scattered through the Granted Petitions and Petitions Not Granted, 1756–1828; Miscellaneous Papers of the General Assembly, folder 8 (1800–1820); folder 10 (1826–1830); folder 11 (1831–1835); folder 12 (1836–1840); folder 13 (1841–1845); folder 16 (1851). These miscellaneous papers, together with the Dorr Manuscripts, vol. 25, in the Thomas W. Dorr Papers in the Special Collections of the John Hay Library at Brown University, show scattered proposals to revive legislative jurisdiction over insolvency cases, and persistent attempts to abolish imprisonment for debt. Even after 1826, the General Assembly continued to pass individual bankruptcy laws. For resolutions and memorials from individuals and town meetings opposing a national bankruptcy law, see Miscellaneous Papers of the General Assembly, folder 13 (1841–1845); and, for attempts to exempt homesteads from attachment, see *ibid.*, folder 18 (1853–1854).

[60] A draft criminal code revision proposed in 1822 set savage punishments for even minor offences. Not until twenty-four years later was it proposed to abolish capital punishment for murder, rape, and arson. See, Miscellaneous Papers of the General Assembly, folder 9 (1821–1825); folder 14 (1846–1848); *Acts and Resolves*, February 3, 1838, pp. 3–46; *Public Laws Passed Since January, 1837*, pp. 961–1004; *Acts and Resolves*, January, 1852, pp. 12–13.

in 1844, the legislature did not abolish imprisonment for debt. Neither the labor movement nor individual reformers succeeded in rousing public opinion on this question.[61] This was probably because most people regarded the statutes as being lenient rather than harsh. For example, the jail limits usually encompassed the town's business section, thereby permitting debtors to pursue their crafts or professions by day. Depending on individual circumstances, debtors had two remedies open to them. An indigent could take the poor debtors' oath. This forced the creditor to choose between releasing the debtor or holding him in jail at his (the creditor's) expense. Obviously, the latter course was a case of throwing good money after bad. The creditor gained vindictive rather than pecuniary satisfaction. A propertied debtor, instead of taking the poor debtors' oath, could petition for the benefit of the Act of June, 1756, which required him to make a full disclosure of his property. The threat of incarceration, or, if he was already in prison, the threat of being kept there, generally forced the debtor to make an honest inventory. If he did not, or if the Assembly suspected him of concealing property, it simply kept him in prison until he admitted possession of undeclared assets, or until it became satisfied with the veracity of the original inventory. Given tolerable jail conditions, the poor debtors' oath, and the bankruptcy procedure, the public saw little reason to abolish imprisonment for debt.

In part, Rhode Island failed to grapple effectively with the social and economic problems of industrialization because its political system frustrated reform efforts and muted the voice of popular protest. Though it was the first American colony to declare its independence from Great Britain, Rhode Island did not follow up its assertion of sovereignty with a constitution embodying prevailing revolutionary sentiments. Instead, it continued to function under the principles of the Charter granted in 1663.[62]

---

[61] The otherwise conservative *Manufacturers' and Farmers' Journal*, June 21, 1827; May 3, 1830; May 21, 1831; April 23, 1835; was an exception. For an 1854 attempt to abolish imprisonment for debt by constitutional amendment, see Field, *Rhode Island*, 1:363. See also, *Public Laws, 1822*, pp. 66–67.

[62] For the Charter, see *Manual of Rhode Island, 1955–1956*, pp. 97–112.

According to this system, the government consisted of a governor, a deputy governor, and six senators elected at large, and
representatives chosen in town meetings. With the exception of
Newport, to which the Charter granted six representatives, each
original town, Providence, Warwick, and Portsmouth, elected four
delegates. Each town incorporated after 1663 received two seats
in the lower house. The formation of Burrillville in 1806 raised
the number of representatives to seventy-two. The governor presided over the Senate, but he had been given only very limited
executive powers.

While the Charter could still be considered comparatively liberal even as late as 1790, it rapidly became outmoded, and by 1840
the state faced a constitutional crisis. When the protagonists of the
status quo denied repeated requests for a fundamental revision of
the Charter system of government, the reformers, led by Thomas
W. Dorr attempted to secure their objectives by extralegal means.
The so-called Dorr War did bring about the adoption of a new
constitution, but the reformers attained only some of their goals
and the General Assembly continued to reflect vested interests
rather than the popular will.

Four major issues—representation, the suffrage, a bill of rights,
and judicial independence—formed the crux of the constitutional
dispute. Some issues arose earlier than others, the intensity of dissatisfaction with the Charter varied from locality to locality, and,
despite the charges and countercharges, the reform question cut
across class, ethnic, and urban-rural lines. Throughout, sectional
interests played a fundamental rôle.

Decade by decade, the industrial revolution gradually altered
the distribution of population in Rhode Island until the question of
legislative reapportionment emerged as the issue underlying the
entire constitutional problem. Like the British Liberals in their
struggle to reform the House of Commons in 1832, Dorr and his
followers aspired to reform the House of Representatives. Though
representation had been reasonably equitable throughout the Colonial period, the rise of manufacturing in some localities but not
in others produced serious inequities in the Charter system. With
each decade of industrialization, the gulf between the over-repre-

sented declining and static towns and the under-represented expanding towns became wider and wider.

By 1840, the situation had become critical and was growing worse. Ten towns, six of them in the expanding group and eight of them in northern Rhode Island, exceeded the state average of

TABLE 23

THE RATIO OF REPRESENTATIVES TO POPULATION, 1790–1840

Towns	Seats in 1840	Number of Residents per Representative					
		1790	1800	1810	1820	1830	1840
Bristol	2	703	839	1,347	1,598	1,517	1,745
Warren	2	561	736	887	903	900	1,218
Cranston	2	938	822	1,080	1,137	1,326	1,451
Johnston	2	660	682	758	776	1,057	1,238
Providence	4	1,595	1,903	2,518	2,942	4,209	5,793
North Providence	2	535	532	879	1,210	1,851	2,103
Cumberland	2	982	1,028	1,055	1,326	1,837	2,612
Smithfield	2	1,585	1,560	1,914	2,339	3,428	4,767
Burrillville	2			917	1,082	1,098	991
Warwick	4	623	633	939	911	1,382	1,681
Expanding Towns	24	947	1,025	1,313	1,506	2,008	2,590
Barrington	2	341	325	302	317	306	274
Glocester	2	2,012	2,004	1,155	1,252	1,260	1,152
Scituate	2	1,157	1,261	1,284	1,417	1,996	2,045
East Greenwich	2	912	887	765	759	795	754
Coventry	2	1,238	1,211	1,464	1,569	1,925	1,716
North Kingstown	2	1,453	1,397	1,478	1,503	1,518	1,454
South Kingstown	2	2,065	1,719	1,780	1,866	1,831	1,858
Richmond	2	880	684	665	711	681	680
Hopkinton	2	1,231	1,138	887	910	888	863
Westerly	2	1,149	1,664	955	986	957	956
Newport	6	1,119	1,123	1,318	1,220	1,335	1,388
Middletown	2	420	456	488	474	457	445
Portsmouth	4	390	421	449	411	432	426
Tiverton	2	1,226	1,358	1,418	1,437	1,452	1,591
New Shoreham	2	342	357	361	477	592	534
Static Towns	36	1,031	1,010	992	1,009	1,079	1,074
Foster	2	1,134	1,228	1,306	1,450	1,336	1,090
West Greenwich	2	1,027	878	809	963	908	707
Exeter	2	1,247	1,238	1,128	1,290	1,291	888
Charlestown	2	1,011	727	587	580	642	461
Jamestown	2	253	250	252	224	207	182
Little Compton	2	771	788	776	790	689	663
Declining Towns	12	907	851	809	883	845	665
Rhode Island	72	983	987	1,070	1,154	1,350	1,512

one representative to each 1,512 residents. They included Providence, Smithfield, and Cumberland, where the ratio was one representative to 5,793, 4,767, and 2,612 residents, respectively. At the other end of the scale, and generally in southern Rhode Island, there were six towns which fell far below the state average. They included Jamestown, Barrington, Portsmouth, Middletown, and Charlestown. There, the ratio ranged from 182 to 461 residents to each representative. In effect, the rapidly expanding towns accounted for over half Rhode Island's population but elected only a third of the representatives. The inequality between individual communities was even more pronounced. Providence, which had four representatives under the Charter, should have had at least fifteen under any apportionment system based strictly on population; and Portsmouth, which also had four seats under the Charter, should have had only one under any equitable arrangement.

Even if the legislature were to be considered as representing property rather than people, the apportionment system still favored the declining and static towns at the expense of the expanding ones. Each year the disparity became more evident. According to the 1796 valuation, the nine expanding towns contained $6,821,000 worth of taxable property. The fifteen static towns contained approximately the same amount, $6,936,000, and the six declining towns a mere $1,789,000. During the early nineteenth century the situation changed very rapidly. By 1824 the taxable wealth of the expanding towns had almost trebled and by 1840 it had reached approximately $39,000,000, or more than sixty-eight per cent of the total. This contrasted with $15,000,000 for the static towns and $3,000,000 for the declining ones. In fact, the taxable wealth of the expanding towns grew even more rapidly than did their population. By 1840 these communities had an average of $622 worth of taxable property per person as compared to $395 for the static towns and $376 for the declining ones.

More important, this difference meant that each member of the lower house of the General Assembly who came from an expanding town represented, on the average, over $1,600,000 worth of taxable property. The comparable figure for the static and declining towns was $427,000 and $250,000 respectively. The disparity between individual communities was even greater. A delegate elected to the House of Representatives from Providence in 1840 represented some $5,400,000 in taxable wealth, but delegates from five of the static towns and from all six of the declining towns represented less than $300,000 each, and a New Shoreham delegate represented a mere $91,000. In short, a coalition of towns representing a minority of wealth were in a position to control public policy. The Dorrites, therefore, set equality of representation as a major goal.[63]

In point of time, the suffrage question, not the apportionment question, was the first to emerge. Because it lent itself to dramatization, it seemed to be the focus of reform agitation.[64] According to the Charter, only freemen could vote. In the seventeenth century

[63] For the reapportionment question, compare *Facts Involved in the Rhode Island Controversy* (Boston, 1842), 12–13, 40; Elisha R. Potter, *Considerations on the Questions of the Adoption of a Constitution and Extension of Suffrage in Rhode Island* (Boston, 1842), 41; [Edmund Burke], *Interference of the Executive in the Affairs of Rhode Island* (28 Congress, 1 session, *House Report no. 546*, serial 447, Washington, 1844), 11. Hereafter cited as *Burke's Report*. See also, Petitions Not Granted, January, 1834; Dorr to Jesse Calder, May 4, 1841, in Dorr Correspondence, 3:55, in the Dorr Papers; *An Address to the People of Rhode Island from the Convention, 1834* (Providence, 1834), 20–26, 38–39; and, for taxable wealth, *Acts and Resolves*, June, 1796, pp. 16–17; January, 1824, pp. 15–16; June, 1849, pp. 18–22; January, 1856, pp. 89–90. For complaints against the 1796 tax apportionment, see *Providence Gazette*, June 25, July 9, 30, 1796. Northern property, ran these protests, was overvalued as compared to southern property. For a comparative table of population, representation, and taxation which served as the basis of an extended discussion of reform issues, see *ibid.*, December 15, 1822.

[64] For the colonial suffrage, see Arthur May Mowry, *The Dorr War or the Constitutional Struggle in Rhode Island* (Providence, 1901), 18–20. For later developments, including the provision that a freeman could ballot for state officers and congressmen only in the town where he held the real property which qualified him as a voter, see Petitions Not Granted, January, 1826; Mowry, *Dorr War*, 20–22; Noah J. Arnold, "The History of Suffrage in Rhode Island," in *The Narragansett Historical Register*, 8:305–307 (October, 1890); Charles E. Gorman, *An Historical Statement of the Elective Franchise in Rhode Island* (Providence, 1879), 6–9; Edwin Maxey, "Suffrage Extension in Rhode Island Down to 1842," in *American Law Review*, 42:541–577 (July-August, 1908); *Providence Journal*, January 11, 1842.

the General Assembly required possession of a "Competent Estate" for admission to the rank of freeman; in the eighteenth century this came to mean ownership or a life interest in a fixed minimum of real property. Most adult male colonists obtained the franchise without difficulty. Land was relatively abundant throughout the Colonial period, the state made occasional grants of land to encourage settlement, especially in western areas, and towns readily admitted residents to the rank of freemen as soon as they acquired sufficient real estate. The suffrage law also permitted the eldest sons of freemen to vote even though they could not meet the property qualification. Thus government rested on a popular base, and the suffrage system never evoked serious criticism. But the acute shortage of land which developed during the generation following the Revolution made it impossible for many potential voters to qualify as freemen, and the rise of manufacturing, particularly in Blackstone and Pawtuxet valley localities, soon created a large and ever-growing but politically impotent class of landless workers.[65]

Critics of the Charter system disagreed among themselves as to the appropriate remedy. Seth Luther and other labor leaders demanded universal manhood suffrage; the Dorrites started out with a much less extreme objective. As philosophical but essentially moderate radicals, they opposed enfranchising the propertyless "rabble," for they feared such people almost as deeply as did the conservative defenders of the *status quo*. Rather, the Dorrites wished merely to extend voting rights to middle-class taxpayers and, perhaps, to militiamen, and they opposed discriminating in favor of landowners and their eldest sons.[66]

[65] The proportion of adult male residents of the expanding commercial and industrial centers who were freemen dropped substantially after 1790. By 1841, barely four out of ten Rhode Island men could vote. Perhaps as few as six per cent of Providence's population were freemen. In rural Jamestown the comparable figure was as high as sixteen per cent. See *Burke's Report*, 12, 120–121, 203–205, 353; *Facts For the People* (Providence, 1842), 4–6, 12; *Providence Journal*, May 3, 1841; Stokes, *Finances and Administration of Providence*, 33, 136–137.

[66] Dorr to Jesse Calder, May 4, 1841, in Dorr Correspondence, 2:55.

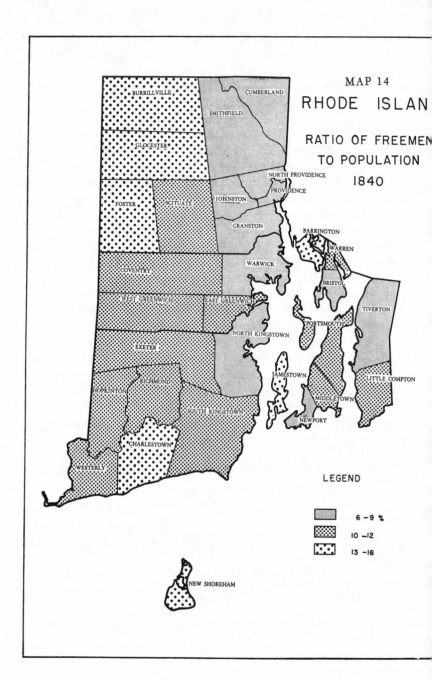

MAP 14

RHODE ISLAN

RATIO OF FREEMEN
TO POPULATION
1840

LEGEND

6 – 9 %

10 – 12

13 – 16

Two other major issues—the demand for a bill of rights guaranteeing fundamental liberties, and the agitation for a truly independent judiciary—were closely connected and reflected dissatisfaction with the concentration of power in the General Assembly. Though the underlying constitutional principles appealed most to educated men of liberal inclinations, they also attracted popular support after 1820, when many Rhode Islanders became imbued with ideas linked to the wider American reform impulses.[67] Complaints of political corruption and chicanery constituted an important though subordinate reform issue. The Dorrites appreciated that Rhode Island politics needed to be changed as much in spirit as in form. They were particularly aware of the pressures to which voters were subjected and argued that this made a mockery of democratic government. As everyone knew, Simeon Potter of Bristol had urged his debtors to vote for his nephew, James DeWolf, in the election of 1802, and Elisha R. Potter of South Kingstown, it had been charged in 1829, controlled the votes of all those freemen who had borrowed from him or from his banks, or who held life interests in his land. Under the latter arrangement, property never even passed to the grantee. Instead, Potter continued to farm it and, in effect, received an annual rent for

[67] For earlier Rhode Island interest in a bill of rights, see the eighteen principles and twenty-one proposed amendments to the Constitution of the United States which the constitutional convention attached to its ratification in 1790 (copy in the Rhode Island Archives); An Act Declaratory of Certain Rights of the People of This State, and An Act Relative to Religious Freedom, and the Maintenance of Ministers, in *Public Laws, 1822*, pp. 66–69. Apparently, the committee appointed to revise the laws proposed these two declaratory statutes. The first was primarily concerned with the judicial process but also declared against imprisonment for debt. The statute merely stated what an individual's rights ought to be. It did not make these principles binding on either the legislature or the courts. The religious freedom statute was more positive. It declared that no man "shall" be compelled to frequent or support any religious worship, place, or ministry, and that his views on religion and involvement or non-involvement "shall" in no wise diminish, enlarge, or affect his civil capacities. See also, "A Rhode Islander" [Francis H. McDougall], *Might and Right* (Providence, 1844), 33–34, 38–39, 49–53, 164; *Address from the Convention*, 57–58; [John Augustus Bolles], *A Review of President Wayland's "Discourse on the Affairs of Rhode Island"* (Providence, 1842), 12, 16–17.

conferring the voting privilege. The Spragues of Cranston were also resourceful election manipulators. They supervised the endorsement of their employees' ballots, a method nicely calculated to secure the election of Sprague candidates or, indeed, of the Spragues themselves. Such local political overlords were understandably opposed to the secret ballot. Land often changed hands on election day merely to enfranchise additional voters, or, especially in such urban areas as Providence, men acquired small parcels of realty by promissory note in a sum considerably in excess of the property's worth. The seller simply manufactured suffrages and he presented the note for payment if the purchaser failed to vote according to instructions. Many freemen supported an extension of the franchise not because they believed in "progress," or in the amelioration of social problems, or in the fundamental goodness of man and his inherent capacity for self-government. On the contrary, they had little sympathy with such Dorrite views. But they did protest the debasement of legal votes, and they supported the reformers as the best hope for eliminating political corruption.[68]

These primary and secondary issues attracted only spasmodic attention between 1776 and 1820; at no time did it appear likely that any basic constitutional changes would be adopted. The first attempt to replace the Charter occurred in 1777, when the General Assembly appointed a committee to draft a new frame of government, but the British occupation of Newport quickly diverted public attention from constitution making to survival, and the committee never completed its work. For the most part, the people considered the Charter eminently satisfactory and they were well-satisfied both in 1777 and 1797 when the legislature voted first to

[68] On Simeon Potter, see Howe, *Mount Hope*, 95. A pamphleteer charged that Elisha Potter publicly supported one candidate but ordered his "slaves" to vote against him. See *What a Ploughman Said* (Kingston, 1829), 4–5. See also, Benjamin Knight, *The Sprague Families*, 15, 18; Petitions Not Granted, May, 1835; Sullivan Dorr to Dorr, May 21, 1835, William Peckham to Dorr, February 3, 1837, in Dorr Correspondence, 1:121, 2:129; Papers Relative to the Election to the 24th Congress, 1835, in the Rhode Island State Archives; Field, *Rhode Island*, 1:335–336.

continue the old system of government in force and then to express the suffrage qualifications in dollar equivalents.[69] Despite some grumbling over the spirit if not the form of politics, the General Assembly was relatively free from pressure to outlaw fraudulent voting practices and to prevent the rigging of elections. As a consequence, the legislature considered it unnecessary to enfranchise taxpayers and militiamen, a proposal advocated in 1811 as a first step toward the elimination of corruption.[70] The Assembly also rejected a scheme to hold a constitutional referendum in 1814,[71] and five years later it set aside Newport complaints that the franchise was as partial as it was defective. The right to vote, asserted these disgruntled freeholders, was "an original, unalienable, and unquestionable right, on the free exercise of which the very existence of our Liberty, and prosperity depends." Rhode Island, like other states, they argued, should adhere to the republican maxim that payment of taxes and performance of militia service constituted not only the legal but the equitable qualification for voting.[72] Dissatisfied with the legislature's intransigence, reformers

---

[69] Mowry, *Dorr War*, 27. The General Assembly had rejected a memorial for a state constitution in 1793. See Bicknell, *Rhode Island*, 3:1117. The *Providence Gazette*, June 21, 1806, reported that some towns instructed their representatives to press for a constitutional convention. The question was not put to a vote in the General Assembly. See also, Dorr Manuscripts, 3:1–5.

[70] Mowry, *Dorr War*, 28–29; Miscellaneous Papers of the General Assembly, folder 8 (1800–1820); Dorr Manuscripts, 3:7, 10. In general, Federalists opposed and Republicans supported reform. Thus the Republicans charged the Providence Federalists with conspiring to use fraud to qualify additional voters. By this means they hoped to use their control of the General Assembly to secure the election of Federalists to the United States Senate. See *Rhode Island American*, March 5, 1811; *Providence Gazette*, March 30, 1811; Field, *Rhode Island*, 1:294–295; Jacob Frieze, *A Concise History of the Efforts to Obtain An Extension of Suffrage in Rhode Island, From the Year 1811 to 1842* (Providence, 1842), 161. Voting on the bill did not follow a sectional pattern. See House Journal, March 2, 1811. An earlier bill (*ibid.*, March 5, 1803) to prevent bribery and corruption was also defeated. The strength of the anti-corruption movement lay in southern Rhode Island. See also, Miscellaneous Papers of the General Assembly, folder 8 (1800–1820), for a bill (proposed in June, 1811) to prohibit the use of money, liquor, or property to influence elections.

[71] Mowry, *Dorr War*, 29.

[72] Petitions Not Granted, February, 1819.

gathered in Providence complaining that "a free people have for more than forty years submitted to a species of government in theory, if not always in practice, as despotic as that of the autocrat of the Russians." They warned the General Assembly that continued opposition to a constitutional convention would force the people to call one themselves.[73]

In 1821, perhaps to forestall popular action, the General Assembly placed the question of calling a constitutional convention on the ballot at the April elections.[74] Most but not all rapidly expanding industrial and commercial towns supported the proposed convention. The static and declining towns generally opposed it. In all, twelve towns voted to call a convention. They included all the expanding towns (except Johnston, Burrillville, and Warwick), and Barrington, Glocester, Scituate, East Greenwich, and Hopkinton among the static towns. Except in a few cases where the voting was close, the freemen voted overwhelmingly for or overwhelmingly against the proposal. In Providence, for example, the vote was 598 in favor and only 7 against; in North Kingstown the vote was 1 in favor and 153 against. Because the ten expanding towns failed to act together on this issue they were defeated by the relatively narrow margin of 1,903 votes to 1,619. However, the constitutional question was complicated by sectionalism and the same coalition of southern and western voters that secured the election of the first governor from Newport in thirty years also combined to defeat the proposal to hold a convention.[75]

[73] Dan King, *The Life and Times of Thomas Wilson Dorr, with Outlines of the Political History of Rhode Island* (Boston, 1859), 28–29. Several reforms were proposed in February, 1819, and in June, 1820. One would have directed freemen to declare themselves on the question of extending the franchise. A second would have regulated the use of printed ballots and election rigging. A third would have granted the suffrage to free, able-bodied, white, adult male American citizens who also met residence and militia service requirements. See, Miscellaneous Papers of the General Assembly, folder 8 (1800–1820), and Granted Petitions, 48:103 (1819–1820).

[74] Mowry, *Dorr War*, 29–30. For opinion favorable to a constitutional convention, see *Providence Gazette*, January 31, February 10, 24, April 18, June 16, 1821. Party maneuvering, though present, was not significant.

[75] *Providence Gazette*, May 9, 1821. The expanding towns cast 1,150 votes in favor and 307 votes against; the static towns cast 461 votes in favor and

In 1822 the majority of freemen again opposed revising the Charter.[76] Nevertheless, two years later the General Assembly took the initiative by calling a constitutional convention into session. Delegates drafted a system of government meeting some but not all the criticisms leveled at the Charter. They formulated a bill of rights, eliminated the special voting privilege enjoyed by

---

1,022 votes against; and the declining town cast 8 votes in favor and 574 votes against. Had Johnston, Burrillville, and Warwick voted "yes" they would have tipped the scales in favor of holding the convention by a majority of almost 200 votes. The northern towns of Cumberland, Scituate, Glocester, Cranston, and Warren supported the constitutional convention but voted for William C. Gibbs, the Newport gubernatorial candidate. Warwick and West Greenwich voted against both the convention and Gibbs. Almost twice as many votes were cast in the election for governor as in the constitutional referendum. Gibbs polled 3,801 votes, Samuel W. Bridgham, 2,801. See also, *ibid.*, September 19, 22, 1821, for further discussion of the constitutional question, and *ibid.*, January 19, 1822, for a report on a statutory revision. It indicated that only unencumbered realty could qualify freemen to vote, a device to check the manufacture of fraudulent votes. It was erroneously reported that the special privilege enjoyed by the eldest sons of freemen had been struck out "as being the relic of feudal times, incompatible with the genius of free institutions." The report was premature. Compare *Revised Laws, 1822*, pp. 90–97.

[76] For support of constitutional reform, especially proposals to limit the powers of the legislature and to make the executive a co-ordinate branch of government, see *Providence Gazette*, March 13, April 10, 1822. The editor also urged that the judiciary be made independent of the legislature, and that the apportionment of seats in the General Assembly be based either on population or on property, or on some combination of the two. Others asserted that the legislature should represent "the *people*, and not the inhabitants of a few rotten boroughs" but considered party feeling too strong to permit a convention to be called. Anyway, any attempt to frame a constitution would only intensify animosity between town and country, merchant and farmer, north and south. See *ibid.*, April 18, 1821; April 13, 17, 1822.

A preliminary tabulation of votes in the referendum indicated much the same results as in 1821; Providence, North Providence, Smithfield, Glocester, and Bristol favored a convention, while Scituate, Warwick, Burrillville, Exeter, Newport, Portsmouth, and Middletown opposed it. See *ibid.*, April 20, 1822. The freemen rejected the proposal by a vote of 1,804 to 843. See Bicknell, *Rhode Island*, 3:1133.

For a reapportionment bill submitted by Elisha R. Potter of South Kingstown in June, 1822, increasing the representation of Providence by three seats, and of Smithfield, Foster, Coventry, the Kingstowns, and Bristol by one seat each, see Miscellaneous Papers of the General Assembly, folder 9 (1821–1825); *Providence Gazette*, June 15, 19, 1822. A year later Potter repeated his proposal for a constitutional convention. See *ibid.*, June 14, 1823.

the eldest sons of freemen, and reapportioned seats in the House of Representatives. But they did not abolish the real property suffrage qualification. Three towns, Newport, Portsmouth, and Warwick, would have lost seats had the constitution gone into effect, and ten towns, Providence, North Providence, Smithfield, Cumberland, Scituate, the two Kingstowns, Coventry, and Bristol, would have gained additional representation. Though the new arrangement would have strengthened the political influence of the growing communities, especially those in the Providence hinterland, it would have reduced, not eliminated, the inequities. The expanding northern communities would still have been underrepresented, and a coalition of static and declining towns would have retained control of the state.[77]

The freemen rejected the proposed constitution by the decisive margin of 3,123 votes to 1,664. Significantly, the margin of difference lay in the sharp increase in the number of freemen who went to the polls. As compared to 1821, the number of favorable votes cast rose by a mere 45, but the number of opposing votes rose by more than 1,200. Moreover, three northern towns, Cranston, Scituate, and East Greenwich, which had favored calling a convention in 1821, opposed the new constitution in 1824, and almost twenty-five per cent more negative votes were cast by the expanding towns in 1824 than in 1821. The voting again followed a sectional pattern. With few exceptions, northern industrial and commercial towns supported reform while southern and western communities opposed it. Many voters regarded the Charter as sacrosanct; others rejected one or more of the proposed reforms.[78]

The decisive defeat of the 1824 constitution intensified political agitation.[79] This pressure culminated in 1829 in a series of reform

[77] *Providence Gazette,* January 3, 17, June 23, 26, 30, July 3, 7, 10, 17, 21, 1824. It was widely believed that Newport would head the southern opposition to the proposal. See, for example, *Providence Patriot,* November 3, 1824.

[78] Frieze, *A Concise History,* 17. Frieze gives totals of 3,206 and 1,668.

[79] Further attempts to alter the apportionment also failed. See *Providence Gazette,* January 15, 19, 1825. A House committee favored the change but disagreed on how to implement it. See Miscellaneous Papers of the General Assembly, folder 9 (1821–1825).

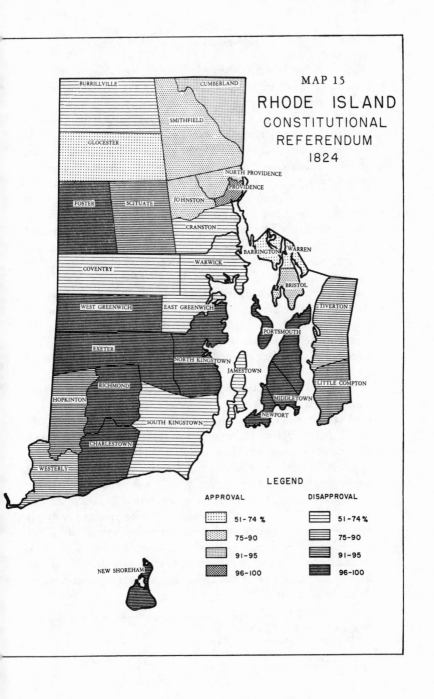

MAP 15

RHODE ISLAND
CONSTITUTIONAL
REFERENDUM
1824

LEGEND

APPROVAL

	51 - 74 %
	75 - 90
	91 - 95
	96 - 100

DISAPPROVAL

	51 - 74 %
	75 - 90
	91 - 95
	96 - 100

petitions. Most memorials urged either the extension of the franchise to all adult taxpaying militiamen, or the prohibition of the use of colored ballot papers, a technique practiced in some towns to influence voting. Collectively or separately, these petitions touched all the major constitutional issues.

One petition concentrated on the legal and political disabilities of the landless class. Except for the right to petition the legislature for divorce or for the benefit of the insolvent debtors statute, the 12,600 non-freemen in Rhode Island enjoyed no more rights than aliens or strangers. Although they had access to the federal courts, these non-freemen could institute suits for debt in state courts only if a freeholder guaranteed legal costs. Nor, it was argued, was ownership of land greater proof of patriotism than willingness to die defending the United States. Yet only land-holding conferred voting rights. "Miserable indeed must be that attachment to our free institutions," asserted the petitioners, "which depends upon the ownership of 134 dollars worth of land, and which can be the subject of bargain, sale and conveyance, by deed signed, sealed and delivered." If the General Assembly insisted on retaining a property qualification, they concluded, it should be extended to personalty, including agricultural implements and mechanical tools.[80]

North Providence petitioners advanced similar arguments, but added that the special voting privilege conferred on the eldest sons of freemen was anti-republican in spirit and contradicted the Revolutionary principle of equality. Condemning the privilege as both unjust and unequal, they asserted that it was "known only in the oppressive codes of monarchy and aristocracy." The petitioners also protested discrimination against enterprising mechanics simply because their work made landed proprietorship unnecessary. They concluded by predicting revolution unless the franchise was extended before further population growth made Rhode Island's limited area incapable of conferring the suffrage on even a majority of the adult males.[81]

[80] Petitions Not Granted, May, 1829, in Outsize Petitions, box 1. See also, McDougall, *Might and Right*, 49.
[81] Petitions Not Granted, May, 1829.

Warren residents also memorialized the legislature, asking whether "the principles of equitable government are better understood by the proprietors of the *soil*" than by the landless. Neither Rhode Island nor Virginia, the only states retaining the real property qualification, managed their affairs more wisely than other states. The eldest sons of freemen, they contended, "whether wise men or fools, are admitted to the Polls:—they—whether rich or poor, can dispose of the money they do not pay."[82]

Finally, Bristol petitioners warned that "unwise and odious" suffrage restrictions evoked "the voice of complaint . . . in every quarter." No advocates of universal suffrage, these Bristol folk opposed enfranchising "murderous Mobs," or opening the gates to "the Rabble," but rather prayed "for their entire . . . exclusion from the rights and privileges of Freemen." Nevertheless, they wondered how many "abject wretches" there were in the ruling class "whose noses only blush for them, whilst they yield votes to the influence of Rum!"[83]

The legislature firmly rejected reform, agreeing with a House committee that the petitions contained nothing, either of fact or of reason, to warrant debate. For "no constitution" had been or could be framed that was "more free and popular" than the Charter. Besides, asserted the committee, the General Assembly was morally powerless to alter the suffrage. Once admit that authority, and voting rights could be restricted so as to establish an aristocracy. Rather, the committee urged non-freemen to follow the safer course of qualifying themselves to vote by acquiring land. "Let strangers . . . treat this instrument with levity," concluded the committee, "but let *us* continue to be proud of it."[84]

The legislature's uncompromising reaction temporarily discouraged agitation, but reformers soon resumed their offensive.[85] In February, 1834, delegates from Newport, Bristol, Warren,

[82] *Ibid.*

[83] *Ibid.*, October, 1829, and an undated petition.

[84] *Burke's Report*, 377–401. See also, five petitions from Burrillville, Glocester, North Kingstown, Smithfield, and Middletown, in Petitions Not Granted, April 15, June 19, 1829; and *Providence Journal*, June 27, 1829.

[85] For a Warren petition, see Petitions Not Granted, May, 1833. It resembled those presented in 1829, and on June 27, 1834, it too was postponed indefinitely.

Cranston, Johnston, Providence, North Providence, Cumberland, Smithfield, and Burrillville convened at Providence to discuss their grievances against the Charter and to form the Constitutional party. Except for Newport, only the rapidly expanding northern towns sent delegates to the conference. In an address to the people prepared by Joseph K. Angell, David Daniells, Thomas W. Dorr, Christopher Robinson, and William H. Smith, the convention declared that the Revolution of 1776 had conferred sovereignty on the people of Rhode Island, thereby empowering them to adopt a constitution whenever they chose to do so. The address also summarized the reform arguments for reapportionment and the extension of the suffrage, and urged the General Assembly to call a constitutional convention to make the necessary changes in the system of government.[86]

The legislature acceded to this request in June, 1834, perhaps responding also to pressure from the Providence City Council, which complained that by any measure—population, wealth, or taxation—the people of the city deserved a stronger voice in formulating public policy. Though Providence contained more than a sixth of Rhode Island's population and a quarter of its wealth, and though it contributed some two-thirds of all taxes paid to the state, the city elected barely a twentieth of the members of the House of Representatives.[87]

The reformers failed to capitalize on this opportunity to secure their objectives.[88] After four attempts to obtain a quorum between

[86] The convention's memorial to the General Assembly is *ibid.*, May, 1834. It too was postponed. The convention's proceedings are in *Burke's Report*, 151–185. See also, *An Address from the Convention, passim*, and, for the Constitutional party's activities between 1834 and 1837, Dorr Manuscripts, vol. 26, and Dorr Correspondence, vol. 1 (1820–1835), vol. 2 (1836–1839), *passim*.

[87] Petitions Not Granted, January, 1834. On June 27, 1834, the House discharged the committee considering the petition and postponed consideration indefinitely.

[88] Dorr moved that all native-born resident citizens be permitted to vote for delegates, provided that within the preceding year they had paid taxes on a minimum of $134 worth of real or personal property. Only three representatives, Otis Mason of Cumberland, John H. Weeden of North Providence, and Levi Haile of Warren, supported Dorr's motion. See Frieze, *Concise History*, 25–26.

the fall of 1834 and the summer of 1835, delegates abandoned the struggle to draft a constitution. Inept, inadequate leadership contributed most to the convention's collapse. Neither the Whigs nor the Democrats identified themselves with the reform cause, and the conviction that voters would reject any system of government proposed doubtless discouraged delegates. So long as the majority of freemen remained content with the Charter and politically apathetic, politicians were satisfied to let sleeping dogs lie. Moreover, the class conscious agitation organized by Seth Luther and his labor supporters alienated many freemen otherwise sympathetic to reform. Though leadership was passing from these extremists to the moderate and thoroughly respectable Dorr, middle-class reformers lacked the capacity to dramatize their ideas or to organize popular support. The Constitutional party struggled vainly to advance its cause.[89]

With the failure of the convention, Dorr, who had been elected to the House of Representatives as a Whig in 1834, urged his colleagues to reform the franchise themselves. Soundly defeated on this question both in 1835 and again in 1836, Dorr nevertheless elevated the reform movement to the lofty plane of high moral and constitutional principle, and he focused popular discontent on fundamental issues. First, he proposed enfranchising all adult males who owned a minimum of $250 worth of property, and second, extending the suffrage to as many sons as a freeman's realty was divisible by $134. Though these measures reflected the essential moderation of Dorr's reform views, the House rejected each bill by an overwhelming majority.[90]

[89] Mowry, *Dorr War*, 41–42; Frieze, *Concise History*, 24. Seven static or declining towns, Scituate, Foster, Barrington, West Greenwich, Richmond, Charlestown, and New Shoreham, failed to elect delegates. For an attempt in November, 1834, to force towns to send delegates, see Miscellaneous Papers of the General Assembly, folder 11 (1831–1835), and for a general discussion, see Frieze, *Concise History*, 26–27. For the working class background of the early agitation, see Dorr Manuscripts, vol. 3 (May 10, 1833), and vol. 17 *passim*; Seth Luther, *Address on the Right of Free Suffrage* (Providence, 1833), *passim*.

[90] Miscellaneous Papers of the General Assembly, folder 12 (1836–1840). For an earlier complaint about the incompetence of some judges, see *Manufacturers' and Farmers' Journal*, October 10, 1829.

Dorr then tried another tactic. He submitted his reform creed to the House for adoption in the form of a resolution. Dorr wished to reduce the power of the legislature, to enact a bill of rights, to establish the independence of the judiciary, and to reform both the franchise and the apportionment systems. He especially protested the concentration of power in the General Assembly, arguing that time had made the Charter system of government as inequitable as it was unjust. Since there were neither legal nor constitutional restraints upon the legislature, it could subordinate the inalienable rights of citizens, including freedom of assembly, speech, religion, and the press, to its arbitrary will. Even the judiciary, Dorr complained, had become "the creature of the Legislature, and the places of most Judges are amicably distributed by the prevailing party among political friends." Republicanism no less than justice, argued Dorr, demanded an end both to the grossly inequitable apportionment of seats in the lower house and to a franchise system which denied the vote to two-thirds of the men.[91] When in 1837 the House of Representatives spurned this eloquent plea for reform the Constitutional party went down to a crushing defeat from which it never recovered.[92]

Though criticism of the Charter attracted virtually no attention during the spirited presidential election of 1840, the Harrison-Van Buren campaign did revitalize the Rhode Island reform movement. Dorr flattered himself that the sudden outpouring of infectious enthusiasm for the cause of justice and good government vindicated his faith in the fundamental common sense of the people. Certainly the fact that less than 9,000 freemen voted in one of the most fiercely contested elections in early American history did not go unnoticed, especially since the suffrage law forced about 15,000 of the 25,000 adult males in the state to stand on the sidelines as mere observers.

[91] Miscellaneous Papers of the General Assembly, folder 12 (1836–1840). For Dorr's efforts to reform the judiciary and judicial procedures, see Dorr Manuscripts, vol. 30 *passim*.

[92] Frieze, *Concise History*, 24–28. For a petition from a Smithfield town meeting held September 9, 1837, supporting reapportionment, see Dorr Manuscripts, 3:12.

But Dorr was naive in supposing that the "licentious republic," as Ezra Stiles had called Rhode Island in the eighteenth century, had overnight abandoned its roguish political ways for the pristine paths of high principle. The shrewd opportunism displayed by Narragansett Bay politicians during the struggle over the ratification of the Constitution of the United States, and the bold pragmatism that carried James DeWolf into the Jeffersonian camp in 1799, still characterized Rhode Island political life. Thus some Democratic politicians, piqued at the Whig victory, which they believed had been won by manufacturing freeholds, and egged on by New York Loco Focos, took up the reform cause, hoping that universal manhood suffrage would defeat the Whigs at the next presidential election. Despite this cynical political maneuver, the constitutional question did not become a party issue. Many Whigs joined Dorr in the Rhode Island Suffrage Association, the organization which replaced the Constitutional party as the reform organization in 1840. With branches scattered throughout the state, a militant determination previously lacking in the reform camp, and a platform closer to the extremism of Seth Luther than to the earlier moderate views of Dorr, the new association spearheaded the attack on the Charter.[93]

Supporters of the *status quo* now faced a critical dilemma. Though they had no wish to concede the Suffrage Association's demands—reapportionment, universal manhood suffrage, separation of powers, a bill of rights, and a drastic reduction in the Assembly's powers—they recognized and feared the revolutionary spirit abroad, particularly the assertion that the sovereign people were competent to formulate and ratify a constitution on their own authority. Under pressure from local suffrage associations as well as from town meetings, the General Assembly therefore decided to convene a constitutional convention. Since the meetings of 1824 and 1834 had relieved tension without forcing concessions, defenders of the Charter doubtless looked forward to a sim-

---

[93] Mowry, *Dorr War,* 50–52. See also, *Preamble and Constitution of the Rhode-Island Suffrage Association . . . 1840* (Providence, 1840), 3–9, for a detailed criticism of the existing system.

ilar result. While the legislature did apportion convention seats so as to increase the representation of the northern industrial and commercial towns,[94] it refused to go as far as the reformers demanded,[95] and it allowed only freemen to elect delegates or to vote in the ratification referendum. In taking the calculated risk of calling a convention, the General Assembly could be reasonably certain, as the reformers well appreciated, that the freemen would reject any but the most conservative constitution.

The legislature's refusal to give the expanding towns equitable representation in the convention, or to allow all men to participate in the voting, stung the Suffrage Association into action. It organized a series of popular demonstrations in Providence in the spring of 1841, then called a constitutional convention of its own.[96] Though all adult white male citizens could vote, only 7,512 of them participated in the election of delegates to the so-called People's Convention. For a while reform leaders feared that public apathy would make a fiasco of their efforts. Nevertheless, delegates completed their deliberations at Providence in November,[97] and a month later the people ratified the constitution by almost 14,000 votes to 52. This was the largest number of voters that had ever participated in any Rhode Island election. Nevertheless, more than 10,000 men had stayed away from the polls, and except in the Blackstone-Pawtuxet valley towns, and Newport, New Shoreham, and Westerly, less than a majority of the freemen had endorsed the People's Constitution. Almost sixty-three per cent of the freemen in the expanding towns voted for the constitution, but in the static towns the comparable figure was only forty-four per cent, and in the declining towns it was a mere twenty-nine per cent. Moreover, in the expanding towns the non-freemen who voted outnumbered the freemen by over twenty-seven per cent. In the

[94] The act calling the convention is in *Acts and Resolves*, January, 1841, pp. 85–86, and the apportionment arrangement is *ibid.*, May, 1841, p. 45. For a supporting petition adopted unanimously by the Smithfield town meeting, see Steere, *Smithfield*, 67–68.

[95] *Providence Journal*, June 26, 28, 1841; *Burke's Report*, 439–441.

[96] Mowry, *Dorr War*, 53–57, 61–71.

[97] *Ibid.*, 94–98.

static towns, by contrast, the freemen outnumbered the non-free-men who voted by over thirty-one per cent, and in the declining towns they outnumbered the non-freemen who voted by almost sixty-nine per cent. Nor is it without point that farming, not manu-facturing, predominated in the nine towns (Burrillville, Barring-ton, South Kingstown, Hopkinton, Portsmouth, New Shoreham, Foster, Charlestown, and Jamestown) where more freemen than non-freemen voted. In short, the People's Constitution received its strongest support in the industrial and commercial towns, where the incidence of freemanship was lowest, and its weakest support in the static and declining towns, where landowning (and there-fore voting rights) was most widespread.[98]

In the meantime, the Freemen's Convention called by the legis-lature had assembled at Providence in November, 1841. When delegates began drafting a document so conservative that it re-tained even the freehold suffrage qualification, anti-reform leaders quickly realized that such intransigence threatened to be self-defeating. It would stimulate, not dissipate, revolutionary senti-ment. Appreciating that judicious but minor concessions could drive a wedge between the extreme and moderate wings of the reform forces, they induced the convention to adopt compromises. The delegates rallied to this principle; they even contemplated enfranchising Negroes. However, in the end they balked at this idea. Instead, they drafted a constitution restricting the suffrage in state and local elections to all white adult male native-born resi-dents. They also reapportioned seats in the House of Representa-tives.[99] As expected, the proposed constitution aroused hostility at both extremes of the political spectrum. Diehard Charterites re-sisted even these modest innovations. Supporters of the People's Constitution did likewise, partly out of distaste for the ambivalent

[98] Over sixty per cent of the 52 negative votes were cast in Little Compton, South Kingstown, and North Providence. The estimate of freemen used in the voting analysis is compiled from *Burke's Report*, 120–121, 203–205, 353. Com-pare the tabulation and commentary in *Facts for the People*, 4–6, 12. There were 4,715 freemen in the expanding towns. Of these, only 2,970 voted. By contrast, 6,009 non-fremen voted.

[99] Mowry, *Dorr War*, 99–100, 119–120.

principles the Freemen's Constitution embodied, but also out of loyalty to the idea of popular sovereignty. Sectional considerations also influenced voting in the referendum held in March, 1842.

With the exception of East Greenwich, which was really a border community, all Blackstone-Pawtuxet towns voted against the constitution, often by substantial majorities. In Glocester, for example, the vote was 387 to 59, in Burrillville, 326 to 52, and in Smithfield, 997 to 334. North Kingstown and Hopkinton also opposed the constitution, but by narrow margins. Voters in the rest of the state, particularly in the south, strongly favored the constitution. In Little Compton the vote was 6 to 202, in Exeter, 32 to 258, and in Middletown, 6 to 152. Although the vote was close only in Westerly, the coalition of static and declining towns, supported by Bristol and Warren among the expanding towns, failed to offset the solid block of opposition mustered in Providence and Kent counties, the two most heavily populated jurisdictions in the state. As a result, the voters rejected the Freemen's Constitution by the narrow margin of 8,689 votes to 8,013. It is notable that this referendum attracted almost twenty per cent more voters than did the one on the People's Constitution. Nevertheless, either because of indifference to the issues involved, or because they did not meet the residence, birth, or, in the case of naturalized citizens, the property qualifications, some 8,500 men stayed away from the polls.[1]

In general, the Freemen's Constitution occupied a middle position between the two extremes represented by the Charter and the People's Constitution.[2] The chief differences lay in the handling of three key issues, the bill of rights, the suffrage, and reapportionment.

Though many provisions of the two declarations of rights closely followed the guarantees of personal freedom laid down in the first ten amendments to the Constitution of the United States, they differed in spirit as well as in specifics. The People's Constitution

---

[1] *Burke's Report*, 105–106. For criticism of Dorrite opposition, see *Providence Journal*, March 24, 1842.

[2] The relevant documents are set out in King, *Dorr*, 298–346; and Frieze, *Concise History*, 129–138.

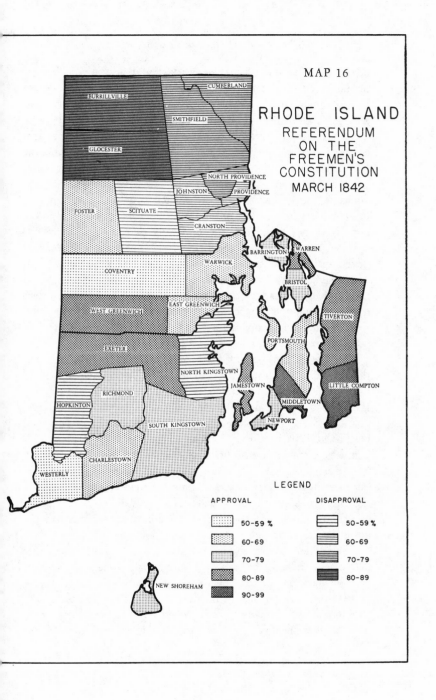

MAP 16

RHODE ISLAND
REFERENDUM
ON THE
FREEMEN'S
CONSTITUTION
MARCH 1842

LEGEND

APPROVAL

50-59 %
60-69
70-79
80-89
90-99

DISAPPROVAL

50-59 %
60-69
70-79
80-89

began with five declarations of fundamental principles. The first upheld freedom of conscience, thought, expression, and action; the second reiterated the ideas expressed in the Declaration of Independence; the third summarized the Dorrite creed: "All political power and sovereignty are originally vested in, and of right belong to, the people," it proclaimed. "All free governments are founded in their authority, and are established for the greatest good of the whole number. The people have therefore an unalienable and indefeasible right, in their original, sovereign, and unlimited capacity, to ordain and institute government, and in the same capacity to alter, reform, or totally change the same, whenever their safety or happiness requires." The fourth condemned discrimination against any individual, party, society, or religious denomination, supported the enactment of legislation for the good of the many instead of the few, and declared that "the burdens of the state ought to be fairly distributed among its citizens." Finally, the constitution directed the legislature to promote free public education.

The Freemen's Constitution, by contrast, made no such declaration of political philosophy, though it did guarantee individual liberties. Moreover, it contained some unique provisions of its own. It declared against imprisonment for debt, prohibited slavery, guaranteed the right of the people to keep and bear arms, and prohibited laws impairing contractual obligations. Of these four points, the People's Constitution touched only one and that obliquely, the slavery question. It gave any person in Rhode Island claiming to be held to labor or service under the laws of any other state the right to a jury trial to determine the validity of the claim. In criminal trials under the People's Constitution juries had the power to judge both law and fact.

Though both constitutions enfranchised all adult white male native-born citizens, they reserved to property owners the right to vote on questions of taxation or the expenditure of public funds, as well as the right to serve on city councils. The Freemen's Constitution allowed holders of realty worth $134 or personalty worth $150 to vote on money matters; the People's Constitution set the qualification at $150 worth of rateable property, whether real or personal. The Freemen's Constitution also established more stringent residence requirements, and it enfranchised only those naturalized citizens who owned $134 worth of realty. Both conventions took an ambivalent stand on enfranchising Negroes.[3] The Freemen's Convention left the question to the discretion of the General Assembly; the People's Convention directed the legislature to settle the matter by a referendum. The two constitutions contained broadly similar provisions dealing with the registration of voters, balloting, and the integrity of elections.

The system of legislative reapportionment also distinguished the constitutions from each other. In general, both recognized the necessity of adjusting to the population changes which had occurred since 1790, but the People's Constitution went much further than the Freemen's in shifting political power northward to the rapidly expanding manufacturing centers. Under the Charter, the expanding towns had one-third of the seats in the House of Representatives. The Freemen's Constitution would have given them slightly more than two-fifths of the seats, the People's Constitution almost half. As a matter of practical politics, therefore, the People's Constitution conferred virtual control on the north. For if the ten expanding towns voted as a block they could dominate the lower house by winning over only three of the forty-two votes distributed among the twenty-one static and declining towns. This was a far cry from the Charter arrangement which made it almost impossible for the expanding towns to control the legislature.

Both constitutions also deviated from the Charter by apportioning seats in the Senate, but neither convention framed an equitable system or succeeded in grouping towns according to economic interest. Thus the People's Convention included the farming com-

[3] In 1831 Providence Negroes began asking for either the suffrage and the right to send their children to public schools, or to be exempt from taxation. Though they secured a tax exemption a decade later, they soon requested that it be repealed. See Petitions Not Granted, January, 1831; January, 1838; June, 1841. For the status of the Negro generally, see Julian Rammelkamp, "The Providence Negro Community, 1820–1842," in *Rhode Island History*, 7:20–33 (January, 1948); and Bartlett, *From Slave to Citizen*, 39–42, 51–56.

munity of Glocester in a district with the manufacturing towns of Scituate, Burrillville, and Johnston instead of with the other hill-country towns of West Greenwich, Coventry, and Foster. It also linked densely inhabited Newport to the isolated farming and fishing communities of New Shoreham and Jamestown. Population

TABLE 24

LEGISLATIVE APPORTIONMENT AND RATIO OF SEATS TO POPULATION UNDER THE CHARTER, THE PEOPLE'S, AND THE FREEMEN'S CONSTITUTIONS, 1841

Towns	Charter		People's		Freemen's	
	Seats	Ratio	Seats	Ratio	Seats	Ratio
Bristol	2	1,745	2	1,745	2	1,745
Warren	2	1,218	2	1,218	2	1,218
Cranston	2	1,451	2	1,451	2	1,451
Johnston	2	1,238	2	1,238	2	1,238
Providence	4	5,793	12	1,931	8	2,896
North Providence	2	2,103	3	1,402	3	1,402
Cumberland	2	2,612	3	1,742	3	1,742
Smithfield	2	4,767	5	1,907	4	2,767
Burrillville	2	991	2	991	2	991
Warwick	4	1,682	4	1,682	4	1,682
Expanding Towns	24	2,590	38	1,635	32	1,942
Barrington	2	275	1	549	2	275
Glocester	2	1,152	2	1,152	2	1,152
Scituate	2	2,045	3	1,363	3	1,363
East Greenwich	2	754	2	754	2	754
Coventry	2	1,717	2	1,717	2	1,717
North Kingstown	2	1,455	2	1,455	2	1,455
South Kingstown	2	1,859	2	1,859	2	1,859
Richmond	2	681	2	681	2	681
Hopkinton	2	863	2	863	2	863
Westerly	2	956	2	956	2	956
Newport	6	1,389	5	1,667	4	2,083
Middletown	2	446	1	891	2	446
Portsmouth	4	427	2	854	2	854
Tiverton	2	1,592	2	1,592	2	1,592
New Shoreham	2	535	2	535	2	535
Static Towns	36	1,075	31	1,312	33	1,172
Foster	2	1,091	2	1,091	2	1,091
West Greenwich	2	707	2	707	2	707
Exeter	2	888	2	888	2	888
Charlestown	2	462	2	462	2	462
Jamestown	2	183	1	365	2	183
Little Compton	2	664	2	664	2	664
Declining Towns	12	666	11	726	12	666
Rhode Island	72	1,517	80	1,360	77	1,413

ranged from 6,475 residents in the twelfth district (Bristol County) to over 11,000 in each of the two Providence city districts. The Freemen's Convention experienced similar difficulties; its senatorial constituencies ranged from less than 3,000 in the least populous district to over 11,500 in the most populous. Nevertheless, since both conventions voted against retaining the Charter system of electing senators at large, the districting plans did have the merit of avoiding the extreme alternative—a Senate representing towns rather than people. This meant that the upper house would be broadly reflective of the popular will and would not offset the gains made by reapportioning the lower house.

In keeping with American tradition, the constitutions separated the powers of government into three distinct categories. However, only the People's Constitution applied this principle unconditionally. It made the governor a truly executive official by relieving him of the presidency of the Senate and by giving him a veto over acts of the Assembly, including militia commissions. This constitution was also unique in that it withdrew original jurisdiction from the legislature in cases of insolvency, divorce, and the sale of real-estate belonging to minors, and it abolished the legislature's appellate jurisdiction in all other cases. The Assembly retained its visitorial powers over corporations under both proposed systems of government, but the People's Constitution contemplated the delegation of this authority to commissions appointed by the legislature. More important, the People's Constitution required a two-thirds majority in each house for any act dealing with a particular corporation, and in the case of banks, it required a popular referendum. All grants of incorporation were made subject to future acts of the General Assembly. Under the Freemen's Constitution, constitutional amendments proposed by the legislature became effective only when ratified by a three-fifths majority of the voters. The People's Constitution required only a simple majority. Thus the insurgents attempted to establish a clearer separation of powers; to reduce and check the authority of the legislative branch; and to effect some fundamental changes, especially in regard to manufacturing and banking corporations.

With the defeat of the Freemen's Constitution in March, 1842, events moved swiftly to a dramatic climax. The Charter forces seized the offensive in three ways. First, the legislature enacted the so-called Algerine Law imposing severe penalties for overt acts against the *status quo*. Persons accepting office or exercising power under the People's Constitution faced arrest either for high crimes and misdemeanors, or for treason.[4] Second, the Charterites followed up their earlier success in dividing the reformers by playing on the sectional, class, ethnic, and religious suspicions previously noted. They cast the constitutional question as an urban-rural conflict between industrial and agricultural towns; they branded the reform movement with a working class, anti-capitalistic bias; and they hinted darkly that industrial and commercial centers could expect sharp increases in tax rates if the Charter system were abandoned. They also conjured up images of the state falling under the control of Roman Catholics by stressing the fact that naturalized citizens, particularly Irishmen, were growing rapidly in number and could be expected to seek special privileges, notably public support for parochial schools.[5] Third, the Law and Order party, as the Charter faction called itself, secured President Tyler's promise of support from the national government in the event of disorders.[6]

The reformers counterattacked by defying the Algerine Law, and in April, 1842, they held statewide elections to form a popular government which, they hoped, would quickly establish itself as the *de facto* regime. All candidates, whether for executive or for legislative posts, were elected unanimously, but even Dorr, who became

[4] See *Report of the Committee on the Action of the General Assembly, on the Subject of the Constitution*, 13–15, bound in with *Acts and Resolves*, March, 1842.

[5] *Manufacturers' and Farmers' Journal*, January 3, 4, 13, 1842; *Providence Journal*, January 1, 6, 12, February 28, March 12, 14, 16, 17, 19, 21, 1842; McDougall, *Might and Right*, 21–22. Archibald Kenyon, the pastor of a Baptist church in Providence, supported the Dorrite position. He contended for a government based on consent and, in good Jeffersonian style, argued that each generation should be free to determine its own political system. See his pamphlet, *The Object and Principles of Civil Government* (Providence, 1842), especially pp. 4–5.

[6] *Burke's Report*, 656–659.

governor in the insurgent administration, obtained only 6,359 votes despite the universal manhood suffrage provisions of the People's Constitution.[7] Though the popularly elected assembly triumphantly convened in a disused Providence foundry in May, 1842, the revolutionaries made no move to seize control of the State House, archives, and courts of law. Indeed, on the second day they adjourned for two months.[8]

Dorr, whose arrest had been ordered by the Charter regime, then secretly slipped away to Washington to plead the reform cause before President Tyler. He left the insurgent government leaderless and on the defensive. Tension mounted as the people of Providence strained to anticipate the tide of events. Rumors, charges, and countercharges confused the issues, business slackened noticeably, and an air of expectant foreboding hung heavily over the city. Timid souls now began withdrawing their support from the People's government, and when Dorr returned from Washington and New York in mid-May he was able to keep the reform movement intact only by exercising considerable skill.[9]

Dorr acted decisively and dramatically in the face of these difficulties, but he succeeded only in precipitating a crisis and in bringing about his own downfall. In a tragi-comic climax, he tried to seize the city arsenal, as much to symbolize popular sovereignty as to gain strategic advantages. Forewarned, the Charter authorities alerted the arsenal's tiny garrison, and the crowd which gathered to witness the siege confused an ill-directed attack. To compound this confusion, a dense fog descended. In the damp atmosphere, Dorrite cannon would not fire. When the morning sun finally lifted the fog, Dorr saw that most of his men had slipped quietly away. Deserted by his militia, and isolated by the arrest or resignation of most of his government, Dorr fled the city. After briefly rallying

---

[7] King, *Dorr*, 73.

[8] Mowry, *Dorr War*, 151–156.

[9] *Ibid.*, 160–164, 174–179. The constitutional problem even affected Providence fire companies. Some threatened to withdraw service from supporters of the Charter government. See *Providence Journal*, April 15, 1842.

his remaining forces at Chepachet in Glocester late in June, he escaped to New Hampshire.[10]

Dorr continued to believe that the people would vindicate him by establishing a government based on the liberal principles he espoused, but, as the Law and Order party correctly judged, the revolution had been crushed. The anti-Dorrites, led by James Fenner, a prominent Democratic politician and former governor, capitalized on the rout by convening a constitutional convention while the tide of reaction was still running strongly against the defeated insurgents. Though the convention was not intended as a delaying device, the Fenner faction determined to make as few concessions as possible. However, the General Assembly did increase the representation of Providence and Smithfield in the convention, and it did authorize all native-born adult male citizens to vote for delegates.[11]

The constitution framed in November, 1842, contained a bill of rights, reapportioned the House of Representatives, and reformed the franchise.[12] In a redistribution of seats even more equitable than under the People's Constitution, the convention gave the ten rapidly expanding northern towns thirty-seven of the sixty-nine seats in the house. However, the convention also set an upper limit of twelve seats for any town regardless of its population. This immediately deprived Providence of two seats and it served as a potential check on the political power of the north. Moreover, the convention gave each town a seat in the Senate. The upper house, by representing towns rather than people, thus threatened to become a bulwark against popular government.

The suffrage provisions, though broader than those applied before the Dorr War, nevertheless discriminated against naturalized

[10] Mowry, *Dorr War*, 181–189. The attack on the arsenal is fully described in *Providence Journal*, May 19, 26, 1842.

[11] See *Acts and Resolves*, June, 1842, pp. 3–5; and Dorr Correspondence, vols. 5–6, for letters to Dorr from B. T. Albro, F. L. Beckford, Franklin Cooley, and John S. Harris, and for letters from Dorr to William Simons and David Parmenter, dated September 18, 26, October 18, 21, 31, November 11, 12, 20, 1842, and January 28, 29, 1843.

[12] *Rhode Island Manual, 1955–1956*, pp. 39–64.

citizens, as well as against non-property owners and non-taxpayers. Foreign-born citizens could vote only if they possessed the traditional $134 worth of real property, and only persons who paid taxes on a minimum of $134 worth of property, real or personal, could vote in the election of the Providence City Council or on any local proposition to impose taxation or to spend public funds. Registered native-born citizens could vote for state and town officials provided they were taxpayers or militiamen. Balloting rather than voice voting was mandatory only for the major posts. Secrecy of the ballot was not guaranteed.

Nor did the constitution alter the General Assembly's judicial powers. Even though it gave judges tenure, they were removable by a simple majority of each house of the legislature. Supreme Court judges were directed to instruct juries on points of law. The General Assembly had to allow an election to intervene between the submission of an application for a charter and the grant of incorporation, but the act did not have to pass by a special majority and it did not have to be submitted to a popular referendum. Finally, the constitution directed the General Assembly to promote public education.

From his refuge in New Hampshire, Dorr urged his followers to boycott the constitutional referendum. Although a mere fifty-nine electors voted against the new form of government in the balloting held in November, 1842, the constitution attracted the support of only a fraction of the qualified voters. Because many Dorrites followed their leader's advice to abstain, and because many diehard Charterites opposed change of any kind, the new constitution went into effect in May, 1843, with the sanction of barely 7,000 men out of a total of over 25,000 in the state. On the average, between two-thirds and three-quarters of the adult males in each town did not vote; in five towns more than four-fifths of the men stayed away from the polls; and in Glocester and West Greenwich more than eighty-five per cent of the men abstained. To be sure, some men could not qualify to vote because they could not meet one or other of the suffrage requirements. Nevertheless, the voters received the new constitution with apathy rather than enthu-

TABLE 25

VOTING FOR THE 1843 CONSTITUTION, WITH LEGISLATIVE APPORTION-
MENT IN 1842, 1843, AND 1851[13]

Towns	Adult Males	Yes Votes Cast	Apportionment		
			Charter	1843	1851
Bristol	765	341	2	2	2
Warren	805	281	2	2	2
Cranston	670	101	2	2	2
Johnston	576	156	2	2	2
Providence	5,013	1,606	4	12	12
North Providence	884	187	2	3	4
Cumberland	1,130	226	2	3	4
Smithfield	1,933	374	2	6	6
Burrillville	524	96	2	1	2
Warwick	1,419	285	4	4	4
Expanding Towns	13,719	3,653	24	37	40
Barrington	133	51	2	1	2
Glocester	637	83	2	2	2
Scituate	1,058	251	2	3	2
East Greenwich	397	144	2	1	1
Coventry	794	255	2	2	2
North Kingstown	726	179	2	2	2
South Kingstown	880	237	2	2	2
Richmond	316	75	2	1	1
Hopkinton	415	106	2	1	1
Westerly	466	124	2	1	1
Newport	1,897	694	6	5	5
Middletown	248	100	2	1	1
Portsmouth	482	192	4	1	1
Tiverton	762	214	2	2	2
New Shoreham	284	48	2	1	1
Static Towns	9,495	2,753	36	26	26
Foster	587	265	2	1	1
West Greenwich	379	53	2	1	1
Exeter	445	131	2	1	1
Charlestown	212	56	2	1	1
Jamestown	102	25	2	1	1
Little Compton	317	85	2	1	1
Declining Towns	2,042	615	12	6	6
Rhode Island	25,256	7,021	72	69	72

siasm; in Foster, the town where the largest proportion of the men
voted, less than a majority of the adult males went to the polls.[14]

[13] Mowry, *Dorr War*, 286–289; *Burke's Report*, 119; *Acts and Resolves*, January,
1851, p. 15.

[14] For the Dorrite reaction to the proposed constitution, see letters to Dorr from
Ariel Ballou, F. L. Beckford, Franklin Cooley, and John S. Harris, and letters

Illogically, the Dorrites did vote for state officials and members of the General Assembly in the election of April, 1843. In the bitter gubernatorial contest, James Fenner, Dorr's arch-enemy, defeated Thomas F. Carpenter, the candidate of the "regular" Democrats, by approximately 9,000 votes to 7,000. Although Dorr might have taken comfort in the fact that over 16,500 men participated in the election, or more than twice as many as in any previous election for governor, he considered Fenner's election a crushing personal defeat, a rejection of his reform principles, and proof that his faith in the people had been misplaced.[15]

The unwillingness of the people to act out the Jeffersonian rôle shattered Dorr's spirit and destroyed his idealistic faith in the common man. He returned to Providence in October, 1843, to give himself up to the authorities. Convicted of treason the following April, he served one year of a life sentence before Charles Jackson, the governor elected on the so-called "Liberation" ticket, signed a bill releasing him. The General Assembly restored Dorr's civil and political rights in 1851. Three years later, over the vigorous protest of the Supreme Court, it reversed the treason conviction. Ironically, one of Dorr's major criticisms of the Charter system had been the legislature's exercise of judicial authority.[16]

---

from Dorr to David Parmenter and William Simons, in Dorr Correspondence, vols. 5–6, September 18, 26, 29, October 18, 21, 31, November 2, 20, 1842. See also, Mowry, *Dorr War*, 286–289; *Burke's Report*, 119; Robert Sherman, "The Dorr Rebellion," *Providence Daily Journal*, January 10, 1874.

[15] For the election of 1843, see letters from B. T. Albro, F. L. Beckford, Walter S. Burges, and Philip B. Stiness to Dorr, and letters from Dorr to Walter S. Burges and William Simons, in Dorr Correspondence, vol. 5, December 15, 1842; January 7, 26, 28, 29, February 26, April 2, 6, 10, 12, 14, 1843; for a resolution (December 16, 1842) urging the Dorrites to vote in the election in April, 1843, see Dorr Manuscripts, 5:113; Mowry, *Dorr War*, 289–291. A decade elapsed before the total number of votes cast in a gubernatorial election exceeded the 16,520 votes cast in April, 1843. In general, the level of voter participation failed to keep pace with the growth of population. For voting statistics, see *Rhode Island Manual, 1961–1962*, pp. 205–217.

[16] King, *Dorr*, 151–175, 189–214; *Providence Gazette*, April 15, June 28, 1845. Dorr's restoration to civil and political rights is in *Acts and Resolves*, May, 1851, pp. 3–4; the legislative reversal of the treason conviction *ibid.*, January, 1854, pp. 249–251; and the Supreme Court's declaration *ibid.*, June, 1854, pp. 4–14. See also, *Providence Journal*, February 28, 1854.

No single factor explains the "Dorr War."[17] Compounded of
many issues, some of them seemingly discrete, the constitutional
struggle shattered traditional loyalties. Though the symbols usually substituted for analysis—democratic workers versus entrenched
vested interests; townsmen versus farmers; foreign-born Catholics
versus native-born Protestants; or Democrats versus Whigs—ac-
curately reflect the political ammunition fired during the conflict,
they actually distort basic forces and conceal inner complexities.[18]
In arresting Seth Luther for his part in the revolution, the Law
and Order regime conveniently curbed the activities of Rhode Island's most militant labor leader, and some manufacturers, notably
the Lippitts of Warwick, did dismiss employees for Dorrist sym-
pathies. But other industrialists, the Spragues of Cranston, for example, initially encouraged the reform movement, defecting only
after Dorr had formed his revolutionary government. They were
not willing to follow Dorr down the road to revolution. As their
cynical exploitation of their workers' votes both before and after
1842 shows, the Spragues were primarily political manipulators.
Their support of Dorrism was at least as much motivated by self-
interest as by sincere dissatisfaction with the Charter system. As
with so many Rhode Islanders, the desire for money and power

[17] For other interpretations, see Brennan, *Social Conditions*, 169–173; Grieve,
History of Pawtucket, 102; *History of Rhode Island*, 41–45; Field, *Rhode
Island*, 1:335–352; Knight, *Sprague Families*, 28; Maxey, "Suffrage Extension,"
565–577; Mowry, *Dorr War, passim*; John Bell Rae, "The Issues of the Dorr
War," in *Rhode Island History*, 1:33–44 (April, 1942); Arthur M. Schlesinger,
Jr., *The Age of Jackson* (Boston, 1945), 410–417; Stickney, "Know-Nothing-
ism," 246–247; Chilton Williamson, *American Suffrage from Property to De-
mocracy, 1760–1860* (Princeton, 1960), 242–259.

[18] One pastor equated reform and infidelity, another denounced Dorrist godless-
ness, and a professor of moral philosophy and metaphysics described Dorr's ideas
as licentious and disruptive. Compare Francis Vinton, *Loyalty and Piety* (Providence, 1842), 23; Mark Tucker, *Discourse Preached Thanksgiving Day* (Providence, 1842), 8; William G. Goddard, *The Civil Government of Rhode-Island*
(Providence, 1843), 13; William Goodell, *The Rights and the Wrongs of Rhode
Island* (Whitesboro, New York, 1842), especially pp. 4–8, 31, 35–37, 39–40, 62–
63, 85–92; *The Close of the Late Rebellion in Rhode-Island* (Providence, 1842),
especially pp. 6–7, 11, 13–16.

dominated Sprague thinking. Politics was simply a means by which to gain those ends.[19]

Fennerite allegations of class war notwithstanding, the insurgent movement challenged rather than bolstered traditional relationships. Like their leader, many Dorrites came from families of affluence and respectability; some had been close to the state's inner councils. They saw Dorr as he saw himself, as a moderate dedicated to conserving rather than to destroying, to purifying rather than to defiling, and they too wanted to revive Rhode Island pride in its political institutions. Dorr considered himself the friend rather than the enemy of his class. Thus the constitutional issue divided families, including Dorr's own, and won the sympathy of many property owners and their eldest sons. And when the state closed ranks behind the Law and Order party in the summer of 1842, the militia, which represented all shades of opinion and all walks of life, remained loyal to the legally constituted authorities. This belied Fennerite assertions that Dorr's course resulted in the setting of class against class.[20]

Though industrialization and urbanization certainly facilitated egalitarian agitation in the Blackstone and Pawtuxet valleys, dissatisfaction with the Charter system stemmed as much from the reapportionment question as from the suffrage issue. In this respect if not in many others, workers and employers made common cause.

[19] Grieve, *History of Pawtucket*, 102; Knight, *Sprague Families*, 28; *Providence Daily Express*, May 18, 1842; *Providence Journal*, July 4, 30, 1842; Stickney, "Know-Nothingism," 246.

[20] Dorr had an impeccable background—Phillips Academy, Harvard College, and legal studies under James Kent. Yet Francis Wayland, in *The Affairs of Rhode-Island* (Providence, 1842), 7–8, accused Dorr of hungering for power. If the reformers had their way, Wayland thought, "the law of force" and "the love of plunder" would quickly replace properly constituted authority. Goddard also believed that Dorrism threatened the rights of property. See his address on *Civil Government*, 28. However, for a contrary view, see William H. Smith to Dorr, September 3, 1842, in Dorr Correspondence, vol. 5, in which Smith complained that "Even our coloured girl Kate was taught to speak disrespectfully of Suffrage folks & to talk saucy to me. The only friendly face in the house was that of an Irish girl, a sincere friend of liberty." See also, McDougall, *Might and Right*, 227, 294–295, 325–332.

Workers hoped to pave the way for reform, manufacturers to make the General Assembly more responsive to industrial needs.

Nor was the reform movement a simple sectional question pitting northern expanding communities against southern and western ones. Most rural areas did oppose Dorrism, but Glocester, a static agricultural town, supported Dorr as enthusiastically as did the burgeoning industrial centers of Providence and Smithfield. Yet landholding, and thus the right to vote, was fairly widespread in Glocester, and the town gained nothing directly from reapportionment. While timber workers and charcoal burners may have assumed the rôle played by disgruntled mill hands in the manufacturing towns, and though the extraordinarily high incidence of insolvency in Glocester suggests the possibility of a parallel to attitudes underlying Shays' Rebellion in Massachusetts, loyalty to the revolutionary movement seems to have stemmed primarily from the leadership of Samuel Y. Atwell, one of Glocester's representatives in the General Assembly and a staunch Dorr supporter.[21] Moreover, the reapportionment system that went into effect in 1843 penalized the northern towns of Barrington and Burrillville, but they still considered that the advantages of the new constitution outweighed the disadvantages of the Charter, and Newport, although the leading southern town and therefore the one most vitally affected by the realignment of political power in the state, divided on the reform question. Many Newporters took the Dorrist side out of dissatisfaction with the Charter suffrage system and a desire to elevate the tone of political life, but others opposed

[21] Glocester freemen acted with the same determination as their counterparts in other towns to prevent election frauds. They challenged applicants for admission as freemen because they were not old enough, or because they possessed insufficient property, or because they were not properly qualified residents. See, Glocester Town Meeting Records, 2:252–265 (1786–1864); Glocester Mortgages, 1:14–15 (April 19, 1837), in Glocester Town Hall; Schedule Five, Seventh Census of the United States, 1850, Rhode Island volumes, 6:315–322; Granted Petitions, volumes 38–53 (1809–1825); Petitions Not Granted, 1807–1828. In all, Glocester residents submitted 120 bankruptcy petitions. This was more than the residents of any other town except Providence. See also, *History of Rhode Island*, 138.

change, mainly because reapportionment threatened to reduce New-port's political influence.

Appearances to the contrary, the reform movement was not a party question either. Dorr and others like him did switch from the Whig to the Democratic camp, and the New York Loco Focos certainly attempted to use the Dorr War as a propaganda weapon against the Whigs,[22] but support for, or opposition to, the in-surgent movement bore little relationship to party affiliation. In-deed, the very unwillingness of political leaders to identify them-selves with the opposition to the Charter hamstrung first the Lutherites then the Dorrites. Politicians withheld their support not out of distaste for reform but because they detected no broad demand for it. Leaders as shrewdly opportunistic as those bred in the cynical Rhode Island climate would never have hesitated to rally to the constitutional cause had they thought it politically ex-pedient to do so.

The fluidity of Rhode Island society prevented the reform ques-tion from dividing the state along clear-cut social, economic, or political lines. On the whole, native Americans did enjoy greater social and economic mobility than did naturalized citizens, but with the great waves of immigration still in the future the lines were not yet sharply drawn. This denied the reformers the support of natural, easily organized interest blocs, delayed the constitutional crisis until the industrial revolution was far advanced, and pro-duced ambivalent results.

The reform movement attracted heterogeneous support. At one extreme stood the Dorrites. They acted from principle and, initi-ally, sought a government controlled by responsible middle-class interests. Offended in their sense of republican propriety by the suffrage and apportionment systems, they also sought to curb the power of the legislature by guaranteeing fundamental rights and by relieving the General Assembly of its judicial functions. To a

[22] Arthur M. Mowry, "Tammany Hall and the Dorr War," in *American His-torical Review*, 3:292–301 (January, 1898); *The Conspiracy to Defeat the Liberation of Governor Dorr!* (New York, 1845), especially pp. 3–22.

lesser extent, they hoped that a reformed political system would be more responsive to the popular will and, in particular, that solutions to pressing social and economic problems might be enacted. At the other extreme stood the Lutherites. Reflecting the popular Jacksonian, Loco Foco position, they demanded universal manhood suffrage as a means to an end—the passage of their radical legislative program. Between these polar positions stood a number of reform sympathizers. Some acknowledged the inequities of the Charter system but cared little about other issues. They merely supported a reasonable extension of the franchise and a just system of apportionment. Others were indifferent to principle. Their interest in constitutional reform was largely a practical one. Expanding the electorate would give them control of more votes, and reapportionment would increase their political power. Significantly, this group defected as soon as the insurgents took their first revolutionary steps.

The Charterites were also heterogeneous in character. The diehards opposed change of any kind, others feared that suffrage reform would lead to mobocracy, and still others wished to prevent the northward shift in political power. Many genuinely feared enfranchising Irish Catholics, but some cynically exploited ethnic, religious, sectional, and rural fears merely to preserve their own political influence.[23]

Despite their initial disappointment in having failed to make the People's Constitution the permanent basis of government in Rhode Island, the Dorrites could take pride in having forced an unwilling regime to extend the franchise, redistribute House seats, and formulate a bill of rights. But the Fennerites gave the state the appearance, not the substance, of reform. The first elections under the new constitution were, if possible, even more blatantly corrupt than before. In many instances, landlords supervised the voting of their tenants and mill owners saw to it that their workers voted as instructed by the overseers. Party leaders paid the registration tax

---

[23] For example, Francis Vinton, in *Loyalty and Piety*, 23, rejected the Dorrite axiom that the people were above constitutions as a radical doctrine that was "subversive of all security." See also, McDougall, *Might and Right*, 227–228.

for non-property owners and dispensed liberal quantities of rum as additional inducements to voters.[24] Such abuses so discouraged political activity that only 4,000 voters participated in the gubernatorial election of 1850.

The rapidly changing character of Rhode Island society gave these political manipulators a relatively free hand, and they were especially quick to appreciate the significance of the flood of immigrants reaching the state from Europe and Canada. At first, economic no less than political conditions combined to keep the foreign-born as a landless, politically mute minority. Even if individual immigrants did save enough to buy land, social pressures discouraged its being sold to them. As a consequence, in 1865 there were only 1,260 naturalized voters out of an immigrant population exceeding 40,000. It was not until the native-born sons of these immigrants themselves reached voting age, therefore, that potentially, at least, the government acquired the popular basis that Dorr had intended. Even so, these voters were easily controlled by employers and politicians,[25] and despite the promises made to immigrants to get them to enlist in the Union Army during the Civil War, the real-property qualification for naturalized citizens remained in the Constitution until 1888.[26]

[24] For evidence of corruption in the 1842 and 1843 elections, see letters to Dorr from B. T. Albro, Ariel Ballou, F. L. Beckford, Walter S. Burges, and Philip B. Stines, and letters from Dorr to Burges and William Simons, dated November 2, 1842; January 7, 28, February 26, April 2, 4, 6, 10, 14, 19, 1843; in Dorr Correspondence, vols. 5–7. See also, Chafee, "Weathering the Panic," 272; McDougall, *Might and Right*, 307–309.

[25] According to the *Manufacturers' and Farmers' Journal*, September 4, 1851, "The landless workingman and mechanic is as eligible to any office . . . as the richest landowner. Yet . . . that class is not represented by a single member either in the Senate or the House of Representatives of this State."

[26] For the 1888 amendment and its rôle in sharply increasing the number of votes cast in gubernatorial elections, see *Rhode Island Manual, 1961–1962*, pp. 66–68, 210–219. Between 1843 and 1874 the total vote exceeded 20,000 only twice. It generally exceeded 20,000 after 1874, and in 1887 and 1888 it exceeded 35,000. The total vote rose to 43,000 in 1889, the first election under the new suffrage law, and the general trend was upward throughout the remainder of the century. Nevertheless, the rate of increase probably failed to keep pace with the growth of the adult male population.

In the long run, therefore, and in a very fundamental sense, the Dorr War failed. It failed to elevate the spirit of Rhode Island political life, it failed to open local and state government to majority rule, it failed to free the judiciary from legislative interference, and, above all, it failed to inaugurate an era of social and economic reform. The fundamental problems inherent in the transformation of Narragansett Bay society were dealt with no more effectively or earnestly after 1842 than they had been before.

For the status of aliens, see, for example, Petitions Not Granted, May, 1846, in which naturalized citizens sought equality of treatment. They protested that it was impossible for them to buy land and that Negroes enjoyed more rights than they did. While they claimed not to despise Negroes, they were not unmindful of the popular belief in Negro inferiority. Compare, *ibid.*, January, 1855, in which some Warwick citizens urged intensification of discrimination against foreign immigrants. They asked the legislature to require twenty-one years of residence in Rhode Island before permitting immigrants to become naturalized citizens. For attempts to abolish the registry tax, see Miscellaneous Papers of the General Assembly, folder 21 (1859–1860). The history of the suffrage after 1843 is discussed in Gorman, *The Elective Franchise*, 11–37; Chilton Williamson, "Rhode Island Suffrage Since the Dorr War," in *New England Quarterly*, 28:43-50 (March, 1955). See also, Hazard, *Economics and Politics*, 119; Massachusetts Bureau of Labor Statistics, *Eleventh Annual Report, January, 1880* (Boston, 1880), 13.

CHAPTER SEVEN

Legacy

RHODE Island had yet to reach the limits of industrial expansion when the Civil War broke out. The factory labor force continued growing by leaps and bounds for another two generations and did not reach its peak until 1919. Nevertheless, the industrial pattern changed relatively little. Already the most highly industrialized American state, Rhode Island retained this distinction throughout the second half of the nineteenth century.

As before, textiles and metals absorbed a disproportionate share of venture capital and, despite an apparent trend toward diversification, the economy remained seriously unbalanced. To be sure, the hosiery, knit goods, and silk industries became increasingly important, but they merely extended textile making to new products. They did not change the direction of economic growth. Similar conditions prevailed in the base metal industry. There, too, the Rhode Islanders expended their main effort on traditional products—machinery, equipment, steam engines, and hardware—and what appeared to be new lines of endeavor were actually projections of the old. Though the Providence Tool Company took up the manufacture of rifles, for example, it simply applied methods of mass production to an old Rhode Island industry; though the Burnside Rifle Works became an important locomotive factory, the seemingly new activity had grown out of the well-established steam engine industry; and though the Nicholson File Company became the world's largest manufacturer of hand files and rasps, the product was not new to Rhode Island. With the exception of machine tools, an important post-Civil War development, the base metal industry thus retained its traditional character. Nor were conditions different in the precious metal industry. The labor force as well as the scale of production continued expanding, but no significant changes occurred either in the types of articles produced or in the concentration of production in the Providence area. The phosphatic chemical and rubber footwear industries did become major new sources of wealth in the second half of the nineteenth century. However, they too had their origins in the pre-Civil War period and, more important, they did not counterbalance the excessive emphasis given to textiles and metals. In effect, therefore, the Rhode Islanders simply exploited their already demonstrated competence in certain specialized fields.

Lucrative though these activities were, the economy remained vulnerable to adverse business trends. Over the short term, particular industries, such as precious metals, were unusually sensitive to fluctuations in consumer demand, and some industrial empires were either so tightly integrated or so sprawling that losses could set off a chain reaction of failures throughout the economy. The latter was the case with the Spragues in the panic of 1873.[1] The family owned or controlled some ten cotton mills, a streetcar company, a steamboat line, seven metal working enterprises, and five banks. In addition, the family had invested heavily in southern water privileges, timber properties, and railroads. Many of these enterprises were totally unrelated to the main Sprague business of textiles, but they all depended upon the family for their working capital and credit. Though their assets totaled $19,000,000 and their liabilities only $11,000,000, the Spragues could not meet their obligations.

Just as the first American bank failure—the Farmer's Exchange of Glocester in 1809—sent a tremor of trepidation across the nation, so the collapse of the multi-million dollar Sprague empire resounded throughout the country. Industrial failures were not new in American business history, but there had never been a disaster of such magnitude. Many Sprague properties had to be disposed of at a fraction of their value as going concerns, thereby entailing enormous losses for the family as well as for their creditors. Two savings banks went down in total ruin; and three commercial banks

[1] Chafee, "Weathering the Panic," 270–293; Carroll, *Rhode Island*, 2:863–864; Field, *Rhode Island*, 3:316–317; Fuller, *History of Warwick*, 254–255.

had to reduce their capital by a total of $600,000 and to assess their stockholders to make good some of the losses.

Although the economy resumed its expansion at the end of the decade, weaknesses soon reappeared. Significantly, eight banks, with combined liabilities of $10,000,000 failed between 1889 and 1898.[2] More important, the Sprague and related failures administered a devastating shock to the Rhode Island entrepreneurial tradition.

Gone was the vitality, the creativity, the daring sense of risk taking—in short, the dynamic quality that had characterized the merchants and industrialists of earlier days. At the very time that business leaders should have been correcting the imbalance in the economy and restoring its flexibility and resilience, they were overwhelmed by the postwar depression. Instead of seizing opportunities, or creating new ways of making money, they reacted cautiously. Many simply intensified their effort within the existing industrial framework. The less enterprising gave up all pretense at entrepreneurship; they shifted their capital to bonds and settled for a safe but sure return.

So long as the nation continued expanding and the South remained agricultural, the danger implicit in the Rhode Island economic structure was concealed. But with nearly six out of every ten factory workers employed in various branches of the textile industry, and over half the labor force engaged in manufacturing or construction, it required only a slight increase in competition or a small shift in consumer preference to jeopardize the state's economic well-being.

Cotton manufacturers felt this pressure earliest and most severely. After 1875, employment in cotton mills increased at only half the rate of the factory labor force as a whole and, after 1923, when the full impact of Southern industrialization became apparent, cotton textile employment fell precipitously. This slowed the overall rate of economic growth so much that during the twentieth century the Rhode Island economy expanded much more slowly than did that of the nation as a whole.

[2] Field, *Rhode Island*, 3:317.

The Rhode Islanders had been too successful. They had industrialized beyond the point of no return; they had blocked off avenues of diversification; without intending to do so, they had built flexibility out of their operations. Traditionally, the state's entrepreneurial class had anticipated and abetted economic trends. In good times, investors had ventured into experimental, high-risk enterprises. Their object had been to diversify their operations, to find new and profitable activities before competitors crowded the field, and to overcome the fundamental shortage of natural resources in Rhode Island. If anything, entrepreneurs had applied such principles even more vigorously during bad times. For then, more than ever, they had to rely on their talents for making opportunities where none existed. In any event, when they succeeded, they earned speculative profits commensurate with the risks they had taken. But manufacturing enterprises lent themselves best to this kind of aggressive opportunism during the experimental phase of development. As each undertaking became well-established, and as the industrial economy itself reached maturity, the routine of keeping the economic machine in sound working order gradually sapped the traditional entrepreneurial spirit. Eventually, but only when it was already too late, business leaders gradually realized that they had irrevocably committed themselves and Rhode Island to a particular pattern of industrial activity. In effect, they had cut off their lines of retreat.

When the crisis came, as it did after the First World War, capitalists and workers alike could only suffer the consequences. They no longer had the capacity to turn adversity to their advantage. Though some factory workers found employment in trades and services, the business climate discouraged economic experimentation.

Rhode Island then experienced a prolonged period of economic stagnation. Between the end of the First World War and the outbreak of the Second, over a fifth of the Rhode Island textile workers lost their jobs and the proportion of factory workers laid off in the state was almost seven times as large as in the nation as a whole.

This problem had its roots, of course, in the distinctive Rhode Island economic pattern and constituted one element of the legacy bequeathed by the industrial revolution.

A second constituent of the legacy bequeathed to posterity was a pattern of investing surplus venture capital outside the state. Initially, much of this money, such as that risked in southern New England manufacturing or even in Cuban sugar plantations, was an extension of or was complementary to the Rhode Island economy and created employment for Rhode Islanders. Increasingly, however, as funds moved further and further afield and especially into activities having no direct connection with the pattern of Rhode Island life, only the profits came home and the investments stimulated the economies of other communities, sometimes competing ones. Such was the case with Newport capital ventured in the New York money market, with Bristol funds risked in manufacturing in Kentucky,[3] or with Providence capital invested in Paraguay.[4] The Browns financed many of the railroads constructed west of the Hudson Valley, developed the Lake Superior iron ore fields, and speculated in western lands.[5] Others formed southwestern mining

[3] *DeWolf vs. Johnson, et al.,* 10 *Wheaton* 367 (1825).

[4] In 1853, a syndicate headed by Edward Carrington, Jr., Samuel Arnold, and Walter S. Burges secured a charter for the United States and Paraguay Navigation Company, a mercantile and manufacturing enterprise with an authorized capital of $900,000. It quickly acquired property in Paraguay, including a cigar factory at Asuncion and a sawmill at San Antonio, but these activities, as well as plans to manufacture hemp, were abruptly halted in 1855, when the government expelled all foreign interests. This immediately doomed the venture. However, negotiations for damages were so protracted that the corporation could not be dissolved until 1891. See *Acts and Resolves,* June, 1853, pp. 172–176; Joan Lawton, "United States and Paraguay Navigation Company," in *Rhode Island History,* 6:108–109 (October, 1947); and *Bank of the Republic vs. Edward Carrington, et al.,* 5 *Rhode Island* 515 (1858).

[5] James B. Hedges, "The Brown Papers: The Record of a Rhode Island Business Family," in *Proceedings of the American Antiquarian Society,* New series, 51:33–34 (April, 1941); Paul Wallace Gates, "Land Policy and Tenancy in the Prairie States," in *Journal of Economic History,* 1:60–82, especially pp. 68, 71, (May, 1941). See also, J. B. Rae, "Asa Whitney's Effort in Rhode Island to Promote a Railroad to the Pacific," in *Rhode Island History,* 3:19–20 (January, 1944).

ventures,[6] and the Spragues acquired land and lumber interests in Maine and water privileges in South Carolina.[7] During the second half of the nineteenth century, difficulties of various kinds forced many banks to reduce their capital, but even then they too had more funds than they could place profitably enough at home.[8]

Though this search for lucrative investments was in keeping with the Rhode Island tradition, it was also symptomatic of the inability of the economy to absorb all the capital available and both reflected and encouraged a declining rate of economic growth. And it was paralleled by a new pattern of business consolidation. Particularly in the textile industry, but also in the base metals, some of the largest enterprises passed into the hands of corporations controlled in Boston and New York. As a consequence, the intense identification of economic leaders with the locality, an identification that had distinguished so much of the early entrepreneurial spirit, waned.

In general, the pattern of population distribution and growth established in the first half of the nineteenth century also persisted. The northern half of the state, especially the Blackstone-Pawtuxet region, expanded more rapidly than the rest of Rhode Island. No fundamental change occurred until during and after the Second World War, when the growth of naval facilities at North Kingstown and Newport stimulated the development of all surrounding areas. After the lapse of more than a century, the sea again became a dynamic factor in the Rhode Island economy.

Industrialization also bequeathed a rapidly changing ethnic and religious pattern.[9] A sixth of the Rhode Islanders were foreign-born in 1850; by 1865 more than a third of them had either been born abroad or had one or more foreign-born parents. Persons of foreign stock constituted approximately half the population in 1875; by 1910 seven out of every ten Rhode Islanders had one or more foreign-born parents, and every third inhabitant was a foreign im-

[6] For the charters of the Tower, Sopori, and Arizona land and mining companies, see *Acts and Resolves*, January, 1854, pp. 287–290; January, 1856, pp. 119–120; May, 1859, pp. 8–15.
[7] Chafee, "Weathering the Panic," 274, 282.
[8] Field, *Rhode Island*, 3:317.
[9] *Rhode Island Manual, 1961–1962*, p. 220.

migrant, the highest proportion in the Union. This pattern emerged despite the reversal of the earlier trend in which Rhode Island had lost more residents to emigration than it had gained from the influx of persons born in other American states.

The composition of these foreign immigrants did change fundamentally over the course of the century. Since the peak of Irish immigration occurred before the Civil War, their proportion of the total population began declining. After 1865, French Canadians arrived in increasing numbers, but after 1890 the inflow of southern Europeans, especially Italians, became the most pronounced.

Throughout the nineteenth century, native-born Protestants of Anglo-Saxon stock retained social, economic, and political power. The situation changed rapidly, especially in the political field, after the turn of the century. The majority of Rhode Islanders described themselves as Roman Catholics in the 1905 census. Two years later the voters elected the state's first Irish-Catholic governor.[10]

From the vantage point of the early twentieth century, the Rhode Islanders could look back at their achievements with considerable pride and solid satisfaction. In the course of almost three hundred years of exciting growth, they had made their reputations first as mariners, then as manufacturers. Held back initially by the tiny colony's meager natural resources, the pioneer settlers had eventually learned to wrest livelihoods from the sea, and some, as Simeon Potter put it, had shown a willingness to "plow the sea to porridge to make money."[11] Whenever possible, they engaged in legitimate coastal and foreign ventures, but whenever the profits justified the risks, they just as eagerly piled up fortunes outside the law. Successful though they were during both the Colonial and Revolutionary periods, after 1790 they encountered increasing hazards and declining profits in maritime trade. They responded to this challenge creatively. Once their experiments with textile manufacturing had proved successful, they plunged into the new form of money making with their customary thoroughness and

---

[10] Kurt B. Mayer and Sidney Goldstein, *Migration and Economic Development in Rhode Island* (Providence, 1958), especially pp. 18–22, 56.

[11] Howe, *Mount Hope*, 85.

relish. By the end of the first quarter of the nineteenth century they had not only abandoned the sea; they had also made Rhode Island a leading industrial state. This was no mean achievement. Apart from its water resources and favorable climate, Rhode Island enjoyed no distinct industrial advantages over other American states. What it did have was ambitious, talented entrepreneurs, especially in Providence. Their determination to advance both their private interests and what they judged to be the interests of the community shaped the speed, direction, and extent of the economic revolution.

However, over the long term the fundamental shift from the sea to the land, from maritime to industrial endeavor, produced ambivalent and, so far as the nation was concerned, prophetic results. For Rhode Island encountered economic sluggishness as early as the opening of the twentieth century, its economy was already seriously depressed long before the Crash of October, 1929, and employment remained slack until after the outbreak of the Second World War. Abnormal wartime conditions provided neither the opportunity nor the incentive to reorganize the economy.

Though progress was made after 1945, Rhode Island's underlying economic problems were not solved. Newport and the southern segment of the state continued to depend heavily on the Navy and the resort business for economic vitality; Providence and the northern region fought a continuing battle to discourage industries from moving out of the state; and Rhode Island, still the most highly industrialized state in the Union, had yet to diversify its manufacturing effort adequately or to regain its earlier economic flexibility. The conversion of textile factories to discount stores or to egg production symbolized the inadequacy of some of the solutions tried, and the rapid growth of some suburban towns, notably Warwick, concealed the underlying malaise. Whether Rhode Island could recapture the vigor and resourcefulness of its first two and a half centuries in its fourth remained to be seen. One thing seemed clear: the prospect for the 1960's was far less bright than it had been for the 1790's.

Index

A. & W. Sprague, 128, 129, 131, 132, 296–297

Albion, Smithfield, 122–123, 134

Albion mills, Smithfield, 196

Algerine Law, 282

Aliens, status of, 244, 247, 268, 294n

Allaire, James P., 143

Allen, Philip, 168, 231, 244

Allen, Samuel G., 130

Allen, William, 168

Allen, Zachariah, 98, 134–135, 214, 231, 249

Almy, Brown, and Slater, 79, 85, 87, 119, 130

Almy, William, 78–79, 83, 131, 168

Almy and Brown, 80, 82, 82n, 83, 113, 131, 162n

American Bank, Providence, 201

American Insurance Company, Providence, 212, 214, 215

American Screw Company, Providence, 146–147, 240

Angell, Joseph K., 270

Ann and Hope, 44

Anti-Catholicism, 242–246

Anti-Masonry, 246

Arkwright Manufacturing Company, Coventry, 83, 169n

Arnold, Asa, 101

Arnold, Samuel, 299n

Arnold, Samuel G., 96

Atlantic and Mediterranean Banking and Navigation Company, Newport, 69–70, 201

Atlantic DeLaine Company, North Providence, 131

Atlantic Insurance Company, Providence, 215

Atlantic Steamboat Company, Providence, 165

Atlas Bank, Providence, 201

Atwell, Samuel Y., 197–198, 290

Babcock, 143

Babcock, John, 143

Baker, William L., 182n

Bank of Commerce, Providence, 201, 215

Bank of Rhode Island, Newport, 188n, 211

Bankruptcy, xi, 252–254, 268, 281, 290

Banks: incorporation of, 113, 183–184, 281; debt collection by, 113, 187, 188n, 192, 194–195, 196, 198n, 212n; liability of shareholders in, 116–117, 187, 197, 197n; taxation of, 118n, 192–194, 196–197; growth of, 182–205, 252, 296–297; location of 184, 186; capital of 184–186; regulation of 190, 192, 197–198, 198n, 199–200, 202–203, 215; crisis of 1814, 192

Barbary pirates, 39, 49

Barrington, R. I.: population of, 16, 21, 72, 154, 220, 222–226, 228; industry in, 105, 153–154, 155; legislative representation of, 256, 257, 280, 286, 290; and constitutional reform, 264, 267, 271n, 275, 277, 286

Barstow, Amos C., 240

Barstow, John, 144

Base metal industry, 101–103, 106, 109, 119, 141–150, 153, 154n, 158, 159, 196, 295, 300

Bates, Barnabas, 57

Benson, George, 130

Bernon, Smithfield, 122

Beverly Mill, Mass., 77

Bill of rights, 255, 261, 261n, 265, 272, 276–278, 292

Blackstone Canal Bank, Providence, 173, 201

Blackstone Canal Company, Provi-

303

dence, 162, 171–174, 176, 217, 242
Blackstone Manufacturing Company, Providence, 130
Blackstone Valley, 7, 13, 15, 67, 77, 83, 85n, 90, 102, 103, 122–123, 128, 141, 154, 157, 171n, 172, 176, 177n, 223, 289
Booth, Clark, 54n
Booth, Reuben, 54n
Borden, Holder, 125n
Boston and Providence Railroad and Transportation Company, 175–176
Boston Exchange Office, Mass., 190
Branch Valley, 87, 122, 141, 177n
Brickmaking, 105, 154, 154n, 158
Bridgham, Samuel W., 265n
Briggs, Nathaniel, 54n
Bristol, R.I.: population of, vi, 12, 15, 16, 21, 72, 107, 154, 156, 220, 222–227; industry in, 35, 38, 65, 83, 109, 117, 122, 124, 126–127, 149, 153, 154n, 155; commerce of, 42–43; slave trade of, 54–57; privateering of, 57–60; decline of, 61, 71; whaling of, 63–64; shipping of, 65; banking in, 117, 184–185, 186n, 191, 193, 195–196, 205, 206; insurance industry in, 211–212, 216; legislative representation of, 256, 280, 286; political corruption in, 261; and constitutional reform, 265n, 266, 267, 269–270, 276, 277, 286
Bristol Bank, 188
Bristol Commercial Bank, 189, 189n
Bristol County, R.I.: population of, 15, 21, 221, 228; industry in, 36, 129, 132, 140, 149; economy of, 158; and constitutional reform, 281
Bristol Insurance Company, 188, 211–212
Bristol Marine Insurance Company, 212
Bristol Union Bank, 197n
Brown, James S., 101, 148
Brown, John (1736–1803), 10, 18–20, 22, 34, 52, 168, 186–188
Brown, John (mechanic), 101, 172
Brown, John C., 201, 299
Brown, Joseph, 10, 34, 142
Brown, Moses, 10, 19–20, 34, 53, 75n, 77–79, 83, 115, 168, 186–188, 210
Brown, Nicholas, 19–20, 34, 47, 83, 130, 168, 172, 175, 210, 299

Brown, Obadiah, 80, 83, 210
Brown and Francis, Providence, 41
Brown and Ives, Providence, 44, 66n, 125n, 130, 131, 209
Brown and Sharpe, Providence, 147
Brown University, 218, 242
Buffum, Benjamin, 165
Burges, Alpheus, 148
Burges, Walter S., 299
Burnside Rifle Works, Providence, 295
Burrillville, R.I.: population of, 72, 154, 220–227; industry in, 87, 93, 94, 97n, 98–99, 122, 124, 126–127, 129, 135–141, 149, 153, 155, 157–158; railroads in, 177; banking in, 205; legislative representation of, 256, 280, 286, 290; constitutional reform in, 264, 265n, 267, 270, 275, 276, 277, 286
Burrillville Bank, 196
Business corporations: formation of, ix, 108, 110–118, 130–132, 141, 218, 281; liability of shareholders in, ix, 111–112, 113–114, 114n, 115n, 116, 117, 145n, 209, 213; sanctity of charter rights of, 66n, 193, 195n; corporate succession in, 110n, 111, 113, 115n, 168; hostility to, 112, 112n, 117, 179; taxation of, 112, 118n, 168, 172; special privileges of, 113; in Massachusetts, 115n
Butler, Cyrus, 115, 130
Butler, Samuel, 31
Butler Hospital, Providence, 250

Canals, 162, 171–174n, 176, 178, 217, 242
Candle making, 10–11, 19, 35, 73, 105, 154n, 158
Capital punishment, 218, 243, 253–254
Carpenter, Thomas F., 287
Carrington, Edward (1775–1843), 31, 83, 130, 172, 175
Carrington, Edward (1813–1891), 229n
Carrying trade, 50–51, 61, 64
Catholicism, 243–246, 301
Centerdale, North Providence, 168
Central Falls, Smithfield, 122–123, 142, 147, 148
Chace, Harvey, 131
Chace, Oliver, 131
Chace, Samuel B., 131

Champlin, George, 44, 68
Charlestown, R.I.: population of, 17, 21, 72, 220, 222, 224–226; industry in, 126–127, 135, 137n, 153, 155; banking in, 205; legislative representation of, 256, 257, 280, 286; and constitutional reform, 267, 271n, 275, 277, 286
Charter of 1663, 218, 252, 254–255
Chemical industry, 158, 296
Chepachet, Glocester, 166, 284
Chepachet River, 122, 141
Child labor, 73, 75, 80, 89, 141, 218, 219, 230, 231, 233–235, 236, 238, 251
Children's Friends Society, 239
Chippewa, 59
Citizens Savings Institution, Woonsocket, 207n
Civil War, 177, 246, 293
Clark, John I., 47
Clark and Nightingale, Providence, 47, 53–54
Clarke, Peleg, 44, 54n
Clinton mill, Cumberland, 123
Clothing industry, 153, 153n–154n, 158, 159
Clyde printing works, Warwick, 128
Coal mining, 76, 105–106, 110, 145n, 154n, 158, 242
Coddington Manufacturing Company, Newport, 133
Coles, Thomas, 110n
Collins, Charles, 55–57
Columbian Fire Insurance Company, Providence, 213
Commerce: illicit, ix, 4, 18, 23, 24, 28; encouragement of, 4; regulation of, 8, 22, 39, 49, 74n, 79; re-export trade, 9, 22–23, 40, 49, 66; organization of, 26–33
  Foreign: Caribbean, 4, 9, 20, 30, 32, 38, 40, 44–46, 48, 49, 52, 58, 61, 66, 66n, 67, 95; British and European, 8–11, 22, 29, 32, 37–49, 66, 67, 69; African, 9, 10, 45, 46, 48, 51–57, 67; Oriental, 26, 29, 33, 38, 40–48, 66, 67, 163, 188; Latin American, 38, 42, 46–48, 66, 67; Canadian, 48–49, 128
  Domestic: 7–8, 22, 32, 40, 50–51, 61, 66n, 89n, 95
Commercial Insurance Company, Bris-
tol, 212
Commercial Steamboat Company, Providence, 165
Common carrier liability, 179, 179n
Congdon, Joseph, 95
Constitution of 1824, 239n, 265–267
Constitution of 1843, 284–287
Constitutional convention of 1834, 270–271
Constitutional party, 270–273
Constitutional referendum of 1821, 264, 265n
Corliss, George H., 144
Corliss Steam Engine Company, North Providence, 145, 147
Cotton industry: growth of, viii–ix, 77–96, 118–133, 134, 136, 137n, 138, 140–141, 154n, 158, 159; climatic and topographic factors in, 71–72; finishing, 71, 93, 109, 121, 122n, 124n, 125, 125n, 128, 130, 131, 132, 218; encouragement of, 75n, 76–77; marketing in, 79, 80, 81, 84–85, 90–91, 106, 119–120, 120n; handicraft stage in, 79–80, 87n, 97n, 230, 237, 242; putting out system in, 80, 82, 87n, 88, 105; factory system in, 96, 106; steam power in, 108–110; corporation in, 112–116; working conditions in, 230–237, 240; decline of, 297
Cove Machine Company, Providence, 145, 147
Coventry, R.I.: population of, 12, 17, 21, 72, 220, 222, 224–226; industry in, 83, 85, 86–87, 93, 94, 101, 124, 124n, 126–127, 135, 137, 139, 149, 153, 155; banking in, 124n, 185, 200n, 201, 205; turnpikes in, 167; legislative representation of, 256, 265n, 280, 286; and constitutional reform, 266, 267, 277, 286
Coventry Bank, 124n
Coventry Manufacturing Company, 82, 85
Cozzens, Benjamin, 120–121
Cranston, R.I.: population of, 14, 16, 21, 72, 156, 220, 222–227, 229; industry in, 84, 86–87, 93, 94, 97, 121, 124 124n, 126–127, 128, 129, 131, 135, 140, 142, 149, 153, 155; turnpikes in, 167; banking in, 185, 201, 205; legislative representation

of, 256, 280, 286; political corruption in, 262; and constitutional reform, 265n, 266, 267, 270, 277, 286, 288

Cranston Bank, 194

Criminal code, 253, 253n

Crompton, Warwick, 247

Cumberland, R.I.: population of, vi, 15, 16, 21, 72, 154, 220, 220n, 222–226, 229; industry in, 86–87, 93, 94, 97n, 98–99, 103, 124–129, 135–137, 139–140, 149, 153, 155; coal mining in, 145n, 158; turnpikes in, 169; banking in, 185, 189n, 200n, 201, 205; legislative representation of, 256, 257, 266, 280, 286; constitutional reform in, 265n, 267, 270n, 277, 286

Curtis, George, 114n, 197–198

Daniells, David, 270

Democratic party, 247–248, 273

Depressions: of 1819, 89, 97, 104, 183, 191, 192, 195, 233; of 1825, 92, 97, 183; of 1829, 92, 97, 103, 141–142, 159, 184, 196, 233, 237; of 1837, 119, 120, 147, 184, 199, 233, 237; of 1850, 125; of 1857, 34, 62, 128, 140n, 147, 184, 201–202, 207, 233; of 1873, 296–297

DeWolf, Charles, 42–44, 55

DeWolf, George, 56–57, 60–61, 195

DeWolf, James (1764–1837), 42–44, 55–57, 59–60, 83, 169n, 196, 212, 261, 273

DeWolf, James (1790–1845), 56, 60

DeWolf, John (1760–1841), 42–44, 55, 60–61

DeWolf, John (1779–1872), 42–44, 55

DeWolf, Levi, 55

DeWolf, Mark A., 54–55

DeWolf, Simon, 55

DeWolf, William, 55

Dexter, Andrew, Jr., 190

Diman, Byron, 61

Dodge, Nehemiah, 104

Dodge, Seril, 104

Dorr, Sullivan, 30, 96

Dorr, Thomas W., 197–198, 200n, 255, 270, 270n, 271–273, 282, 285, 287, 288, 289, 289n, 293

Dorr War, 197, 200n, 243, 255, 274–294

Douglass, William, 68n

Duncan, Alexander, 130

Durfee, Job, 123–124

Dyer, Benjamin, 111, 115

Dyer, Cyrus, 111, 115

Dyer, Paris, 111, 115

Eagle Bank, Providence, 197n

Eagle Screw Company, Providence, 146

East Greenwich, R.I.: population of, 17, 21, 72, 154, 220, 222, 224–226; industry in, 35, 86–87, 93, 94, 101, 109, 112, 123, 124, 126–127, 128, 135–136, 153, 155; fishing industry of, 45n; banking in, 185, 190, 202, 205, 206; insurance industry in, 215; legislative representation of, 256, 280, 286; and constitutional reform, 266, 267, 276, 277, 286

East Greenwich Manufacturing Company, 112–113

Education, 218, 219, 230, 236, 238–242, 251, 278, 279n, 285

Edward Carrington and Company, Providence, 44, 47

Ellery, William, 52, 54–57

Embargo of 1808, viii–ix, 39, 48, 49, 68, 71, 84, 191, 211–212

Erie Canal, 171n

Ethnic conflicts, 237, 242–248, 282, 288, 292

Exchange Bank, Newport, 199, 203

Exchange Bank, Providence, 189, 210–211

Exeter, R.I.: population of, 15, 17, 20, 21, 72, 220, 222, 224–226; industry in, 86–87, 93, 94, 97n, 124, 126–127, 135, 137, 139, 153, 155; banking in, 185, 200n, 205; legislative representation of, 256, 280, 286; and constitutional reform, 265n, 267, 276, 277, 286

Factory system, 79–80, 88, 95–96, 106, 218, 230

Fairbanks, Bancroft and Company, Providence, 144

Fairbanks, Clark and Company, Providence, 143–144

Fall River, R.I.: railroads to, 176–178; banking in, 185–186, 201, 206; population of, 220, 220n, 225n, 226

Fall River, Tiverton: industry in, 109, 123–125, 128, 130; population of, 223, 227

Fall River Bank, 202

Fall River Manufactory, 83

Fall River Union Bank, 194

Fall River, Warren and Providence Railroad Company, 177

Farmers and Mechanics Bank, Pawtucket, North Providence, 196, 204

Farmer's Exchange Bank, Glocester, 189–191, 296

Farmers Mutual Fire Insurance Company, East Greenwich, 215

Farming, 4, 5, 7, 8, 10, 11, 13–14, 15, 16–17, 21, 22, 73, 158, 188

Fayles, David G., 148

Fayles, Jencks and Sons, Central Falls, Smithfield, 147

Fenner, James, 284, 287

Firefly, 163

Fishing industry, 4, 7, 9, 11, 13, 14, 15, 45n, 66n, 73–74, 74n, 154n

Flanagan, Mary, 243n

Food processing, 8, 9, 10, 11, 73, 74, 74n, 75, 76–77, 82, 105, 154n, 158, 160

Footwear industry, 153n, 159, 296

Foster, R. I.: population of, 21, 72, 220, 222, 224–226; industry in, 87, 93, 94, 97n, 124, 135, 153, 155; turnpikes in, 167; banking in, 185, 199; legislative representation of, 256, 265n, 280, 286; and constitutional reform, 267, 271n, 275, 277, 286

Franklin Bank, Glocester, 191, 203

Franklin Foundry and Machine Company, Providence, 148–150

Freemen: qualifications of, 187, 258–259; eldest sons of, 259, 265–266, 268; ratio to population, 259n, 260

Freemen's Bank, Bristol, 191

Freemen's Constitution, 1841, 275–282

French Revolutionary Wars, viii, 26, 29, 39, 45, 49, 52

Fulton, 163

G. and A. Richmond, Providence, 104

Gardner, Caleb, 44, 54n

Gardner and Dean, Newport, 54n

Gay, Gamaliel, 116–117

George Washington, 22, 41

Gibbs, William C., 265n

Gibbs and Channing, Newport, 44, 54n

Gilmore, William, 82, 82n, 88, 91, 101, 218

Gin distilling, 36, 75, 105, 159

Globe Bank, Providence, 201

Globe Printing Company, Tiverton, 130

Glocester, R.I.: population of, 14, 16, 21, 72, 220, 222, 224–227; industry in, 86–87, 93, 94, 98–99, 122, 123, 124, 126–127, 129, 135, 140, 149, 153–155; turnpikes in, 166; banking in, 185, 189–190, 191, 205, 296; legislative representation of, 256, 280, 286; and constitutional reform, 264, 265n, 267, 276, 277, 284, 285, 286, 290

Glocester West Turnpike Company, 166, 171n

Goddard, William G., 130, 289n

Gordon, John, 243

Gorham, Jabez, 104, 151

Gorham, John, 151

Gorton, Samuel, 5

Greenwich, R.I., 13, 14

Gyles, William, 54n

Haile, Levi, 270n

Hamilton, Alexander, 23, 73

Hamlet, Smithfield, 122–123

Handicraft industries, 73, 79–80, 97n, 105–106, 158, 233, 242

Harris, Edward, 134, 136

Harris Lime Rock Company, Smithfield, 110, 134

Hazard, Benjamin, 83, 196

Hazard, Isaac P., 101, 134, 136, 138, 168, 231

Hazard, Rowland, 95

Hazard, Rowland G., 101, 134, 136, 138, 168, 179–181, 181n, 231, 235, 249

Hazard, Rowland H., 80–81n

Hazard, Thomas R., 250

Hill, Thomas J., 150

Hodgson, Adam, 69n

Hope Furnace, Scituate, 10, 20, 34

Hope Iron Foundry, Providence, 147

Hope Manufacturing Company, Providence, 130

Hopkinton, R.I.: population of, 17, 21, 72, 220, 222, 224–226; industry in, 93, 94, 97, 101, 124, 126–

127, 135, 137, 139, 141, 153, 155; and railroads, 180n; banking in, 185, 205; legislative representation of, 256, 280, 286; constitutional reform, 264, 267, 275, 276, 277, 286

Hopkinton Bank, Westerly, 202

Hopkinton City, Hopkinton, 171

Hoppin, William A., 247

Humphrey, Hosea, 76

Illiteracy, 230, 241–242

Immigration, 107, 219n, 229, 230, 241–242, 249, 291, 293, 294n, 300–301. *See also* Aliens; Nativism

Imprisonment for debt, ix, 236, 253, 253n, 254, 261n, 278

India Point, Providence, 163, 175

Industrialization, viii, 106–107, 122, 157, 162, 223, 227, 230, 230n, 246–247, 289

Insurance companies: marine, 53, 207–213, 216; incorporation of, 113; liability of shareholders in, 116–117; banking affiliations of, 188–189; fire, 208, 211, 213–216

Intestacy law, 230

Iron industry, 4, 7, 10–11, 33–34, 73, 110–111. *See also* Base metal industry

Ives, Moses B., 115, 175, 201

Ives, Thomas, 130

Ives, Thomas P., 115, 172, 175, 187–188, 201

Jabez Gorham and Son, Providence, 152

Jackson, Andrew, 250n

Jackson, Charles, 287

Jackson, Richard, 83, 210

James, Charles T., 145n, 150

Jamestown, R.I.: population of, 13, 15, 16, 21, 72, 220, 222, 224–226, 228–229; legislative representation of, 256, 257, 280, 286; and constitutional reform, 267, 275, 277, 286

Jefferson, Thomas, 55

Jenckes, Ebenezer, 54

Jencks, Alvin, 148

Jewelry industry. *See* Precious metal industry

John Jay, 44

Johnston, R.I.: population of, 16, 21, 72, 156, 220, 222–226; industry in,

86–87, 93, 94, 97, 97n, 98–99, 105, 121, 124, 124n, 126–127, 128, 129, 149, 153, 155, 158; turnpikes in, 167; banking in, 185, 205; legislative representation of, 256, 280, 286; and constitutional reform, 264, 265n, 267, 270, 277, 286

Joint-stock partnerships, 81, 106, 108, 110, 113, 115n, 118n

Judiciary, 230, 251–254, 271, 285; independence of, 255, 261, 265n, 272

Juno, 42–43

Kent Bank, Coventry, 194

Kent County, R.I.: population of, 15, 17, 21, 221, 228; industry in, 36, 85n, 129, 132, 140, 149; turnpikes in, 169; and constitutional reform, 276

Kenyon, Abial S., 181–182n

Kenyon, Archibald, 282n

Kingstown, R.I., 13, 14

Knight, Benjamin B., 131n, 201

Knight, Robert, 131n, 201

Knowles, John W., 95

Know-Nothing movement, 247–248

Labor movement, 229–230, 235–238, 242. *See also* Child Labor; Women

Law, Darius, 137n

Law and Order party, 282, 284, 288, 289

Legislative apportionment, 255–258, 265n, 266n, 270, 272, 272n, 275, 276, 279–281, 284, 289–292

Lime industry, 7, 9, 10, 11, 74n, 105, 110, 154n

Lime Rock Bank, Smithfield and Providence, 199

Limited partnerships, 114, 114n

Lippitt, Warwick, 247

Lippitt Manufacturing Company, Warwick, 86, 125, 288

Little Compton, R.I.: population of, 15, 16, 20, 21, 72, 220, 222, 224–228; industry in, 153, 155; legislative representation of, 256, 280, 286; and constitutional reform, 267, 275n, 276, 277, 286

Lonsdale, Smithfield, 122–123

Lonsdale Company, Smithfield, 128, 129, 130, 132

Lotteries, 76, 116, 117, 145n, 168, 224–245
Louisquissett turnpike, 167–168
Lowell, Francis C., 91, 133
Lucy, 55
Lumbering, 4, 7, 10, 11, 14, 15, 22, 73–74, 74n, 76–77, 82, 105, 154n, 158
Luther, Seth, 235, 239, 259, 271, 273, 288
Lyman, Daniel, 82n, 96
Lyman Manufacturing Company, North Providence, 82, 83

Man, Thomas, 235, 236–237
Manchester, Job, 101
Manton, North Providence, 168
Manufactories, 75, 76, 105–106
Manufacturers Mutual Fire Insurance Company, Providence, 214
Manufacturing: encouragement of, 4, 75, 75n, 76–77; rise of, 4, 10–11, 71, 73–77; as ancillaries to maritime trade, 10–11, 19–20, 33–38; effect of Revolution on, 19–20; organization of, 71, 81, 91–92, 101–102, 106, 108, 110–118, 130–132, 138, 141, 152–153, 218; importance of, 71, 106–107, 132–133, 138, 140–141, 153–154, 156–157, 219–229; regulation of, 73–74, 74n, 75, 218, 237, 240–241; labor supply for, 73, 79, 230–231; health hazards in, 74–75; working conditions in, 75, 230–232, 232n, 233–234; mechanization of, 91, 141, 230; diversification of, 95, 157–160; factorage system in, 119–120, 120n, 133; capital in, 153, 153n–154n, 155; paternalism in, 231–232; wages in, 233, 233n
Manville, Smithfield, 122–123
Manville Mills, Cumberland, 128, 132
Marchant, Henry, 128
Marine Insurance Company, Providence, 212
Martin, Joseph S., 96
Mason, John, 83, 209
Mason, Otis, 270n
Mathew, Theobald, 244
Mechanic lien law, 237
Mercantile Bank, Providence, 201
Merchants Bank, Newport, 191

Merchants Bank, Providence, 194, 199
Merchants Insurance Company, Providence, 215
Merino factory, Johnston, 97
Middletown, R.I.: population of, 16, 21, 72, 220, 222, 224–227; economy of, 67, 156; railroad in, 178; legislative representation of, 256, 257, 280, 286; and constitutional reform, 265n, 267, 276, 277, 286
Mill dam statutes, 76–77
Mill River, 123
Monroe, James, 57
Moshassuck Valley, 90, 128, 152
Mount Hope, 163
Mount Hope Bank, Bristol, 117, 196
Mount Vernon Bank, Foster, 199
Murfree, 209–210

Napoleonic Wars, viii, 29, 45, 49, 211
Narragansett, 165
Narragansett, South Kingstown, 45n
Narragansett Bank, North Kingstown, 190
Natick, Warwick, 247
Natick mill, Warwick, 84
Nativism, 242–248, 249n
Negroes, 4, 13–14, 247, 248, 275, 279, 279n, 294n
New England Association of Farmers, Mechanics and other Workingmen, 236
New England Bank, Boston, Mass., 194
New England Pacific Bank, North Providence, 195
New England Screw Company, Providence, 146–147, 240
Newport, R.I.: commerce of, 3, 4, 8, 9, 22, 34, 44, 67; slaving of, 9, 52, 54; industry in, 10, 35, 36, 37, 38, 83, 83n, 85n, 93, 94, 95, 101, 106, 109, 123, 124, 126–127, 135, 136, 137, 139, 149, 153, 155; population of, 13, 15, 16, 21, 72, 154, 220–228, 299; whaling of, 63–64; shipping of, 65; decline of, 66, 67–71, 108, 161, 191, 239n; transportation industry in, 163–164, 174n, 178; banking in, 183–186, 188, 191, 193, 199, 200n, 201, 205, 206; insurance industry in, 211, 216; education in, 239n; temperance

movement in, 249; legislative representation of, 255, 256, 280, 286; and constitutional reform, 263–267, 269–270, 274, 277, 286, 290–291; economy of, 299, 302

Newport Bank, 188, 188n, 189

Newport County, R.I.: population of, 13, 15, 16, 21, 221, 228; industry in, 36, 88, 129, 130, 132, 140, 149; economy of, 158; banking in, 188, 189n

Newport Insurance Company, 211

Newport Savings Bank, 206

New Shoreham, R.I.: population of, 13, 15, 16, 21, 72, 156, 220, 222, 224–226, 228–229; industry in, 153, 155; banking in, 185n–186n; legislative representation of, 256, 258, 280, 286; and constitutional reform, 267, 271n, 274, 275, 277, 286

Nicholson File Company, Providence, 295

Nightingale, Edwin J., 144

Nightingale and Jenckes, Providence, 47

Northam, Stephen T., 143

North Kingstown, R.I.: population of, 14, 17, 21, 72, 154, 220, 222, 224–226, 228; industry in, 35, 87, 93, 94, 97–99, 124, 126–127, 135, 137, 139, 152, 153, 155; banking in, 185, 190, 191; legislative representation of, 256, 265n, 280, 286; and constitutional reform, 264, 266, 267, 276, 277, 286; economy of, 300

North Kingstown Farmers Bank, 202

North Providence, R.I.: population of, 16, 21, 72, 154, 156, 220–226, 229; industry in, 35, 75, 77, 83, 84, 86–87, 93, 94, 98, 99, 103, 121, 124, 126–129, 131, 134–135, 137, 139–140, 145, 148, 149, 152, 153, 155, 158; commerce of, 50; transportation industry in, 168–169; banking in, 185, 200n, 201, 205; insurance industry in, 214; Catholicism in, 243–244; legislative representation of, 256, 280, 286; and constitutional reform, 265n, 266–270, 270n, 275n, 277, 286

Norwich and Worcester Railroad Company, 177

Ogden, Samuel, 82

Olneyville, North Providence, 131

O'Reilly, Bernhard, 247

Packet industry, 161–166, 169, 175–176, 178

Palmyra, 47

Pascoag, Burrillville, 177

Pawcatuck, Westerly, 45n, 97, 143, 150, 169, 175, 227

Pawcatuck Valley, 7, 174n

Pawtucket, North Providence: industry in, 10, 80n, 89n, 100, 101, 102–103, 122–123, 141–142; commerce of, 50; transportation industry in, 168, 169, 171, 176; banking in, 196, 206; insurance industry in, 215; urbanization of, 227; labor movement in, 235; Catholicism in, 244; rowdyism in, 247; temperance movement in, 249

Pawtucket and Providence East Turnpike Company, 169n, 171, 174, 176–177

Pawtucket River, 76

Pawtucket Institution for Savings, North Providence, 206

Pawtucket Mutual Fire Insurance Company, North Providence, 215

Pawtuxet Valley, 7, 13, 67, 83, 85n, 87, 90, 102, 124n, 128, 154, 157, 169n, 223, 289

Peace Dale, South Kingstown, 95, 101, 134, 168, 223, 227, 231, 250

Peace Insurance Company, Providence, 212

Peck, Perez, 101

People's Constitution, 274–275, 276–283, 292

People's Savings Bank, Providence, 206

Peters River, 123

Phoenix, Warwick, 247

Phoenix Bank, Providence, 201, 204

Phoenix Company, Providence, 110

Phoenix Iron Foundry, Providence, 144, 148

Phoenix Village Bank, Westerly, 203

Philip Allen and Sons, Providence, 130, 132

Phillips, James, 42

Piracy, ix, 3–4, 24, 28, 58n, 60, 64

Pitcher, Larned, 101, 148

Political corruption, 261–262, 263,

263n, 264n, 265n, 290n, 292–293
Poor debtors' oath, 254
Poor relief, 219, 230, 231, 249–251
Portsmouth, R.I.: population of, 13, 15, 16, 21, 72, 220, 222, 224–225, 225n, 226; fishing industry of, 45n; economy of, 67; industry in, 87, 93, 94, 96n, 97–99, 123, 135, 137, 139, 143, 153, 155; coal mining in, 105–106, 145n, 242; legislative representation of, 255, 256, 257, 280, 286; and constitutional reform, 265n, 266, 267, 275, 277, 286
Potter, Abijah, 54
Potter, Elisha R., 261–262, 262n, 265n
Potter, Simeon, 54, 239n, 261, 301
Powdermill turnpike, 171n
Precious metal industry, 104, 106, 109, 119, 150–153, 154n, 158, 159, 295–296
Privateering, 3, 8, 9, 18, 20, 28, 50, 57–61, 62, 64. *See also* Piracy
Providence, R.I.: population of, vi, 13–16, 21, 72, 220–229; entrepreneurs in, viii, 30–31, 63, 132–133, 302; steam power in, x, 108–109; commerce of, 4, 8, 9, 10, 15, 16, 22, 29, 31, 37, 40–42, 44, 46–50, 63, 66–67; industry in, 9, 35–38, 77, 80, 82, 86–87, 87n, 93–94, 97, 99–104, 120–130, 135–156, 296, 302; slave trade of, 53–54; whaling industry of, 63–64; shipping of, 63, 67; contributions to New England cotton industry, 83–84; business corporations in, 110–111, 110n, 130–131; urbanization of, 156; economic growth of, 158–160, 217; transportation industry in, 161–182; banking industry in, 159, 182–190, 193–194, 197n, 200n, 205, 206, 207; insurance industry in, 207–216; labor movement in, 236; education in, 238; child labor in, 240–241; illiteracy in, 241; anti-Catholicism in, 242, 247; Catholics in, 244, 245, 246n; Negroes in, 248, 279n; temperance movement in, 248–249; legislative representation of, 255–258, 260, 270, 280–281, 284, 286; and constitutional reform, 264, 265n, 266–267, 270, 274, 275, 277, 282n, 283, 283n, 286, 290

Providence Abolition Society, 53
Providence and Boston Railroad Company, 174
Providence and Boston turnpike, 169n
Providence and Norwich turnpike, 171n
Providence and Pawcatuck Turnpike Company, 171
Providence and Pawtucket turnpike, 169n, 171, 174
Providence and Plainfield Railroad Company, 175n
Providence and Springfield Railroad Company, 177
Providence and Worcester Railroad Company, 173–174, 176, 176n
Providence Association of Mechanics and Manufacturers, 96n, 238, 249
Providence Bank, 187–188, 188n, 189, 209, 210–211
Providence City Council, 270, 285
Providence County, R.I.: population of, 15, 21, 221; industry in, 34, 36, 85n, 97n, 98, 119, 129, 132, 138, 140, 146–147, 149; and Fall River, 123; turnpikes in, 169; banking in, 189n; and constitutional reform, 276
Providence "Cupola," 103, 150
Providence Dyeing, Bleaching and Calendering Company, 132, 144
Providence Gas Company, 154n, 160
Providence, Hartford and Fishkill Railroad Company, 177, 215
Providence Institution for Savings, 206
Providence Insurance Company, 208–211
Providence Iron Company, 146–147
Providence Iron Foundry, 111, 131
Providence Journal, 247–248
Providence Machine Company, 147, 150
Providence Manufacturing Company, 82, 169n
Providence Mutual Fire Insurance Company, 213, 215
Providence Mutual Fire Society, 213
Providence-Plantations Canal Company, 172
Providence River, 152, 163
Providence Steam Engine Company, 145n
Providence Tool Company, 295
Providence, Warren and Bristol Railroad Company, 177, 177n
Providence-Washington Insurance Company, 211–215
Providence Woolen Manufacturing Company, 96, 142

Quarrying, 7, 75, 105–106

Railroads, 162, 168n, 170, 171, 174–182, 252; regulation of, 175, 175n, 176, 178–182, 182n
Randall, E. K., 96
Religious conflicts, 242–248, 282, 288, 292
Reservoirs, 90, 110, 130
Rhode Island Central Bank, East Greenwich, 190, 202
Rhode Island Cloth Hall Company, Providence, 120
Rhode Island Coal Company, Portsmouth, 110
Rhode Island Silk Company, Providence, 116
Rhode Island Society for the Encouragement of Domestic Industry, 120
Rhode Island Steam-Boat Company, Providence, 143
Rhode Island Suffrage Association, 273–274
Rhode Island Union Bank, Newport, 188, 188n, 189, 211
Richmond, 165
Richmond, R.I.: population of, 15, 17, 21, 72, 220, 222, 224–225, 225n, 226, 228; industry in, 87, 93, 94, 97n, 124, 126–127, 135, 137, 139, 149, 153, 155; railroads in, 181n–182n; banking in, 185, 205; legislative representation of, 256, 280, 286; and constitutional reform, 267, 271n, 277, 286
River Machine Company, Providence, 65–66
Robinson, Christopher, 270
Robinson, James, 44
Roger Williams Insurance Company, Providence, 212
Ropemaking industry, 11, 33, 37–38, 154n, 158, 159
Rosalie, 63
Rum distilling, 9, 10, 11, 33, 36–37, 37n, 45n, 75, 159
Rushlight, 143
Russell, 44

Sackett, Davis and Company, Providence, 151
Sailmaking, 11, 37, 76
Sanford, Peleg, 8
Saugatucket River, 95

Saunders, Isaac, 181n
Savings banks, 118n, 206–207, 231, 296
Sayles, Welcome, 240–241
Scituate, R.I.: industry in, 10, 34, 87, 93, 94, 97n, 105, 124, 126–127, 129, 135, 149, 153, 155, 158; population of, 14, 16, 21, 72, 220, 222, 224–226; turnpikes in, 167; banking in, 185, 205; legislative representation of, 256, 280, 286; and constitutional reform, 264, 265n, 266, 267, 271n, 277, 280, 286
Scituate Silk Company, 117
Sectionalism, 255, 258n, 263, 264, 266, 276, 282, 290–291
Seekonk River, 50, 163, 175
Semiramis, 44
Shipbuilding, 9, 11, 33, 34–35, 143, 153n, 159
Sickel, Frederick E., 145n
Silk industry, 76, 116–117
Sisters of Mercy Convent, Providence, 247
Slater, John (1776–1843), 82, 83, 120, 231
Slater, John (1815–1884), 82n, 88, 120, 231
Slater, Samuel, 77–79, 79n, 80n, 82, 83, 84, 88, 89n, 108, 111 114, 115, 120, 131, 168, 169n, 218, 231n, 233–234, 235, 250n
Slater steam mill, Providence, 128, 130, 150
Slater system, 231
Slatersville, Smithfield, 122–123
Slave trade, 9, 10, 15, 28, 30, 36, 45, 50, 51–57, 61, 64, 67, 209, 212, 218; regulation of, 51–53, 56–57, 68
Smith, Amasa, 54
Smith, James Y., 201
Smith, William H., 270, 289
Smith, Dee, and Eddy, Warren, 151
Smithfield, R.I.: population of, 14, 16, 21, 72, 154, 220–226, 229; industry in, 75, 83, 86–87, 90, 92–94, 103, 105, 110, 119, 122, 124, 126–127, 128, 129, 131, 135–137, 139–140, 152, 153, 155, 158, 235; turnpikes in, 167–168, 169; banking in, 185, 195, 199, 205; legislative representation of, 256, 257, 280, 284, 286; and constitutional reform, 265n, 266,

267, 270, 272n, 274n, 277, 286, 290
Smithfield Manufacturing Company, Providence, 110n
Smithfield Union Bank, 189, 189n
Smuggling, ix, 18, 23, 24, 28
South County Bank, South Kingstown, 202
South Kingstown, R.I.: population of, 14, 17, 21, 72, 154, 220, 222, 224–228; industry in, 86–87, 93, 94, 95, 97, 97n, 98–99, 124, 135–137, 153, 155; railroads in, 179, 181n; banking in, 185, 200n, 201, 202, 205, 206; legislative representation of, 256, 280, 286; political corruption in, 261; and constitutional reform, 265n, 266, 267, 275, 275n, 277, 280, 286
Sprague, Amasa (1798–1843), 84, 131, 262, 288
Sprague, Byron, 201, 300
Sprague, William (1773–1836), 84, 131, 244, 262
Sprague, William (1799–1856), 84, 131, 201, 262, 288
Sprague, William (1830–1915), 300
Steam engine: manufacture of, 109, 142–145, 158, 159
Steam power, ix–x, 96, 108–110, 115, 117, 118, 121–122, 123, 125, 128, 130, 132, 133, 135–136, 141–142, 151n, 152, 159, 218, 233
Stephen Jenks and Sons, Pawtucket, 103, 196
Sterry, Cyprian, 54
Stonington railroad, 168, 171, 174n, 175–176, 178–180, 182n, 201
Suffolk Bank, Boston, 194, 198
Suffrage, 236, 255, 258–260, 263, 265–266, 268–269, 270, 270n, 271–272, 276, 278–279, 279n, 284–285, 289–292, 293n

Taber, Constant, 54n
Tariff protection, 79, 89n, 90, 97, 117, 136n–137n; tariff of 1816, 88; of 1824, 136–137; of 1828, 125n, 136–137; of 1833, 121, 137; of 1846, 138
Taunton River, 128
Taxation, 118n, 120, 168, 172, 179, 192–194, 219, 239, 245, 251, 278, 279n
Temperance movement, 36, 219, 232,

248–249, 251
Textile industry, 106, 109, 153, 154n, 157, 158, 196, 216, 230–237, 295, 297, 298, 300
Textile machinery industry, 98, 100–101, 103, 130, 147–150, 154n
Thorpe, John, 100, 148
Thurston, Robert L., 142–143
Thurston, Gardner and Company, Providence, 145
Tiverton, R.I.: population of, 15, 16, 21, 72, 220, 220n, 222–227; industry in, 83n, 87, 121, 123, 124n, 126–127, 128, 130, 135, 137, 139, 153, 155; railroads in, 125; banking in, 185, 200n; legislative representation of, 256, 280, 286; and constitutional reform, 267, 277, 286
Tiverton Savings Bank, 206
Tompkins, Joseph, 111
Topham, John, 54n
Transportation industry, 66–68, 73, 80, 133, 159, 161–182, 216–217
Trident Mutual Insurance Company, Providence, 215–216
Turnpikes, 113, 162, 166–171, 168n, 178, 188, 252
Tyler, George W., 117
Tyler, John, 282, 283
Tyler, William, 244

Union Bank, Providence, 197
Union Broadcloth mill, East Greenwich, 135
Union Butt Company, Cranston, 147
Union Insurance Company, Providence, 212
Union Mill, Warwick, 86, 88–89
United States and Paraguay Navigation Company, Providence, 299n
Urbanization, viii–ix, 223–227, 230n, 246–247, 289
Usher, Aaron T., 60
Usher, Thomas J., 60

Valentine Silk Company, Providence, 117
Valley Falls, Cumberland, 122–123, 134
Valley Falls Company, Smithfield, 131
Valley Falls mills, Smithfield, 196
Village Bank, Smithfield, 194
Vinton, Francis, 292n

Wadsworth, James A., 143

War of 1812, ix, 34, 39, 49, 57–59, 68, 71, 84, 86, 96, 103, 171n, 191, 211, 212

Ward, Samuel, 41

Warren, R.I.: population of, 15, 16, 20, 21, 72, 107, 154, 220, 222–227; industry in, 34, 35, 36, 38, 83n, 109, 126–127, 149, 151, 152, 153, 155; slave trade of, 54, 55; whaling of, 63–64; railroads in, 178; banking in, 184, 185, 186, 205, 206; insurance industry in, 212, 216; legislative representation of, 256, 280, 286; and constitutional reform, 265n, 267, 269, 270n, 276, 277, 286

Warren Insurance Company, 212, 212n

Warwick, R.I.: population of, 13, 14, 17, 21, 72, 154, 220–222, 224–226, 228, 302; fishing industry of, 45n; industry in, 76, 82, 84, 86–87, 92, 93, 94, 96n, 97, 121, 124, 124n, 126, 127, 128, 137, 139, 149, 153, 155; banking in, 185, 205; legislative representation of, 255, 256, 280, 286; and constitutional reform, 264, 265n, 266, 267, 277, 286, 288; nativism in, 294n

Washington Bank, Westerly, 188, 190

Washington County, R.I.: population of, 15, 16–17, 21, 221, 223, 228; transportation industry in, 67, 169, 174n, 178, 180; industry in, 85n, 88, 98, 129, 132, 136, 138, 140–141, 145, 149; economy of, 158; banking in, 188n, 189n; temperance movement in, 249

Washington Insurance Company, Providence, 210

Washington Silk Company [South Kingstown?], 117

Water power, ix, 71, 72, 77, 95, 108, 109, 125, 141

Wayland, Francis, 242, 289n

Weaving, 80, 82, 88, 98, 105, 218, 242

Webster, Henry L., 151

Weeden, John H., 270n

Wenscott Valley, 90

West Greenwich, R.I.: population of, vi, 15, 17, 21, 72, 220, 222, 224–227; industry in, 87, 93, 94, 124, 126, 127, 153, 155; legislative representation of, 256, 280, 286; and constitutional reform, 265n, 266, 267, 277, 285, 286

Westerly, R.I.: population of, 13, 14, 17, 20, 21, 72, 154, 220, 222, 224–227, 229; industry in, 35, 93, 94, 97–99, 106, 124, 135, 137, 139–141, 149, 153, 155; banking in, 185, 186, 188, 190, 202, 205, 206; legislative representation of, 256, 280, 286; and constitutional reform, 267, 274, 276, 277, 286

Weybosset Bank, Providence, 197

Whaling, 22, 36, 50, 61–64, 117, 154n

What Cheer Company, Providence, 201

Wheelock, Joseph B., 200n

Wheelock, Otis A., 200n

White Rock, Westerly, 227

Wickford, North Kingstown, 45n, 66n, 191

Wilkinson, Abraham, 100, 115, 150, 168, 196, 204

Wilkinson, David, 100, 103, 111, 114, 115, 150, 243–244

Wilkinson, Isaac, 100, 103, 115, 150, 168

Wilkinson, Oziel, 100, 102, 115, 150, 168

Williams, Roger, 4, 5

Williams, Thomas R., 95, 101

Williams, William P., 165

Williams and Brown, Providence, 152

Women: employment of, 73, 89, 141, 146, 151, 236; rights of married, 218

Wood, William, 44

Woodley, Robert D., 244–245

Woolen industry: putting out system in, 73, 80, 80n–81n, 230, 233; fulling mills in, 82, 105, 135; rise of, 95–99; corporations in, 110, 110n; organization of, 118–119, 138; expansion of, 133–141; importance of, 138, 140–141, 157–158, 159; working conditions in, 230–237

Woonasquatucket calico printing works, North Providence, 132

Woonasquatucket Valley, 13, 76, 82, 90, 128, 131, 168, 177

Woonsocket, Cumberland: industry in, 122, 122n, 123, 134, 136, 138; railroads in, 177n, 181, 181n; banking in, 186n, 189n, 206; urbanization of, 227; labor movement in, 235–236, 237; Catholicism in, 246

Yankee, 59